Stephanie Dimond-Bayir

with Caroline Nixon and Michael Tomlinson

Map of the book

	Vocabulary	Grammar	Literature	Cross-curricular	Exam
1 In style Mission: Write a review Page 4	Clothes Parts of clothes **Pronunciation:** plural pronunciation of 's'	**Comparative adjectives, adverbs and *as…as*** *On the first site, the shoes were much more expensive.* *I took the T-shirt out of the box as quickly as I could.* **The present simple with future meaning** *The bus leaves at quarter past six.*	***King Canute's day on the beach*** A story Social and emotional skill: dealing with frustration	**Clothes throughout history** Learn about clothes and materials in the past, present and future.	A2 Key for Schools: Reading and Writing Part 1 A2 Key for Schools: Listening Part 1
2 Future technology Mission: Recommend new technology Page 16	Technology Verbs for using computers **Pronunciation:** syllabus stress in two-syllable words	**The first conditional** *If my mum says it's OK, then I'll go.* **The zero and first conditional** *If the floor is dirty, a robot drives around and cleans.* *If I'm hungry, I'll ask the freezer, "What ice cream have we got?"*	***The IAST Times*** A newspaper article Social and emotional skill: dealing with jealousy	**How to make an app** Learn what an app is and what you need to make one.	A2 Key for Schools: Speaking Part 1 A2 Key for Schools: Reading and Writing Part 2
3 Jim-nastics Mission: Invent a new sport Page 28	Sports Sporting actions, people and equipment **Pronunciation:** contracted forms	**The passive (present simple)** *Dog surfing competitions are organised by people all around the world.* **Modal verbs** *Birch may have made a mistake.* *This could be the most important point today.* *The ball might go into the net!* *Shall we watch that goal again?*	***The Spartan Princess*** A comic book Social and emotional skill: perseverance	**How athletes prepare for sport** Learn how athletes train, eat and sleep before competitions.	A2 Key for Schools: Listening Part 2 A2 Key for Schools: Reading and Writing Part 5
Review units 1–3					
4 Be careful! Mission: Find out about emergency services Page 42	Accidents and illnesses Health and medicine **Pronunciation:** sentence stress	**The present perfect with *how long*, *for* and *since*** *I haven't been well for a week.* *She's had a problem with her heart since April.* **The present continuous for future plans** *We're taking her to the vet this evening.*	***The £20,000 adventure*** A story Social and emotional skill: dealing with fear	**Changes in medicine** Learn about vaccinations and treatments.	A2 Key for Schools: Reading and Writing Part 4 A2 Key for Schools: Listening Part 4
5 Fun foods Mission: Take part in a cooking competition Page 54	Cooking ingredients Cooking actions and equipment **Pronunciation:** verb endings in the past	***Rather* and *prefer*** *I prefer carrots to broccoli.* *I'd rather have salmon.* **The passive (past simple)** *The sandwich wasn't made from bread.* *It was made from two cookies and some ice cream.*	***The very, very interesting diary of Juana Sánchez*** A diary Social and emotional skill: apologising and showing empathy	**Food groups** Learn about why some foods are good for you.	A2 Key for Schools: Listening Part 5 A2 Key for Schools: Reading and Writing Part 7

	Vocabulary	Grammar	Literature	Cross-curricular	Exam
6 Environmentally friendly Mission: Share ideas to protect your environment! Page 66	Home The environment **Pronunciation:** schwa	***A lot of, lots of, a few, a little, many, much*** *There's a lot of water from our town's river.* *There are lots of fish living in the water.* *Many people don't believe me.* *My house doesn't use much electricity.* *When we have a little rubbish, we try to use it.* *We only throw away a few bags each year.* **Tag questions** *Everyone recycles a lot, don't they?* *You couldn't recycle, could you?*	***The fall of a Mayan city*** A story Social and emotional skill: looking after the environment	**Ecosystems in the city** Learn about the animals that make their home in the city.	A2 Key for Schools: Speaking Part 2 A2 Key for Schools: Reading and Writing Part 6
	Review units 4–6				
7 Feeling it Mission: Make a 'feelings wheel' Page 80	Feeling and emotions Wellbeing **Pronunciation:** /b/ /v/ /w/	***Needn't, have to, should, ought to, must, mustn't*** *I have to wait until I'm older.* *If your parents say you can't have a snake, you must listen to them!* *You mustn't get a snake without telling your parents!* *You needn't worry if some of your ideas aren't very good.* *You should try to be satisfied with what you have.* *You ought to write about something you love.* ***Such … that / so … that*** *It's so fun that my mum and I always laugh a lot!* *It's such a relaxing place that I once fell asleep there!*	***The cowboy who cried wolf*** A story Social and emotional skill: telling the truth	**Emotional awareness** Learn about empathy and how we show emotions.	A2 Key for Schools: Reading and Writing Part 3 A2 Key for Schools: Listening Part 3
8 Pretty cities Mission: Plan a city visit Page 92	A tour of a city Visiting new places **Pronunciation:** intonation in questions	**Indirect questions** *Do you know how many paintings there are?* ***Used to / didn't used to*** *They used to make the air very dirty.* *Today the trains are electric, but they didn't use to be.*	***The case of the Butterfly Diamond*** A novel Social and emotional skill: managing stress	**Responsible tourism** Learn how to look after places when you go on holiday.	A2 Key for Schools: Reading and Writing Part 4 B1 Preliminary for Schools: Reading Part 6
9 Lights, camera, action! Mission: Make a scene for a film or TV show Page 104	TV and film genres Television **Pronunciation:** word stress	**Causative *have/get*** *Mum's having a special superhero cake made for me.* **The second conditional** *If I had $250 million, I'd buy cameras and costumes for the actors.*	***The Monster in our Homes!*** A poem Social and emotional skill: identifying and expressing an opinion	**Special effects** Learn how special effects are used in films.	A2 Key for Schools: Reading and Writing Part 7 B1 Preliminary for Schools: Writing Part 1
	Review units 7–9				
	Pronunciation				
	Grammar reference				

Checklist for A2 Key for Schools Preparation

Paper	Part	Task	Practice
Listening 30 minutes	1	Discrete 3-option multiple choice (visuals)	*Preparation*: Pupil's Book Unit 1 Page 14 *Practice*: Activity Book Unit 1 Page 14
	2	Gap fill	*Preparation*: Pupil's Book Unit 3 Page 37 *Practice*: Activity Book Unit 3 Page 37
	3	3-option multiple choice	*Preparation*: Pupil's Book Unit 7 Page 90 *Practice*: Activity Book Unit 7 Page 90
	4	3-option multiple choice (text)	*Preparation*: Pupil's Book Unit 4 Page 52 *Practice*: Activity Book Unit 4 Page 52
	5	Matching	*Preparation*: Pupil's Book Unit 5 Page 63 *Practice*: Activity Book Unit 5 Page 63
Reading and Writing 60 minutes	1	Discrete 3-option multiple choice	*Preparation*: Pupil's Book Unit 1 Page 13 *Practice*: Activity Book Unit 1 Page 13
	2	Matching	*Preparation*: Pupil's Book Unit 2 Page 26 *Practice*: Activity Book Unit 2 Page 26
	3	3-option multiple choice	*Preparation*: Pupil's Book Unit 7 Page 89 *Practice*: Activity Book Unit 7 Page 89
	4	3-option multiple choice cloze	*Preparation*: Pupil's Book Unit 4 Page 51 *Practice*: Activity Book Unit 4 Page 51 *Preparation*: Pupil's Book Unit 8 Page 101 *Practice*: Activity Book Unit 8 Page 101
	5	Open cloze	*Preparation*: Pupil's Book Unit 3 Page 38 *Practice*: Activity Book Unit 3 Page 38
	6	Writing – Short message	*Preparation*: Pupil's Book Unit 6 Page 76 *Practice*: Activity Book Unit 6 Page 76
	7	Writing – Story (35 words or more)	*Preparation*: Pupil's Book Unit 5 Page 64 *Practice*: Activity Book Unit 5 Page 64 *Preparation*: Pupil's Book Unit 9 Page 113 *Practice*: Activity Book Unit 9 Page 113
Speaking 9–10 minutes	1	Interview	*Preparation*: Pupil's Book Unit 2 Page 25 *Practice*: Activity Book Unit 2 Page 25
	2	Candidate discussion	*Preparation*: Pupil's Book Unit 6 Page 75 *Practice*: Activity Book Unit 6 Page 75

Checklist for B1 Preliminary for Schools Preparation

Paper	Part	Task	Practice
Listening 35 minutes	1	3-option multiple choice (visuals)	See Level 6
	2	3-option multiple choice (gist)	See Level 6
	3	Sentence completion	See Level 6
	4	3-option multiple choice (long text)	See Level 6
Reading 45 minutes	1	Discrete 3-option multiple choice	See Level 6
	2	Multiple matching	See Level 6
	3	4-option multiple choice	See Level 6
	4	Gapped text	See Level 6
	5	4-option multiple choice cloze	See Level 6
	6	Open cloze	*Preparation*: Pupil's Book Unit 8 Page 102 *Practice*: Activity Book Unit 8 Page 102
Speaking 10–12 minutes	1	Short conversation between the interlocutor and each candidate	See Level 6
	2	Individual long turn	See Level 6
	3	Collaborative task	See Level 6
	4	A discussion on topics related to the collaborative task in Part 3.	See Level 6
Writing 45 minutes	1	Candidates write an email based on an annotated input task	*Preparation*: Pupil's Book Unit 9 Page 114 *Practice*: Activity Book Unit 9 Page 114
	2	Candidates write one from a choice of two specified text types.	See Level 6

About Power Up

Power Up

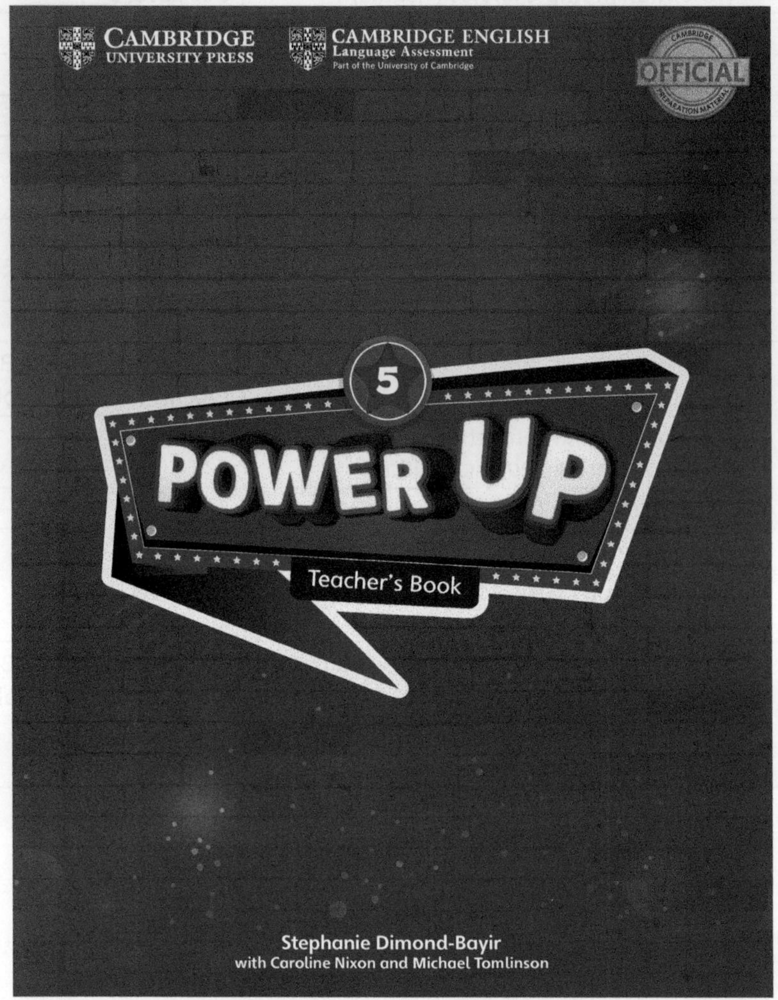

What is Power Up?

Power Up is an engaging and effective approach to learning which uses:

- Lively activities with clear objectives
- Age-appropriate, engaging topics which support learner progress and collaborative learning
- Real-world contexts and language
- Development of life competencies and test skills
- Scaffolded tasks which support learners of all abilities
- A unifying learner-centred methodology which supports life-long learning.

Power Up provides both general English and comprehensive preparation for Cambridge English Qualifications, jointly published with Cambridge Assessment English. Student-centred learning is a core part of the course, with ongoing unit tasks giving ample opportunity for collaborative learning.

Key features of Power Up

Activities are based on real-world skills and situations that learners find engaging and fun. All four skills – reading, writing, listening and speaking – are used to explore interesting topics. The activities scaffold the learning to support both stronger and weaker learners. Grammar and vocabulary are developed through communicative activities which have a clear purpose and encourage learners to use language naturally. All new language is heard, read, written and spoken as learners acquire it and the language is then consolidated throughout, building as the units progress.

Power Up and the Cambridge Framework for Life Competencies

In addition to language learning, *Power Up* develops the life competencies of learners.

Power Up is one of the first generation of courses to integrate the Cambridge Framework for Life Competencies. This is an ongoing research initiative into how thinking and learning skills are developed over different life stages. Each unit of *Power Up* is mapped to a component within the Cambridge Framework for Life Competencies to ensure a wide range of skills are covered. This also provides opportunities for formative assessment and a broad view of each learner's development.

Missions

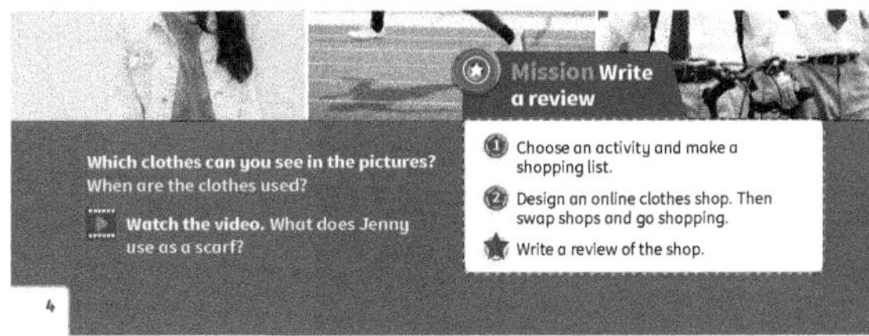
Mission Write a review

Which clothes can you see in the pictures? When are the clothes used?

Watch the video. What does Jenny use as a scarf?

1 Choose an activity and make a shopping list.

2 Design an online clothes shop. Then swap shops and go shopping.

Write a review of the shop.

4

The Life Competencies framework is a key feature of the unit Missions, where learners are building on social skills by practising collaboration and communication. The enquiry-led approach used in the Missions also builds on learners' thinking and learning skills, through the creativity, critical thinking, problem solving and decision making employed in each stage of the Mission.

Each unit is structured around a 'Mission' which helps learners to set objectives at the beginning and understand their end goal and learning outcomes. Outcomes are also clearly stated at the beginning of each lesson so that learners can understand and think about them. The teacher's notes suggest creative ways to share these with the learners. The Missions are based on real-world contexts with a focus on real English. They give learners the opportunity to build up a portfolio of their work as evidence of their learning and help them to reflect and evaluate their own learning even at a young age. In Level 5, the Missions are flexible and open, allowing the teacher and learners to decide how much time to assign to their completion. Learners have increased autonomy in deciding how to achieve their goals. Each mission includes skills that students need for real-life activity. As part of this approach, there are frequent opportunities for learners to reflect on what they have learnt and help them plan for the next stage of learning, with practical tips on how teachers can help learners do this.

Literature

The Life Competencies framework also features in the Literature spread, where learners are building on emotional skills and social responsibilities. Each story holds a message that learners can identify with and explore, making it relevant to their own contexts. They learn about emotions, empathy and how to respond to others appropriately through identifying with the characters in the stories.

Cross-curricular learning

The cross-curricular sections also develop life competencies through critical thinking and wider world knowledge.

Cross-curricular learning is used in *Power Up* to refer to any teaching of a non-language subject through the medium of a second or foreign language. It suggests a balance between content and language learning. The non-language content such as natural and social sciences, arts and history is developed through the second language, and the second language is developed through the non-language content. Cross-curricular learning can be seen as an educational approach which supports linguistic diversity and is a powerful tool that can have a strong impact on language learning.

Why cross-curricular learning is important for language learning

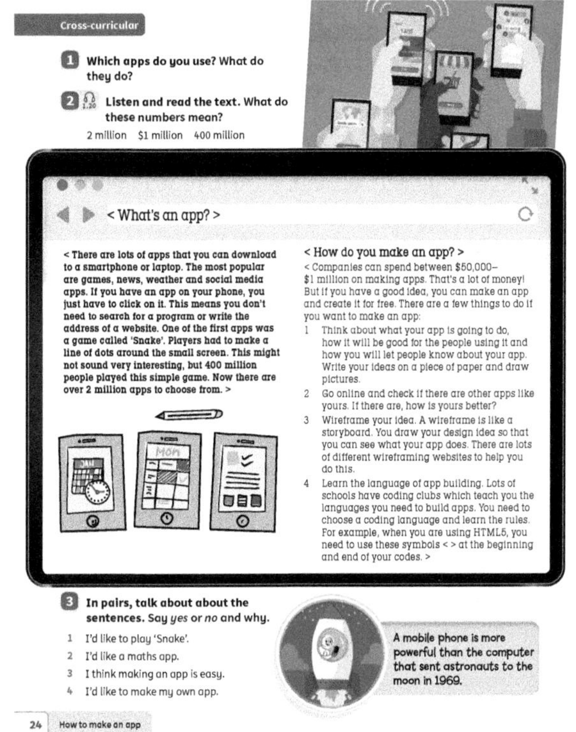
Cross-curricular

1 Which apps do you use? What do they do?

2 1.20 Listen and read the text. What do these numbers mean?

2 million $1 million 400 million

< What's an app? >

< There are lots of apps that you can download to a smartphone or laptop. The most popular are games, news, weather and social media apps. If you have an app on your phone, you just have to click on it. This means you don't need to search for a program or write the address of a website. One of the first apps was a game called 'Snake'. Players had to make a line of dots around the small screen. This might not sound very interesting, but 400 million people played this simple game. Now there are over 2 million apps to choose from. >

< How do you make an app? >

< Companies can spend between $50,000–$1 million on making apps. That's a lot of money! But if you have a good idea, you can make an app and create it for free. There are a few things to do if you want to make an app:

1 Think about what your app is going to do, how it will be good for the people using it and how you will let people know about your app. Write your ideas on a piece of paper and draw pictures.
2 Go online and check if there are other apps like yours. If there are, how is yours better?
3 Wireframe your idea. A wireframe is like a storyboard. You draw your design idea so that you can see what your app does. There are lots of different wireframing websites to help you do this.
4 Learn the language of app building. Lots of schools have coding clubs which teach you the languages you need to build apps. You need to choose a coding language and learn the rules. For example, when you are using HTML5, you need to use these symbols < > at the beginning and end of your codes. >

3 In pairs, talk about about the sentences. Say *yes* or *no* and why.

1 I'd like to play 'Snake'.
2 I'd like a maths app.
3 I think making an app is easy.
4 I'd like to make my own app.

A mobile phone is more powerful than the computer that sent astronauts to the moon in 1969.

24 How to make an app

Research on second language acquisition has shown that exposure to naturally occurring language is necessary to achieve a good level of competence in the language. Acquiring a second language is a long and natural process. Learners need to have access to spontaneous speech in an interactive context and the cross-curricular lessons in *Power Up* provide learners with this access. Learners have to expand their linguistic resources in order to deal with the demands of content learning. Using a second language to grasp non-language content requires a depth of processing which leads to improved language acquisition. Learning is a problem-solving activity and cross-curricular learning requires learners to solve problems through a second language.

The benefits of using cross-curricular learning in the classroom

- Cross-curricular learning relies on intrinsic motivation, that is, the learners are involved in interesting and meaningful activities while using the language. Lessons provide opportunities for incidental language learning. Incidental learning has been shown to be effective and long lasting.
- Through exposure to interesting and authentic content, cross-curricular learning leads to greater involvement and helps increase learner motivation.
- Through the interactive and co-operational nature of the tasks, cross-curricular learning helps boost self-esteem, raise self-confidence, build learner independence and teach learner organisational skills.
- Through the integration of language and content, cross-curricular learning encourages creative thinking.
- Cross-curricular learning fosters learning to learn through the use of learning strategies and study skills.

In Primary 5 and 6, learners can move in a linguistic environment that promotes a complete development of the language. The difficulty now falls on the changes in the learner's maturity and their reluctance to stand out from their peers. This shyness affects the interactive nature of the CLIL classes, but it can be countered by the increased use of pair and group work. Throughout the learning process of children at this level, teachers are able to talk without paying special attention to the English language. Learners will have acquired a natural perception of the second language and a linguistic level that allows them to understand most of the language structures. There is however an increased demand for accurate reading and writing skills as they have to practise for the external language exams. The topics covered in the CLIL pages have been chosen to interest learners and to motivate them to extend their knowledge by further investigation.

Pronunciation and Spelling

When learning another language, pronunciation and spelling are two of the most challenging aspects. English, in particular, has a complicated spelling system, so learning and practising the rules and patterns, as well as any exceptions to those rules, is the key to success!

In *Power Up* levels 5 and 6, the focus is predominantly on pronunciation and stress patterns. There are pronunciation activities for every unit at the end of the Pupil's Book and within every unit in the Activity Book. The activities focus on a variety of potentially challenging pronunciation aspects of the English language. They focus on areas such as sounds non-native English speakers often find more challenging, or particular spelling patterns that sometimes pose more difficulties. In addition, they focus on stress patterns in words, sentences and questions, as well as intonation. The nuances of English pronunciation can affect the meaning of a statement or question, so it is important for students to familiarise themselves with these nuances and practise them as much as possible.

The Pupil's Book pronunciation activities are designed to practise key sounds or spellings that occur in the words taught in the unit, so that the words and their meanings are already familiar to the students, therefore making the focus more about pronunciation than on reading and comprehension. The Activity Book activities are based on the audio from Lesson 6 of each unit.

The teaching notes support the pronunciation focus along with the accompanying audio. Any key pronunciation points are outlined in the teaching notes for each unit and there's also a pronunciation tip for each of the Activity Book pronunciation activities, for the teacher to discuss with the children. Gradually, the children will learn the patterns for pronunciation and sentence stress through lots of practice and, over time, their pronunciation will become more and more accurate as their ear becomes attuned to hearing the British/American pronunciation.

Preparation for Cambridge A2 Key for Schools and B1 Preliminary for Schools in Level 5

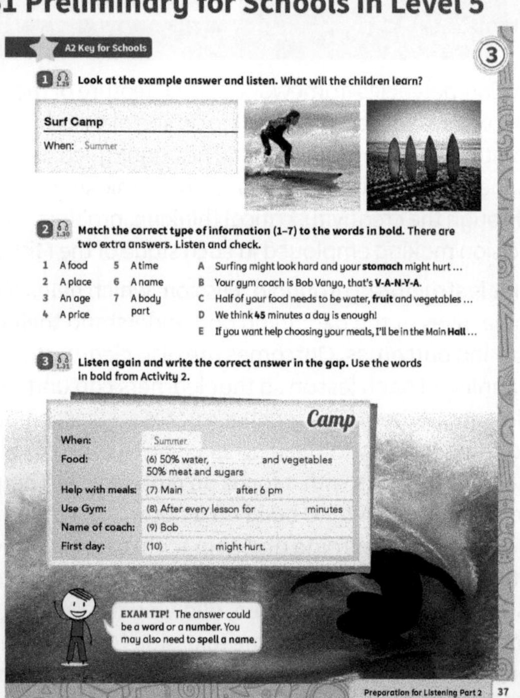
A2 Key for Schools

3

1 **Look at the example answer and listen. What will the children learn?**

Surf Camp

When: Summer

2 **Match the correct type of information (1–7) to the words in bold. There are two extra answers. Listen and check.**

1 A food
2 A place
3 An age
4 A price
5 A time
6 A name
7 A body part

A Surfing might look hard and your **stomach** might hurt …
B Your gym coach is Bob Vanya, that's **V-A-N-Y-A**.
C Half of your food needs to be water, **fruit** and vegetables …
D We think **45** minutes a day is enough!
E If you want help choosing your meals, I'll be in the Main **Hall** …

3 **Listen again and write the correct answer in the gap. Use the words in bold from Activity 2.**

Camp

When:	Summer
Food:	(6) 50% water, ... and vegetables 50% meat and sugars
Help with meals:	(7) Main .... after 6 pm
Use Gym:	(8) After every lesson for .... minutes
Name of coach:	(9) Bob ....
First day:	(10) .... might hurt.

EXAM TIP! The answer could be a **word** or a **number**. You may also need to **spell a name**.

Preparation for Listening Part 2 37

Through a unique partnership between Cambridge Assessment and Cambridge University Press, *Power Up* is the first course to naturally integrate test preparation and formative assessment in a fun and effective English course. This well-rounded formula equips learners with the skills and abilities to approach Cambridge English tests with real confidence.

Power Up contains a motivating 'test builder' stage in each unit which develops the skills needed for test success and test strategies for younger learners. It familiarises learners with Cambridge test formats in a positive context which prioritises progress in learning and develops confidence. Learners complete their preparation for A2 Key for Schools and partially prepared for B1 Preliminary for Schools during Level 5 of *Power Up*.

The unique partnership between Cambridge University Press and Cambridge English Assessment means that *Power Up* has been developed with a new, integrated approach to the Cambridge Exams.

Throughout *Power Up*, learners are given practice in Cambridge exam-style tasks, indicated by the ☆. In Level 5 Units 1–4, learners experience test tasks in the style of A2 Key for Schools. Then in Units 5–9, they progress to Preliminary for Schools.

In each unit of Level 5, the two Pupil's Book Exam preparation pages focus on two parts of the A2 Key for Schools or B1 Preliminary for Schools tests. Each page breaks down a task and focuses on the skills needed to complete it step by step. The lesson trains learners and provides tips and insights into what learners can do to achieve their best.

The Activity Book follows on by giving learners an opportunity to practise the task in full, building on what they have learnt in the Pupil's Book.

As a final step, the *Power Up Test Generator* includes full Key for Schools and Preliminary for Schools practice tests.

The Cambridge exams provide colourful and motivating tasks which test real-life skills. All the exams help learners develop their everyday written and spoken English. This means that preparing for the exams also supports effective learning. Each exam tests the four skills: listening, reading, writing, speaking. *Power Up* bridges the gap between the topics of the exam and the lives of the learners in a humorous and inspiring way, presenting the topics in a fun and engaging style. Exam-style tasks therefore develop the skills of the learners effectively in a step-by step-progression, allowing learners to build on what they know and increase their confidence. B1 Preliminary for Schools now has practical language skills and the content is aimed a school-age learners so it continues to build on the knowledge learners have developed when preparing for Key for Schools. Information about the revised tests is available here: www.cambridgeenglish.org/exams-and-tests/

 Audio visual material

The audio visual material in *Power Up* both as a learning aid and as a tool to increase learner motivation.

Power Up Levels 5 and 6 feature two videos per unit:, plus another interactive quiz video in each of the three review sections.

- A unit opener video introduces the unit topic, activates prior knowledge and helps establish both unit and individual learning objectives.
- Speaking test videos, designed to focus on one part of Cambridge Key for Schools or Preliminary for Schools Speaking Test, appear in Speaking practice. They feature two exam candidates answering questions in the style of the test. These serve as a model for learners to follow and also reduce anxiety by giving learners an idea of what to expect. There is also a still from the video on the Activity Book page, followed by an activity.
- The interactive review quizzes in the three review sections consolidate the learner's knowledge and assesses how they have progressed in relation to the learning objectives.

Components

Pupil's components

Pupil's Book

Activity Book with access to online activities

Home Booklet

Teacher's components

Teacher's Book

Teacher's Resource Book

Test Generator

Class audio CDs

Presentation Plus

Downloadable class videos (videos diaries, practice Speaking Test videos, interactive quizzes)

Posters

Visit www.cambridge.org/powerup to find all the information you need on the wide variety of components of *Power Up* and how they can be combined to meet your needs. In the following section of this introduction we focus on the Pupil's Book followed by the unit opener page and sounds and spellings sections found in the Activity Book.

The Pupil's Book

The Pupil's Book features:

- nine core units with audio and audio visual content
- three Review units

Pupil's Book unit walk-through

In *Power Up* 5, Jim and Jenny Friendly are living in the city and produce funny vlogs (video diaries) about different subjects. They share their ideas and adventures with their friends Mark and Sam.

This is followed by nine core units, each with 12 lessons. The Teacher's Book contains a 'Warm-up' and an 'Ending the lesson' activity for each of the 12 lessons and the Review units. The 'Warm-up' is designed to prepare learners for the lesson and engage them fully. The 'Ending the lesson' activity is designed to consolidate what they have learnt in the lesson. The Review sections appear after every three units.

The 12 lessons in each core unit are:

- Lesson 1 Unit opener and Mission set up
- Lesson 2 Vocabulary 1 presentation
- Lesson 3 Language presentation 1
- Lesson 4 Language practice 1 & Mission Stage 1
- Lesson 5 Vocabulary 2
- Lesson 6 Language practice 2 & Mission Stage 2
- Lesson 7 Literature – text focus
- Lesson 8 Literature – response to text / social & emotional skills
- Lesson 9 Cross-curricular
- Lesson 10 Exam builder
- Lesson 11 Exam builder
- Lesson 12 Review & Mission in action

Lesson 1

Unit opener and Mission set up

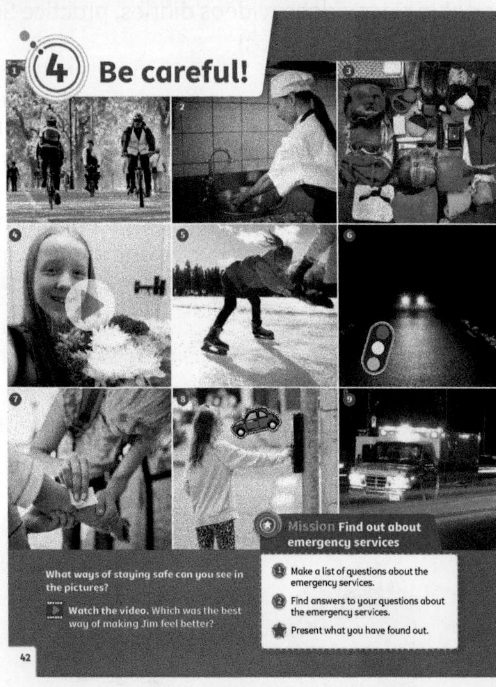

Lesson 1 opens the unit with theme-related pictures which set up the context for the unit and introduces some of the core language that follows.

SA Learners are introduced to their first self-assessment in a self-assessment spot. They are invited to think about how much they can do at this stage of learning. This will allow them to see how much progress they have made by the end of the unit. At this stage:

- learners have a chance to think about the topic and what they already know about it.
- they are asked to assess which language they know and what they can't say yet.

- Learners then watch a vlog (video diary) and complete a task which encourages them to think about what will follow in the rest of the unit. This task also personalises the learning and makes it relevant to their lives.
- The unit Mission is then set up. Three stages and a Mission completion are clearly outlined. The Activity Book contains a corresponding Mission statement page which is revisited as the learners progress through the mission.

Lesson 2

Vocabulary 1 presentation

The first focus on vocabulary is presented and practised in Lesson 2 based on the topic of the unit and with colourful images to contextualise the language. This shows typical real world situations and contextualises the vocabulary to present meaning.

- Learners see and hear the new language first of all and are required to give a response as they recognise the vocabulary.
- Learners are encouraged to produce the language accurately in an engaging activity.
- This is followed by a consolidation task, usually requiring learners to respond to questions using the new vocabulary.

Lesson 3

Language presentation 1

Lesson 3 provides a related context using pictures, audio or text which practices the new vocabulary and introduces the grammar point to follow.

- Learners listen and read the language using the pictures to help them understand.
- The teacher's book provides comprehension checks for the teacher to use to support and check understanding.
- At this stage, the learners are only exposed to new language. The activities and pictures help to establish the meaning and are often related to the types of task found in the exam.
- There may be an exam tip box which gives learners a technique to help them with exam questions.

Lesson 4

Language practice and Mission Stage 1

In lesson 4, the new grammar point is practised and Mission Stage 1 is completed.

- The 'grammar look' box highlights the target language which learners have heard in the previous lesson and gives learners a chance to say and hear the language. It highlights key features of the language form in a simple, age-appropriate way. Pronunciation can also be corrected at this point.
- There is a further exam tip highlighting how the skills used in this lesson can be helpful in the exam.
- This is usually followed by a task requiring the learners to read and write using the new language.
- Learners are also directed to additional grammar tasks at the back of the book to provide further controlled practice of the language.
- Learners then complete Mission Stage 1 using the language they have learnt so far in the unit. The Mission Stage 1 activities usually involve listening and speaking

collaboratively to complete a topic focused task. It requires learners to make decisions and be creative in order to complete the task.

Lesson 5

Vocabulary 2

This lesson uses a reading or listening text to develop the topic and introduce further new vocabulary.

- Learners complete simple tasks which encourage them to produce the new language.
- This is usually followed by an activity or game that provides further practice and develops one or more skills – listening, reading, writing or speaking.

Lesson 6

Language practice 2 and Mission Stage 2

This lesson begins with a listening task requiring learners to select a picture by understanding the new language.

- There is a second **Grammar look** box which again highlights the target language and gives learners a chance to hear the language and say it correctly.
- Learners are directed to further grammar practice and a pronunciation task at the back of the book which encourages them to practice a feature of pronunciation related to the target language.
- In the final part of the lesson, learners use the new language to complete Mission Stage 2. This builds on Mission Stage 1 and again activities usually involve listening and speaking collaboratively to complete a topic focused task.
- SA Once Mission Stage 2 is completed, learners are directed to complete a reflection and self-assessment from the Mission statement page in the Activity Book.

Lessons 7 and 8

Literature – text focus and response to text / social and emotional skills

In this section, learners read and listen to a text and then respond to it. The text uses language from the unit in a context which learners can relate to. The pictures and illustrations support understanding and help learners follow the text as they listen. It also helps them prepare for the activities that follow.

- Each text generally begins with an introductory speaking task which helps the learners to focus on the topic and encourages them to look at the titles and pictures of the story before they read.
- Learners then listen to the text as they read which helps bring it to life and understand the content.
- Teacher's notes provide comprehension tasks to help support comprehension and to check understanding stage by stage as learners listen and read.
- In the second lesson, learners complete follow up activities using reading, speaking, writing and listening. Tasks include answering questions, talking about personal experience related to the topic, discussing ideas and identifying how people or characters feel about situations. The activities help develop learners' emotional competencies and encourage them to develop social and life skills such as kindness, sharing and politeness.

Lessons 9

Cross-curricular

This lesson introduces a topic which relates to the main focus on the unit but which is linked to other subjects in the school curriculum. This encourages learners to think about other learning areas using English and develops their vocabulary further. It also develops critical thinking skills and encourages broader knowledge of the world around them.

- Tasks and pictures are provided to help learners understand the topic and its relevance to them.
- A variety of practice activities follow: these can involve listening, reading, writing and speaking and give learners to the chance to practise language, develop their skills and improve their critical thinking.
- There is an exam tip which gives the learners useful strategies for the exam.

Lessons 10 and 11

Key for Schools and Preliminary for Schools Cambridge Exam skills builder

In lesson 10, there is a focus on familiarising learners with the Cambridge A2 Key for Schools and B1 Preliminary for Schools exams. Each lesson focuses either on listening, speaking, reading and writing. It allows learners to develop exam strategies and tips. It enables them to become familiar with the exam rubrics and task types of the exam. It also allows both the learners and teacher to see how well they might perform in the KfS or PfS exams.

- Learners complete tasks typical of the KfS or PfS exams. These include matching tasks, completing texts and writing about pictures.
- Notes in the teacher's book give advice on how to develop learners' exam strategies including confidence building tips. There are also more exam tip boxes.

Lesson 12

Unit review and *Mission in action*

The final lesson reviews the language covered in the unit through the final Mission stage. This brings together all the previous stages in a collaborative and practical task. As such it recycles all the language and skills developed in the unit.

- Learners are encouraged to follow all the stages of the Mission and has a final outcome. This might be acting out a scenario, doing a presentation or showing a final plan or piece of work.
- SA Once the *Mission in action* is completed, learners are directed to complete a final reflection and self-assessment from the Mission statement page in the Activity Book.

Review units

A review unit is included every three units and appears after unit 3, 6 and 9. Each review is two pages and recycles and consolidates the language from the preceding units. The topics are similar to those in the core units but encourage the learners to apply their new language and knowledge into new contexts.

- Each review begins with a video quiz which learners can complete to see how much they can remember. This quiz can be repeated after the review is completed to measure progress after the review activities are complete.
- This is followed by listening tasks, tasks based on pictures to encourage speaking practice and personalised writing tasks.
- There is also a flowchart which provides learners with some techniques for learning and retaining vocabulary autonomously. This develops their study skills.

Unit opener page in the Activity Book

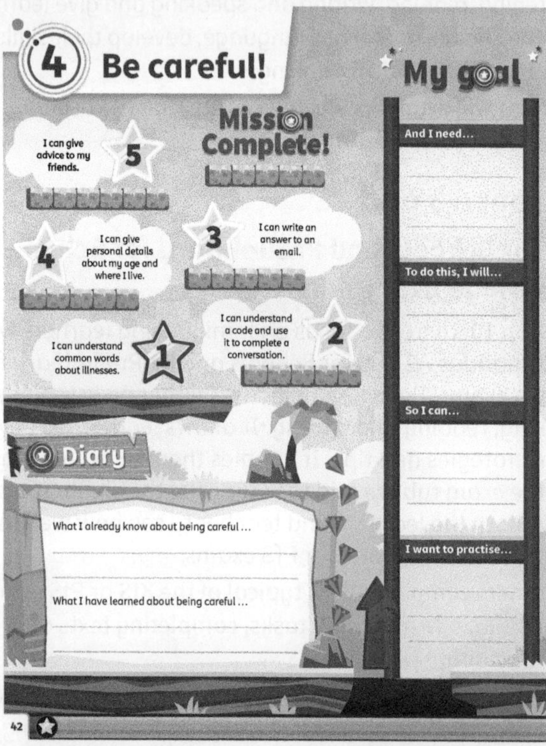

The unit opener in each unit of the Activity Book is actually a page for you and your learners to refer to throughout each unit. It has three key parts: the Mission Complete, a 'My unit goals' ladder and 'My mission diary'. The following section provides you with the teaching notes for this page of the Activity Book which you can return to as you progress through each unit.

Mission Complete

Go through the mission statements with the learners at the beginning of the unit. You can read these or if you prefer you can put them onto the board or a poster. Ask learners to think about how confident they are with each step. Learners can discuss in pairs and small groups or just think about what they can do on their own. Remember to go back to the mission complete sentences at the end of each Mission stage during the unit and review them. Learners can tick the stars as they progress. Quickly check what each learner is doing at each stage to get a sense of their own assessment. **Fast finishers** and **stronger learners** can work in pairs and give examples of the language they have learnt that helped them complete each stage. **Extra support** – learners can go back to their books to copy words or language they have been learning.

My mission diary

At the start of each Mission stage, ask learners to think about what they already know about the main topic of the unit. Ask them to fill in the first part of the diary. They can do this alone or discuss in pairs or small groups and then complete the information for themselves. Go back to this at the end of each Mission stage and ask them to complete the second part of the diary highlighting what they know about the topic after completing the different parts of the unit.

My unit goals

This section is in four parts and forms a 'ladder'. After learners are familiar with the mission goals, and have finished the first part of the unit, e.g. after the unit opener, ask learners to think what they would like to do by the end of the unit. **Stronger learners** might come up with their own ideas. **Extra support** – some learners might need to use the Mission statements to think about something they want to learn. Tell them to think about what they need to learn and do in order to achieve this. You can give an example if you like, e.g. *I want to practise describing a city so I can say if it is a good place to live. To do this, I will read about cities and I need new vocabulary*. Check the ideas that learners have and what they think they need to do.

Practical techniques for using the word stack

1 Test yourself

- Learners go through their word stack and write a selection of words onto small cards. They can draw a picture on the other side of the card. Put the learners into pairs. Their partner holds up the card to show the picture and the learner says the word.
- Pairs then swap roles.

2 Test each other

- Learners choose a selection of words from their own word stack.
- Put the learners into pairs.
- Learners take it in turns to say a word to their partner. Their partner should draw, mime or give an example sentence of all the words they know. If they are asked a word they don't know their partner should explain or show it to them.

3 K/M/F charts

- This is a play on the K/W/L chart. Learners go through their word stack and choose five words they feel confident about, three they think they know, and two they can't remember.

- They create a poster with the letters *K*, *M*, *F* at the top. *K* is for words they **know**; *M* is for words they **might** know, and *F* is for words they have **forgotten**. They can write the words into the columns or add sticky notes to each column.
- Learners then work in small groups of three or four and present their K/M/F charts to the rest of the group. Other learners in the group should remind them of the three words in the *F* list. If no-one can remember the words, they should check in their books.

4 Learner quiz

- Learners work in groups of four or five. They look at their word stacks and create three questions to ask the rest of the class about some of the words. The questions can be based on drawings (*What is this? / What are these?*) or on an action (*What do I feel?* – miming angry or happy) or a question (*Is Harry big or small?*).
- Once the learners have prepared their questions, they sit in their groups. Each group takes it in turns to ask the rest of the class one of their questions.
- The first group to answer gains one point. If any group can ask a question the other learners don't know, they get a bonus point.

Speaking and spelling in the Activity Book

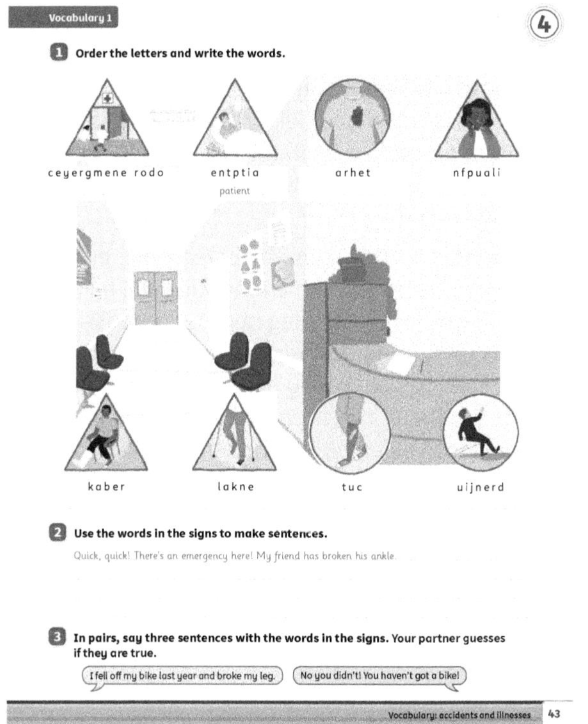
Vocabulary 1

4

1 **Order the letters and write the words.**

ceyergmene rodo

entptia

patient

arhet

nfpuali

kaber

lakne

tuc

uijnerd

2 **Use the words in the signs to make sentences.**

Quick, quick! There's an emergency here! My friend has broken his ankle.

3 **In pairs, say three sentences with the words in the signs.** Your partner guesses if they are true.

I fell off my bike last year and broke my leg.

No you didn't! You haven't got a bike!

Vocabulary: accidents and illnesses 43

When learning another language, pronunciation and spelling are two of the most challenging aspects. English spelling can seem very complicated, but there are many patterns and rules which will help learners achieve success.

There are speaking and spelling practice activities in every unit of the Activity Book. The activities focus on particular words that learners often find challenging, or particular spelling patterns that sometimes pose difficulties, such as certain spelling patterns pronounced in different ways, as well as words pronounced the same but spelt differently.

The focus vocabulary used in these activities is drawn from the first vocabulary set of each unit, as well as any relevant revision vocabulary from prior units and levels where appropriate. The activities are designed to practise key words and expressions taught in the unit, so that the words and their meanings are already familiar to the learners, thereby making the focus more about sounds and spelling than reading and comprehension.

Power Up and its methodology

Power Up features a systematic approach to language learning in which the learner and teacher are in a partnership. It aims to develop the language and skills of the learner, but also helps them achieve better life-long progress in learning.

What does it involve? The *Power Up* methodology helps teachers and learners to plan learning effectively, measure progress and identify areas for improvement in learning. In practice this means that all activities, inside and outside the classroom, can be integrated with assessment. More traditional summative assessment still continues. External 'tests' can be used alongside the classroom-focused formative assessment activities. For teachers, this should not feel strange: using external assessments to check progress and performance is familiar; monitoring learners' progress and adapting teaching to support them is also routine. *Power Up* simply combines these elements in a systematic way. In *Power Up*, you will see that classroom activity is designed to allow the teacher to monitor for evidence to measure progress and also includes tasks that are similar to those in formal summative tests such as Cambridge English Key for Schools and Preliminary for Schools.

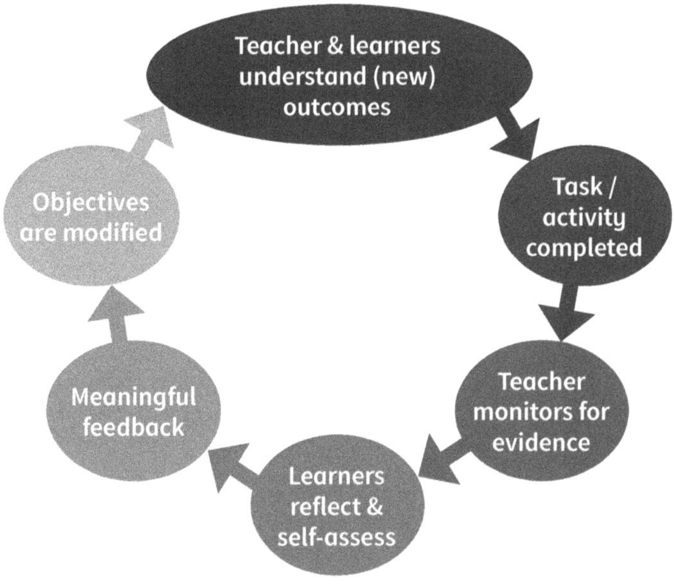

How does it work in the classroom? In *Power Up*, learners are given more independence to understand their own strengths and weaknesses, both immediate (e.g. in a lesson) and longer term (e.g. over a school term). In the classroom, this begins with making sure learning objectives are clear to both learner and teacher. In *Power Up*, these are identified by the outcomes at the beginning of each lesson. Once outcomes are established, both the learner and the teacher think about how each activity can support a learning outcome. After the activity is finished, they reflect on performance in relation to that outcome and use this evidence to adjust what happens in later lessons – this might be reviewing and practising some language again or moving on more quickly depending on the performance. Normal classroom activities therefore combine learning with assessment to provide meaningful feedback to learners. Being involved in the process helps learners improve outcomes and gain confidence. In addition, if the activities and content are linked to the language and skills of more formal language tests, classroom activities can also be benchmarked against formal tests.

No matter how young a learner might be, this process can help learners develop their skills and learn about the world around them. *Power Up* aims to develop skills such as collaboration and encourages learners to understand their own progress and think about how they can improve. Learners can begin to do this even when they are young. *Power Up* therefore includes multistage projects which encourage learners to collaborate and work together helping them develop better life skills, and regular self-assessment stages.

What kind of activities are used in class? *Power Up's* methodology can be integrated into everyday learning to support progress in different ways and these have been integrated into the course:

Power Up prioritises real-life language and activity. It therefore includes learning activities which reflect **real-world tasks** and offer topics designed to engage the learners.

Power Up asks teachers and learners to understand objectives. Expected outcomes for each lesson are shown at the beginning of each lesson in *Power Up* and Mission statements are also provided in learner-accessible style; these can be shared in creative ways with the learners. This helps learners understand what they are trying to achieve in each activity they complete. In Level 5, the Missions are more flexible giving learners the opportunity to decide how much work they want to do to achieve each stage.

Using *Power Up*, learners begin to **reflect on their own performance and measure progress** in achieving those outcomes. Learners complete multistage projects in *Power Up* and consider how well they have done at each stage of the project using suggested self-assessment techniques. This encourages **autonomy**. Learners are also given opportunities to make choices during their activities and Missions, which encourages self-confidence and independence.

Teachers using *Power Up* can collect information about the learners through their classroom activities, completion of tasks and self-assessment, and this allows both teacher and learners to **plan learning** more effectively as they work through the material.

Links can be made between classroom activities and some of the performance measures of formal tests so that **formative and summative assessment** is linked together.

Self-assessment guide

It is important for learners to understand the purpose of lessons and to think about how well they achieve learning outcomes. They can begin to do this at a young age: their learning in all areas, not just language, will benefit. In this book, each unit of learning therefore includes stages:

- asking learners to think about what they will learn – making the outcomes for each lesson clear to them
- helping them to think about their progress – asking them to self-assess through simple activities.

When to use Self-assessment

These stages are labelled **Self-assessment**. You can use any of the techniques explained below at these stages. Choose one of the techniques each time. You can do this at the beginning and end of each lesson and/or at the beginning and end of each unit.

When you do this at the beginning of learning, **encourage the learners to be honest** – the language will be new, so they should recognise this. They need to be reassured that if you can't do something, knowing this and showing you need more support is a positive way to help yourself. There is an added benefit: when you repeat this assessment at the end of activities, they will be able to recognise what they have learnt. They can also indicate if they are still not confident, which will help you, and them, to see which areas of learning will need more attention.

Techniques for the classroom

Some of the techniques are suitable for the start, mid and end of lessons or units in the self-assessment spots. Other techniques are quick and preparation free (or need preparing once and are reusable) and could be used in the self-assessment spots but also for individual activities if it would be useful to include.

1 Self-assessment cards

Create a simple self-assessment card and make a 'post box' by using a cardboard box with a 'letter box' cut in the lid. Learners complete their self-assessment and put it into the post box.

An example (which can be adapted for different tasks and activities) is below:

Ask learners which outcomes they are trying to achieve and help them complete the sentences – you can direct them to the lesson outcomes to support, e.g. I understand words about computers. Then tell them to think about how close they feel to achieving the outcome and choose a phrase that describes this.

Lesson outcomes: what we want to achieve	How I feel
I understand words about	This is true. This is mostly true. This isn't true yet.
I can say	This is true. This is mostly true. This isn't true yet.
I know	This is true. This is mostly true. This isn't true yet.

Variation:

- Learners keep a notebook and write their self-assessment notes in this rather than cards.
- If learners have access to mobile devices or PCs, they can complete an online self-assessment using a tool such as *doodle* and send it to you.

2 Instant messaging

Use an instant messaging service for your group. At the end of an activity or lesson ask learners to message you their self-assessment choosing from appropriate phrases, e.g. *I'm confident I can .../I'm not sure about .../I can't ....*

3 Learner journals

Learners keep a journal. Spend five minutes at the end of each lesson encouraging the learners to fill in their journal. They can be provided with stem sentences (as in example 1) or they can write anything they feel about their performance with no input from you.

4 K/W/L charts

Before beginning work on new language, create a poster with the letters K, W, L at the top. K is for words they know; W is for words they would like to know. Give the learners different words from the activities they are about to do. Ask them which words go into the K column and which go into the W column. If learners choose to put the words into the K column, they should explain or give an example using the word. After the lesson or activity sequence, go back to the poster and review the words in the W column. Learners can move them to the L column if they are confident (L is for words they have learnt) or leave them in the W column if not. You can ask them for examples of all the words in the K and L columns. If any words are left in the W column, you may need to teach them again.

Variations:

- Have one large poster and the words on cards. Use sticky tack and select learners to come up and pin them into the columns.
- Have several large posters. Divide learners into groups – one poster per group. Choose a group leader to stick the words up for the group or, for a more dynamic activity, allow all the learners to stick up some words. Words can be written on cards with sticky tape on the backs or onto sticky notes- ask the learners to copy the new words out themselves.
- Have several large posters. Divide learners into groups – one poster per group. Give each group a marker pen to write the words into the columns. (They can cross out the words at the end when they change position.)

5 Scales reordered

Create a long arrow from cardboard and stick it on the side of the board or on the wall. Inside the very top, draw a smiley face and write 100%. At the bottom do a frowning face and write 0%. (This is re-suable so you only need to prepare it once.) Give out slips of paper and paper clips to the learners. They write their name on the paper. At the end of an activity, ask them to bring up their name and to paper-clip it to the edge of the arrow, showing where they think they are on the scale.

6 Red and green cards

These cards can be prepared in advance. Although this takes preparation, these can be reused in class for a long time. Use thick green card and red card and cut these into squares approximately 12 cm x 12 cm. You will need one card of each colour per learner. If possible, laminate the cards. Punch a hole in the top left corner and tie together one red and one green card with string or a treasury tag.

Tell the class to use their cards to demonstrate how they feel about what they are learning. Hold up:

- green for 'confident'
- red for 'not sure'

Learners can also leave these on their desks as they work, leaving red up if they want help from the teacher.

Variation:

If you don't have red/green cards, ask learners to draw an empty square on a card and put it on their desk at the beginning of the lesson. During the lesson, stop at an appropriate point and ask them to colour in the square: red for 'I don't understand'; green for 'I understand'.

7 Traffic flags

Get learners to make flags. Give each learner paper. They cut out three large rectangles or triangles of paper and colour or paint them red, green and yellow. Give each learner three drinking straws and sticky tape. Ask them to stick the rectangles/triangles to the straws to make flags. When you complete an activity, the learners wave a flag according to how they feel: red – not confident, yellow – OK but need more practice, green – very confident.

8 Baskets

Put three plastic baskets or boxes on your desk (a red, a yellow and a green one).

Learners write their names onto pieces of paper and drop their name into the basket that shows how they feel.

Variation:

- If learners have completed a piece of writing or homework task, they can hand this in by placing it into the baskets to show how they feel they have done on that particular task.
- Just have red and green, without yellow to keep reflection simple.
- Paint or colour three paper plates in the three different colours or label three boxes with the different colours.

Quick 'on the spot' SA techniques

1 Thumbs up

Tell the class to use their thumbs to demonstrate how they feel about what they are learning. They can use:

- thumbs up (+ smiling) – 'I feel very confident'
- thumbs mid position (+ neutral face) – 'I think I know this' (optional)
- thumbs down (+ shaking head) – 'I'm not confident'

2 High fives

Tell the class to show how they feel about the learning using 'high fives' (the learner holding out their hand and slapping hands with another learner or the teacher):

- high five (holding the hand up high to slap) – 'I feel very confident'
- low five (holding the hand lower near the waist) – 'I'm not confident'

Even with a big class, you can go around quite quickly to 'high five' or 'low five' each learner.

Alternatively you can ask them to go to one side of the room to 'high five' and to the other side of the room to 'low five' each other, giving you a quick visual of how learners are feeling.

3 Washing lines

Give each child two pegs ¬– preferably one red and one green. Ask them to write their name on both using indelible marker pens. Set up two string lines at the front of the classroom (e.g. across a display board). After an activity, ask the learners to put either their red peg ('I don't understand') or their green peg ('I understand') on the line. If you can't find coloured pegs use simple wooden ones for learners to write on; have two lines (one with the sign 'I understand' and one with the sign 'Let's try again' next to them).

4 Sticky notes

Put a large poster on one side of the room with I can do this at the top. Put another on the other side with a saying I'm not confident yet. Learners write any words or grammar they feel confident about and something they aren't sure about, on two different sticky notes. They add one to each poster.

If many learners choose the same word to try again, you may need to revisit it with the whole class. You can ask learners to write their names on the sticky notes to help you identify individual learners' reactions.

5 Sticky spots

Create a poster divided into three columns. In the column headings, write I can do this / I'm not sure / I can't do this yet. At the end of any activity, give learners a sticky dot or sticky label. Ask them to write their name on it. As they leave the class, they stick their name into one of the columns.

6 Mini whiteboards

Give each learner a mini whiteboard if you have these. Alternatively you can make them by using laminated card which can be reused a few times.

At appropriate points, stop and ask learners draw on the card to show how they feel. You can ask them to draw a smiley or frowning face. Alternatively learners write OK / Not OK, OR write a word/phrase they are confident about at the top and a word or phrase they don't fully understand at the bottom.

They can either hold up their mini whiteboard or leave it on the desk as they work so you can see them as you monitor.

7 Jump up / Sit down

Call out some of the words or language learners have been learning, and ask learners to jump up if they are confident, but sit down if they aren't sure. You can do this with more than one item.

Teacher's classroom assessment:

As we have seen, *Power Up* involves assessing learners during everyday activities along with more traditional types of assessment or test-type activities. This information will help the teacher adjust learning aims and lesson plans so that areas of difficulty can be reviewed and areas that are easy can be dealt with quickly. This responsive style of teaching allows better progress. The teacher will also take into account how the learners are feeling: even if a learner answers questions correctly, if they don't feel confident about a particular area they may still need some extra practice.

The teacher's role

To use this approach successfully, during teaching you need to:

a. identify language outcomes clearly at the start of lessons/tasks
b. use 'closing language' regularly to highlight the achievements made
c. monitor effectively during specific activities
d. keep formative assessment notes on the group and individual learners
e. alternatively use checklists to record assessment of skills and life skills (e.g. planning / collaborating / working autonomously / sharing.)
f. encourage learners to engage in self-assessment.

After teaching you need to:

a. keep or update anecdotal records
b. use scoring rubrics to measure achievement against external scales
c. use 'portfolio' building / record keeping for individual learners.

This will give you a full record of assessment for each learner alongside any results from tests. This can help you when writing reports for learners, making them evidence-based and more detailed. It will give you an idea of how well learners are doing against external measures.

Practical techniques for the teacher's role: in class

Identifying outcomes

Each unit contains an opening stage which shows you how to set up the Mission clearly for learners. There is a Mission poster to help you track progress in the Activity Book. In this way setting outcomes and reviewing them are built into the materials.

You can:

- tell learners what you will do at the beginning of the lesson
- write the outcomes on the board
- write the outcomes on a poster and stick it on the wall; at the end of the teaching cycle you can then return to this and tick the items, or encourage a learner to come up and tick them
- put two posters on the wall: 'What we are learning', 'What we learnt': write each outcome for your lesson on a large card and stick it under the 'What we are learning' poster; at the end of the teaching cycle move the card or encourage a learner to move it to under the 'What we learnt' poster. All the outcomes from the term can gradually be added here giving a visual record for learners of what they have achieved.

Use 'closing language' regularly to highlight the achievement

- After the activity go back to the outcomes and use this to 'close' the task, e.g. *Well done. You've used lots of new language to talk about cities and described them in detail. You could answer questions after you listened to the information.*
- You can use the language from the outcomes to help close the task.
- If learners have found something difficult, make sure you praise their work even if you need to do more on this area, e.g. *Well done – you've worked really hard and described cities. Let's try again later and we can start to add more detail and use more new words.*

Monitor effectively during specific activities

- Once you have set up an activity, do a quick check around the room to make sure the learners are 'on task' and provide more guidance if any have not understood what to do. To keep the activity moving, it might be necessary to use a little L1 to help them. Try to avoid doing this too much or you will find learners 'switch off' during English instructions as they know you will repeat in L1.
- Once all the learners are on task, monitor the group, listening carefully to what they say and looking at their work especially if they are writing words. You may need to feed in words in English or answer questions if they ask you for help.
- If everything is going well, you might want to praise their progress briefly in English, but don't step in too much. If you always step in, learners will stop doing tasks and expect you to be involved. This is fine sometimes but you want to see how they work and collaborate together and if you are involved all the time you can't do this. Learners will soon get used to you monitoring without intervening.
- Use this time to note how they are doing. If you have a large group, make a list of all the learners and plan to monitor different members of the group closely during each activity, e.g. monitor learners 1–5 closely in Activity 1, monitor learners 6–10 closely in Activity 2, and so on. In this way, over a few lessons you will have monitored each individual closely.

Keep formative assessment notes on the group and individual learners

- You can use monitoring, the activities learners complete and any classroom-based tasks and homework to gather evidence about learner progress.
- Keep a notebook and pen with you during lessons to make notes; alternatively use a mobile device, e.g. tablet.
- You can prepare your notebook in advance with a page or half page for each learner. This can be updated during and after activities. See below for examples of notes on language and the skills of speaking and writing (you could include listening and reading).

Example of notes:

Learner	Overall	Vocab	Grammar	Pron	Speaking	Writing
Maria	Good progress – motivated.	Fine. Good range. Tries new words quickly.	Good word order. Forgets 'am/is/are'.	✗ Word stress	✓ Fluency ? Turn taking	✓ Spelling
Simone	Not doing homework. Progress limited.	? uses a lot of L1	✗ Tends to use single words not sentences.	✓ Accurate when using English. Uses L1 a lot.	? Lacks confidence.	✓ Strongest skill. Enjoys copying. Accurate.
Alex	Progress OK but not motivated.	Limited range but remembers.	Pres simple questions inaccurate.	? OK but problem with adding /ə/ before vowels.	✓ Fluent ? Turn taking	? OK – has to check text book a lot for words.

Use checklists for skills and life skills (planning / collaborating / working autonomously / sharing, etc.)

- Alternatively – or in addition to notes – checklists can help you to keep evidence of progress. The lists need to be prepared in advance and can be based on outcomes and/ or descriptors of level such as those in CEFR. See below for examples of a checklist for listening, reading and life skills. (You could include vocabulary, grammar, pronunciation, speaking and writing.) See the next section for information on CEFR.

Example of checklist:

	Maria	Simone	Alex
Listening – understanding gist	✓	✗ tries to understand everything	✓
Listening – understanding details	✓ some errors	? often incorrect	✓
Listening for specific information	✓ good at predicting strategies	? some errors	✓
Reading for gist	✓	✓ slow but can manage	✓
Reading for specific information	✓	✓	✓
Collaborating for group work	✓	✓	✗ not motivated – doesn't do much
Sharing	✓	✓	✓
Working autonomously	✓	✗ tries but lacks confidence	✗ needs encouragement

Encourage students to engage in self-assessment

See notes on self-assessment.

Practical techniques for the teacher's role: after class

After teaching you can use the information and evidence you have collected to ensure you have full records for learners. This information can be reviewed, along with the learners' self-assessment, to decide on what kind of teaching and learning will follow as well as to produce reports.

Keep or update anecdotal records

You can use your notes to add to any records you keep for learners. If you used a digital device you can cut and paste the notes you made. Along with formal test results, this will give you evidence and detailed information if you need to write reports for your learners.

Use scoring rubrics

You can combine in-class assessments with results of class tests, e.g. percentage scores, and all this information can be matched against external standards to give you an idea of how well learners are doing overall. For example, you can look at the 'can do' statements for each skill in CEFR scales. Look here for more information about CEFR:

http://ebcl.eu.com/wp-content/uploads/2011/11/CEFR-allscales-and-all-skills.pdf

We really hope you enjoy teaching with *Power Up* and look forward to supporting you throughout this journey with your learners.

1 In style

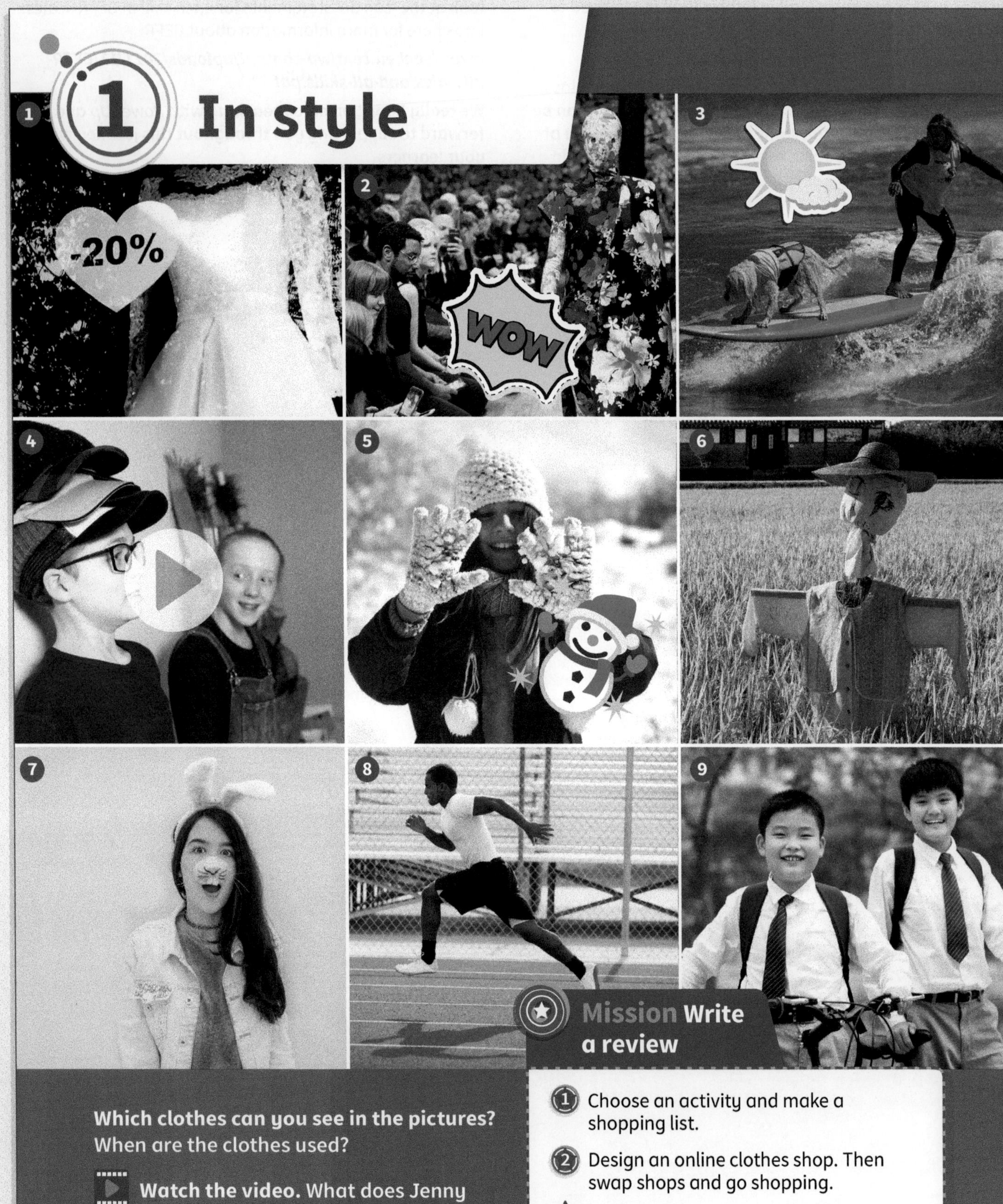

Mission Write a review

1. Choose an activity and make a shopping list.
2. Design an online clothes shop. Then swap shops and go shopping.
3. Write a review of the shop.

Which clothes can you see in the pictures?
When are the clothes used?

Watch the video. What does Jenny use as a scarf?

Unit 1 learning outcomes

In Unit 1, learners learn to:

- describe clothes
- use comparative adjectives and adverbs
- use present simple to talk about the future
- read and listen for general and specific information
- understand people all have similar feelings
- read and develop ideas about clothes in history

Materials video, two pictures (a rainy day, a raincoat) colouring pens and paper

Self-assessment

- **SA** Show pictures from the unit. Hold a copy up and point. Ask what they think they will learn about. Learners discuss in pairs then share.
- Ask learners to complete the self-assessment (see Introduction). Say *OK. Let's learn.*

Pupil's Book, page 4

Warm-up

- Ask learners to mingle around the room. If possible, play music (if not, clap a rhythm). Tell them when the music stops, they freeze. Tell them to stand back to back with the person nearest them so they can't see their partner. If there is a learner without a partner, pair with them.
- Say *What's your partner wearing? Don't look – can you remember? Tell each other.* Learners describe each other's clothes. Monitor as they speak.

Which clothes can you see in the pictures? When are the clothes used?

- Say *Open your books at page 4.* Point to the picture of a wedding dress. Ask *What's this? (a wedding dress). When is it used? (for a wedding).* Learners repeat.
- Say *We wear different things for different activities. Which clothes can you see? When are the clothes used?*
- Put learners into groups of three. Tell them they have 2 minutes to name as many items as they can. Call out *Stop* after 2 minutes. The group with the most items wins.
- Point to each one. Ask the name and what it is for. Say the name of the clothes clearly. Highlight the stress. (It is often on the first syllable.) Learners repeat.

Key: 1 wedding dress – at a wedding 2 strange dress – at a fashion show 3 wetsuit – watersports 4 hats – sunny weather 5 gloves - cold weather 6 shirt/blouse – autumn 7 fancy dress – parties 8 (running) shorts – athletics 9 ties – school

Watch the video. What does Jenny use as a scarf?

- Show a picture of a rainy day. Ask *What's the weather like? (rainy and cold). What do you wear in this weather?* Learners suggest ideas. If not suggested, show a raincoat (or picture of a raincoat). Ask *What about this? Would this be OK? (Yes) What is it? (a raincoat).* Learners repeat.
- Tell learners they will watch Jenny's vlog about organising clothes. Ask *What does Jenny use as a scarf? Think about why.* Learners watch, and then compare ideas.
- Say *How many other clothes did you see? Let's make a list.* Learners call out ideas. Write a list on the board as they say them. Say *Watch and check. Did you miss any?*
- Play the video. Learners watch and tick off items or add them.

Key: Jenny uses a raincoat as a scarf. They are giving away any clothes they can't wear and she wants to keep her raincoat, but she is wearing too many clothes.
Possible items: T-shirt, blouse, jumper, raincoat, football T-shirt, hat, trousers.

Mission Write a review

- Say *We're going to review a shop. What is a review? (It tells us about a place and what is good or bad about it).*
- Learners suggest ideas. Ask learners to read the Mission Statement in pairs to see if their ideas are right.
- Ask *Why do we use shopping lists? What would you like in your favourite clothes shop?*, e.g. types of clothes, big mirrors, free sweets.
- Tell learners to close their books. Ask learners to try to remember the Mission. Check. Say *This is our Mission.*

Activity Book, page 4

See pages TB126–141.

My unit goals

- Go through the unit goals with learners. Read these or put them onto the board or a poster (see suggested techniques in 'Identifying outcomes' in Introduction).
- Go back to these unit goals at the end of each Mission stage and review them. Say *This is our Mission page.*

Ending the lesson

- Put learners into groups of four. Give them colouring pens and paper. They take turns to draw an item of clothing. They keep drawing until others guess the item.
- The learner able to draw the most clothes which their partners can guess is the winner.

Learning outcomes By the end of the lesson, learners will be able to describe clothes, pronounce /s/ and /z/ sounds, and listen for specific detail.

New language *handbag, trainers, tights, blouse, jewellery*

Recycled language *tracksuit, jumper, raincoat, suit, swimming costume, tie*

Materials audio; dice (one per pair of learners)

Warm-up

- Draw a stick figure or simple outline of a person on the board for learners to copy it. Next to the figure write: *1 hat, 2 T-shirt, 3 trousers, 4 shoe, 5 scarf, 6 shoe*. Put learners into pairs. Give each pair a dice. Explain that if you throw 1, draw a hat. If you throw the same number twice, don't add anything.
- Tell learners to play in pairs and take turns throwing the dice. The first learner to dress their stick figure wins.

  Fast finishers label their drawings and add additional words using a dictionary if they wish, e.g. jumper, coat.

Pupil's Book, page 5

1 1.02 Listen and point to the clothes. Then match the clothes (1–11) to the words in the box.

- Say *Do you ever choose clothes online? Why / Why not?* Learners offer ideas.
- Read the introductory sentence. Say *Let's see what she wants for her birthday.*
- Say *We are going to listen to some sentences. But is it helpful to think and look at all the information we have before we listen? (Yes, it helps us listen better.)*
- Ask learners to look at the pictures quickly for 15 seconds. Then they close their books. Put them in pairs. Learners try to remember any clothes they saw.
- Say *Well done! Let's listen now. Point to the clothes when you hear them. Let's do the first one together.* Play the first sentence from the audio (*The handbag is green*). Check learners are pointing at A. Say *Now do the rest.*
- Play the audio. Learners point and say the name of each item.

  Track 1.02

  The handbag is green.
  The tracksuit is pink.
  The jumper is red and striped.
  The trainers are white.
  The tights are light blue.
  The raincoat is purple and white.
  The suit is dark blue.
  The swimming costume is pink and orange.
  The blouse is yellow.
  The tie is purple.
  The jewellery is silver.

  Extension Ask learners to look at the picture. Say *Find something yellow*. Learners call out *blouse*. Put learners into small groups Learners take it in turns to say *find something (colour)*. Their group answer.

Key: A handbag B jumper C raincoat D suit E swimming costume F tie G tights H tracksuit I trainers J jewellery K blouse

2 In pairs, read the sentences. Are they true for you?

- Read out the example: *My teacher's wearing jewellery.* If you are wearing any jewellery, show them. Ask the learners *Is it true or false*
- Learners read the sentences and answer.
- Check answers.

  Extension Learners stand in circles of six. They take it in turns describing the clothes of the learner to their right, e.g. *Alex is wearing red trainers. False making either a true or false statement' Alex is wearing white trainers.* The group call out *True* or *False*.

3 1.03 PRONUNCIATION Listen and repeat. page 118

- Write the three words on the board. Write /s/ and /z/. Ask *Which sound did you hear in each word? (suits /s/, jeans /z/, blouses /z/).*
- Tell learners to listen and repeat again paying attention to the sounds. Play the audio again.

  Track 1.03

  suits
  jeans
  blouses

- Tell learners to turn to page 118 to do Pronunciation Activity 1. (See page TB124.)

Activity Book, page 5

See pages TB126–141.

Ending the lesson

- Draw a Venn diagram on the board with *winter* in one circle and *summer* in the other.
- Ask learners what they wear at different times. Learners come to the board and write up words or work in small groups. Encourage them to explain their answers, e.g. *swimming costume – I wear this in summer at the beach.*

Vocabulary 1

1  **Listen and point to the clothes. Then match the clothes (1–11) to the words in the box.**

handbag jumper raincoat suit swimming costume
tie tights tracksuit trainers jewellery blouse

I love looking at clothes online, and here are some of my favourites. I'd love to get some of them one day … and it's my birthday soon!

1 You can put your phone in this.

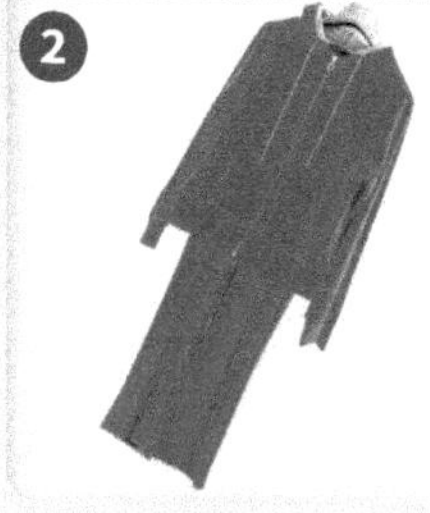

2 Great for riding my bike in the park.

3 I ♥ this. It's warm and cosy!

4 You'll love [rain] if you wear this coat.

5 Something for my brother (if he ever gets married?!?)

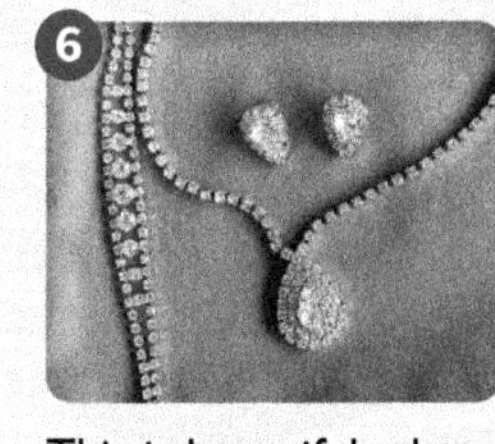

6 This is beautiful – but more $ than some cars!

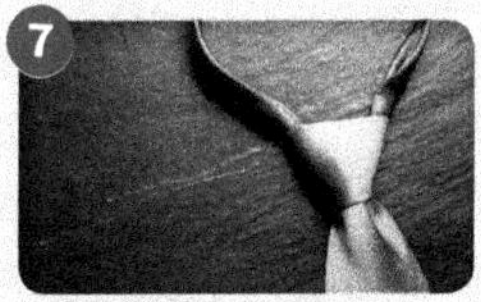

7 My geography teacher wears this! It's awesome!!!!

8 My favourite tennis player wears these!

9 This is perfect to wear in spring.

10 These are cute! And they look really comfortable.

11 This is more beautiful than a sunny day at the beach.

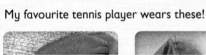

2 **In pairs, read the sentences. Are they true for you?**

My teacher's wearing jewellery.
No, she isn't.

My teacher's wearing jewellery.
I've got a handbag at home.
I've got a swimming costume.
My teacher often wears a tie.
There's a raincoat in my bag.
I'm wearing a jumper.
My mum's got a tracksuit.
I'm wearing black tights.
I've got a yellow blouse.
There are trainers in my bag.
My dad's got a blue suit.

3 1.03 PRONUNCIATION **Listen and repeat.** page 118

①

Language presentation 1

1 Read Jim's blog and answer the questions.

1 What did Jim and Jenny want? ______
2 What were the problems with the things they bought? ______
3 What is a shopping fail? ______

Jim's Big Blog

Online Shopping Fails

22nd March @12:25 pm

Last week, I bought a T-shirt online to wear at my friend's birthday party. I found a few websites where you can write on T-shirts. On one site, the T-shirts weren't as expensive as on other sites, and they looked nicer too. My friend is learning Spanish with me so I asked for 'Happy Birthday' in Spanish on the T-shirt.

The T-shirt arrived more slowly than I hoped. In fact, it arrived a few minutes before my friend's party. I put it on as quickly as I could then I left to go to the party. The T-shirt felt great – it wasn't bigger or smaller than I wanted.

When I arrived, I showed the T-shirt to my friend and he started laughing. I was confused – but then he told me about the problem with my T-shirt. It didn't say 'Feliz cumpleaños' on the back. It said, 'Happy Birthday in Spanish'! 😱

At first, I was angry – but my friend said that the T-shirt made him happy on his birthday. Then I felt a lot better. 😊

22nd March @12:45 pm

Last month, I made an online shopping mistake that was as bad as Jim's.

My feet are growing quickly so I needed a bigger pair of trainers for tennis club. I looked at two different websites. On the first site, the shoes were much more expensive. But on the second site I saw a pair of shoes I loved – they were bright red and they were very cheap.

My mum ordered the trainers for me but when they arrived I was surprised. The box was very small. Then, when I opened the box, I was shocked. The trainers were a lot smaller than my feet. And they were smaller than my toes too! In fact, they were trainers for a doll! 👟 What a mistake!

Now, I always check the size of the things I buy online.

2 Read the blog again. Who says each sentence – Jim or Jenny?

1 'My old ones are too small.'
I think Jenny says this.
2 'Great! I love the colour and they're not expensive.'
3 'Wow! This is really comfortable.'
4 'This is awful! I look so silly.'
5 'That's strange. Why's this so small?'
6 'I'm happy it made you laugh.'

Learning outcomes By the end of the lesson, learners will be able to read and understand comparatives in a text.

New language *online, blog*

Recycled language *clothes, angry, surprised, shocked,* comparative adjectives

Materials pictures of trainers, a T-shirt, a mobile phone and books; 2 cards and colouring pens for each pair of learners

Pupil's Book, page 6

Warm-up

- Write *keys* and *snacks* on the board. Ask *Which ends with the sound /s/ and which ends with /z/? (keys /z/; snacks /s/).*
- Put learners into pairs. Give each pair two cards and a colouring pen. Tell learners to write /s/ on one and /z/ on the other.
- Tell learners to decide which sound they hear, /s/ or /z/. When you say *Show me now*, learners hold up the correct card. Each pair gains a point for a correct answer.
- Do an example: say *keys*. Say *Show me now*. Check learners are doing the task correctly and gradually increase speed. (Words: days (z), trainers (z), suits (s), jobs (z), tights (s), jeans (z), shoes (z), ties (z), newspapers (s), cups (s). Add more if you wish.)

Presentation

- Say *We're going to read Jim's blog about buying clothes online on the Internet*. Say *online*. Learners repeat.
- Show pictures of trainers, a T-shirt, a mobile phone, a book.
- Say *Sometimes, when we buy things online, we don't get what we want. What problems could you have with these things online?* Discuss the picture of the trainers together, e.g. *they are the wrong size or colour*.
- Put learners into pairs to discuss the other items. Share their ideas. Ask *Which of these is expensive and which is cheap?* Check meaning if learners don't know the adjectives (*mobile phone is expensive; book or T-shirt is cheap*). Read the questions aloud.

1 Read Jim's blog and answer the questions.

- Ask *Can you read every word carefully in 2 minutes? (No).* Say *Can you find the information? (Yes).* Say *Let's find out.*
- Learners read the text alone. Monitor for progress and finish after 4 minutes.
- Put learners into pairs to check answers. Check with the class.

Key: 1 Jim wanted a T-shirt with 'Happy Birthday' written on it in Spanish, Jenny wanted a new pair of trainers.
2 Jim's T-shirt said 'Happy Birthday in Spanish' on it, Jenny's trainers were for a doll.

2 Read the blog again. Who says each sentence – Jim or Jenny?

- Tell learners that they will read again to find out more.
- Look at number 1 together. Ask learners for their answer, and then the reason.
- Put learners into pairs. Learners read and answer numbers 2–6 together. Give up to 5 minutes, but monitor for progress.
- For each answer, ask learners what Jim or Jenny said the comment about and where they found the sentence.

Key: 1 Jenny (she needs a bigger pair of trainers)
2 Jenny (she sees a pair of shoes she loves, they're red and very cheap) 3 Jim (when he puts the T-shirt on, it feels great – not bigger or smaller than he wanted)
4 Jim (his friend laughs and laughs and Jim feels angry)
5 Jenny (she's surprised when she sees the box)
6 Jim (he feels better because he made his friend laugh on his birthday)

Activity Book, page 6

See pages TB126–141.

Ending the lesson

- Divide the class into two groups. Half the class look at Jim's blog, and the rest look at Jenny's. Pair learners with a learner reading the same blog.
- Tell them they will complete a reading race to find some information in the blog. They must write their answers quickly. Give an example, e.g. say '*What does Jenny buy?' (a T-shirt for Jim;)*. Say the pair that finish first will win.
- Reveal the questions. *When did they look at the website (Jim: last week; Jenny: last month); Was the size OK? (Jim: yes; Jenny: no); Did their shopping arrive quickly enough (Jim: no; Jenny: yes); Find an adjective that describes how Jim/Jenny felt (Jim: confused or angry; Jenny: shocked).*
- Learners work in pairs and answer the questions as fast as possible. Check answers with the class.

1 Language practice 1

Lesson outcomes By the end of the lesson, learners will be able to use comparatives accurately in written and spoken English and make comparisons between clothes.

New language *...er than ..., more ... than, as ... as* for comparisons, *vintage*

Recycled language adjectives, clothes

Materials colouring pens and outline picture of body, large paper

Pupil's Book, page 7

Warm-up

- Put learners into groups of five. Give out colouring pens and a body outline or ask them to copy one. Learners have 5 minutes to create an outfit for a fashion show and describe it.
- Hold the fashion show. Invite the groups to bring their picture to the front. They present their outfit, e.g. *He is wearing lovely black jeans and a bright red T-shirt. He's got red trainers.*
- Once all the groups have presented, ask one learner from each group to stand at the front with their designs.
- Choose two designs each time. Tell the class to vote. Ask *Which clothes are more colourful?* Learners vote. Repeat with other questions: *Which clothes are warmer/ smaller/ longer/more unusual?* Finish by asking *Which is the best?*

Presentation

- Ask *What did Jim get online? (a T-shirt). What did Jenny get? (trainers).* Ask them to look at Jenny's blog on page 6.
- Ask *How small were the trainers? (very small) Why? (Because they were for a doll).* Say *Can you find a sentence that shows how small they were?* Write onto the board *The trainers were smaller ...* invite learners to call out the rest of the sentence. *(... than my feet/toes).*
- Ask *Why didn't Jenny buy the trainers on the first website?* Write on the board *They were much more ... (expensive).*
- Say *These are comparatives we use them to show a difference between two things.* Underline *smaller than* and *more expensive.* Say *Which adjective is short? (small).* Say *If it is short, we add ...(-er)* and *than.* Ask *What do we do with expensive? (add more ... than).*
- Ask *Does Jenny think her mistake was worse? (No). Does she think the mistakes were similar? (Yes).* Write on the board *I made a mistake that was as ... (bad as Jim's).* Ask *Are the mistakes similar or different? (similar).* Say *If we are comparing two similar things, we can use as... as.*

Grammar look: comparative adjectives, adverbs and *as ... as*

- Put learners into pairs. Show the sentences in the left of the grammar look box. Invite a learner to read them out. Tell learners to read the questions on the right and choose the correct option in pairs. Monitor and check.
- Ask learners to complete the rules 4-7 at the bottom of the grammar box in their pairs. Check answers with the class.

Key: 1 Jenny's feet, 2 on the first site, 3 they were similar, 4 –er than, 5 more than, 6 similar, 7 different

1 Make sentences to compare the pictures.

- Ask learn *Are 'vintage' clothes old or new? (old).* Ask *What kind of clothes can you see? (a tracksuit, a dress, trousers).* Ask *When were they made? (1860s, 1970s, 1990s)*
- Read the fact box about dresses aloud. Ask which picture shows that type of dress (the first). Ask *Is the dress older than the tracksuit? (Yes)* Put an example sentence on the board. *The dress is older than the tracksuit.*
- Put learners into threes. Check answers with the class.
  Extra support Give learners a list of adjectives changed into comparative, e.g. *wider, newer, older, more interesting.*

Key: Sample answers The dress is wider than the trousers. The tracksuit is newer than the trousers.

Complete the Grammar look on page 120.
(See pages TB125–126.)

Mission Stage 1

- Put learners into groups of four. Give each group paper. Ask them to write a list of at least six activities they could do in their free time. Show them the example (*hiking*).
- Tell learners to choose one of the activities on their list and think about what they need to wear. Say *Make a shopping list.*
- Invite each group to explain their activity and their list.
  Extension Use a picture or learner dictionary. Learners find one new word to add to their list.
- Keep a note of the activities and group members for the rest of the Mission.

Activity Book, page 7

See pages TB126–141.

Ending the lesson

- Keep learners in groups. Ask them to compare online shopping and buying things in a market or shop, e.g. *You can try clothes on in a shop. You can find cheaper things online.*

Grammar look: comparative adjectives, adverbs and *as … as*

'The trainers were a lot smaller than my feet.'

'On the first site, the shoes were much more expensive.'

'Last month, I made an online-shopping mistake that was as bad as Jim's.'

1 What is bigger? **the trainers / Jenny's feet**

2 Where did the shoes cost more? **on the first site / on the second site**

3 Whose mistake was worse? **Jim's / they were similar**

4 With short adjectives (one or two syllables long), we make comparisons with *-er than / more … than*.

5 With long adjectives (three or more syllables long), we make comparisons with *-er than / more … than*.

6 We use *as … as* to say something is the same or **similar / different** to something else. For example: 'I took the T-shirt out of the box as quickly as I could.'

7 We use *not as … as* to say something is **similar / different** to (and usually less than) something else. For example: 'The T-shirts weren't as expensive as on other sites.'

page 120

1 Make sentences to compare the pictures.

The tracksuit isn't as old as the trousers.

Did you know?

In the 1860s, some dresses were as wide as doors. Women often got stuck when they walked between rooms!

My bag: 0 items
Register/Log in
Search
Vintage Online
Look cool fast with clothes from the past!
Search by year >
Search by item >
Price: £295
Size: medium;
made in the
1860s
Price: £25
Size: extra large;
made in the 1990s
Price: £295
Size: small;
made in the
1970s

Mission Stage 1

Choose an activity and make a shopping list.

Hiking
a warm jumper, a cosy hat, trainers, a raincoat, trousers

Vocabulary 2

1 1.05 **Match the sentences (1–7) to the clothes (A–G). Then listen and check.**

It's got gold buttons.

The dress.

1 It's made of **cotton.** It's got a picture of the sun on it.

2 It's made of **leather.** It looks good for cold weather.

3 It's got a blue **collar** and it's made of **silk.** It's got gold **buttons,** too.

4 It's got a parrot **pattern.** You wear it round your neck.

5 There's a small **size** and a large **size.** You use them when you go walking.

6 It's got long **sleeves** and it's got a price **label.** It costs £25.

7 It's got a **chain.** There's a crocodile on it, too.

SOUTH AFRICA

25

A B C D E F G

2 ★ **In pairs, talk about what you like wearing at the weekend.**

3 1.06 **Listen to Safi and Rav packing. Do they need winter or summer clothes?**

EXAM TIP! Write times as numbers (for example, **12:15**) not words (for example, quarter past twelve).

4 1.07 ★ **Listen again. Complete the timetable.**

School trip timetable

Tuesday:	Airport bus leaves at: **(1)** 6:15
Flight:	10 am–9 pm
Wednesday:	go to the **(2)** ______
Thursday morning:	shopping
afternoon:	**(3)** ______ at the hotel
Friday:	go **(4)** ______
Saturday:	whale watching at **(5)** ______

Learning outcomes By the end of the lesson, learners will be able to describe clothes and what they are made of, and listen to hear general and detailed information.

New language *buttons, collar, cotton, leather, pattern, price label, silk, sleeves, it's made of*

Recycled language clothes, comparative adjectives

Materials audio; a leather belt, a silk scarf, a cotton blouse with buttons and a collar (or use pictures)

Pupil's book, page 8

Warm-up

- Put learners into groups of four. Give each group a word card with three objects. Duplicate the cards if you have a large class. *(bike/car/plane; giraffe/elephant/ant; laptop/ smartphone/tablet; big house/flat/tent; beach/city/village)*.
- Give learners 3 minutes to make comparisons.
- The winners are the group with most correct sentences.

Presentation

- Show learners items made of different materials, e.g. a leather belt, a silk scarf, a cotton blouse with buttons and a collar (or use pictures). Show the scarf. Ask *What is it? (A scarf)*. Ask *What's it made of?* Let some learners feel the material. *(It's made of silk.)* Learners repeat. Repeat with the leather belt. Say *<u>lea</u>ther* and ask learners which part/ syllable is stressed *(the first syllable)*. Learners repeat.
- Repeat with *<u>co</u>tton blouse, sleeve, <u>co</u>llar, <u>bu</u>ttons*.
- Put the items into a bag. Tell a learner to put their hand into the bag without looking and say what they can feel, e.g. *It's the belt. I can feel it's made of leather…* Repeat with a few learners.

1 1.05 Match the sentences (1–7) to the clothes (A–G). Then listen and check.

- Say *Look at the pictures. What can you see?* Learners give ideas. Ask *Can you see any pictures?* Learners point to the scarf. Say *Yes it's a… (parrot). But it has lots of parrots. This is a pattern. Pattern.* Learners repeat.
- Put learners into pairs. Ask them to say the sentence and point to the clothes. Monitor and check.

Track 1.05

Boy: It's got a blue collar and it is made of silk. It has got gold buttons, too.
Girl: The dress.
Boy: It's got long sleeves and it has got a price label. It cost £25.
Girl: The shirt.
Boy: It's made of cotton. It has got a picture of the sun on it.
Girl: The T-shirt
Boy: It's made of leather. It looks good for cold weather.
Girl: The jacket
Boy: There's a small size and a large size. You use them when you go walking.
Girl: The bags
Boy: It's got a chain. There is a crocodile on it, too.
Girl: The necklace.
Boy: It's got a parrot pattern. You wear it round your neck.
Girl: The scarf.

Key: dress, shirt, T-shirt, jacket, bags, necklace, scarf

EXAM TIP! Say *In the exam, write times and prices and dates as numbers not words. Can you see a sentence with numbers? (£25). So in the exam, write …* put £25 on the board. *Don't write …* put twenty-five pounds on the board.

- Learners copy the sentences. Check they write numbers.

2 ★ In pairs, talk about what you like wearing at the weekend.

- Put learners into pairs to talk.
- Ask learners to tell the class what their partner likes wearing.

3 1.06 Listen to Safi and Rav packing. Do they need winter or summer clothes?

- Read the instructions. Play the audio.
- Put learners into pairs to check answers.

Key: winter clothes (*It's winter in South Africa in July.*)

See audioscripts on pages TB118–123.

4 1.07 ★ Listen again. Complete the timetable.

- Ask *What does this show? (a timetable)*.
- Ask *What kind of information is missing? Look at the gaps.* Learners suggest ideas, e.g. places, activities, times. Say *Now listen again to fill them.*
- Play the audio again. Check answers with the class.

Key: 2 forest 3 party 4 camping 5 2.30

Activity Book, page 8

See pages TB126–141.

Ending the lesson

- Put learners into pairs to describe their clothes to each other. Put pairs together into fours. Each pair tells the other a sentence, e.g. *Nothing I'm wearing has a collar.* Their partners say which person is being described, e.g. *That's Jane because Sam has a collar.*

1 Language practice 2

Lesson outcomes By the end of the lesson, learners will be able to use present simple for the future and speak about future timetables accurately.

New language *trip, safari, city names*

Recycled language clothes, present simple, times, language of shopping, comparatives

Materials paper, colouring pens, sticky tack, copies of Mission worksheet (Teacher's Resource Book page 14)

Warm-up

- Write a list of daily activities on the board, e.g. *wake up; have breakfast*. Say *I will describe my day. Write down the times I do each thing.* Ask if they will write numbers or words *(numbers)*.
- Talk about your day, including times, e.g. *I usually wake up at quarter past six and I have breakfast at half past six.* Learners write the times, e.g. 6:15/6:30.
- Ask learners the time of each activity and write it on the board.
  Extension Learners can repeat the activity in pairs and tell each other their routines and times.

Pupil's Book, page 9

Presentation

- Show a picture of a train. Say *Tomorrow I'm going on a trip by train. It leaves at 8 o'clock.* Draw a timeline across the board. Put an arrow to the centre labelled 'now'. Draw a train shape to the right of the arrow on the line labelled '8.00'.
- Point to the 'now' arrow. Say *Is the train now? (No).* Point to the train picture. *Is it in the future? (Yes).* Write *The train leaves at 8* above the timeline. Say *Is the sentence in the present simple or the future? (present simple).* Say *Is there a timetable for the train? (Yes). So, we use the present simple.*
- Write *lessons* on the board. Say *What time did lessons start today?* (e.g. *9 o'clock*). Say *What time do lessons start tomorrow? (Lessons start at 9 tomorrow too).*

Grammar look: the present simple with future meaning

- Tell learners to read the **Grammar look** box.
- Put learners into pairs to choose the correct options. Check answers.

Key: 1 present simple 2 the future 3 future

1 Put the words in order.

- Put learners into pairs to put the words into the correct order to make questions. Check answers with the class.

Key: 1 When does the flight leave? 2 Where does the trip start? 3 Where does the tour finish? 4 What time is dinner? 5 What day is the party?

2 Choose one of the school trips. Ask and answer the questions from Activity 1.

- Say *You are going to talk about a school trip.* Ask learners to look at the three pictures to guess where the places are and what you can do there (Spain – windsurfing, South Africa – safari, Turkey – hiking).
- Put learners into pairs. Tell them to choose one of the trips but not to say which one. Give them a minute to read their text. Say *Ask your partner the questions in Activity 1.* Demonstrate the task with a strong pair encouraging person A to ask person B the first question. They guess which trip their partner chose. Monitor, checking answers.
  Fast finishers Learners suggest another activity trip of their own describing where to go and what they can do.

Key: **Spain** 1 5:30 2 Barcelona 3 Barcelona 4 6 pm 5 Saturday; **South Africa** 1 8 pm 2 Cape Town 3 Johannesburg 4 7:30 5 Saturday; **Turkey** 1 10 pm 2 Istanbul 3 Istanbul 4 6:30 5 Friday

Mission Stage 2

- Put learners into the same groups as Mission Stage 1. Give each group a copy of the Mission worksheet (Teacher's Resource Book page 14). Show examples of shops online, and then ask them to design their own using the worksheet.
- Tell them to design an online shop selling clothes. Say *Make a list of what you need to do,* e.g. choose clothes; decide the prices, choose a name for the shop.
- Learners design clothes. They can use photos of real clothes or draw them. When drawing, they add notes to the picture, e.g. gold buttons, long sleeves, and show what sizes the items are available in. Learners 'buy' from other groups' shops. Encourage them to ask questions. They talk about what they bought, e.g. *I liked the T-shirt. It's a nice colour and it was cheaper than the other T-shirts.*

Activity Book, page 9

See pages TB126–141.

Ending the lesson

- **SA** Ask learners to complete their self-assessment (see Introduction).

Grammar look: the present simple with future meaning

When does the bus leave?

At 6:15!

1 What tense is the question? **present simple / *going to* future**

2 What time is the question talking about? **the present / the future**

3 The present simple is used to talk about timetables (for example, for buses, for lessons at school or for a holiday) in the **future / past**.

page 120

1 Put the words in order.

1 flight / When / does / leave? / the

2 Where / start? / does / the / trip

3 does / tour / Where / the / finish?

4 is / time / dinner? / What

5 the / day / What / party? / is

2 Choose one of the school trips. Ask and answer the questions from Activity 1.

1

Windsurfing in Spanish seas

- Flight leaves at 5:30.
- Start and end in Barcelona.
- Dinner is at 6 pm every day.
- There is a party every Saturday at the hotel.

2

South African Safari
@ 8 pm Cape Town
(trip starts and ends in
Johannesburg)
7:30
Saturday

3

Trek Turkey

We leave the airport at 10 pm

Start and end in Istanbul

Dinner: 6:30

Party: Friday evening

Mission Stage 2

Design an online clothes shop. Then swap shops and go shopping.

Literature

1 Look at the pictures. Which sentences do you think are true? Read and check.

- The story is about a king. ______
- The king's servants help him with everything. ______
- The king goes swimming one day. ______
- The king finds a fish in the sea. ______

1.08 King Canute's day on the beach

I am a servant to the great King Canute. He is a good and powerful king who can do anything. My friend says that she saw him climb the castle as fast as a spider! And my dad told me that he can swim to the bottom of the sea to talk to jellyfish.

This morning, the king was sitting at the breakfast table, looking at the fish on his gold plate. 'Oh dear,' he said, 'I just want fruit for breakfast today!'

'Oh no!' I thought. 'I'm so sorry, your majesty,' I said. I immediately picked up the fish and someone brought a bowl of fruit that was as big as the table! 'I will do whatever you want. You are our good and powerful king,' I said. 'Thank you,' the king said, but he looked annoyed. 'People always say things like that to me, but I don't like it!' After breakfast, the king went to his bedroom to get dressed. I took his silk shirt, suit and best leather shoes from the wardrobe. His cloak and crown were on his bed. 'Oh dear,' said King Canute in a loud, angry voice. 'I just wanted to wear comfortable trousers, a shirt and boots.' I rushed in with the clothes the king wanted. 'I'm so sorry, your majesty. You are our good and powerful king.'

Again, the king looked annoyed. 'People always say things like that to me!' he complained. 'Why does everyone always, always say "yes" to me?' 'Because you're the king, your majesty,' I replied. I helped him with the buttons on his cotton shirt and I didn't say anything else.

Learning outcomes By the end of the lesson, learners will have read about a king's problem and how he solved it.
New language *complain, obey, tide, throne*
Recycled language *competition*
Materials audio; pictures

Warm-up

- Put learners into groups of four. Say *In the past, there was often a king who was the most important person in a country. And the people who did all the work were … (servants)*. Write *king* and *servant* on the board.
- Tell half the groups they are kings and half the groups they are servants. Write on the board: home/clothes/food/work/activities.
- Ask them to think about each one and what they think their life was like as a servant or a king. Learners discuss in groups.
- Swap two learners from each group so new groups have two 'servants' and two 'kings'. Tell them to describe their lives.
- When they have finished, invite the 'kings' to tell the class about their lives and the 'servants' to talk about their lives.

Presentation

- Ask them where a king sits (*on a throne)*. Say *throne.* Learners repeat. Ask what a king wears and what it is made of *(expensive clothes, e.g. silk shirts/ leather shoes, a crown, a cloak)*. If necessary, draw or show a picture of a crown and a cloak. Say *crown*. Learners repeat. Say *cloak*. Learners repeat.
- Ask *Who do you think is happier? Why?* Learners share ideas.
- Say *The servants have to obey the king. They have to do what he wants. Obey*. Learners repeat. Ask them *Do you have to obey anyone or anything?* (e.g. *parents; school rules*.)
- Say *If you don't like this, you can complain. You can say you aren't happy about something. Complain*. Learners repeat. Say *complain* and ask which sound is stressed. (second syllable). Learners repeat. Ask *What kind of things do we complain about?* (e.g. *if someone does something bad; if we buy clothes that aren't good quality*)
- Put them back into groups. Ask them to make some sentences to compare their lives, e.g. *The king's life is easier than the servants.*
- Ask learners if they think the king has any problems. Listen to their ideas, but don't comment.

Pupil's book, Page 10

1 Look at the pictures. Which sentences do you think are true? Read and check.

- Ask learners to open their books at pages 10 and 11. Ask them to look at the title and pictures. Say *Can you see a throne?* Learners point. Say *Can you see the sea?* Learners point. Say *When the sea comes into the beach what is it called? (the tide)*. Learners repeat.
- Say *What kind of text is it? (A story)*. Put learners into pairs. Ask them to read the sentences in Activity 1 and guess which ones are true.
- Check their ideas.
- Now ask them to read the story quickly. Remind them they don't need to understand every word. Tell them to find the answers to the questions.

1.08 King Canute's day on the beach

- Play the audio. Learners read and listen.
- Put learners into pairs to compare their ideas.
- Check answers.

Key 1 True 2 True 3 False 4 True

- Write the words *sorry, annoyed, excited, surprised* on the board. Tell learners to find someone in the story who feels these things.
- Check their ideas.

Key: He's annoyed because everyone does everything he wants all the time; He's sorry because the King was annoyed; He was excited because he thought the King would stop the tide; They're shocked because the sea doesn't obey the king.

- Put the learners into pairs. Say *The king can wear* 8 things *in the story. Who can find them quickly?*
- Learners look for: silk shirt, suit, shoes, cloak, crown, jeans, shirt, trainers. The first pair to finish are the winners.

Activity Book, page 10

See pages TB126–141.

Ending the lesson

- Put learners into pairs. Ask learners to read the story again and find three words they don't know.
- Give them dictionaries or use an online dictionary to find out what the words mean. Monitor and check.
  Extra support Give learners three words, e.g. powerful (having a lot of power to control people and events) / strange (unusual or surprising) / boring (not interesting or exciting) and the three meanings in random order. Learners match the words and meanings.

Lesson outcomes By the end of the lesson, learners will have responded to a text using critical thinking and emotional intelligence.

New language *powerful,* words chosen by learners

Recycled language clothes, conditionals, adjectives

Materials audio; paper and colouring pens, sticky tack, marker pens

Social and Emotional Skill: dealing with frustration

- After reading the story, ask learners *What does the king complain about? (His servants always saying he's powerful.) How do you think he feels? (annoyed, frustrated, angry)*. Ask *Do you think the servants understand his feelings? (No)*
- Say *When other people don't understand or ignore how you feel, it is frustrating. It is best to act to stop feeling frustrated, like the king does.* Ask *What does he do? (He sits in the sea to prove he doesn't have superpowers because the sea doesn't obey him.)*
- Write the following on the board and tell learners to think about what they would do in each of these situations: *1 A classmate thinks you copied them in an exam, but you didn't. 2 You can't do your maths homework. You don't understand it. 3 Your mother says you should be more talkative.*
- Learners work in pairs to discuss times they felt frustrated, either when people don't understand them or when they weren't able to do something. They share their situations and think of ways to help their partner.

Warm-up

- Put learners into groups of six. Each group sits in a circle. Give each group a bean bag (or alternative object). Tell them to look back at the pictures on pages 10–11.
- Ask learners to retell the story. Give the bean bag to one learner to begin. The learner tells the first line of the story and passes the bag to the next learner who continues. If they get stuck, they say *pass* and give the bag to the next learner.

  Fast finishers Tell the story again, passing the bag faster.

Pupil's Book, page 11

Presentation

- Tell learners to look at the story on pages 10-11 again.
- Put learners into pairs. Tell them to describe what the king normally wears and the clothes he wears to the beach. Invite some pairs to share their descriptions.
- Ask learners to think of words to describe the king. Encourage them to include *powerful*. Ask them to think of three good things about being powerful and three bad things. Let them use dictionaries.

Key: normal: silk shirt, suit, leather shoes; beach: jeans, trainers, cotton shirt with buttons; **Sample answers:** you can do what you want; it's difficult to make friends.

2 In pairs, talk about the questions.

- Put learners into groups of four. Ask them to look at the four questions and discuss.
- Ask groups to share their ideas with the class.

  Fast finishers If learners suggest useful vocabulary, add it to the board. Then Ask them to repeat.

Key: Sample answers 1 A good person because he doesn't want everyone to agree with him just because he's king. 2 He doesn't like them saying yes to him because it is boring. 3 Learners' own ideas 4 He's frustrated because they don't treat him like a normal person. They think he has superpowers, so he tries to stop the sea to show he doesn't.

Activity Book, page 11

See pages TB126–141.

Ending the lesson

- Put learners into groups of three to five. Give each group a set of sticky notes. Tell to write at least three new words the story onto the notes.
- When each group has completed their notes, tell them to think of the meaning and an example for each one. Then they should stick the sticky notes on the wall.
- Tell groups to move in front of the notes of another group. Ask them to find out how many words are the same as theirs and how many are different. If any are different, they check that they understand them and say another example.
- Ask them to stick their sticky notes on the board.
- Put learners into pairs. Ask each pair to look at the board and choose a word. They ask a question related to the word, e.g. *throne – What does the king sit on?* The others say the answer. If it is correct, remove it from the board. Continue until all the notes have been removed.

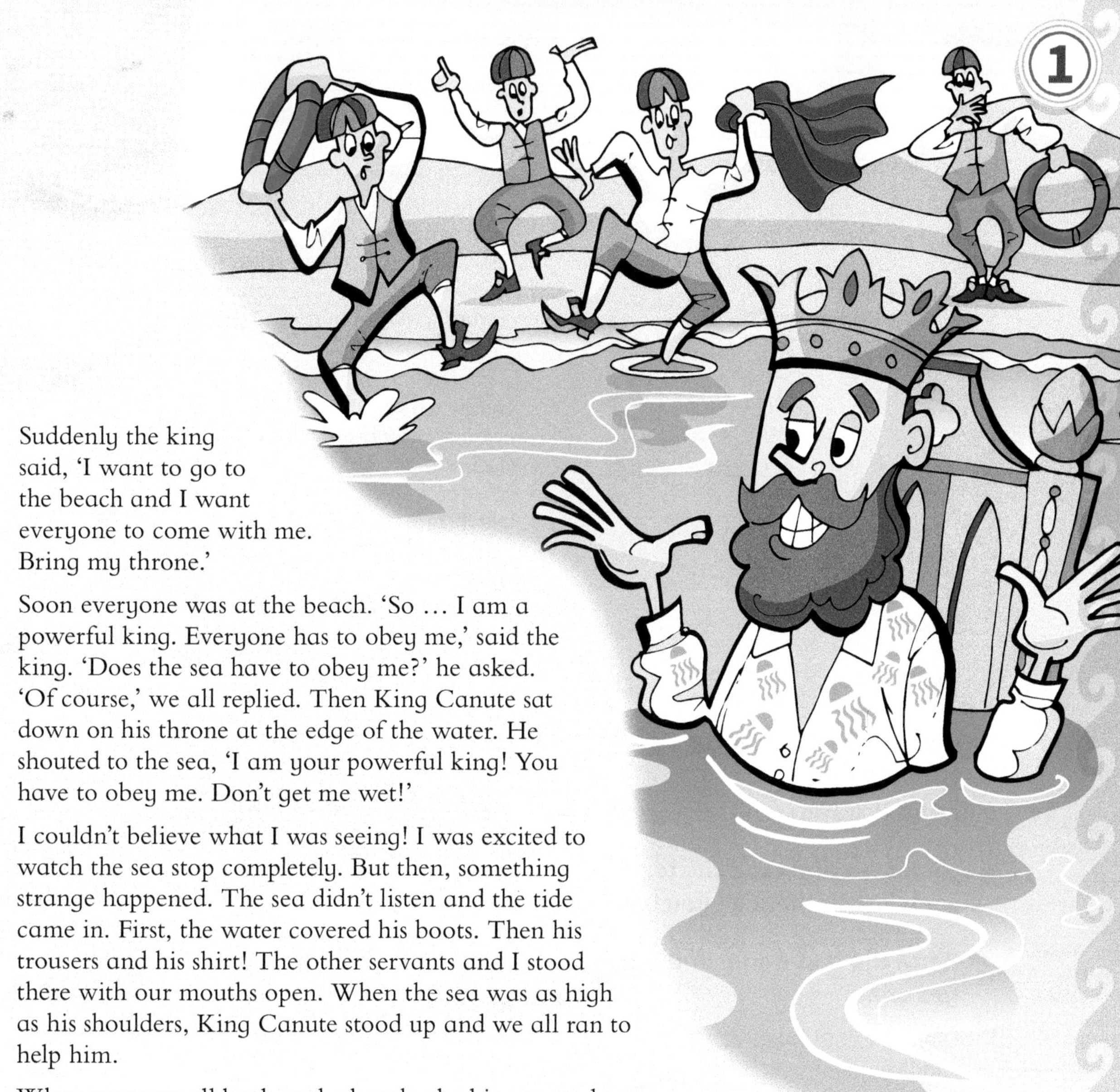

Suddenly the king said, 'I want to go to the beach and I want everyone to come with me. Bring my throne.'

Soon everyone was at the beach. 'So ... I am a powerful king. Everyone has to obey me,' said the king. 'Does the sea have to obey me?' he asked. 'Of course,' we all replied. Then King Canute sat down on his throne at the edge of the water. He shouted to the sea, 'I am your powerful king! You have to obey me. Don't get me wet!'

I couldn't believe what I was seeing! I was excited to watch the sea stop completely. But then, something strange happened. The sea didn't listen and the tide came in. First, the water covered his boots. Then his trousers and his shirt! The other servants and I stood there with our mouths open. When the sea was as high as his shoulders, King Canute stood up and we all ran to help him.

When we were all back at the beach, the king turned to us and said, 'You see, I am very wet. I am your king but I don't have superpowers. I can't control the sea. The sea doesn't obey me. So, stop always saying "yes" to me. It's very boring!'

2 In pairs, talk about the questions.

1 Do you think King Canute is a good person or a bad person?
2 What doesn't the king like about his servants?
3 Why does the king feel frustrated? What does he do to solve the problem?
4 Imagine you are a servant. What would you say to the king after what happened at the beach?

Cross-curricular

1 **Look at the pictures and answer the questions.**

1 When did people wear these clothes?
2 What do you think the clothes are made of?
3 Which styles do you like the best?

2 1.09 **Listen and read the text. What clothes can you find?**

3 **Read the text again and say *yes* or *no*.**

1 Everyone could wear silk in the Middle Ages.
2 Cotton is a manmade textile.
3 You need 25 plastic bottles to make a fleece.
4 Fleece is better for the planet than wool.
5 Smart textiles can change shape.

4 **In pairs, talk about the questions.**

1 Which materials is your shirt made of?
2 How do you think we will use smart textiles in the future?

Clothes in the past

In the past people used natural materials to make their clothes like animal fur and skin. They also used leaves and plants. In the Middle Ages, most people wore warm woollen clothes which came from sheep. Shoes were very simple and they were made of leather. Only very rich people could wear silk and colourful clothes, as dyed fabrics were expensive.

What we wear today

Today, we still use many natural materials for our clothes like cotton, wool, silk and leather. We also use manmade textiles, like acrylic, polyester and nylon. People like them because they are cheaper than natural textiles. They have different qualities too – swimwear is made of manmade materials because they dry faster. Our clothes often have both natural and manmade materials. Check the label on your T-shirt!

Fleece is a very special, manmade fabric. It's made from recycled plastic bottles. You need 25 plastic bottles to make a fleece sweater or a blanket! Fleece fabric keeps us warm, it's waterproof and it helps us to look after the planet.

What will we wear in the future?

In the future, we could all be wearing smart textiles. These clothes have little sensors hidden inside and they catch energy from our body. They can change colour, light up and even grow. Smart textiles are important for sport. For example, a T-shirt could help keep a football player cool during a match. Smart textiles can also be fun. Imagine your friends' faces when your T-shirt changes colour at a party!

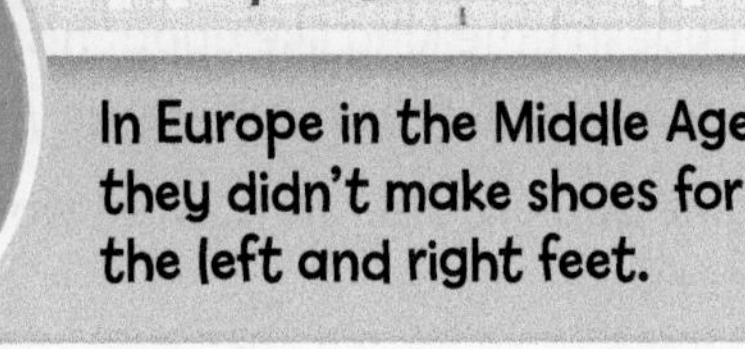

Did you know?

In Europe in the Middle Ages, they didn't make shoes for the left and right feet.

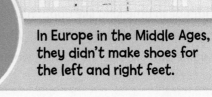

Learning outcomes By the end of the lesson, learners will have read a text about clothes throughout history, using critical thinking skills (analysis, application, creative).

New language *fabric, material nylon, waterproof*

Recycled language *leather, silk*

Materials items/clothes made of leather/silk/wool/nylon, a waterproof item

Warm-up

- Ask learners to write down some dates. Remind them to use numbers not words. Say *1900s, 1960, today.*
- Put learners into small groups. Ask them to choose a date in their group and find out the types of clothes from that time. They can use their imagination.
- Each group writes a description including what the clothes are made of. Ask each group to read their description to the class. The class guesses which date the group chose.

Pupil's Book, page 12

Presentation

- Bring in items or pictures of items made of leather/silk/wool/nylon/a waterproof item, e.g. waterproof jacket.
- Say *Look at these. These are all made of different kinds of material. Material.* Learners repeat. *Fabric.* Learners repeat. Say *Another word for material is fabric. Fabric. Learners repeat.*
- Show the items made of leather then silk. Ask *What's it made of? (leather/silk).* Repeat with the nylon item. Learners say *nylon*. Show the waterproof item. Say *This kind of material doesn't let water go through so it stops you getting wet. It is water…(proof).* Learners say *waterproof*.
- Write the words *material/fabric* in the centre of the board and circle them. As learners repeat the words back to you, add them to the mind map. Add *leather/silk/wool/nylon/waterproof* and any others learners can think of.
- Put learners into groups of three. Say *What kind of clothes are made of these materials? You have 2 minutes to find one piece of clothing for each type of material.* Check answers.
  Extension Ask learners to copy the mind map. Clean the board. In pairs, one learner says the name of a material and the other says a type of clothing. Then they swap.

1 Look at the pictures and answer the questions.

- Put learners into pairs. Tell them to look at the pictures, choose the clothes they find most interesting, and tell their partner why. Share their ideas.
- Ask learners to write down some dates: *500 BC, 13th century, 1800s, 1970s, today.* Ask what people's clothes were made of on each date. Read the questions aloud to check understanding. Tell learners to answer in pairs.
- Monitor and support. Check answers with the class.
  Extra support Write the adjectives *leather/silk/wool/nylon/waterproof* on the board.

Key: 1 13th century, 500 BC, 1800s

2 1.09 Listen and read the text. What clothes can you find?

- Tell learners to read the text again quickly and find as many different clothes as they can. Before they start, say Give me an example of words you could look for. (e.g. *shirt, tie, shoes*).
- Give learners approximately 4 minutes to read, but monitor for progress. Put learners in pairs to compare answers.
- Check with the class.

Key: swimwear, T-shirt, sweater

3 Read the text again and say *yes* or *no*.

- Learners continue in pairs, read the sentences together and say 'yes' or 'no'. Tell them to go back to the text and check the information. Say *Do you need to read quickly or more slowly now? (more slowly). Are you looking for particular information? (yes).* Learners read and discuss in pairs.
- Check answers with the class. Ask them to find the part of the text that helped them answer.

Key: 1 no 2 no 3 yes 4 yes 5 yes

4 In pairs, talk about the questions.

- Learners work in pairs and discuss the questions.
- When pairs have finished, put them into fours and ask them to compare ideas. Check answers with the class.

Did you know?

- Ask a strong learner to read out the fact. Discuss with the class.

Activity Book, page 12

See pages TB126–141.

Ending the lesson

- Put learners into small groups. Ask them to think of someone they know who they think dresses well. Tell them to write about the clothes that person wears. Each learner describes the person. The group guess who it is, e.g. *Usually older men wear suits. Is it your dad?*

Learning outcomes By the end of the lesson, learners will be able to understand strategies for reading effectively, understand different text types and read for key information.

New language *text message, label*

Recycled language clothes, parts of clothes, materials

Materials messages hand written onto large sheets of paper or on slides ('1 Do not wash in hot water'; '2 shoes, shirt, shorts, socks'; '3 Hi ☺ Don't forget your swimming costume for the trip!'); slips of paper (one per learner)

Warm-up

- Put learners into groups of six. Say *You are going to make a word chain using categories.* Everyone will say one word. Say *I will give you a starter word and you have to continue giving words connected to that word.* Say *clothes … What letter is at the end of the word? (s).* Say *OK 's' … so a word beginning with 's' is … ? (shirt).* The first learner repeats. Point to the next learner and ask *What does shirt end with? (t). So you say a word beginning with 't', for example … (tie).*
- Arrange each group in a circle. Say *Let's begin the chain. Your starting word is 'clothes'.* Groups make word chains.
- Repeat with other words and new categories, e.g. hobbies. **Extra support** Learners who find this challenging can begin the chain.

Pupil's Book, page 13

Presentation

- Tell learners they are going to read some information. Write *shopping list, text message, label* on the board.
- Now tell them they are going to read each message in 5 seconds. Ask *Is this OK?* If learners say *no*, say *Let's try.*
- Tell them they will see each text for 5 seconds and they have to choose which type of message it is.
- Show slides of the messages for 5 seconds each. If you don't have slides, write the messages on poster paper and hold each up for 5 seconds. (1 'Do not wash in hot water'; 2 'shoes, shirt, shorts, socks'; 3 'Hi ☺ Don't forget your swimming costume for the trip!').
- Learners discuss their answers in pairs.
- Check answers. Say *Well done! You did it in 5 seconds!*
- Ask how this might help in an exam. *(In reading exams, you can understand the main message by reading fast. Think about the type of text to help you do this).*

EXAM TIP! Ask a learner to read the exam tip aloud. Say *We can think about where we see the message to help us understand what it means. Do you know when we do this in the exam? (In KfS, Reading and Writing Part 1).*

1 Match the text types in the box to the examples A–D.

- Ask learners to read the texts quickly and decide which type they are. Tell them to use pictures to help them e.g. *Is it on a sign? Is it on a phone?*
- Learners work for 2–3 minutes on their own to match.
- Put them into pairs to check ideas. Check answers with the class.

Key: A an advert B a note C a notice D a short email

2 Look at the texts again. Match the titles (1–4) to the texts (A–D).

- Tell learners to look at the texts again. Tell them to think about the type of message and where they might see it.
- Put them into pairs. Say *Decide quickly which title matches each text.* Check with the class.

Key: 1 D 2 B 3 C 4 A

3 Read the text and answer the questions.

- Read question 1. Say *Look at the text really quickly. What kind of text is it?* Check ideas. Remind them to look quickly for the most important information. Give them a minute.
- Put them into pairs to check answers. Check with the class.

Key: 1 a note 2 Dad 3 Buy his uncle a birthday present. 4 C is the correct answer because it is the only one that means the same as 'after your lessons'.

Activity Book, page 13

See pages TB126–141.

Ending the lesson

- Put learners into pairs. Say *You are going to write a text message. It should be less than 10 words, beginning 'Don't forget …' Make it about something true.*
- Learners write their messages.
- Put learners into groups and take their slips of paper. Hand them out randomly. Each learner reads their message aloud. The group guesses who wrote it.

1 **Match the text types in the box to the examples A–D.**

a short email a note
an advert a notice

EXAM TIP! Think about where you would see each message. What sort of words do you use in those places?

A

Clean clothes as fast as a car!

Two shirts for the price of one!

B

Sara,

Don't wash your clothes in the washing machine. It broke this morning. You can use the sink in the kitchen.

See you later,

Mum

C

IMPORTANT NOTICE

PLEASE TAKE OFF YOUR SHOES BEFORE YOU ENTER SECURITY

D

Dear Bill,

We change your towels daily and clean your room every morning after breakfast.

We hope you have a great time!

Janet Mills

(Manager)

2 **Look at the texts again.** Match the titles (1–4) to the texts (A–D).

1 Hotel information ......

2 A machine that doesn't work ......

3 Airport information C

4 A special offer ......

3 **Read the text and answer the questions.**

George,

Uncle Bob will be here for dinner tonight. Please buy him a nice birthday present after your lessons. He loves funny ties!

Dad

1 What kind of text is it?

....

2 Who wrote the message?

....

3 What does George need to do?

....

4 When should George look for a present?

A at dinner time

B before school

C after school

A2 Key for Schools

1 1.10 **Listen and match.** Put the pictures in the correct order.

I've marked your test and I've got some good news!

That's E.

A

B

E

C

D

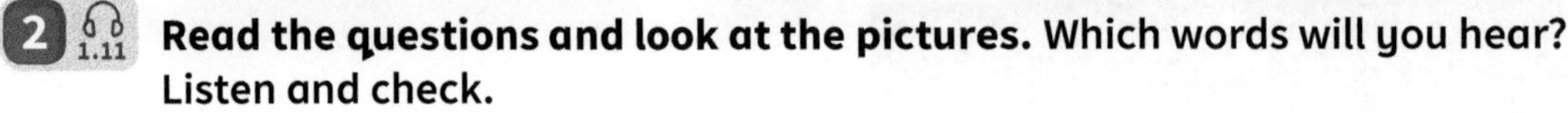

2 1.11 **Read the questions and look at the pictures. Which words will you hear? Listen and check.**

1 Why can't Karen help her mum?

A
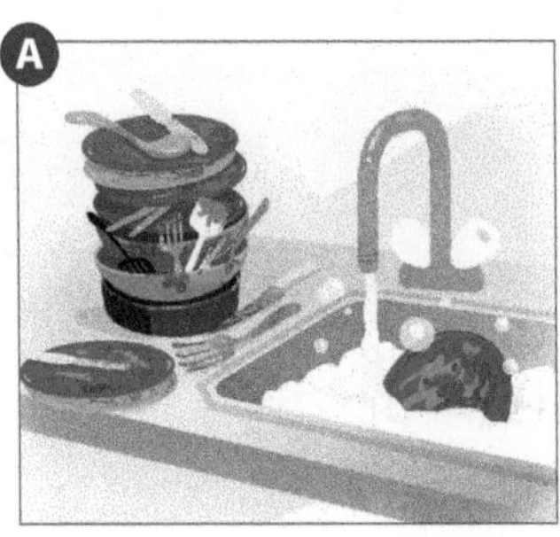

B

C

2 Which trainers does the boy take?

A
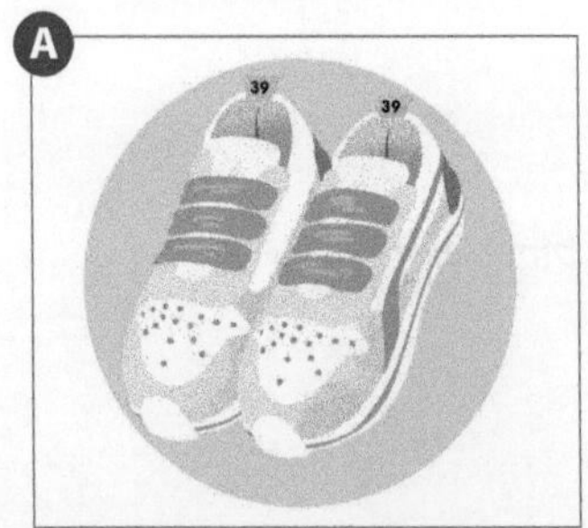

B

C
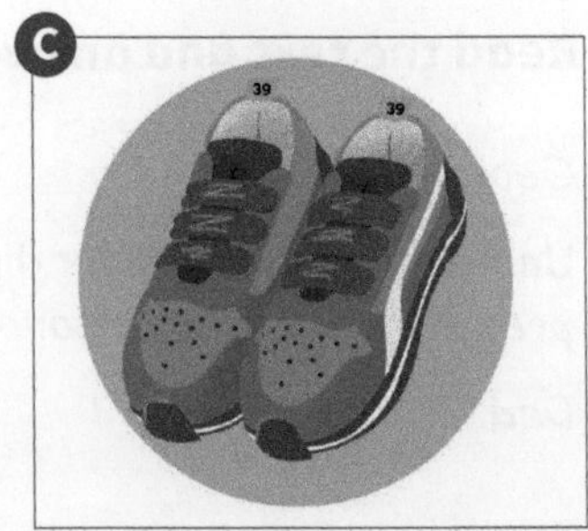

3 1.12 **Listen again and choose the correct answer.** Why is this correct?

EXAM TIP! Use the **first** listening to choose an answer. You can check your answer the **second** time you listen.

Learning outcomes By the end of the lesson, learners will understand strategies for listening effectively and listen to find the correct structural words to complete sentences.

New language *noun*

Recycled language clothes, activities

Materials 4 pictures (a person skiing, a person on a beach/a person in a class/ a person at the gym)

Warm-up

- Put four pictures on the walls of the classroom: people in a skiing outfit / on a beach / in a class / in the gym. Point to pictures and ask questions: *What is he/she doing? What kind of clothes is he/she wearing?* Share ideas.
- Tell learners to listen and stand under the correct picture as quickly as possible. (Or learners can point to the pictures.)
- Give the first sentence. *I need to wear good trainers to run well. (gym)* Check learners have chosen the correct picture. Ask them what they heard that helped them *(trainers, run)*.
- Continue giving different sentences while they listen. More can be added. e.g. *Have you got a scarf to cover me up – I'm getting sunburnt. (beach). My feet are getting wet. I think my boots are broken. (skiing).*

  Extra support Give learners the clues with answers in brackets to read before the activity; they try to remember.

Pupil's Book, page 14

Presentation

- Say *It helps to look at information and try to understand before we listen. We can understand a lot from pictures.*
- Put learners into pairs. Ask them to look at the pictures and think about who the people are. Do the first one together, e.g. *They're both the same age. Maybe they're friends.*
- Say *Let's guess what the people might talk about. Who might talk about directions? (the tourist and bus driver).*
- Tell learners to discuss what the people in the picture might be talking about. Share ideas.

1 (1.10) Listen and match. Put the pictures in the correct order.

- Explain learners will listen and match the picture with the conversation. Tell them to read the exam tip.

EXAM TIP! Say *In Listening Part 1, how many times will you listen? (twice). You can check your answers the second time.*

- Play the audio.
- Put learners into pairs to compare answers. Play the audio again.
- Learners finalise their answers in pairs. Check answers.

Key: E, C, B, D. A

See audioscripts on pages TB118–121.

2 (1.11) Read the questions and look at the pictures. Which words will you hear? Listen and check.

- Ask learners what they can see in pictures A–C *(washing-up; school book; football; trainers)*. Play the audio.
- Put learners into pairs to compare ideas. Check answers.

Track 1.11

Woman: Karen, can't you do the washing-up tonight?
Girl: Oh, Mum! I've got to read 10 pages about jewellery for my History homework!
Woman: And what about your brother? Can't he do it either?
Girl: He's gone to the football match with his best friend. He'll be home late.
Boy: Excuse me?
Woman: Yes? Can I help you?
Boy: Yes, I'd like to change these trainers I bought last week. They're too small.
Woman: I see. What size are you?
Boy: I'm a size thirty-seven, but they're not for me! They're for my sister, she's a thirty-nine.
Woman: We have got a size thirty-nine, but I'm afraid they're purple.
Boy: That's OK. She likes purple too.

Key: B *(too much history homework about jewellery)*

3 (1.12) Listen again and choose the correct answer. Why is this correct?

- Play the audio. Learners check in pairs.
- Check answers. Point out that they hear *small* and *large*, but only one is correct.

  Fast finishers Learners choose another sentence from the email and copy it out missing out one of the words. They show it to a partner who says what they think the missing word is.

Key: 1 B 2 C

Activity Book, page 14

See pages TB126–141.

Ending the lesson

- Ask learners to work in groups of three to think about the listening tasks. Tell them to give exam tips to another student. They need to think of three tips to pass on.
- Pick groups to suggest ideas. The other groups should check if they have similar tips or different ones.

Learning outcomes By the end of the lesson, learners will have used language from the unit to talk about sport and revised the language and skills from the unit.

Recycled language unit language

Materials 12 cards or pieces of paper per 6 learners

Warm-up

- Show learners pictures of different clothes, e.g. on a slide or from magazines.
- Tell learners they have 2 minutes to find as many different clothes as they can and make a list.
- Learners create a list.
- Stop after 2 minutes and ask how many clothes they have on their list.
- Tell each learner to choose an item of clothing from the list and act out putting it on. The rest of the group say which word it is.
- Monitor and check.

  Fast finishers Ask them to write four sentences comparing their clothes, e.g. *My shirt is darker than Tom's shirt.*

Pupil's book, page 15

1 Complete the sentences.

- Ask learners to look at the sentences. Ask them what kind of sentences they are *(comparatives)*.
- Look at the examples together.
- Put learners into pairs. Ask them to complete the sentences.
- Monitor and support.
- Check answers.

Key: 2 expensive than the red raincoat 3 smart as my suit 4 comfortable as my silk ones 5 than my new jumper

2 Complete the sentences. Use the correct form of the words in the box.

- Ask learners to look at the example sentence and answer.
- Put learners into pairs. They say the correct verb for each sentence. Point out that there may be more than one correct answer.
- Check answers.

Key: 1 open 2 arrive/leave 3 finish/start 4 closes 5 start/finish 6 arrives/leaves

3 Choose ten words from this unit. Record the words using the steps below.

- Say *Well done. You've learnt a lot of new language. Let's think about how to learn.*
- Tell learners to look at the flowchart. Ask *What do you think this can help you do? (understand new words).*
- Say *Let's try. If I have a new word, where can I look? (Internet or dictionary). And when I find it what can I do? (write it down). Is it enough to write the word and its meaning? (No, we can write the opposite too). What can we do after? (use it; test our friends).*
- Give learners an example, e.g. *sandals*. Learners choose ten words and repeat this process, using the flowchart.
- Check answers.

Mission in action!

- Put learners into the same groups as earlier in the Mission. Remind them that Stage 3 of the Mission is to write a review of a shop.
- Ask each group what kind of shop they designed in the earlier Mission stages. As they tell you make a list on the board.
- Tell each learner to choose one of the shops they visited (not their own) to review.
- Ask learners the type of information they might read in a review.
- Put their ideas on the board, e.g. *the clothes, the prices, if the shop looks nice.*
- Ask the learners to write a review of the shop they chose.
- Monitor and support as the learners write.
- Once they are complete, ask learners to swap their review with a partner. Their partner should read and see if the review is good or bad.
- Tell learners to find one good thing and one bad thing in the review, e.g. *There are a lot of good descriptions, but I wanted to know more about the prices.*

Activity Book, page 15

See pages TB126–141.

Ending the lesson

- SA Complete the self-assessment (see Introduction).

Review

1

1 Complete the sentences.

1 My jumper is old, but my tracksuit is older.
My jumper is newer than my tracksuit.

2 The red raincoat is expensive, but the blue one is more expensive.
The blue raincoat is more ________ .

3 My raincoat is smart and so is my suit.
My raincoat is as ________ .

4 My cotton socks are comfortable and so are my silk ones.
My cotton socks are as ________ .

5 My old jumper is big, but my new jumper is bigger.
My old jumper is smaller ________ .

2 Complete the sentences. Use the correct form of the words in the box.

finish open leave start close arrive

1 When does the toy shop ________ again?
At 9 am tomorrow.

2 When does the bus ________ ?
In fifteen minutes.

3 What time does the film ________ ?
At 12:30.

4 The school ________ after lunch on Saturday.

5 The concert doesn't ________ until 8 pm.

6 The train ________ in two hours.

3 Choose ten words from this unit. Record the words using the steps below.

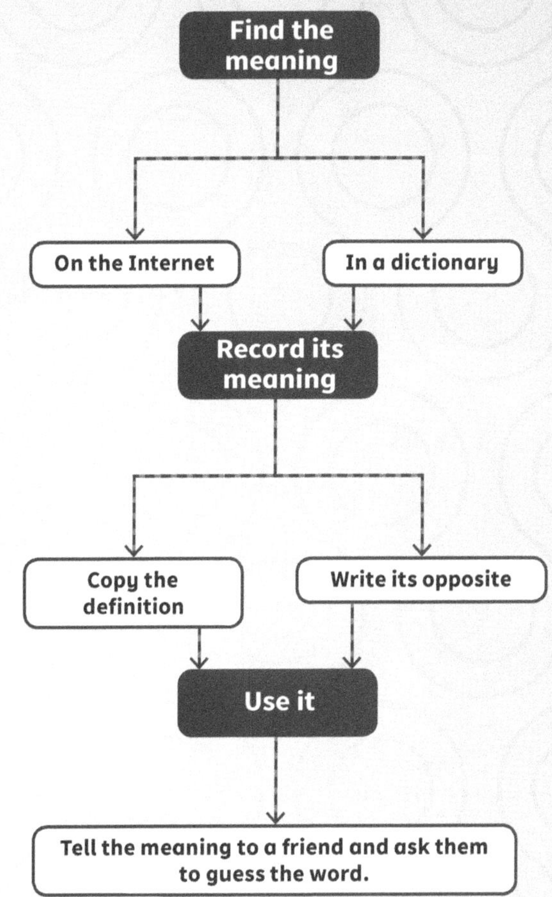

We wanted to buy clothes for a party. So we chose Jaun's disco shop.

Mission in action!

- Say what activity you had to buy clothes for.
- Say why you chose the shop.
- Write a review of the shop.

The silk blouse was the correct size and colour. The order arrived in perfect condition. I can recommend this online shop for smart clothes. ★★★★★

2 Future technology

Is the technology in each picture useful?
Why? Which would you like to use the most?

Watch the video. Why does Jenny need to clean Jim's earphones?

Mission Recommend new technology

1. Find the class's technological needs.
2. Show how a piece of technology works.
★ Present your group's best option.

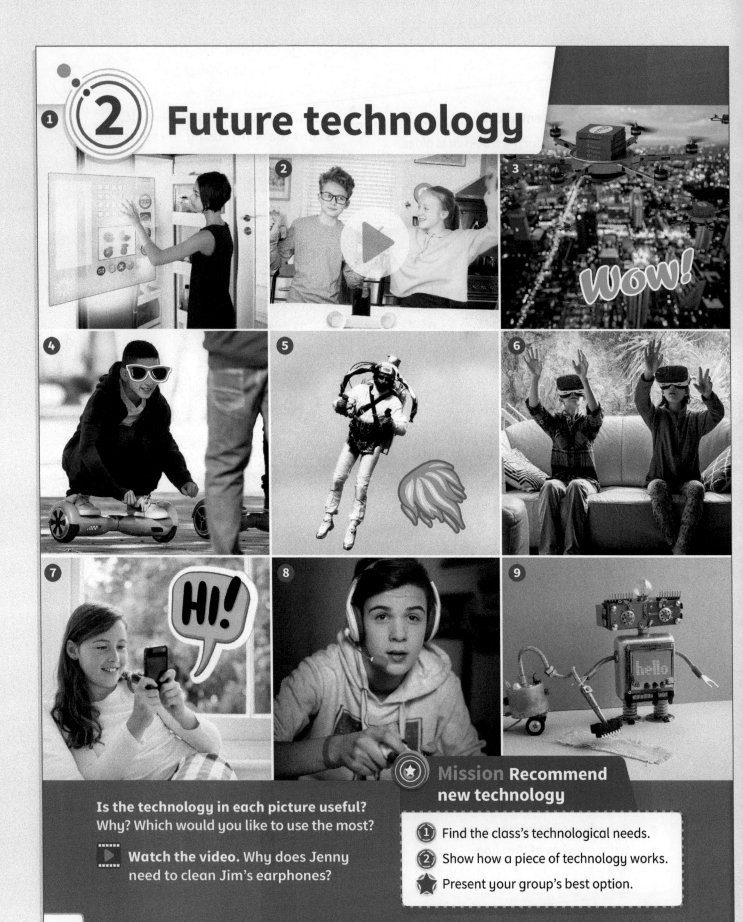

Unit 2 learning outcomes

In Unit 2, learners learn to:

- use vocabulary to describe technology
- use the first conditional and zero conditional
- understand and use verbs connected to computers
- read and listen for general and specific information
- understand how to deal with jealousy

Materials video, large word cards (drone, vacuum cleaner, freezer, hoverboard, jet pack, virtual piano, hardware, headphones), sticky tack

Self-assessment

- SA Write the unit topic on the board. Underneath write: *computer, app, first conditional, newspaper.*
- Put learners into groups of three. Give each group one of the words and ask how we use it. Share their ideas.
- Show the unit outcomes (write/project them on the board).
- Ask learners to complete self-assessment (see Introduction). Say *Let's learn.*

Pupil's Book, page 16

Warm-up

- Write *technology* on the board. Ask *How do you use technology every day?* Write learners' ideas across the bottom of the board, e.g. *mobile phone to text people.*
- Give each learner a sticky note to write their name. Ask them which item is most important to them. Invite them to add their sticky note above the item on the board which is most important. See which is most popular.
- Pair learners who have chosen different things. They say why they think their item is important.

  Fast finishers In pairs, learners look at the most and least popular item and decide why.

Is the technology in each picture useful? Which would you like to use the most?

- Say *What can you see in the pictures?* Put learners into groups of three. Ask them to name the technologies.
- Write numbers 3–9 down the side of the board and stick large word cards (*drone, vacuum cleaner, freezer, hoverboard, jet pack, virtual piano, hardware, headphones*) in a random order on the board. Point to each picture on page 16. Ask a learner to choose one of the cards and stick it next to the correct number. Say each word. Learners repeat.
- Mix the cards again and ask learners the correct word. Point to the number. Learners call out the correct word.

Key: 1 freezer 3 drone 4 hoverboard 5 jet pack 6 virtual piano 7 hardware 8 headphones 9 vacuum cleaner

Watch the video. Why does Jenny need to clean Jim's earphones?

- Say *Are you good at using technology?* Give an example, e.g. *I can use a computer easily, but when it goes wrong, I can't fix it. I ask for help.* Put learners into pairs to discuss.
- Say *We're going to watch Jenny and Jim's vlog. They fix some problems with technology. What do you think they did?*
- Say *Let's find out what they did and why Jenny has to clean Jim's earphones.*
- Play Jenny's vlog. Put learners into pairs to compare answers. Check with the group.

  Extension Learners try to remember how to make the speakers or phone holder and explain to a partner.

Key: Because she had put them in her nose.

Mission Recommend new technology

- Write on the board: Recommend new technology. 1 What technology do we need? 2 How does the new technology work? 3 Which option is best? Tell learners each question is part of their mission. Say *Let's make the first question a Mission statement.* Write *Find the class's technological needs.*
- Ask learners to turn the next two questions into mission statements. Check their ideas. Show the Mission statement in the book. Say *This is our Mission.*

Activity Book, page 16

See pages TB126–141.

My unit goals

- Go through the unit goals with the learners. (See suggested techniques in 'Identifying outcomes' in Introduction).
- Go back to these unit goals at the end of each Mission stage and review them. Say *This is our Mission page.*

Ending the lesson

- Write some anagrams on the board: *potlap, bilmeob hopen, redno, kcpa tej.* Put learners into pairs to solve these.

Key: laptop mobile phone drone jet pack

Learning outcomes By the end of the lesson, learners will be able to use vocabulary to describe computers and how we use them, and listen for general understanding.

New language *drone, freezer, hardware, hoverboard, keyboard, laptop, mobile phone, mouse, program, printer, screen, software*

Recycled language vocabulary related to technology, comparative adjectives, present simple

Materials audio; sticky notes

Pupil's Book, page 17

Warm-up

- Give a sticky note to each learner. Ask them to write down their favourite activity on the computer.
- Put learners in groups of five. Ask them to sit in a group.
- Learners put their sticky notes into the middle of the table. Each learner picks up one sticky note, reads it out then guesses who wrote it. After guessing, they ask a follow-up question, e.g. *Which is your favourite game?*

Presentation

- Show learners a picture of a computer or a real one. Put learners into groups of four. Ask them to name the parts of the computer they know. Monitor and check.
- Say *Choose a word you are sure about.* Invite one of each pair to write the word on the board. Read out their words and invite the class to point at the part in the picture. Say each word clearly. Add any they have missed: *keyboard, mouse, screen, printer.* Learners repeat.
- Ask *What do we call all of these parts? (hardware)* Learners repeat. Ask *What do we call all the games and tools that run on the computer? (software/programs)* Learners repeat.

1 (1.13) Listen, point and say the numbers.

- Ask learners to look at the picture for 5 seconds. Count down from 5, then say *Shut your books.* Ask *What do you remember from the picture?* Learners give ideas. Say *Let's listen and check.*
- Play the audio. Stop after each item. Learners say the numbers.

Key: 4 (laptop) 10 (screen) 8 (program) 2 (hardware) 3 (keyboard) 7 (printer) 6 (mouse) 5 (mobile phone) 1 (disc) 9 (software)

See audioscripts on pages TB118–123.

2 Match the words in the box to numbers 1–10 in the picture.

- Ask learners to look at the words in the box. Ask them which words only have one syllable. (*disc, phone, mouse, screen*) Say each word clearly and encourage the learners to repeat.
- In pairs, learners work out which syllable in the other words is stressed. Do the first as an example. Say *hardware*. Learners repeat. Learners work on the other words.
- Put learners into pairs. They take turns to say a number. Their partner gives the correct word.

Key: 1 disc 2 hardware 3 keyboard 4 laptop 5 mobile phone 6 mouse 7 printer 8 program 9 software 10 screen

3 Look at the words in Activity 2 and complete the challenges.

- Put learners into groups of three. Give them 5 minutes to complete the questions.
- Check answers.

Key: 1 keyboard, laptop, mobile phone, mouse, printer, screen 2 Learner's own answers 3 laptop, mobile phone, printer, screen 4 **Sample answers** computer program, Internet connection, app

Activity Book, page 17

See pages TB126–141.

Ending the lesson

- Put learners into two groups. Ask them to stand facing each other at opposite sides of the room with a mixture of stronger and weaker learners each side. Put a marker e.g. a book, to show a centre point between the two groups.
- Say *When I give a clue, put up your hand if you know the answer.* Tell them if they shout out they won't get a point. Give an example clue: *This is a tool we can use to surf the Internet and chat to our friends and can carry in our pocket or bag. (mobile phone)*
- Choose the first learner to raise their hand and ask them the answer. If they are wrong, go to the second person. If they are right, ask their group to spell the word. If they get the spelling wrong, go to the next clue. If they get the spelling correct, the whole group can take a step forwards. Continue the game with different clues until one group reaches the middle point of the room and wins.
- Use a learner dictionary to create clues.

Extension Learners create a mini 'technology' dictionary. They list words and create definitions.

1 1.13 Listen, point and say the numbers.

This is my laptop. I use it …

Number 4.

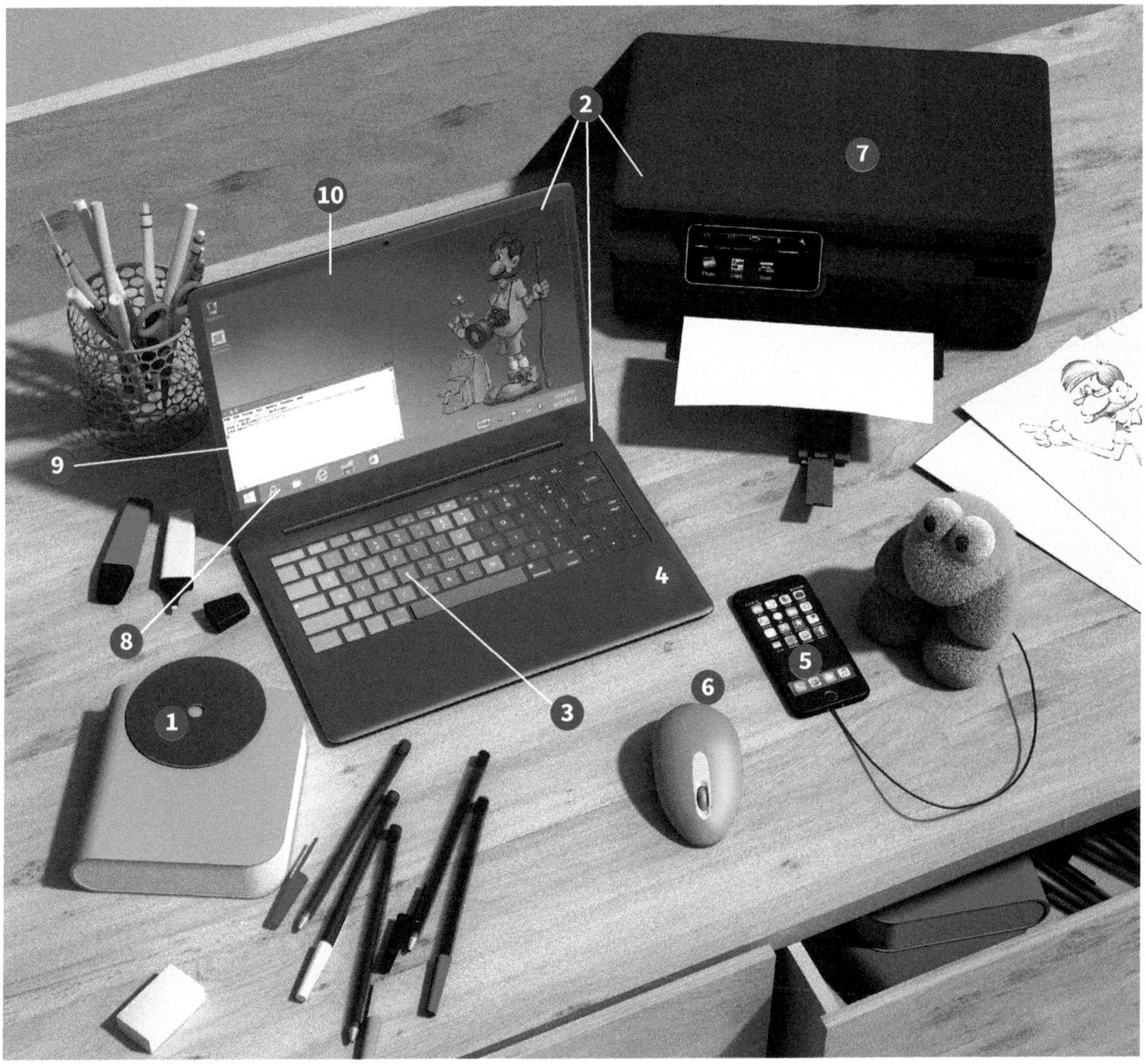

2 Match the words in the box to the numbers 1–10 in the picture.

software disc hardware laptop
screen mouse printer
computer program keyboard mobile phone

Number 8 is software.

3 Look at the words in Activity 2 and complete the challenges.

1 Find the six kinds of hardware.
2 Write a sentence that uses the words 'disc' and 'program'.
3 Find three things that turn on and off.
4 Name three pieces of computer software.

Language presentation 1

1 **Look at the poster.** What can you see? What would you like to look at?

Look! There's a robot dog.

TECHNOLOGY SHOW TODAY
at The Palace Hotel Tickets £8 5 pm – 10 pm
For more information email information@technology.com

2 1.14 **Listen to Tom talking to a friend about a technology show.** What's the address of the show's website?

____

3 1.15 **Listen again.** Match the people (1–5) to the objects (A–H).

1 ☐ 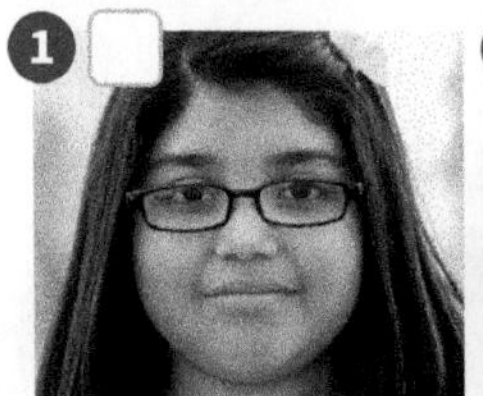
Sarah

2 ☐
Dale

3 ☐ 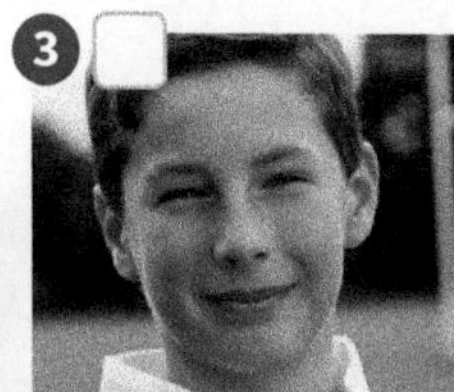
Brian

4 ☐ 
Courtney

5 ☐ 
Scott

A 
mobile phones

B 
laptop

C 
keyboards

D 
screen

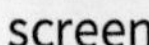

E 
digital printer

F 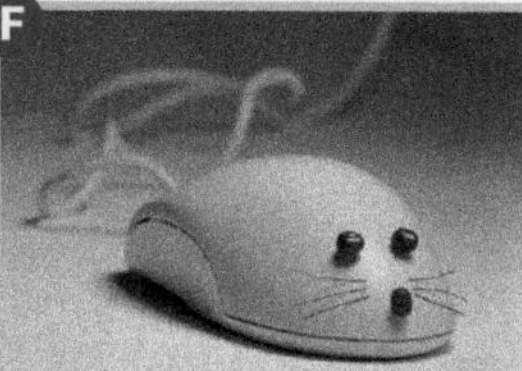
mouse

G 
software

H 
robot dog

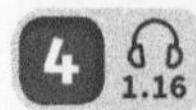

4 1.16 **PRONUNCIATION Listen and repeat.** page 118

EXAM TIP! Remember that there are **three options** that aren't used.

Learning outcomes By the end of the lesson, learners will be able to listen effectively using words to locate information and use the correct language to describe websites.

New language *www, dot, at, com*

Recycled language computer parts, words related to technology

Materials audio, mobile devices or access to Internet if possible

Pupil's Book, page 18

Warm-up

- Put learners into two lines so that each learner is facing a partner. Ask *Which person in your family is best at understanding technology?* Learners discuss in pairs for 1 minute.
- Ask a learner from the end of one line to walk down to the other end of the line so that all the learners in the line have to move up by one, re-pairing them. Repeat before each question to re-pair.
- Ask *If your mobile phone or computer stops working, what do you do?* Learners discuss for 1 minute. Repeat with *Which technology do you need the most: your phone, your laptop or your tablet? Why? What is your favourite website and why?*

Extension Repeat the game with the category of computers.

Presentation

- Tell learners about a website you like to use. Explain what it is and tell them the address, e.g. I love English games. There is one called Academy Island and it has different levels. It is w-w-w dot cambridgeenglish dot org.
- Write the example website on the board. *www.cambridgeenglish.org* Point to the first part and ask How do we say this? *(w-w-w)* Learners repeat.
- Point to the . and ask *How do we say this? (dot)* Learners repeat. Point to the .org. Ask *How do we say this? (dot org).* Learners repeat.
- Add to the board *.com.* Say *We often see this on websites instead of .org. How do we say this? (dot com).*
- Say *Which parts are in the address of most websites? (w-w-w, dot, com).*
- Write @ on the board. Say *How do we say it? (at).*
- Say *We're going to listen to some people talking about a technology show. Would you like to go to this kind of show?* Learners give answers.

1 Look at the poster. What can you see? What would you like to look at?

- Read the questions aloud. Show the example.
- Put learners into pairs to answer the questions.
- Check their ideas.

2  Listen to Tom talking to a friend about a technology show. What's the address of the show's website?

- Say Let's listen to Tom and his friend talking about the show. Find out the website of the show.
- Ask Which words will you need to listen for? (w-w-w, dot, com).
- Play the audio.
- Put learners into pairs to check their answer.
- Check with the class.

See audioscripts on pages TB118–123.

Key: www.information@technology.com

3  Listen again. Match the people (1–5) to the objects (A–H).

- *Say Remember there are three extra answers you don't need.*
- Ask a strong learner to read out the exam tip.
- Say *First let's check the names. Who can you see?* Learners say the names. *And what can they look at? Learners say the objects. So what can you listen for? (names and objects).*
- Play the audio again. Learners complete the task.
- Check answers.

Key: 1 G, 2 E, 3 F, 4 A, 5 H

4 PRONUNCIATION Listen and repeat. 

- Say *Let's practise. Listen and repeat.*
- Play the audio pausing for repetitions. Correct errors.

  Track 1.16

  Sarah: keyboard, printers, robot
- Write up words on the board. Encourage learners to say each one with correct stress. *(keyboard, printers, robot)*
- Tell learners to go to page 118 to do the activities. (See page TB124.)

Activity Book, page 18

See pages TB126–141.

Ending the lesson

- Ask learners to think of their favourite website. Tell them to speak to at least one other learner and give the website address. The learners write down the addresses.
- If possible, tell learners to use their devices to look at the websites and tell their partner if they like it or not.

2 Language practice 1

Learning outcomes By the end of the lesson, learners will be able to use first conditional to describe possibility accurately.

New language *if* (present simple) + *will*

Recycled language vocabulary related to technology, *will*, present simple

Material coloured board markers, paper and colouring pens, (optional: mobile devices or access to internet if possible)

Pupil's Book, page 19

Warm-up

- Divide the learners into three groups numbered 1, 2 and 3. Write three phrases on the board: *1 If I lose my phone, I'll … 2 If I surf on the Internet, I'll … 3 If I get a new computer, I'll …*
- Put learners into pairs within their groups and ask them to talk about ways to finish their sentence.
- Regroup learners into groups of three. Each group should have a learner from group 1, group 2 and group 3.
- Tell them to report back to their original groups.

Fast finishers Learners create their own additional sentences for the two numbers they didn't do.

Presentation

- Ask learners where Sarah went in the listening task before. *(the technology show)*. Ask *What was she thinking about buying? (a new keyboard).*
- Say *But she only wants one if it is cheap enough. Can you remember what she said?* If learners can't remember, give them the first part of the sentence. Write it on the board: *I think I'll buy one, if it's not … (too expensive)* and underline each clause in a different colour.
- Say *Is Sarah definitely buying a new keyboard? (no, because it might be expensive). So it depends on the price? (yes). Is it possible she will buy a keyboard (yes) Yes, she might buy one. When? Now or in the future? (future). It is conditional – it depends on – the price. So what kind of sentence is this? (first conditional).*
- Say *Which part shows the thing she'll do – the action? (I think I'll buy one). Which verb tense is used? (future simple).* Point to 'if it's not'. Say *And this is the 'if' part … What tense is the verb? (present tense of* to be*)*

Grammar look: the first conditional

- Put learners into pairs. Show the sentences at the top of the **Grammar look** box. Invite a learner to read them out. Tell learners to choose the correct option for 1 and 2 in pairs.

Key: 1 Maybe 2 might

1 Which sentence is correct? Choose A or B.

- Put learners into pairs. Ask them to look at the sentences and find any grammar mistakes.
- Show the first pair of sentences. (A) Ask learners if they can see a mistake. Ask how they can correct the sentence. (*I'll go.*)
- Learners complete the rest of the activity in pairs.

Extra support Check progress and underline the error.

- Check answers with the class.

Key: 1 B 2 B 3 A 4 A 5 A 6 A

2 Complete the sentences. Use your own ideas.

- Put learners into pairs. Ask them to look at the sentences and finish them using their own ideas.
- Monitor and support as necessary. Check answers.

3 In groups, share your sentences. Who wrote the most interesting sentence?

- Learners compare sentences in groups of four. Share their ideas.

Complete the Grammar look on page 121.
See pages TB125–126.

Mission Stage 1

- Ask *What ideas do you have for learning English better?* e.g. *You can watch videos online in English.*
- Put learners into groups of five. Tell them to read the example on page 19 and to think of three ideas in their group.
- Pair learners from different groups to swap ideas. Learners report back to their group and choose the best idea.
- Give a large piece of paper and pens to each group. Ask learners to create a list or infographic showing their idea, what technology they have chosen, what it is used for and how it will help in class.

Extension If possible, learners can create their own simple online infographic using a free online tool and present to the class.

Activity Book, page 19

See pages TB126–141.

Ending the lesson

- Learners present their idea to the class. Give them an example, e.g. *We could use tablets to help us learn. When we are learning new words, we could look them up on the tablets. We could use them to watch videos and to write our ideas.*
- Each group presents their idea.

Grammar look: the first conditional

'If my mum says it's OK, then I'll go.'

1 Will Sarah's mum say it's OK? **Yes** / **Maybe**

2 We use the first conditional to talk about things that **might** / **won't** happen.

page 120

1 Which sentence is correct? Choose A or B.

1 A If my mum says it's OK, I'm going to the park this weekend.
  B If my mum says it's OK, I'll plant some tomatoes tonight.

2 A I get a new hat if it's not too expensive.
  B I'll buy a new keyboard if it's not too expensive.

3 A I'll have fun if I join the school basketball club.
  B I'll have fun if I'll play video games tonight.

4 A Kim will email her aunt if she finishes her homework in time.
  B Courtney goes too if she finishes her homework in time.

5 A If I go to the fair, I'll see all my friends.
  B I go to the school disco, I'll see all my friends.

6 A If I go to the fair, I'll look at the robots.
  B If it rains, have to stay inside.

2 Complete the sentences. Use your own ideas.

1 If my mum says it's OK, ________.
2 ________ if it's not too expensive.
3 I'll have fun if ________.
4 ________ if she finishes her homework in time.
5 ________ I'll see all my friends.
6 If I ________, ________

3 In groups, share your sentences. Who wrote the most interesting sentence?

I'll have fun if this toy helicopter flies on Sunday!
I'll have fun if I play games on my brother's tablet after school.

Mission Stage 1

Find out the class's technological need and choose your group's favourite!

What do you think we need in our classroom?
I think these tablets help us to learn a lot!

Tablets ✓✓✓
Laptop ✓

2

Vocabulary 2

1 **Read the school webpage. Who has a robot that gives food to cats?**

Wall | Find friends | Chat | Profile

Hi friends,
How will computers be different in 10 years' time? How will they help us? I'm making a poster about the future of computers and need ideas!
Thanks
Jim

In 10 years' time, I think there will be lots of computers in our homes. In fact, I think that we'll **chat** to computers all day.
The computers will help us a lot. If I'm hungry, I'll ask the freezer, 'What ice cream have we got?' Or if I take photos, I'll ask my phone to **upload** them to my blog. – Ibcat2

In 10 years' time, I think we'll stop using mice. Instead, we'll control our computers using our bodies. When we want to **click** on something, we'll close one eye. And, when we want to **download** a game or a film, we'll look down at the floor.
If we want to **turn on** a computer or **turn** it **off**, maybe we'll jump in the air! – CoolJen

If a computer has a small problem, like a broken 'enter' key, people often throw it away. But in the future computers will be easier to repair. Maybe we'll be able to **install** programs or borrow robots that repair our computers? And if our computers break, they'll be easy to recycle. – SofySky

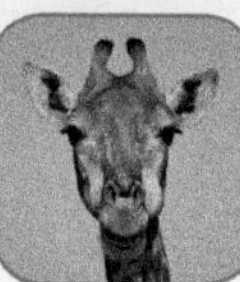

My uncle's got lots of robots. If the floor is dirty, a robot drives around and cleans it. Another robot feeds his cats if they're hungry and **texts** his mobile phone when he needs to buy more cat food!
In 10 years' time, the computers in robots will be able to do almost anything. They'll help us by writing **emails** and doing our homework! – Jungles17

2 1.18 **Match the icons (1–9) to the words in bold on the webpage. Then listen and check.**

1 is 'chat'.

3 **Read the webpage again. Who says each sentence?**

1 'My friends and my sister are helping me with a project.'

I think Jim said this.

2 'Before I go outside, my cupboard will tell me if I need an umbrella.'
3 'Computers in the future will be easier to fix.'
4 'In the future, we'll be able to install programs by smiling.'
5 'In 10 years' time, a computer will be able to make Jim's poster for him.'

4 **Say sentences with the words from Activity 2.**

I chat with my friends online on Saturdays.

Learning outcomes By the end of the lesson, learners will be able to understand and use verbs related to technology, and read to identify types of messages.

New language *chat, click, download, install, text, turn off/on, upload*

Recycled language technology-related vocabulary

Materials audio 3 large cards (A, B, C), sticky tack

Pupil's Book, page 20

Warm-up

- Put three letters up on the board – *A B C* or write on cards and stick up on the walls.
- Learners stand up at the front. Tell them to listen to your questions and possible answers. Explain that they will choose the correct answer by standing under the correct letter. Give a simple example e.g. *My shirt is A red, B blue, C green.* Learners go and stand under the correct letter. Ensure they do this in a line so there is enough space.
- Tell learners they will gain 1 point for each correct answer and they need to remember their own points… honestly!
- Read out sentences and correct answers:
  If want to use my computer, I turn it: A up, B off, C on. (C)
  I can type using a: A mouse, B keyboard, C screen. (B)
  If you have a tablet, you can see websites by choosing: A apps, B a mouse, C hardware. (A)
  If you email a file to someone, they can see it by: A uploading, B deleting, C downloading.(C)
  If you want a new program, on your computer you need to: A install it, B copy it, C type it. (A)
- Learners move to the correct place.
- Finally, learners add up their points to see if there is a winner.

1 Read the school webpage. Who has a robot that gives food to cats?

- Ask learners to look at the text on page 20 and read the question. Ask *What kind of text is this? (an email).*
- Tell the learners to read the email quickly and find the answer to the question. Remind them that they don't need to read everything in detail but just quickly.
- Learners read. Put them into pairs to compare answers.
- Check with the class.

Key: Lucas's uncle

- Say *So Lucas thinks robots will feed cats and do other tasks. What do the others think? (Ibrahim: computers will do jobs in the house; Jenny: we will control computers with our bodies; Sofia: programs or robots will fix computers.)*

2 (1.18) Match the icons (1–9) to the words in bold on the webpage. Then listen and check.

- Tell learners to look at the icons in the pictures and guess what they might represent. Do the first one together as an example *(chat).* Learners work in pairs.
- Say *Listen and check.* Play the audio. Learners check.
- Check answers. As you do so, check learners understand each item by asking questions, e.g. *If I use a mouse, what is the action we do? (click).*

Track 1.18

1 chat	4 download	7 turn off
2 click	5 upload	8 text
3 email	6 turn on	9 install

Extension Give learners a simple process, e.g. send an email with a file. Ask them to describe the process in pairs, e.g. *First turn on your computer and click on the 'email' app to open it. Make a new message and upload the file … .*

Key: 1 chat 2 click 3 email 4 download 5 upload 6 turn on 7 turn off 8 text 9 install

3 Read the webpage again. Who says each sentence?

- Ask learners to read the sentences and think about who might have said them. Learners discuss and predict.
- Ask them to read and check their ideas.
- Check with the class.

Key: 1 Jim 2 Lucas 3 Jenny 4 Sofia 5 Ibrahim

4 Say sentences with the words from Activity 2.

- Put learners in pairs. Tell them to read the example sentence and to make sentences of their own using the words from Activity 2.
- Invite strong learners to say one sentence each to the class.

Activity Book, page 20

See pages TB126–141.

Ending the lesson

- Put learners into groups of four. Write the words from Activity 2 on the board. Each team chooses a referee to watch and make sure there is no cheating.
- Ask learners to test each other. They take it in turns to pick a word and try to get their partners to say it using anything they like without saying the word, e.g. mime, explanation, definition, example.

Language practice 2

Learning outcomes By the end of the lesson, learners will be able to use zero conditional to describe possibilities now.

New language zero conditional (*if* … present simple + present simple)

Recycled language verbs and nouns related to technology, first conditional

Materials sticky notes, paper and colouring pens, copies of Mission worksheet (Teacher's Resource Book page 14)

Warm-up

- Give out sticky notes.
- Ask learners to think of a word connected to technology and write it on the sticky note. Stick these around the wall. If there are several notes with the same word, only put up one.
- Put learners into pairs and ask them to circulate and look at the words. For each one, they think of a sentence using that word and beginning with *If*, e.g. *If my screen breaks, I'll take it to the shop and get it fixed.*
- Learners circulate and discuss.
- Monitor and listen to learners' sentences.

Pupil's Book, page 21

Presentation

- Use one of the sentences learners gave in the warmer or a sentence of your own that has first conditional, e.g. *If I need to study a lot, I turn off my mobile.* Write it on the board.
- Ask learners *Do you remember the sentences we made with 'if'? How many parts were there? (two). What is different about this sentence? (The second part doesn't have 'will', it has another present simple).*
- Ask *Do you turn off your mobile now when you study? (yes). So is this information about facts and habits now? (yes).*
- Add in the word *will* before *I turn off*. Say *Is this something I do now or in the future? (future).*

Grammar look: the zero conditional and first conditional

- Tell learners to look at the **Grammar look** box.
- Put learners into pairs. Ask them to choose the correct option in each question. Check answers.

  Fast finishers Learners think of statements about computers. Remind them of the previous lesson, e.g. *If I click on this app, I will see an online dictionary.*

Key: 1 Yes, it will 2 Zero conditional 3 Yes, he might 4 First conditional

1 What do you do now and what will you do in the future? Ask and answer.

- Ask learners to look at the sentences. Do the first one together. Start the question by asking *What do you do … (if your computer doesn't turn on?).*
- Encourage a stronger learner to answer pointing to the example: e.g. *my computer doesn't turn on, I ask my dad to help me.* Ask *Is this about now or the future? (now).*
- Encourage another learner to answer by reading out the second example. Point out the use of *will*.
- Learners complete the rest asking questions and giving answers about now and the future. Monitor and support.
- Check answers.

Key: 1 Shall we 2 I'd like to 3 can 4 bring 5 might

2  Write notes about how computers will be different in 10 years' time. How will they help us?

- Put learners into groups of five or six.
- Give each group a large poster paper and colouring pens. Tell them to think of five ideas and to create a mind map showing the ideas. Monitor and support.
- When they finish put the posters up on the wall. Learners circulate around the room and decide which of the ideas they like best.

  Fast finishers Design one of the new pieces of technology and label the parts. They describe what the technology can do and why it is useful.

  Complete the Grammar look on page 121.
  See pages TB125–126.

 Mission Stage 2

- Put learners into the same groups as Mission Stage 1. Remind them of the ideas they created at Stage 1 and decide if they want to keep it or use a new idea.
- Give learners a copy of the Mission worksheet (Teacher's Resource Book page 23). Tell them to create a diagram showing how their technology works in a cause–consequence chart.

Activity Book, page 21

See pages TB126–141.

Ending the lesson

- **SA** Ask learners to complete their self-assessment (see Introduction).

Grammar look: the zero and first conditional

'If the floor is dirty, a robot drives around and cleans.'

'If I'm hungry, I'll ask the freezer, "What ice cream have we got?"'

1 When the floor is dirty, how likely is it that the robot will clean? **Yes, the robot will clean. / Yes, the robot might clean.**

2 What kind of sentence is this? **Zero conditional / First conditional**

3 Will the boy be able to talk to the freezer in the future? **Yes, he will. / Yes, he might.**

4 What kind of sentence is this? **Zero conditional / First conditional**

5 We use the first conditional to talk about things that might happen. We use the zero conditional to talk about things that are **never / always** true.

page 120

1 **What do you do now and what will you do in the future?** Ask and answer.

1 Your computer doesn't turn on.
2 Your keyboard's 'enter' key is broken.
3 You want to chat to your friends.
4 You want to download a game.
5 Your floor is dirty.

At the moment, if my computer doesn't turn on, I ask my dad to help me.

In the future, if my computer doesn't turn on, I'll be able to repair it on my own.

2 **Write notes about how computers will be different in 10 years' time.** How will they help us?

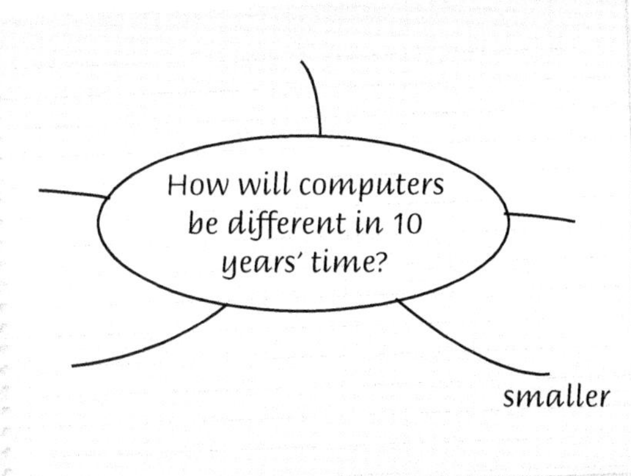
How will computers be different in 10 years' time?
smaller

Mission Stage 2

Show how your piece of technology works.

If you install this program you can practise your English.

Literature

1 **What are the most popular newspapers in your country?** Does your school have its own newspaper or news section on its website?

THE IAST TIMES

1.19

If it happens, we write about it

Friday 28th May | iasttimes.co.tr | No 134

AZRA WINS!

The winner of The Istanbul Academy of Science and Technology's Design-an-app Competition surprised everyone. Emre Erdem tells us what happened.

This Monday there was a surprise winner of Dr Şafak's Design-an-app Competition. Azra Guner, who only joined the Academy last month, won first prize for her brilliant Timetabler app, which helps students organise their time.

Dr Şafak announced the competition at the beginning of May. She said, 'The app must be easy to install and use on a mobile phone, and it must help students with their schoolwork. It shouldn't use lots of battery.' Throughout the month this newspaper followed the competition. We spoke to students about possible winners and everyone said the same thing: 'If Burak Gül enters it, he'll win it.' 'Burak knows everything about computers,' said Ahmet Terim. 'His parents teach him.' 'He'll be the Steve Jobs of Turkey one day,' said Mira Balta.

Everyone was surprised when Dr Şafak announced the winner of the competition. Azra Guner is new to the school and very quiet. Nobody knew that she designed her first app when she was only seven years old. Now, she is the star of the software class and everyone wants to talk about her app. 'It makes it easy to plan your time!' said Hasan Can. 'I love it!' said Ecrin Bartu. 'With Azra's app, I can make a timetable really quickly!'

PROFILES

Name: Burak Gül
Age: 11
Interests: chess, reading

Name: Azra Guner
Age: 11
Interests: video games, music

Learning outcomes By the end of the lesson, learners will be able to recognise text types and read a newspaper article and understand the problems of jealousy.

New language *app, icon*

Recycled language *click, install, mobile phone, program, software, timetable*, zero and first conditional

Materials audio, copies of newspapers if possible, pictures of app icons

Warm-up

- Show learners a simple flowchart for an online tool on the board or on a slide, e.g. *1 Turn on your computer and go online. 2 Download the program from www.fungamesforenglish.com. 3 Press the 'play' icon. 3 Play the game. 4 Press the 'stop' icon if you finish the game. 5 Turn off the computer.*
- Put learners into groups of five and give each a number 1–5.
- Tell each learner they have 1 minute to read and remember their point in the process – learner 1 should try to remember point 1 and so on. After one minute hide the instructions and ask the learners to stand in groups of five and remember the sequence. Explain they don't need to remember the exact words, just the meaning.
- Choose a group to show their process in front of the class.

Pupil's Book, page 22

1 What are the most popular newspapers in your country? Does your school have its own newspaper or news section on its website?

- If possible, bring in some examples of local newspapers. Show these and ask the learners what they are.
- Put the learners into groups of three and ask them what kinds of things they can see in a newspaper. Give them 2 minutes to discuss, then ask for their ideas.
- Ask if they ever read any newspapers and what parts of it they look at. Share their ideas.
- Ask learners to discuss question 1 in pairs. Learners share their ideas.

  Extension If you have enough copies of newspapers for one per group of five learners, put them into groups and ask them to find examples of specific things, e.g. *weather forecast, reviews, sport*. Learners find each section and hold it up saying the word.

Key: learners' own ideas.

Presentation

- Tell learners they are going to read a newspaper article.
- Write the words *competition, app, winner* on the board.
- Learners work in pairs to predict what they might read about in the article. Confirm or guide until they guess it is about a competition to design a new app.
- Look at the pictures on page 22. Tell learners to look at the profiles of the two students and the headline. Ask them *Who won? (Azra).*

1.19 THE IAST TIMES

- Tell learners people were surprised that Azra won the competition. Ask them what kind of app they think she designed. Ask why they think people were surprised.
- Learners discuss in pairs. Share their ideas, but don't respond. Now ask them to read and listen to the article and find out if they are correct.
- Play the audio, but stop after *'you'll be able to read all about it in the IAST Times'* and before the interview with the winner.
- Put learners into pairs to compare answers. Check answers.

Key: Azra designed a timetabling app. People were surprised because Burak is very good at computing and Azra was new and very quiet. People didn't know she was good at computing.

- Tell learners they are going to hear an interview with Azra talking about her app. Ask them what they think it does.
- Learners discuss in pairs.
- Say *You will also hear an interesting fact about one of the first computer programmers. Find out who this person was.*
- Ask them to listen and check. Play the rest of the audio.
- Check answers.

Key: The app helps you make a timetable and plans when you study for your exams. The computer programmer was Ada Lovelace – interesting because it is a woman from 1843!

Activity Book, page 22

See pages TB126–141.

Ending the lesson

- Put learners into groups of three.
- Show some examples of 'app icons' (find pictures online or use your own device). Say *What do we call this type of picture for an app? (icon).* Learners repeat. Tell learners they should design the icon for Azra's app. Tell them to think about what should be in the picture, the colours and if they want to include any letters.
- Learners discuss and create a design.
- Each group present their app and describe why they chose it.

  Extra support Learners can design and label the app.

  Stronger learners can give the presentation.

Learning outcomes By the end of the lesson, learners will be able to recognise text types and read a newspaper article, and understand and consider ways of dealing with jealousy.

New language *jealous, jealousy, successful*

Recycled language *app, click, install, mobile phone, program, software, timetable,* zero and first conditional

Materials pictures of successful people (e.g. a sports winner, a famous actor, a politician, a singer)

Social and Emotional Skill: dealing with jealousy

- After reading the story, ask *What type of competitions do you enter? How do you feel if you win/lose?*
- Point out that it's OK to feel unhappy if you don't win. The important thing is to recognize and talk about your emotions.
- Ask *Can jealousy be positive? (It can make you work harder next time.)*
- Point out that it's hard to lose, but always try to congratulate the winner.
- Learners write a paragraph about feeling jealous about something. Then they write a list of all the things they feel positive about and things they are good at. When they appreciate what they have, they could feel less jealous of others.

Warm-up

- Show learners pictures of successful people, e.g. a sports winner, a famous actor, a politician, a singer. Learners name the different people if they know them and say what their jobs are. Ask them what these people have in common. *(They are successful.)* Put learners into pairs. Ask them what characteristics they might have, e.g. *hard working.*
- Learners discuss in pairs. Share their ideas.

Pupil's Book, page 23

Presentation

- Look at the pictures of successful people again. Say *Imagine you are the friend of one of these people. How might you feel if they are very successful?* Learners suggest ideas, e.g. *happy for them.*
- Write *jealous* on the board. Ask if learners can give you the definition of the word: *When we are jealous, we feel angry because someone has something that we want or can do something that we wish we could do.*
- Give the pronunciation of *jealous*: /ˈdʒeləs/. Learners repeat.
- Ask learners when we might feel jealous of someone, e.g. your friend does better than you do in a test in school, a friend gets something for their birthday that you want but don't have, somebody plays the guitar better than you can.
- Write on the board: *surprised, happy, unhappy, jealous.*
- Put learners into pairs. Ask them to open their books to review the story or read it again quickly. Ask who felt like this.
- Learners compare ideas. Check answers.

Key: Everyone was surprised, Azra was probably happy; Burak was unhappy and maybe he was jealous.

2 In pairs, role play a conversation. Imagine you are Azra and Burak.

- Ask learners to think of more words to describe how Azra and Burak feel after the competition, e.g. *Azra is surprised, happy, excited; Burak is surprised, jealous, angry, sad.*
- Put learners into pairs and ask them to role play a conversation. The conversation should be difficult at first (because Azra knows that Burak feels jealous), but should become easier as Azra and Burak discover they are both interested in design, technology and software.
- Learners plan then act out their role play.
- Choose a few pairs to present their role play for the class.
  Extra support Learners prepare some of their sentences first then try to use the sentences while they role play.

Activity Book, page 23

See pages TB126–141.

Ending the lesson

- Ask learners to think of a time they felt jealous. Put them into pairs. Learners talk about how they felt, what happened and why they were jealous.
- Put learners into groups of four. Tell each group to think of some advice they might give to someone who is feeling jealous.
- Monitor and check that each group has some advice.
- Give learners 5 minutes. Learners mingle and talk to different people about the time they felt jealous and why. Their partner gives them advice.
- Put learners back into their groups. Ask them to decide what they can say to Burak.

Although Burak was very unhappy when he lost the competition, some students say that he and Azra are going to design a new app together. If that happens, you'll be able to read all about it in the *IAST Times*.

AN INTERVIEW WITH THE WINNER

What does your app do?

AZRA It makes a timetable for students.

Can you explain that?

AZRA Of course! You tell the app what exams you need to study for. You also tell it when the exams are. Then you click on the special 'plan' button and the app makes a timetable for you.

Do you mean it tells you what to study and when?

AZRA Yes, that's right! That means you have more time for studying because the app does the planning for you.

Technology Fact of the Week

Ada Lovelace was an English mathematician and one of the first computer programmers. In 1843 she wrote a program for a type of computer that was invented by an Englishman called Charles Babbage.

2 **In pairs, role play a conversation.** Imagine you are Azra and Burak.

STUDENT A You are Azra. You feel happy because you won the competition. You have lots of ideas for new apps. Ask Burak if he would like to help you design a new app.

I can't believe I won!

STUDENT B You are Burak. You feel jealous of Azra because you wanted to win the competition. Ask Azra about her app.

Cross-curricular

1 **Which apps do you use?** What do they do?

2 1.20 **Listen and read the text.** What do these numbers mean?

2 million $1 million 400 million

< What's an app? >

< There are lots of apps that you can download to a smartphone or laptop. The most popular are games, news, weather and social media apps. If you have an app on your phone, you just have to click on it. This means you don't need to search for a program or write the address of a website. One of the first apps was a game called 'Snake'. Players had to make a line of dots around the small screen. This might not sound very interesting, but 400 million people played this simple game. Now there are over 2 million apps to choose from. >

< How do you make an app? >

< Companies can spend between $50,000–$1 million on making apps. That's a lot of money! But if you have a good idea, you can make an app and create it for free. There are a few things to do if you want to make an app:

1 Think about what your app is going to do, how it will be good for the people using it and how you will let people know about your app. Write your ideas on a piece of paper and draw pictures.
2 Go online and check if there are other apps like yours. If there are, how is yours better?
3 Wireframe your idea. A wireframe is like a storyboard. You draw your design idea so that you can see what your app does. There are lots of different wireframing websites to help you do this.
4 Learn the language of app building. Lots of schools have coding clubs which teach you the languages you need to build apps. You need to choose a coding language and learn the rules. For example, when you are using HTML5, you need to use these symbols < > at the beginning and end of your codes. >

3 **In pairs, talk about about the sentences.** Say *yes* or *no* and why.

1 I'd like to play 'Snake'.
2 I'd like a maths app.
3 I think making an app is easy.
4 I'd like to make my own app.

A mobile phone is more powerful than the computer that sent astronauts to the moon in 1969.

Learning outcomes By the end of the lesson, learners will have read a text to identify specific information and learnt to think about the role of technology in the world and how we use it.

New language *code, coding*

Recycled language *app, click, icon, install, mobile phone, program, software, timetable*, zero and first conditional

Materials pictures of apps, access to internet and example apps if possible

Warm-up

- Put a code up on the board as follows: 0 = A 01= B 02=C 03=D 04=E 05=F 06=G 07=H 08=I 09=J 010=K.
- Ask learners to complete the rest of the code in pairs and do a quick check, e.g. *What is the code for 's'? (018). And for 'w'? (022).*
- Write up a code on the board: *<08> <011 014 021 04> <0 015 015 018>* Put learners into pairs to work out what it means. Tell them spaces between numbers mean there is a new letter and the < > symbols show each separate word. *(I love apps).* Now ask the learners to write a short sentence and change it into code in pairs.
- When they have finished, they pass their code to another pair to work out. See which pair can work out their clue quickest.

Pupil's book, page 24

Presentation

- Ask learners what kind of language is put into computers to make them work. (*numbers and symbols ordered in a special way, a bit like the ones in the previous activity*)
- Ask what this is called (*code or computer coding*). Say the word. Learners repeat.
- Put learners into pairs and ask *Would you like to be a computer coder. Why or why not?* Learners discuss. Share ideas.

1 Which apps do you use? What do they do?

- Ask learners to explain what an app is. Remind them of the competition from the previous lesson.
- Learners discuss in pairs and suggest ideas.
- Tell learners to look at page 24 and read the definition. Ask them to guess what the apps might be.
- Put learners into groups of four. Tell each learner to draw a picture of their favourite app icon if they can remember it. Tell them to show their group. The other learners should guess which app they like. If they can't remember, they can draw a picture that gives a clue.
- Learners work in groups sharing clues.
- Ask *Which other apps do you use? What do they do and why do you like them?* Learners discuss. Listen and support.

  Fast finishers Learners find out which apps are most popular in their group and used by more than one person.

2 🎧 1.20 Listen and read the text. What do these numbers mean?

- Tell learners they will read the text again but this time they need to find numbers. Ask if they can remember what types of numbers were given e.g. *dates, prices?* Learners suggest ideas.
- Ask *When you read this time what will you look for? (numbers). Which part of the text will you read carefully? (The sentences with numbers to understand what they describe.)*
- Learners read the text. Put them in pairs to compare answers.
- Check answers.

Key: 2 million: number of apps to choose from, $1 million: the amount of money to make an app, 400 million: number of people who played 'Snake'

3 Read the sentences and talk in pairs. Say *yes* or *no* and why.

- Ask learners to sit in groups of four. Give each member a letter A, B, C and D. Tell them to discuss questions with their partner till you clap your hands. Tell A and B to work together and C and D to work together.
- Ask them to read the first question, say *yes* or *no* and discuss why. Learners discuss in pairs. Clap your hands.
- Tell A and C to work together and B and D to work together. Repeat with the second question. Learners discuss. Clap your hands.
- Tell A and D to work together and B and C to work together. Repeat with the third question. Clap your hands.
- Tell learners to work in fours and discuss the final question.

Activity Book, page 24

See pages TB126–141.

Ending the lesson

- Ask learners to think of a new app that would make their life easier, e.g. *I'd like an app that organises my clothes for me. If I'm going to a party, it will tell me the best way to put my clothes together. If I'm going to play tennis, it will remind me to take my sports shoes.*
- Learners work with a partner and tell them about their ideal app. Their partner says if they would like to use the app too.

Learning outcomes By the end of the lesson, learners will be able to understand strategies for speaking effectively, learn how to analyse a question before answering and use question words.

New language question words

Recycled language present simple, personal information

Materials video

Warm-up

- Put learners into pairs. Write on the board: *daily routine, hobby, likes/dislike, family, friends, study.*
- Say *Think of one question for each category.* Do the first together, e.g. *For daily routine, we could ask 'What time do you … (get up/have breakfast).*
- Learners work together and write questions. Monitor and check as they work. Put each pair of learners together. Each pair take it in turns to ask and answer questions.
- Repeat with other starter words and new categories, e.g. animal; hobbies.

Pupil's Book, page 25

1 Watch the video to see an example of Speaking Part 1.

Presentation

- Tell learners they are going to practise answering questions. Say *Before you speak you need to think about the question. Which information in the question helps you answer well? (the question word)* Ask learners to think of some question words, e.g. *Who/What/How.*

2 Match the question words with the phrases. What information should the answer have?

- Ask learners to look at the question and answer bubbles. Tell them to read the questions and match with the correct answer by thinking about what information should be in the answer.
- Learners work for 2–3 minutes on their own to match. Put them into pairs to check ideas. Check answers.

Key: What …? A thing, Where …? A place, Who …? A person, When …? A time, Tell me about … A short description, An irregular verb – not used.

3 Match the questions and answers.

- Tell learners to look at the questions in Activity 3. Tell them to think about the question word and the kind of information in the answer. Go through examples: *Question 2 and 4 say 'Where…' so both answers will have….(a place). But one is about where you live and one is about where you went on holiday so think carefully.*
- Learners work on their own to match. Put them into pairs to compare answers. Check with the class.
- Ask *Is the answer one word or more? (more).* Say *When you answer you need to give long answers not just one word.*
- Tell learners to think how they could answer themselves.
- Learners role play in pairs. Tell them to take it in turns to be the examiner. The examiner asks the questions and the learner answers. Then they swap roles and repeat. They give answers that are true for them. Monitor and listen.

Extra support Learners make notes for their answers to use them in the role play.

Key: 1 B 2 A 3 D 4 C 5 F 6 E

EXAM TIP! Ask a strong learner to read it aloud. Say *In Part 1 of the test, you must speak clearly even if you are nervous. So practise speaking as much as possible.* Say *First of all, let's think about how to do well.* Ask learners for their ideas and put them on the board, e.g. speak clearly; use good pronunciation; think about the question before you answer; give long answers; don't just use one word.

4 In pairs, ask and answer the questions.

- Tell learners to look at the questions quickly and think about their answers. Put them into new pairs: A and B. Point to the list on the board and remind them that they need to do these things when they speak.
- Tell learner A to be the examiner and learner B to answer. Ask them to role play the questions. Monitor and listen.
- When they finish, ask learner A to give feedback to learner B using the ideas on the board, e.g. *You spoke really clearly, but your answers were a bit short sometimes.*
- Learners swap roles and repeat the sequence.

Activity Book, page 25

See pages TB126–141.

Ending the lesson

- Tell learners that, at the start of Part 1 in Key exams, the examiner also asks for the mark sheet, their name and surname and how to spell their surname. Give an example. Say *My surname is Vesta. It's spelt V-E-S-T-A.*
- Put learners into new pairs. Learners take it in turns to ask *What's your surname? How do you spell it?*

1 **Watch the video to see an example of Speaking Part 1.**

2 **Match the question words with the phrases. What information should the answer have?**

What…?	A thing
Where…?	A time
Who…?	A place
When…?	A short description
Tell me about…	A person

3 **Match the questions (1–6) to answers (A–F).**

1 What's your family name?
2 Where are you from?
3 What do you like about your school?
4 Where did you go on holiday last year?
5 Who usually cooks in your house?
6 Tell me something about a new hobby you would like to try.

A I'm from Seville but I live in Madrid.
B It's Bowring.
C My family and I went to Corfu in Greece.
D It's got a big gym and a modern computer room.
E When I finish my exams, I'll start a short course on writing programs for computer games.
F My parents usually do the cooking but my brother is quite good at making curries and desserts!

4 **In pairs, ask and answer the questions.**

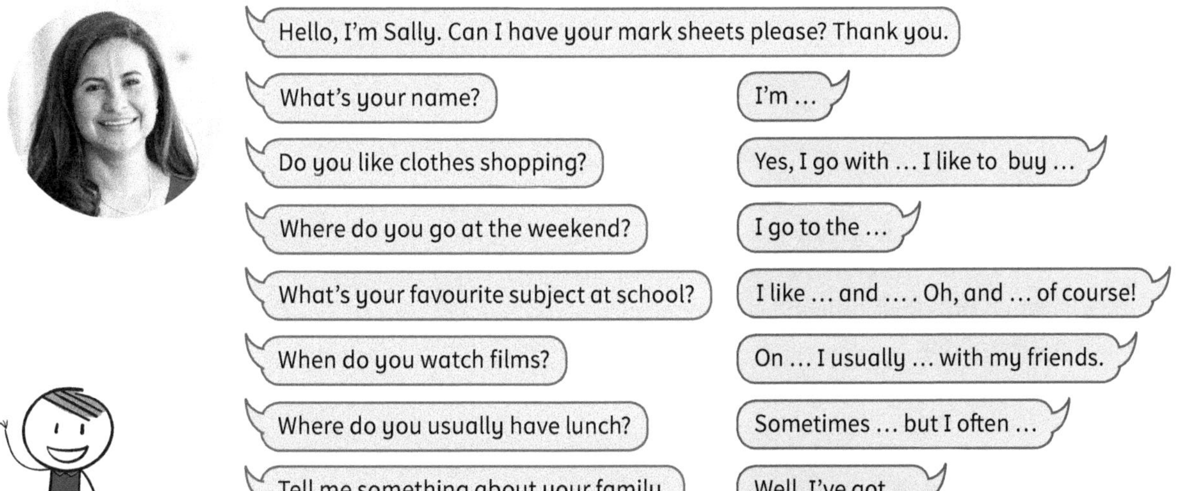

Hello, I'm Sally. Can I have your mark sheets please? Thank you.
What's your name?
I'm …
Do you like clothes shopping?
Yes, I go with … I like to buy …
Where do you go at the weekend?
I go to the …
What's your favourite subject at school?
I like … and …. Oh, and … of course!
When do you watch films?
On … I usually … with my friends.
Where do you usually have lunch?
Sometimes … but I often …
Tell me something about your family.
Well, I've got …

EXAM TIP! Try to **speak clearly** and remember to give **as much information** as you can!

A2 Key for Schools

1 Do the quick quiz.

1 What is a blog?
 a a sauce b an animal
 c something to read

2 Who can write a blog?
 a anyone b children
 c adults

3 Where can I read a blog?
 a in a comic b online
 c in a book

2 In the exam you read about three people talking about the same thing. You have to decide which person says something. What do you think is the best way to do this? Choose and put the sentences in order.

A read each text once C choose a letter ______ ______
B read the questions D read the three texts again ______ ______

3 Choose the correct answer.

1 Which person doesn't write as much as before?
 a Now I'm nineteen and I don't write my blog very often.
 b I post a message once a week.

2 Which person sometimes gets a message they don't want?
 a … sometimes I get emails from my school.
 b Sometimes I get a strange message on the screen but I don't mind … I just delete it immediately!

3 Which person was the youngest when they started their blog?
 a I started my blog when I was thirteen.
 b I started blogging when I was twelve.

4 Which person needs some help to write their blog?
 a My computer is so slow! Sometimes I need to ask if I can use my brother's.
 b When the wifi is broken I can't post a new blog.

EXAM TIP! Don't worry if you see some words which you don't know. You will still be able to answer the question.

Learning outcomes By the end of the lesson, learners will be able to understand strategies for reading and answering questions effectively, and understand how to deal with unknown vocabulary.

New language *blog*

Recycled language technology-related vocabulary, question forms

Materials access to Internet and example blogs if possible

Warm-up

- Learners work in pairs. Ask them to talk about things they can read online or on a mobile, e.g. *text message*.
- Ask learners for their ideas. If they haven't included 'blog', add this to the list and check meaning. Say *a blog is a kind of online diary or place for people to share their ideas.*
- If possible, show some example blogs online (check that they are suitable for the age range in your class). Ask them which ones they think look interesting.

  Alternative If learners have access to individual devices, put them into groups of three and give each one a blog to look at. (If you have a large group, choose three or four blogs and assign each to more than one group). Tell learners to find out what kind of information is in the blog, who writes it and if it is good. Learners report back to the rest of the class.
- Ask learners if they have written a blog. Learners share ideas.

  Extra support Give learners some topics to choose from.

Pupil's Book, page 26

Presentation

- Say *It is good to look at information and try to understand before we listen. We can understand a lot from pictures.*
- Tell learners to discuss what the people in the picture might be talking about. Share ideas.

1 Do the quick quiz.

- Tell learners to read and answer the quiz questions as quickly as possible. Put learners into pairs to check answers.
- Check answers with the class.

Key: 1 c 2 a 3 b

2 In the exam, you read about three people talking about the same thing. You have to decide which person says something. What is the best way to do this? Choose and put the sentences in order.

- Tell learners that, in this part of the exam, they will read about three people and have to choose the correct person. Say *Sometimes it is difficult because they all talk about similar things. We need to think about how to do this best.*
- Put learners into pairs. Tell them to read the points in Activity 3 and decide on the best order.
- Go through the answers one by one. Explain that they need to understand the topic first, so start with the title. They read each text once to get a general idea. Then they should read the questions. At this point, they can choose one text that is not appropriate. This will mean they only have to choose between two possible answers.

  Fast finishers Learners cover the answers and test each other on the correct sequence.

Key: A read each text once B read the questions D read the three texts again C choose a letter

3 Choose the correct answer.

- Ask learners to work in groups of three. Do the first one together. Say *Which words in the question are important? (which person … as before).* Say *We need to think about something which tells us they have changed from before.*
- Ask a strong learner to read out the two possibilities. Say *What do we know about Stephen? (he's nineteen; he doesn't post very often). What do we know about Julie? (she posts once a week).* Say *Read the sentence about Stephen again. He says 'Now I'm nineteen and I don't post very often.'* Emphasise *now*. Say *Did he post more when he was younger? (yes).* Say *Which answer is correct? (a).*
- Ask learners to continue to work in their groups and think carefully about their answers. Monitor and support.
- Check answers with the class.

EXAM TIP! Go to the exam tip. Clarify that they might read some words they don't know, but they will still be able to complete the questions. They shouldn't spend time on the unknown words.

Key: 1 a 2 b 3 b 4 a

Activity Book, page 26

See pages TB126–141.

Ending the lesson

- Put learners into pairs. Ask them to discuss what they might put in a blog if they wrote one. Share ideas.

Learning outcomes By the end of the lesson, learners will have used language from the unit to talk about technology and revised the language and skills from the unit.

Recycled language unit language

Materials poster paper and colouring pens

Warm-up

- Draw three columns on the board. Put *beginning/middle/end* at the top of each column. Say *Let's listen for sounds. The first sound is /t/.* Learners repeat the sound. Say *Listen: laptop. Is /t/ at the beginning, in the middle or at the end? (middle).* Write the word in the second column. Learners repeat.
- Do the same with other words adding them to the columns *chat (end), computer (middle), text (beginning and end), software (middle), turn on (beginning).*
- Repeat but this time with the sound /p/: *program (beginning), app (end), computer (middle).*

  Fast finishers Ask them to write four sentences using the words that are true for them, e.g. *My favourite app is Angry Birds.*

Pupil's Book, page 27

1 Match the sentence halves.

- Ask learners to look at the beginnings and ends of the sentences. Ask them what kind of sentences they are *(conditionals).*
- Look at the first example together (1 C).
- Put learners into pairs. Ask them to match the beginnings to the ends of the sentences. Monitor and support.
- Check answers.

Key: 1 C 2 B 3 E 4 A 5 D

Read the email. Choose the correct answer.

- Tell learners they will choose the correct words for the text.
- Say *Sometimes we don't know all the words in a question or an exam. How can you make sure you know a lot of words?*
- Learners suggest ideas. If they don't mention it, tell them that reading a lot of different things – webpages, books, cartoons, and so on – will help them improve their knowledge.
- Ask learners to read the text quickly and not worry about the gaps. Ask them what the text is about.
- Learners read. Put them into pairs to discuss then check their ideas.
- Ask learners to read the text again and to think about the kind of word that fits. Do the first one together. Say *We need a verb and the sentence is in the present simple. So which one is best? (arrive).* Learners complete the rest of the questions in pairs.
- Check answers.

Key: the text is about how pizzas will be delivered in the future 1 A 2 C 3 C 4 A 5 B

3 Look at the new words from this unit. Make puzzles with the words using the steps below.

- Say to learners *Well done. You've learnt a lot of new language. Let's practise it now. We're going to make a word puzzle.*
- Tell learners to look at the flowchart. Show them the first instruction: four kinds of hardware + one other word. Tell them to call out some examples of hardware (e.g. *screen, laptop, keyboard, mouse*). Write their answers on the board. Ask *What other word did we learn that isn't hardware?* (e.g. *program, app*). Write this up. Say *We've made a puzzle. You have to find the odd word out.*
- Say *Let's try*. Put learners into pairs and ask them to complete the second instruction: four verbs + one other clue. Learners complete. Monitor and support.
- Share their ideas.
- Finally, ask them to do the two instructions under 'Make one more puzzle'. Monitor and support.
- When they have finished, ask them to swap puzzles with a partner and test each other.

Mission in action!

- Put learners into the same groups as earlier in the Mission.
- Ask each group to think about the gadget or technology they designed earlier and how it works.
- Tell each group to prepare their idea to show to the class. Give out paper and colouring pens so they can create a poster with labels and diagrams of how it works.
- Each group presents their idea explaining what the technology is, how it works and how to use it.
- When the groups have presented their ideas, ask the class to vote on the idea they think will help the class most. (They can't vote for their own idea.) Choose a winning idea.

Activity Book, page 27

See pages TB126–141.

Ending the lesson

- SA Complete the self-assessment (see Introduction.)

1 Match the sentence halves.

1 If the laptops are cheap, …
2 If I can't go to the park, …
3 If I want to do my homework on a computer, …
4 If you press 'enter', …
5 If her keyboard is broken, …

A the program will download.
B I'll chat to my friends online.
C I'll buy a new one today.
D Grandma won't be able to email me.
E I'll need a printer.

2 ★ Read the email. Choose the correct answer.

Hi Jim,

Sorry for replying so slowly!

At the moment, when you order pizzas, they often (1) ______ slowly. When there (2) ______ a lot of traffic, the pizza can get cold too! In the future, I think that flying robots will carry pizzas. So (3) ______ you want one, it will be at your house in less than five minutes. (4) ______ you want the pizza cut up, the robot (5) ______ do that for you too!

– Mike

	A	B	C
1	arrive	arrive	arriving
2	was	will	is
3	while	because	if
4	When	Can	Are
5	able	will	is

EXAM TIP! Read the text **once** to understand it. Then read the text **again** and choose the best word for each space.

3 Look at the new words from this unit. Make puzzles with the words using the steps below.

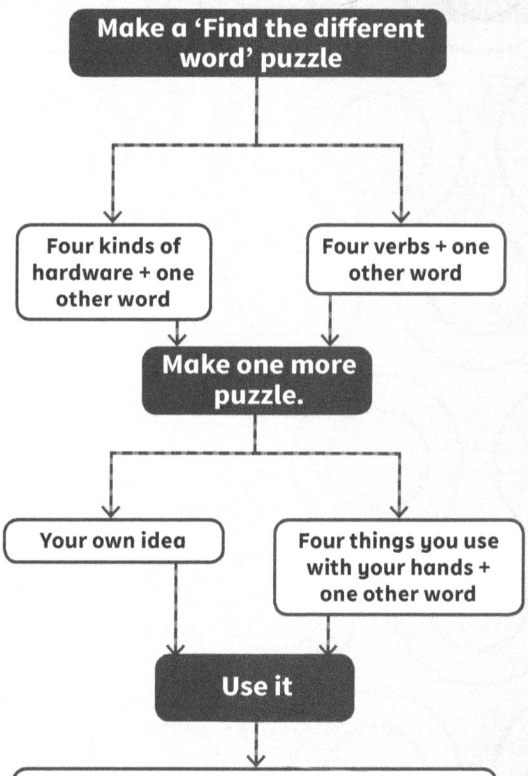
Make a 'Find the different word' puzzle
Four kinds of hardware + one other word
Four verbs + one other word
Make one more puzzle.
Your own idea
Four things you use with your hands + one other word
Use it
Challenge a friend to find the different words in each of your puzzles.

Mission in action!

- Present your group's ideas.
- Choose the best new technology for the class.

This is a great new …

3 Jim-nastics

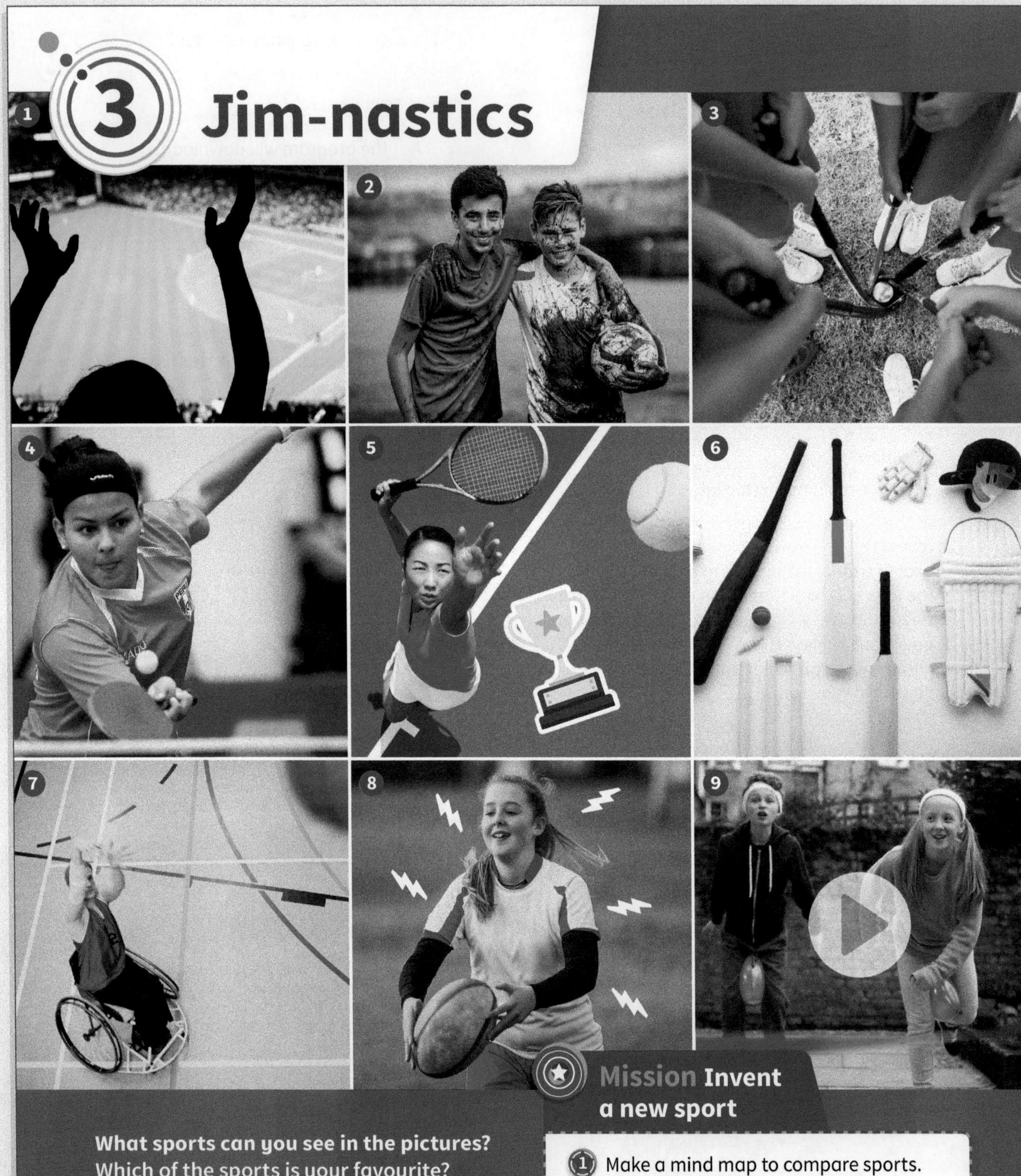

What sports can you see in the pictures?
Which of the sports is your favourite?

Watch the video. What goes wrong when Jim and Jenny play cricket?

Mission Invent a new sport

1. Make a mind map to compare sports.
2. Invent and describe a new sport.
★ Play the sport and vote for the best one!

Unit 3 learning outcomes

In Unit 3, learners will learn to:

- use vocabulary to describe sports and equipment
- use the present simple passive to describe facts and habits
- use modal verbs to describe possibilities
- read and listen for general and specific information
- understand the idea of perseverance
- develop ideas about health and physical activity

Materials video, pictures of athletics, (optional: a video, e.g. of the Olympics)

Self-assessment

- **SA** Write or project the unit outcomes on the board. Put learners into six groups, assign a learning outcome to each group. Ask them to remember. Hide the outcomes.
- Give each group a large piece of paper and tell them to work together and write their learning outcome in their own words.
- Invite each group to show their learning outcome to the class. Correct any issues and clarify if necessary.
- Ask learners to complete self-assessment (see Introduction).
- Put a large plastic box or bin at the front of the class and invite one person from each group to scrunch up their outcome into a paper ball and throw it into the box. Encourage learners to shout *'Good shot'* each time a paper lands in the box.
- Say *Let's learn.*

Pupil's Book, page 28

Warm-up

- Write *sport* on the board. Ask learners to call out sports they know. Write these on one side of the board. Learners work in pairs and use the list to answer questions. Pick different pairs to answer each time. Ask *Which has a ball / has more than two players / is played indoors/outdoors / needs you to run fast?*

  Fast finishers Cover the words and ask for the spelling.

What sports can you see in the pictures? Which of the sports is your favourite?

- Learners look at page 28. Ask *Can you see any of the sports you wrote?* Learners answer. Say *What sports can you see in the pictures?* Learners work in groups of three and discuss.
- Point to each picture and ask the name. Say each sport clearly. Clap the stress for words with more than one syllable, e.g. *football; hockey; cricket*. Learners repeat. Ask *Is the stress on the first or second syllable? (first).*
- Put learners in pairs. Ask *Which sport is your favourite? Why?* (e.g. *I love table tennis because it helps me relax and feel good.*) Choose learners to report back on their partner.

Key: 1 baseball 2 football 3 hockey 4 table tennis 5 tennis 6 cricket 7 basketball 8 rugby 9 [TBC???]

Watch the video. What goes wrong when Jim and Jenny play cricket?

- Say *Which sport is this?* Mime golf. Learners call out the name. Repeat with *cricket.*
- Show pictures (or a video clip) of athletics, e.g. at the Olympic Games. Ask *What name do we use for these sports?* Learners say *athletics.* Say *athletics* and clap on the stress. Learners repeat.
- Say *Jenny and Jim are playing sports. What can go wrong when you play cricket?* Learners suggest ideas. Ask them to watch and find out if they are right and to find out why the three sports they play are unusual.
- Play the video. Learners watch.

Key: Jim hit the ball out of the garden. The three sports are: running with a balloon; French Cricket; and golf with a hairdryer and cup.

Extension Learners watch again and find out which sport Jim likes best. *(golf).*

Mission Invent a new sport

- Write on the board: *A think of some new ideas; B share and organise information; C choose your favourite.*
- Ask learners to read the Mission statement. Tell them to match the activity on the board with the correct statement. Check their ideas. Say *This is our Mission.*

Key: 1 B 2 A 3 C

Activity Book, page 28

My unit goals

- Go through the unit goals with the learners. (See suggested techniques in 'Identifying outcomes' in the teachers' in-class guide in Introduction.)
- Go back to these unit goals at the end of each Mission stage during the unit and review them.
- Say *This is our Mission page.*

Ending the lesson

- Put learners in groups of four. Tell them to take it in turns and mime their favourite sport and one they dislike playing. The rest say the sports and guess which the person likes and which they dislike.

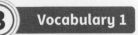

Learning outcomes By the end of the lesson, learners will be able to use vocabulary to describe sports and equipment.

New language *ice-hockey, cycling, diving, surfing, surfboard, boxing, gymnastics, water-skiing*

Recycled language *golf, athletics, rugby, cricket*

Materials audio, sticky notes, pieces of card/paper or mini-whiteboards

Pupil's Book, page 29

Warm-up

- Give a sticky note to each learner. Learners draw a sport they like to watch and stick it on their front.
- Learners mingle and talk to three other learners. They guess each other's sports and find out why they like watching it, e.g. *Is your sport swimming? Why do you like it? I like watching tennis because the players are really good.*

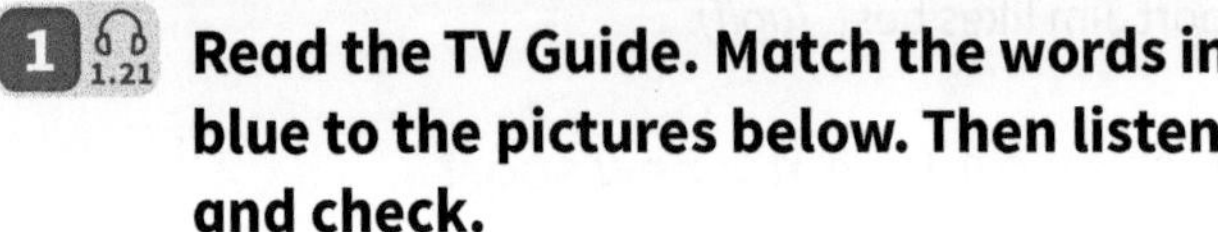

1 (1.21) Read the TV Guide. Match the words in blue to the pictures below. Then listen and check.

- Learners look at the guide quickly while you count to five and then close their books. Ask *What is it? (a TV guide). What kind of programmes can you see? (sports).*
- Say *Well done. You have understood a lot just looking quickly.*
- Learners look again in pairs and find the names of sports in bold then match the words with the pictures 1–11. Do the first one together as an example.
- Say *Let's listen and check.* Play the audio. Stop after each item and encourage learners to repeat. Write the numbers 1–11 on the board and add each word.

Track 1.21

1 cycling
2 gymnastics
3 athletics
4 water-skiing
5 surfing
6 diving
7 rugby
8 golf
9 cricket
10 ice-hockey
11 boxing

Key: rugby – 7, diving – 6, golf – 8, cricket – 9, cycling – 1, ice-hockey – 10, surfing – 5, boxing – 11, gymnastics – 2, athletics – 3, water-skiing – 4

- Give out pieces of card/paper or mini-whiteboards to pairs of learners. Ask *Which sport needs a ball?* Learners write down their answers, e.g. *cricket, golf,* and hold it up. Choose the two quickest pairs and ask them to call out their answers.
- Say *Let's play.* Give clues *(a sport you play on water; a sport with a bike; a sport you play outside; a sport you do inside; a sport with a small ball; a sport with a big ball).*

2 Write the sports.

- Learners look at the three headings in the table. Give an example, e.g. *I've tried diving. I did it when I was on holiday.*
- Learners put the sports into the correct column. They compare their lists in groups of three and find out if they have tried the same sports.

3 Do you like the sports in Activity 1? In pairs, say why or why not.

- Show a picture of rugby. Ask *Which sport is this? (rugby).* Draw a smiley face on one side. Say *I like rugby because …* Learners suggest ideas, e.g. *it's exciting / it's a fast game.* Draw a sad face on the other side. Say *I don't like (rugby) because …* Learners suggest ideas, e.g. *It's easy to get hurt. / It's difficult to play.*

EXAM TIP! Say *When we talk in the exam we can help our partner. We can ask questions or ask them to repeat things if it isn't clear.* Ask learners what they could say, e.g. *Why do you think that? Sorry can you explain again?*

Ask them what a good discussion should include, e.g. *use interesting vocabulary, ask your partner questions.* Write the list on the board. Learners copy it. Ask learners to look at the list of sports in pairs and decide why people like them or not.

Put pairs together in groups of four. One pair discuss which sports they like or dislike. The second pair watch. They give feedback to the first pair using the list. Repeat with pairs swapping roles.

Activity Book, page 29

See pages TB126–141.

Ending the lesson

- Put 11 cups or small boxes around the room. Write a letter under each one (C G A W S D R G C I B). Use a ping pong ball (or ball made of paper). A learner throws it into a box or cup. If they succeed, they lift it up to see the letter and name a sport that begins with that letter.
- When learners understand the game, give out a second ball so that two can be circulated at once.

Vocabulary 1

1 1.21 **Read the TV guide.** Match the words in blue to the pictures below. Then listen and check.

Rugby is number 7.

Wednesday, 9 October

	7:00	7:30	8:00	8:30
Sport 1	Rugby tonight: Wales vs. Australia			Deep diving: Daniel swims with sharks
Sport 2	Small white ball: Exciting golf from around the world		Cricket chat: A review of today's cricket matches	
US Adventure	Cycling: A woman, her bike and America's biggest mountains	Ice-hockey special: See the skaters on the ice for Russia vs. Canada		Surfing: Hawaii's best surfers surf the ocean's biggest waves
FIT1	Be fit boxing: Get your gloves on and get fit	Gymnastics at home: Jump, dance and stretch with Paul	Be fit boxing: Get your gloves on and get fit	Gymnastics at home: Jump, dance and stretch with Paul
AllStars	Sports stars of tomorrow: Watch athletics stars run, throw and jump to prepare for the Olympics		Snow idea: Snow skiers try water-skiing for the first time on Lake Tahoe	

2 **Write the sports.**

Sports I've tried:
Sports I've not tried but would like to try:
Sports I just want to watch on TV:

3  **Do you like the sports in Activity 1? In pairs, say why or why not.**

I love cycling. I go every week with my dad and my brother. It's a great way to see the countryside. Do you like cycling?

EXAM TIP! Be ready to help your partner by repeating what you say or asking them questions.
For example:
Why don't you like …?
What do you think about …?
How about …?

Language presentation 1

1 **Read Jim's blog.** How many dogs can stand on a surfboard?

Jim's Big Blog

If you think that sports like golf or gymnastics aren't interesting enough, you might want to try something a little stranger. I've found three really unusual sports to tell you about.

The world's three strangest sports

The Mud Olympics

The Mud Olympics is held every year in a small German town called Brunsbuettel. Around 50 teams from different countries meet and play football and other sports in deep mud. As you can see, the players get very dirty! Yuck! There are lots of prizes – and people love playing in the mud – but the main reason that the event is arranged is to get money to give to charities.

Man versus Horse

This athletics event is held in Llanwrtyd Wells in Wales. At the event, men and women race a horse for 35 kilometres. People often think that the horse will win easily – but the race is planned so that the horse and runners finish at nearly the same time. How's that done? Well, there are lots of mountains near Llanwrtyd Wells and horses are very slow at going down hills!

Dog surfing

In this sport, the dog usually surfs with a person, but sometimes the dog surfs alone or two dogs surf on one board. Dog surfing competitions are organised by people all around the world. At one competition in the USA, someone took a photo of 18 dogs on a surfboard. That's the largest number ever! I wish I took that photo!

2 **Read the sentences and choose the correct event.**

	The Mud Olympics	Man vs. Horse	Dog Surfing
1 Pets do this event on their own, in pairs, or with a man or woman.	A	B	C
2 Groups do the event together.	A	B	C
3 The event happens in an area where there are lots of hills.	A	B	C
4 People collect money at the event.	A	B	C
5 Competitions happen in many different places.	A	B	C
6 The person or animal who finishes this event first is the winner.	A	B	C

EXAM TIP! Focus on the **general meaning** of the text and don't worry if there are some words that you don't know.

Learning outcomes By the end of the lesson, learners will be able to read for general understanding and understand the present simple passive in a text.

New language *mud, team, player, competition*

Recycled language *golf, gymnastics, football, sports, surfing*

Materials 2–4 balls, map of the UK, picture of mountains, picture of mud (or jar of mud), large sheets of poster paper, colouring pens, (optional: sticky tack)

Pupil's Book, page 30

Warm-up

- Divide learners into two to four groups. Ask *What do we call a group in sports? (team). What do we call the people in the team? (player).* Ask the learners to choose a team name. Say *We're going to have a competition. A competition is a game where there is a winner.* Learners repeat *competition*.
- Get each team to put their chairs in a line, one behind the other with a gap between them, and sit down. Give the learner at the back of each line a ball. Learners pass the ball down the line without the person in front turning around or looking (by putting their hands out behind their heads). If the ball is dropped it goes back to the start of the line.
- Once they understand, play again. This time each player calls out a sport before they pass the ball. They can't repeat a sport once it has been said by a player in their line.
- **Extension** Repeat the game twice with the category of *clothes* then *computers*.

Presentation

- Say *We're going to read Jim's blog about sports. But first let's check some words.* Put up a map of the UK. Point to Wales. Ask *Which country is this?* Ask *What do you think it is like? Is it hot or cold? Is it green?* Learners suggest ideas. Show them a picture of mountains and ask them what they can see. Tell them *Wales has a lot of mountains and hills.*
- Show a picture of mud (or bring some in a jar). Ask *What is it?* Learners repeat. *(mud).*
- Say *Open your books at page 30. Remember we can understand a lot with a quick look.* Point to Jim's blog. Ask *How many sports does he write about? (three). Which one has lots of mud?* Learners point. *Which one do you think is in Wales?* Learners point.
- Point to the third picture (the dog surfing). Ask *What is happening? (the dog is surfing).* Say *Let's find out more.*

1 Read Jim's blog. How many dogs can stand on a surfboard?

- Ask learners *How many dogs can stand on a surfboard?* Learners suggest ideas. Say *OK. Let's read and find out.*
- Tell learners to read the blog. Give up to 5 minutes but monitor for progress.
- Learners compare in pairs. Check with the class.
- Ask learners which sport they would like to see the most. As they offer ideas ask questions, e.g. *Why? Would you like to try it?*

Key: 2 dogs

EXAM TIP! Read the exam tip and remind students that they don't need to understand every word to get information. Say *You can find answers to questions even if you don't understand everything.*

2 ★ Read the sentences and choose the correct event.

- Tell learners that they will read again to find out more information.
- Show them the questions. Learners read and answer in pairs. Give up to 5 minutes but monitor for progress.
- Check answers. For each answer, ask learners where they found a word or sentence that helped. *(1 the dog usually surfs with a person, but sometimes the dog surfs alone or two dogs surf; 2 around 50 teams … play; 3 there are lots of mountains; 4 to get money to give to charities; 5 competitions are organised by people all around the world; 6 people often think that the horse will win easily).*
- Put learners into pairs. Ask them to decide which sport they think is the most difficult and the easiest and why. Learners discuss. Ask for their ideas.

Key: 1 C 2 A 3 B 4 A 5 C 6 B

Activity Book, page 30

See pages TB126–141.

Ending the lesson

- Write *surfing* at the centre of the board and add categories, e.g. *place, equipment, clothes*. Ask what learners would include in each category. Learners discuss.
- Give each group one of the other sports – *Mud Olympics* or *Man versus Horse* – and repeat.
- When they finish, compare ideas.

3 Language practice 1

Learning outcomes By the end of the lesson, learners will be able to use the present simple passive accurately.

New language *kick, goal, organise, plan*

Recycled language *cycling, gymnastics, athletics, water-skiing, surfing, diving, rugby, golf, cricket, ice-hockey, boxing, tennis, football, sports*

Materials a set of pictures (water skis, a football goal, a cricket bat, a surfboard, a tennis net, a boxing glove, a golf club, a cycle, a snorkel, a rugby ball, ice skates), a picture of a football player with a ball, examples of mind maps (online), poster paper, colouring pens, Mission worksheets (Teacher's Resource Book page 32)

Pupil's Book, page 31

Warm-up

- Hide a set of ten pictures around the room (*a football goal, a cricket bat, a surfboard, a tennis net, a boxing glove, a golf club, a cycle, a snorkel, a rugby ball, ice skates*).
- Learners work in pairs and choose a runner and a writer.
- The runner searches for the picture, then runs back to tell their partner what sport to write in a list, e.g. show them a picture of water skis and ask which sport to write. *(water-skiing)*.

  Fast finishers Learners look at their list for 1 minute, then cover it. They test each other to see how many of the words they can remember.

Presentation

- Stick or draw a picture of a player with a football on the right side of the board. Add the picture (from the Warm-up) of the goal on the left side (or draw one). Ask learners what the pictures are. Ask *What does the player do with the ball? (kicks it into the goal).*
- Under the pictures write *The player kicks the ball into the goal.* Take down the picture of the player. Say *I want to write the same thing but not use the word 'player'. How can I say it? (The ball is kicked into the goal).* Write on the board.
- Draw a line in a different colour between the word 'ball' in the first and second sentences. Point to the first sentence and underline *player*. Say *We often say who does something.* Point to the second sentence. Say *But here the ball is the most important. What kind of sentence is this? (passive).*
- In the passive, highlight 'is'. Say *Which word is this?* Draw a box around 'kicked'. Say *What do we use here? (kicked).* Give other examples of past participles. Add an 's' to the word ball and point to 'is'. Say *The balls is … ? (no, the balls are …).* Change 'is' to 'are'. Say *Yes, we use 'is' or 'are'. This is passive.*

Grammar look: the passive (present simple)

- Ask a learner to read the sentences at the top of the **Grammar look** box. Learners choose the correct option in pairs.

Key: 1 We don't know 2 people all around the world 3 by 4 don't know 5 isn't

Complete the Grammar look on page 121. See pages TB125–126.

1 Complete the sentences. Use the words in brackets and the passive in the present simple.

- Learners look at the pictures. Say *Which event is planned? (dog surfing).* Explain that the sentences describe the plans.
- Complete the first sentence together. Learners complete the rest in pairs. Check answers with the class.

Key: 1 are discussed 2 are made 3 is given 4 are taken 5 are shared 6 are cleaned

3 In pairs, say sentences and say which sport it is.

- Tell learners to read the facts again to find clues to ask their partners. They take turns to ask and answer about each sport in pairs. Monitor and check.

Mission Stage 1

- Put learners in groups of four. Give each group a photocopy of the Mission worksheet (Teacher's Resource Book page 32). Learners work individually to choose some sports to compare and contrast them in the mind map. They write where the sport is played/practised and show whether it is an individual or group sport.
- Groups compare whether they have done the same analysis, e.g. *Surfing is practised in the sea. Ice-hockey is played on an ice-rink.*

  Extension If possible, show learners a picture dictionary or online picture dictionary and how to find words.
- Give out poster paper and colouring pens. Learners create mind maps in their groups. Encourage them to include pictures of some of the words. Monitor and support by suggesting additional words and checking spelling.

Activity Book, page 31

See pages TB126–141.

Ending the lesson

- Learners present their mind maps. Give them an example, e.g. *For football, we can pass the ball to another player. We can kick the ball. But in cricket, the ball is hit with a bat.*

Grammar look: the passive (present simple)

'The race is planned so that the horse and runners finish at nearly the same time.'

'Dog surfing competitions are organised by people all around the world.'

1 Who plans the races in Man vs. Horse? **We don't know / The runners**

2 Who organises dog surfing competitions? **We don't know / people all around the world**

3 Which word says who organised the dog surfing competitions? **the / by**

We use the passive when we **(4) know / don't know** who does something or when it **(5) is / isn't** important who does something.

page 121

1 **Complete the sentences.** Use the words in brackets and the passive in the present simple.

How to plan a dog surfing competition

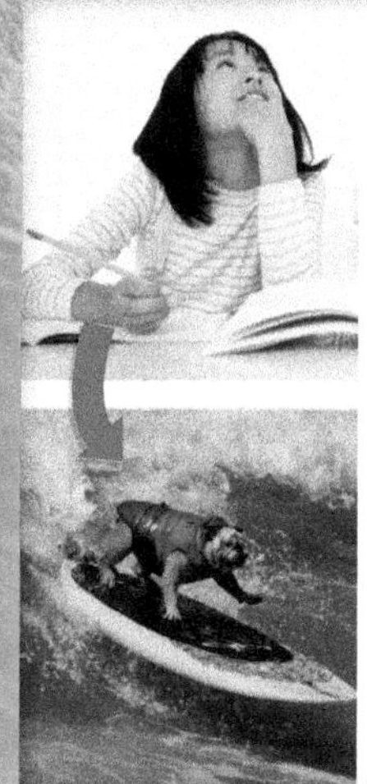

Ideas for the dog surfing event **(1)** are discussed (discuss). Plans **(2)** ________ (made) to be sure that the event is safe.

The dog surfers meet and the event starts. The winner of each competition **(3)** ________ (give) a prize – it could be a golden dog toy!

Photographs of the event **(4)** ________ (take) and **(5)** ________ (share) on the Internet.

Dog food, balls and other litter **(6)** ________ (clean) from the beach and everyone goes home.

Mission Stage 1

Make a mind map to compare your feelings about different sports.

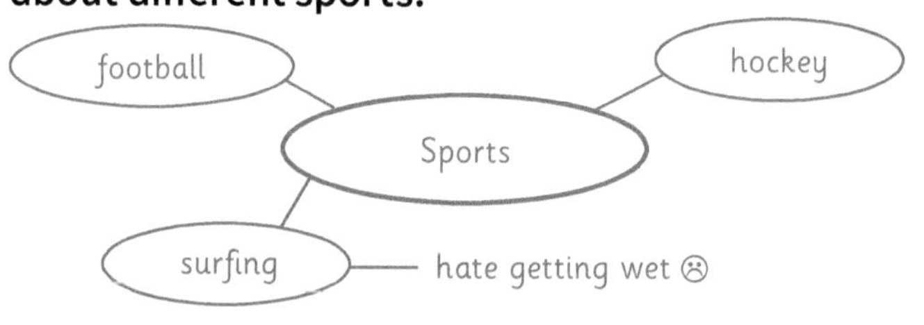

2 **In pairs, say sentences and say which sport it is.**

It's held every year.

The Mud Olympics.

Yes!

3

Vocabulary 2

1 1.22 **Listen. Match the sports commentaries (1–4) to the photos (A–D).**

2 1.23 **Match the definitions (A–K) to the words (1–11). Listen and check.**

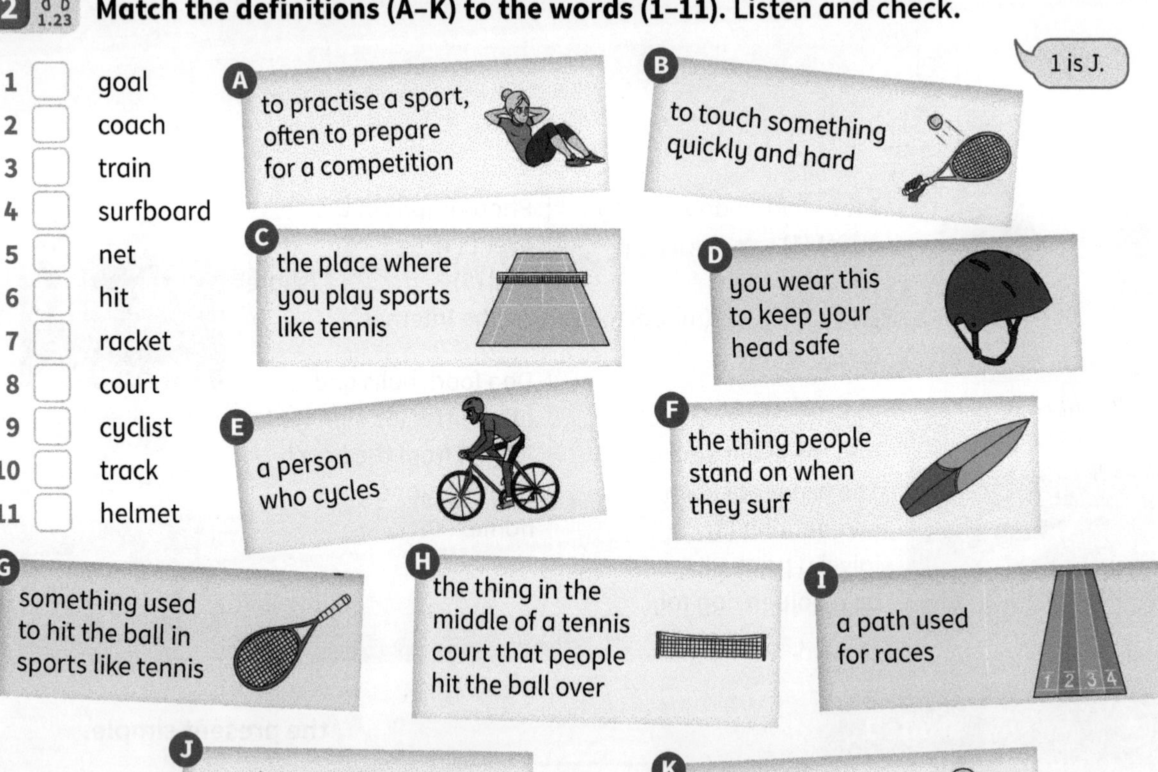

1 is J.

1. goal
2. coach
3. train
4. surfboard
5. net
6. hit
7. racket
8. court
9. cyclist
10. track
11. helmet

A to practise a sport, often to prepare for a competition

B to touch something quickly and hard

C the place where you play sports like tennis

D you wear this to keep your head safe

E a person who cycles

F the thing people stand on when they surf

G something used to hit the ball in sports like tennis

H the thing in the middle of a tennis court that people hit the ball over

I a path used for races

J a point scored in a game like football

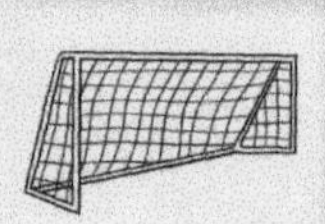

K someone who prepares a team to play sport

3 1.24 **Listen again. Why are the numbers below important?**

 three minutes 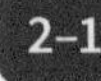 2–1 · 35 minutes · 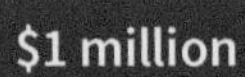 $1 million · one point · two metres ·  ten · eight

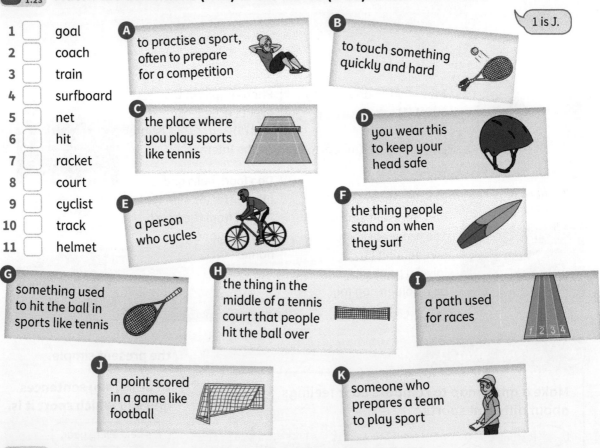

Learning outcomes By the end of the lesson, learners will be able to use vocabulary about sports equipment.

New language *coach, train, net, hit, kick, racket, court, cyclist, track, helmet, stretch*

Recycled language *cycling, gymnastics, athletics, water-skiing, surfing, diving, rugby, golf, cricket, ice-hockey, boxing, tennis, football, sports, goal, surfboard*

Materials audio, (optional: coloured paper cut into strips for matching task)

Pupil's Book, page 32

Warm-up

- Demonstrate a few movement verbs, e.g. *kick, hit, run, stretch, jump*. Complete the actions and say the words. Learners copy and repeat. Ask the learners if they know any other similar words. Write them on the board as they call out.
- Show a short warm-up routine using some of the words, e.g. *First jump three times then kick to the left and the right. Now use your hands to hit up high. Now stretch.*
- Learners listen and follow the routine.
- Put learners into groups of three. Each learner describes and acts out a warm-up activity as the other learners copy.

Presentation

- Ask learners to look at the four pictures. Ask which sport they think each one shows.
- Put learners into pairs. Tell them they have 3 minutes to look at the pictures in detail and name as many things as they can see in the pictures. After 3 minutes stop the activity. Ask learners to call out their words. Learners repeat the words. For any words missed out, add these yourself.

Key: 1 cyclist, track, helmet 2 net, court, racket 3 surfboard, surfer 4 goal

EXAM TIP! Say *Remember when we read we don't need to understand everything. And when we listen it is the same. If you listen for the most important words you can understand a lot.*

1 1.22 Listen. Match four commentaries (1–4) to the photos (A–D).

- Tell learners they will hear four commentaries of events. Ask learners *Where can you hear a commentary? (on TV or the radio)*. Ask *What kind of event is the person talking about? (sports). And what do they talk about? (they describe what is happening)*. Play the audio.
- Learners work in pairs and check answers. Play the audio again if necessary. Check answers.

See audioscripts on pages TB118–123.

Key: 1 C 2 D 3 B 4 A

2 1.23 Match the definitions(A–K) to the words (1–11). Listen and check.

- Ask learners to look at the definitions A–K in pairs and try to guess the word. Now ask them to read the words in bold.
- Say *In which sport do you score a goal? (football). So which card shows where you score a goal? (J).*
- Learners work in pairs Check answers.

Key: 1 J 2 K 3 A 4 F 5 H 6 B 7 G 8 C 9 E 10 I 11 D

3 1.24 Listen again. Why are the numbers below important?

- Tell learners to guess what they think the numbers might be. Learners call out their ideas. Play the audio.
- Learners check answers in pairs.

Key: A 3 minutes left in the match. B Team United are beating Team City two goals to one. C The surfing competition starts in 35 minutes. D The surfboard costs $1 million. E If Tim wins 1 point, he'll win the competition. F The ball falls 2 metres outside the court. G The 10 fastest cyclists in the world are racing. H 9 cyclists fall down.

Activity Book, page 32

See pages TB126–141.

Ending the lesson

- Write on the board: *tennis, football, cycling*. Put learners into groups of three. Ask them to choose a sport to make a short commentary.
- Each group read out their commentary while another group act out the action.

Language practice 2

Learning outcomes By the end of the lesson, learners will be able to use modal verbs accurately.

New language *could, may, might, will, can, shall*

Recycled language *cycling, gymnastics, athletics, water-skiing, surfing, diving, rugby, golf, cricket, ice-hockey, boxing, tennis, football, sports*

Materials a set of large cut-out shapes (enough for one per group of five learners), e.g. racket / surfboard / goal / golf club / rugby ball, three large cards with words on them (*may be, might be, could be*)' sticky tack, colouring pens and paper

Warm-up

- Cut out large shapes from card or paper, e.g. *racket; surfboard; a goal; a golf club, a rugby ball.* Stick these around the walls. Learners guess what the shapes are.
- Point to each shape and ask for their ideas. Encourage learners to use *may* or *might*, e.g. *It might be a racket.*
- Learners work in groups of five and choose a shape. They think of three unusual things they could use their shape for, e.g. *We could use the racket as snow shoes.*

Pupil's Book, page 33

Presentation

- Draw a racket shape on the board. Write *It is a racket.* Underline is. Say *But it might be a guitar, so we can't say 'is'. Shall we change the sentence?*
- Stick three large word cards to the side of the board (*may, might, could*). Say *Which other word can we use if we aren't sure?* Invite a stronger learner to stick the alternative word into the sentence. Other learners can call out alternatives.
- Ask *Are we sure or are we guessing? (we're guessing).* Say the sentence. Learners repeat. Encourage the learner to swap the cards again, e.g. replace might with *may*. Ask *Are we sure or are we guessing? (guessing).* Say the sentence *It may be a racket.* Learners repeat. Repeat the sequence for *could.*

Grammar look: modal verbs

- Put learners into pairs. Ask them to choose the correct option in each sentence. Check answers.

Key: 1 are 2 don't 3 do 4 aren't

Complete the Grammar look on page 121.
See pages TB125–126.

1 1.25 **PRONUNCIATION**
Listen and repeat.

- Say *Listen and repeat.* Play the audio. Learners repeat.

Track 1.25

Boy: Shall we watch the goal again?
Girl: She wouldn't be happy if her surfboard was stolen.
Man: The surfing competition will start in about 35 minutes.

- Learners complete the activity on page 118 (see TB124).

2 Read the dialogue and choose the correct words.

- Ask learners to read the dialogue quickly and find out what they are going to play. *(tennis or table tennis).*
- Learners read the dialogue in pairs and choose the correct words. Monitor and check as necessary.
- Choose stronger learners to act out their dialogue.

Key: 1 Shall we 2 I'd like to 3 can 4 bring 5 might

3 Act out the dialogue. Then act it out again, changing the underlined words.

- Ask all learners to act out the dialogue again in pairs.
- Point to the underlined words. Say *Let's change the words.* Encourage the learners to suggest an alternative for 'play tennis', e.g. *play football.* Put learners into pairs. Learners act out the dialogue replacing all the underlined words.

4 Choose a sport and write a short sports commentary. How many modal verbs can you use?

- Tell learners to write their own commentary.
- Ask some learners to read their commentary to the class. The others count how many modals are used.

Mission Stage 2

- Remind learners of sports they have read about: dog surfing, Man vs. Horse and Mud Olympics. Say *We are going to think of a new sport. What do we need to think about? e.g. people, place, equipment.* If they don't suggest it, add *rules for the game*. Write these on the board.
- Put learners into groups of four. Give out colouring pens and paper. Learners plan their game and create a picture of the game in action with labels/notes.

Activity Book, page 33

See pages TB126–141.

Ending the lesson

- **SA** Ask learners to complete their self-assessment (see Introduction).

Grammar look: modal verbs

'Birch may have made a mistake.'
'This could be the most important point today.'
'The Silver Beach surfing competition will start in about 35 minutes.'
'Hugh hits it back well but the ball might go into the net!'
'Can Waldek shoot?'
'Shall we watch that goal again?'

1 Modal verbs **are** / **aren't** followed by the infinitive form of a verb without 'to' (e.g. *speak*, *go*, *walk* etc.)
2 When you use *he* or *she*, you **do** / **don't** need to add an 's' to the modal verb.
3 To make a question, you **do** / **don't** change the order of the modal (e.g. *might*, *will*, *can* etc.) and the subject (e.g. *I*, *you*, *he*, *she* etc.).
4 There **are** / **aren't** *-ing* forms of modal verbs.

page 121

1 1.25 PRONUNCIATION **Listen and repeat.** page 118

2 **Read the dialogue and choose the correct words.**

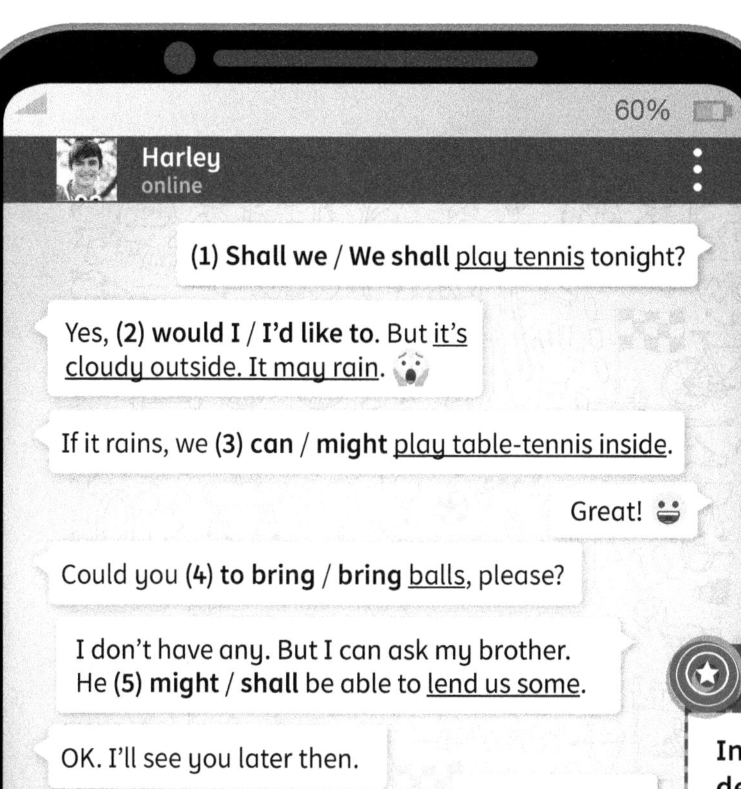

60%
Harley
online
(1) **Shall we** / **We shall** play tennis tonight?
Yes, (2) **would I** / **I'd like to**. But it's cloudy outside. It may rain.
If it rains, we (3) **can** / **might** play table-tennis inside.
Great!
Could you (4) **to bring** / **bring** balls, please?
I don't have any. But I can ask my brother. He (5) **might** / **shall** be able to lend us some.
OK. I'll see you later then.
See you later!

3 **Act out the dialogue.** Then act it out again, changing the underlined words.

4 **Choose a sport and write a short sports commentary.** How many modal verbs can you use?

We're here at the lake to watch the water-skiing today, and we might be lucky with the weather ...

Mission Stage 2

Invent and describe a new sport.

Literature

1 **Look at the pictures. What kind of text is it? Do you like these kinds of stories?**

THE SPARTAN PRINCESS

1.27

In Ancient Greece, around 428 BCE …

Cynisca is a young Greek princess. She is a Spartan. It's hard being a Spartan. They are only interested in being very fit. Boys practise fighting and do athletics and girls also do a lot of exercise. It isn't different for Cynisca even though she's a princess. Her dad, Archidamus, King of Sparta, has encouraged her to do all kinds of sports since she was very young, such as riding and running just like her brother Agesilaus. Cynisca's favourite sport is chariot racing.

Wait for me!
Catch me if you can!
One day I'm going to the Olympics and I'm going to win.
But girls can't enter competitions, so how are you going to do that?

I want four of your best horses.
These are the best horses in all of Sparta.

When the king dies, Cynisca receives half of his money. Agesilaus gets the other half and becomes King. Cynisca really wants to compete in the Olympics so she decides to buy the horses and the chariot she needs.

It's so unfair. I'm ready for the games but they won't let women into the stadium to compete.
Well, you can't be the rider of the chariot but if you find a charioteer, you can enter as an owner and trainer. There's no law against that.

Cynisca trains the horses for the chariot races every day for a year.

Text type: a comic book

Learning outcomes By the end of the lesson, learners will be able to read about sport in Ancient Greece and understand the main ideas of a text.

New language *riding, chariot, charioteer, race, stadium, statue, compete, king, princess*

Recycled language *competition, helmet*, passives, modal verbs

Materials audio, pictures of the Olympic Games, Ancient Greek sports, sports in the middle ages, current sports

Warm-up

- Show learners pictures of sports in the past (e.g. Ancient Greek disc throwers), the middle ages (e.g. archery) and sports now (e.g. athletics).
- Put learners into groups of three and ask them to guess when each sport was played.
- Share ideas.
- Ask learners which sport they think is the most interesting and if they know anything about them.

Pupil's Book, page 34

1 Look at the pictures. What kind of text is it? Do you like these kinds of stories?

- Ask learners to look at the text and pictures. Say *What kind of text is it? Do you like these kinds of stories?*
- Learners share their ideas.

Key: a comic book, learners' own ideas

Presentation

- Show pictures of recent Olympic Games. Ask learners to describe what they can see. Ask if they know what the event is. *(the Olympic Games).*
- Ask *When did the Olympic Games begin? (thousands of years ago).* Ask *Where did they begin? (in Greece).* Tell learners they are going to read a story about the Olympics.
- Say *Open your books at page 34.* Ask the learners to look at the pictures and the title. Point to the picture of the Spartan king and his crown. Ask *Who is he? (the king).* Point to Cynisca. Say *She is his daughter, so she is a … (princess).* Learners repeat the words.
- Now point to the pictures and ask learners for the words: *chariot, charioteer, stadium, statue.* Say each word clearly. Learners repeat. Tell learners *The story is about a race. What happens in a race? (people try to win by being fastest).* Say *a race.* Learners repeat.
- Ask learners to find a picture of a race from the story. Learners show the first picture of Cynisca racing her brother. Ask *What kind of race is this? (a chariot race).*
- Say *We can race against each other. So 'race' is a verb and a noun. Another word for this is compete.* Say *'compete'.* Learners repeat. Ask *Compete is a verb but what is the noun? (competition).*
- Put learners into pairs. Ask them to look at the pictures and predict what happens in the story.
- Share their ideas, but don't confirm if they are correct or not.

1.27 The Spartan Princess

- Tell learners to read and listen to the first page of the story. Say *Find out what Cynisca wants to do. Why is it difficult?*
- Play the audio.
- Put learners into pairs and ask them to compare their ideas. Check answers. *(she wants to race in the Olympics; she can't because she is a girl).* Ask *Can she go to the race? (yes, but as an owner and charioteer).*
- Now ask learners to predict the end of the story. Learners call out their ideas.
- Tell learners to listen and read the end of the story on page 35. Say *Check if your ideas are correct.* Play the audio. Learners listen and read.
- Put learners into pairs and ask them to compare their ideas.
- Check answers. *(Cynisca enters and wins the race).* Ask *Why do people know about Cynisca? (there is a statue of her).*
- Put learners into groups of six. Ask the learners to read the story aloud – choose a stronger student per group to be the narrator. Allow learners to assign the other roles.
- Monitor and support.

Activity Book, page 34

See pages TB126–141.

Ending the lesson

- Tell learners to close their books. Write some key words onto the board: *King of Sparta, girls, horses, Stadium of Zeus, race, champion, statue.*
- Put the learners into groups of three and ask them to look at the key words and retell the story using the words.
- Monitor as they work helping learners as needed.
  Extra support Tell learners to keep their books open and read if they need to.
- Ask learners to recreate the story as a class. Point to the first key word and choose a learner to begin the story. Work through each key word and choose a learner to continue through the story until it is complete.

Learning outcomes By the end of the lesson, learners will be able to respond to a text using critical thinking and emotional intelligence, and understand the idea and benefits of perseverance.

New language *persevere*

Recycled language *riding, chariot, charioteer, race, stadium, statue, compete, king, princess, competition, helmet*

Materials audio, paper and colouring pens, sticky tack, marker pens

Social and Emotional Skill: perseverance

- After reading the story, ask *Why couldn't Cynisca do what she wanted? (Women weren't allowed into the stadium.) What did she achieve in the end? (She found a different way and won the chariot race as the owner of a chariot.)*
- Ask *What qualities did Cynisca show? (strength and determination). We can learn a lot from her example of perseverance.*
- Learners work in pairs. They think of a difficult situation that needs perseverance. One learner is Cynisca and imagines what she could say. The other asks how Cynisca felt and what advice she can give.

Warm-up

- Put learners into groups of three. Tell them to discuss something they found difficult and to talk about it and how they felt, e.g. *I'm really bad at singing. When I was young, I wanted to be in the choir, but I couldn't because my singing was terrible. I felt really miserable and decided to stop. But my sister told me we should sing for fun. I joined a group and i really enjoy it!*
- Ask learners to share their idea. Be careful not to specify particular learners if they are not comfortable; ask general questions, e.g. *How does it feel when you find something hard? What can you do?*

Pupil's Book, page 35

Presentation

- Put learners into pairs. Give each pair paper to sketch a word or sentence from the story, e.g. the statue (*'I, Cynisca who won with a four-horse chariot, put up this statue'*).
- Learners create their images. Stick the images around the classroom like an art gallery. Tell the pairs to walk around and decide, for each picture, what word or sentence it shows. Ask each pair to stand by their picture. Ask other learners to call out what the picture shows.
- Play the audio again. Learners hold their pictures in the air at the point it appears in the story. Ask each pair to find three things that might be difficult for Cynisca. Learners discuss in pairs.

Key: Sample answers She's a girl, so she couldn't enter the race; she has to train very hard; she isn't allowed into the stadium.

2 In pairs, talk about the questions.

- Put learners into groups of four. Ask them to look at the three questions and discuss. Monitor and support.
- Draw out the idea of perseverance and not giving up. Say *If something is difficult but we keep trying, we persevere.* Say *persevere.* Learners repeat. Ask learners to think of a time they persevered and discuss in pairs.

Key: Sample answers 1 She felt upset and angry because she's good at racing and can't do it because she is a girl. 2 She's a strong girl (determined) who keeps trying even if things are hard. She didn't give up when she couldn't enter the games. She found a different way to do it.
3 They might not get on well because she can win races and beat him, but he's a boy, so has a lot of advantages.

Activity Book, page 35

See pages TB126–141.

Ending the lesson

- Put learners into groups of five. Ask them to think of things that are difficult to do, e.g. *learning to swim*. Each group sends a member up to write their ideas on the board. If another group has put up the idea, they can't repeat it. Give each group a sticky note. Ask them to choose a group name and write it. Each group adds their sticky note to the board to claim one of the problems. Give them 30 seconds to choose a problem. Say *Go!* Each runner claims a problem. Now each group races to find three possible solutions to their problem.
- Say *Start now.* When the first group raise their hands, ask them to explain their three solutions.

3

No! Go faster when you turn! Look behind you as you do it. We only have a few months before the competition!

Cynisca finally finds a charioteer. He's perfect for the job. He's thin, tall and young. She is a strong instructor.

The summer of 396 BCE …

Finally, the day of the Olympic Games arrives. Cynisca travels with her brother and horses to the great stadium of Zeus at Olympia. The games are held here every four years. The streets are crowded. People come to watch and take part in the games from all over the world, from as far away as Spain and Turkey.

Can I come into the stadium? I'll put on a helmet and dress like a man.
No, it's too dangerous. If they catch you, they'll punish you.

You've won! You've won!

Cynisca sits outside the stadium and listens to the crowds shouting and screaming. The four-horse chariot race is always the most spectacular race in the Olympics.

My family and I were Kings and Queens. I, Cynisca who won with a four-horse chariot, put up this statue. I am the only woman in Greece to win this prize.

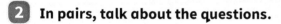

Cynisca wasn't able to take part herself in the Olympic Games, but she won the chariot race twice in 396 BCE and again in 392 BCE.

2 In pairs, talk about the questions.

1. How do you think Cynisca felt about not riding the chariot herself in the games?
2. What kind of person was Cynisca? How did this help her enter and win the Olympic Games twice?
3. What was Cynisca's relationship with her brother?
4. Why do you think there is a statue to remember Cynisca?

3

Cross-curricular

1 **Look at the pictures.** How do these activities help you to prepare for a sports competition?

2 1.28 **Listen and read the text.** How many hours a day does each athlete train?

Every four years the Olympics is shown on TV. It takes years of training and hard work to compete at an Olympic Games and there are many things that an athlete has to think about before they run around the track, hit a ball or put on a helmet for that important race.

Gymnasts

Training: Gymnasts train for six hours a day. As well as this, they swim, cycle and run to make their legs stronger. It's important that they stretch every part of their body before and after they practise or they might get injured.

Food: Gymnasts need to eat a lot of protein (chicken and fish) and healthy snacks like bananas and strawberries.

Rest: They have one rest day a week and try to get a good night's sleep too. It's difficult to train if you are tired.

Simone Biles has got the most medals of any American gymnast.

Divers

Training: Divers also train for about six hours a day, but before they get into the pool, they have to practise in the gym. They lift weights and do handstands to make their forearms strong. After training in the pool they often put ice on their triceps to help them recover.

Food: Food is very important for divers. Cereal with lots of iron in is good and it's important in the evening to eat snacks with carbohydrates like toast with chocolate spread – this helps with energy levels.

Rest: After training all day, divers often have a massage and they are in bed by 10:30 pm.

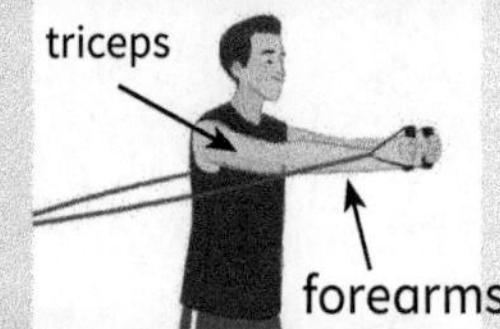

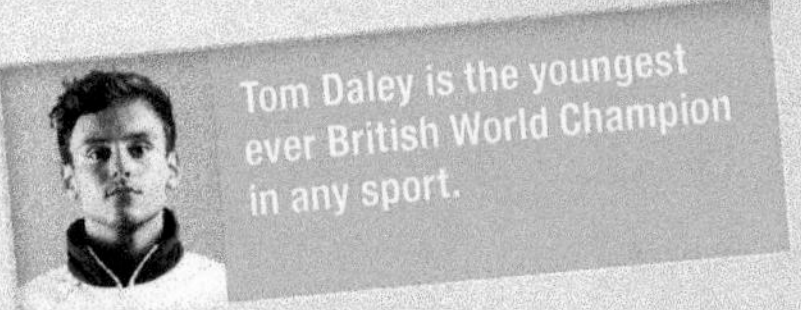

Tom Daley is the youngest ever British World Champion in any sport.

3 **Read the text again and answer the questions.**

1 How often can you watch the Olympic Games?

2 What do athletes need to do before competing?

3 Why should athletes stretch before and after training?

4 Why shouldn't athletes go to bed late?

5 How do athletes look after their muscles?

6 Write examples of each of the food groups:
Protein: … Iron: … Carbohydrates: …

Learning outcomes By the end of the lesson, learners will be able to understand healthy lifestyles including food and exercise and read using critical thinking skills (analysis and application).

New language *protein, carbohydrate, iron, forearms, triceps, exercise band, scrambled eggs*

Recycled language *jump, train, compete, helmet, hit, race, gymnast, diver*, passives, modals

Materials food flashcards: one set per six learners (chicken, burgers, sausages, spinach, broccoli, peas, biscuits, cake, cole, rice, pasta, bread), sticky tack

Warm-up

- Put up a picture of some chicken, green vegetables, rice and biscuits. Learners say which they like best and why, e.g. *I like biscuits because they taste good!*
- Put learners into groups of six. Give each group a set of food flashcards (*chicken, burgers, sausages, spinach, broccoli, peas, biscuits, cake, cola, rice, pasta, bread*). Ask them to decide which foods are healthy and divide the cards into two groups. *(all are healthy except biscuits, cake and cola).*
- Check answers by having one group bring their cards to the board and stick the pictures up on two sides of the board: 'healthy' and 'not so healthy'.

Pupil's Book, page 36

Presentation

- Point to the biscuits. Ask *Why are too many biscuits bad for you? (They contain a lot of sugar).* Point to the chicken. Ask *Why is it good for you? (It contains protein which makes our bodies strong).* Learners repeat *protein*. Ask for other foods with protein (e.g. *meat, eggs, milk*). Repeat with *spinach. (It contains iron which helps us stay healthy).* Learners repeat *iron*. Ask for other food with iron (e.g. *green vegetables*).
- Repeat with *rice. (It contains carbohydrate which gives us energy.)* Learners repeat *carbohydrate*. Ask for other foods with carbohydrate (e.g. *pasta, bread*).
- Say *Look at the pictures on page 36. What other ways to stay healthy can you see? (sleeping, exercise).*
- Mime stretching and ask *What am I doing? (stretching my muscles).* Learners repeat. Stretch out your arms and say *I'm stretching out my forearms*. Show this part of your arms. Say *forearms.* Learners repeat. Flex your arms up and point to your triceps. Say *And now I'm working my triceps.* Say *triceps.* Learners repeat.
- Ask the learners to stand up and follow your instructions. Say *Stretch out your forearms. Now show your triceps.* Learners complete the stretches.

1 Look at the pictures. How do these activities help you to prepare for a sports competition?

- Learners think about preparing for a sports competition. Tell them to look at the pictures and think about how each one might help.

  Extra support Put a list on a handout or on the board with suggested answers to match with the pictures.

Key 1 Exercise makes you fitter. 2 Food has protein for strength and carbohydrates for energy. 3 Stretching helps your muscles. 4 Sleep helps your body rest and recover.

2 1.28 Listen and read the text. How many hours a day does each athlete train?

- Tell learners they are going to find out about how gymnasts and divers train. Learners read quickly and find out how many hours a day each athlete trains. Allow 4 minutes but monitor for progress.
- Learners compare answers in pairs. Check answers.

Key: about six hours a day

3 Read the text again and answer the questions.

- Learners continue working in pairs and discuss the questions.
- Check with the class.

Key 1 Every four years 2 They train and work hard for years. 3 Stretching stops them getting injured. 4 It is difficult to train if you are tired. 5 They stretch before they train, they do different exercise to make them strong, they put ice on them to help them recover. 6 Protein: chicken, fish, scrambled eggs; Carbohydrates: toast; Iron: cereal

Activity Book, page 36

See pages TB126–141.

Ending the lesson

- Ask learners to choose a famous sports star they admire. Tell them to talk about the person's life and the class will guess who it is. Give them time to practise what they will say in groups.
- Each group presents the daily routine of their personality. The class guess who it is.

  Extension After the activity learners imagine they are writing a blog for the sports star. They create a blog to describe his/her day. If they have access to computers, they can add photos and illustrations.

Learning outcomes By the end of the lesson, learners will be able to understand strategies for listening effectively and listen for key information.

New language *predict, camp*

Recycled language *surfing, surfboard,* present simple passive

Materials pictures of a beach and a forest

Warm-up

- Put up the pictures of a beach and a forest. Put learners into groups of four and say they are going to organise a summer holiday camp. Learners choose a location.
- Write on the board: *activities, food, entertainment*. Explain that each group should organise daytime activities, food and evening entertainment for their camp.
- Learners plan in groups. Share ideas with the class.

Extension Learners present their plans to the class and the class vote on the best summer camp at the end.

Pupil's Book, page 37

Presentation

- Ask learners to listen to information about surfing and write down what you say. Tell them that you will speak quickly, so they can't write everything – just the important words.
- Write clues on the board: *place, number, name*. Ask learners the kind of words they can listen for to get this information, e.g. *places (city or country names, oceans), numbers (one, two, hundred, etc.), names (people, animals).* Tell them to write numbers and not words when they hear things like 20 or a thousand.
- Read sentences at normal speed: *Surfing is very popular. The oldest picture of surfing was found in Peru and is five thousand years old. Now people surf all over the world. A man called Kelly Slater, who is surf champion, earned three million dollars one year from surfing. But surfing can be dangerous and many surfers are injured each year.*
- Read the sentences again. Learners check in pairs.
- Learners rebuild the text in pairs to create the same meaning. Accept the ideas if they create the general meaning. Ask learners *Did you hear any numbers? (5,000 years old; 3,000 000 dollars).* Ask *Did you hear a place? (Peru). Did you hear the name of a person? (Kelly Slater).*
- Discuss how clues or questions can help them predict then find answers more easily. Check 'predict' (guess something using information they have). Ask how it might help them if they do an exam. *(Exam questions are like the clues and help you predict and find key information).*

1 (1.29) Look at the example answer and listen. What will the children learn?

- Ask them to read the question and think about the answer.
- Play the first part of the audio (*Good morning … to Summer Surf Camp!*) then stop. Check answers.

See audioscripts on pages TB118–123.

Key: Surfing

2 (1.30) Match the correct type of information (1–7) to the words in bold. There are two extra answers. Listen and check.

- Learners predict the answers in pairs. Don't check or confirm.
- Play the audio and ask learners to listen and match.
- Check with the class.

Key: 1 fruit 2 Hall 5 45 6 Vanya 7 stomach

EXAM TIP! Read the exam tip aloud. Explain that in this type of listening test they might have to write numbers. Ask *Which is easier to write – the number or the word for the number … (the number).*

Tell learners they might also hear words spelt out so they need to know the alphabet.

3 (1.31) Listen again and write the correct answer in each gap. Use the words in bold from Activity 2.

- Ask learners to look at the completed example and the rest of the gaps. Learners predict the type of word that might go into each gap, e.g. a name or a verb.
- Play the audio. Learners listen and write their answers.
- Check answers.

Key: 6 fruit 7 Hall 8 45 9 V-A-N-Y-A 10 stomach

Activity Book, page 37

See pages TB126–141.

Ending the lesson

- Put learners into groups of four. Ask them to choose five of the words from the listening tasks. Each learner takes it in turns to test their group with a word from their list. Their group try to write down the words with the correct spelling.

1 1.29 **Look at the example answer and listen.** What will the children learn?

Surf Camp

When: Summer

2 1.30 **Match the correct type of information (1–7) to the words in bold.** There are two extra answers. Listen and check.

1 A food
2 A place
3 An age
4 A price
5 A time
6 A name
7 A body part

A Surfing might look hard and your **stomach** might hurt …
B Your gym coach is Bob Vanya, that's **V-A-N-Y-A**.
C Half of your food needs to be water, **fruit** and vegetables …
D We think **45** minutes a day is enough!
E If you want help choosing your meals, I'll be in the Main **Hall** …

3 1.31 **Listen again and write the correct answer in the gap.** Use the words in bold from Activity 2.

Camp

When:	Summer
Food:	(6) 50% water, ________ and vegetables 50% meat and sugars
Help with meals:	(7) Main ________ after 6 pm
Use Gym:	(8) After every lesson for ________ minutes
Name of coach:	(9) Bob ________
First day:	(10) ________ might hurt.

EXAM TIP! The answer could be a **word** or a **number**. You may also need to **spell a name**.

3

A2 Key for Schools

1 Read the text and answer the questions.

1 Who is Billy? (Billy is Henry's friend.)
2 Where is he?
3 What sport is he doing?
4 Who is he writing to?

From: Billy **To:** Henry

Hi Henry,

How (1) are you? I'm trying a new sport called cricket. It's not like baseball but it's very popular here (2) in India! I've got (3) a great coach. He's called Kishan and before he became a coach he played in a famous (4) team.

Yesterday our group practised in the park. Kishan showed (5) us how to hold the bat and hit the ball. Later, Mum and I watched a match. Kishan (6) was playing with his new team and they won! Afterwards Kishan said I could keep the ball!

I'll send you (7) some photos after my lesson.

Write to me soon!

Billy

2 Look at the underlined words in Activity 1. What type of words are they?

- verb
- indefinite article
- preposition
- pronoun
- auxiliary verb
- noun

3 Complete the email. Use the words in the box.

went I my the for

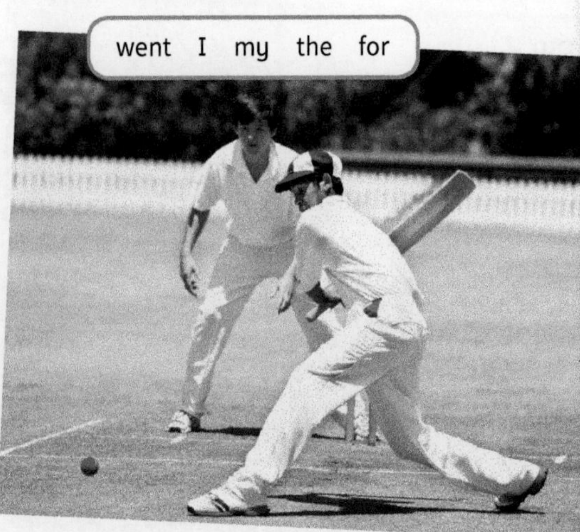

From: Henry **To:** Billy

Dear Billy,

Thanks (1) ________ your message. Cricket sounds like a lot of fun.

I'm on holiday with (2) ________ family in Sri Lanka, which is near India. We (3) ________ cycling this morning and then I took my surfboard to (4) ________ beach in the afternoon.

Talk soon!

Henry

Learning outcomes By the end of the lesson, learners will be able to understand strategies for reading effectively and read to find the correct structural words to complete sentences.

New language *noun, verb, article, preposition, pronoun, quantity*

Recycled language *surfing, surfboard,* present simple passive

Materials 6 large cards with words (noun, verb, article, preposition, pronoun, quantity), sticky tack, a picture of sports in action (one picture per 4 learners)

Warm-up

- Put six large cards with word types (*noun, verb, article, preposition, pronoun, quantity*) around the walls. Ask learners for an example of each word type, e.g. *cricket, play, a, on, she, some.*
- Put learners into three groups. Give each group a colour: red/blue/yellow. Tell them they must listen for the words for their colour, then stand by the correct word type.
- Call out the groups then words, e.g. *blue – sport*. Blue learners move to the correct word card (*noun*). Say the next group and word, e.g. *red – the* (*article*); *yellow – under* (*preposition*).
- Continue giving different words and speed up.
- Possible words: sport/the/under; it/many/play; an/organise/they; a lot / tennis / a; jump/she/camp.
  Extra support Give learners words on cards with the word type in brackets to call out the words and confirm if their classmates are correct.

Pupil's Book, page 38

Presentation

- Write on the board: *I really ______ basketball. It is ____ great game.* Point to the first gap and then the word *basketball*. Say *There is a noun at the end here, but a very important type of word is missing from the sentence. So, what do we need? (verb).* Point to the second gap and say *We have a verb already* (point to 'is') *and a noun* (point to 'game'). *What do we need to go with the noun? (an article).*

1 Read the text and answer the questions.

- Ask learners to decide what kind of writing it is. *(email message).* Ask them to read the questions, then read the text quickly and answer the questions. Tell them not to worry about the gaps. Give them 2–3 minutes.
- Put learners into pairs to compare answers. Check answers.

Key: 1 Henry's friend 2 In India 3 Cricket 4 Henry

EXAM TIP! Ask a strong learner to read the exam tip aloud. Ask *How many words go into each gap? (one).* Say *What do we need to think about? (the type of word).* Say *Let's try.*

2 Look at the underlined words in Activity 1. What type of words are they?

- Ask learners to look at the text quickly. Ask *Who wrote this email? (Henry).* Point to the underlined answers. Say *Let's remember what to do. First, we read quickly. Then … (think about the type of word we need).* Learners match the words to the types.
- Put learners into pairs to compare answers. Check answers.

Key: are = auxiliary verb, in = preposition, a = indefinite article, team = noun, us = pronoun, was = auxiliary verb, some = indefinite article

3 Complete the email. Use the words in the box.

- Tell learners to look at the gaps in the first email. Remind them about using the whole sentence to help them think about the type of word that is missing.
- Put learners into pairs to look at the list of word types and decide which goes into each gap. Check answers.

Key: 1 for 2 my 3 went 4 the

Fast finishers Learners can choose another sentence from the email and copy it out, missing out one of the words. They show it to another student who has to say what they think the missing word is.

Activity Book, page 38

See pages TB126–141.

Ending the lesson

- Put learners into groups of four. Give out pictures of different sports in action, e.g. a footballer scoring a goal, a tennis player hitting the ball with a racket.
- Ask each group to write three or four sentences about their picture without using the name of the sport. Put the pictures up onto the board.
- Ask a learner from each group to read their first sentence. The other learners guess which picture is being described.

Learning outcomes By the end of the lesson, learners will have used language from the unit to talk about sports and revised the language and skills from the unit.

Recycled language unit language

Materials 12 cards or pieces of paper? per 6 learners

Warm-up

- Give groups of six learners 12 blank cards or pieces of? paper.
- Tell each group to write six verbs that describe actions (e.g. *run, stretch*). Learners mix the cards up and place the pile face down. Tell each group to think of six sports and write them onto the other cards, then mix them and place them face down.
- Learners take it in turns to pick up a verb card and a noun card. They make a sentence using the two words. Tell them they get a point for each correct sentence and an extra point if they use a modal verb. Give an example, e.g. *I have 'stretch' and 'tennis'. If you play tennis you have to stretch to hit the ball.*

  Fast finishers Learners mix the cards and repeat.

Pupil's Book, page 39

1 Rewrite the sentences in the passive. Don't use the underlined word.

- Learners look at the example sentence and answer. Ask which is active and which is passive. *(the second is passive).* Ask why we often use passive. *(when we don't know who does something or it isn't important).*
- Learners look at the passive sentence. Highlight the subject of the sentence. Ask what comes next. *(is).* Ask what follows the 'am/is/are' in a present simple passive. *(past participle).*
- Learners write the sentences 2–5 in passive form in pairs.
- Check answers.

Key: 2 Lots of different sports are played there. 3 Football is played. 4 Tickets are sold to raise money for charity. 5 Prizes are given to the winners of the competition. 6 Lots of showers are needed at the event.

2 Write the sentences in the negative and question form.

- Ask *What happens to the verb to make a negative? (we add 'not'; we don't add -s for he/she/it; we don't use 'to' before the main verb).* Ask what happens to the order of the words in a question. *(the modal verb goes before the subject).*
- Learners write the sentences in negative and question form.
- Check answers.

Key: 2 I couldn't hit the ball. Could I hit the ball? 3 You shouldn't train every day. Should you train every day? 4 We can't go water-skiing here. Can we go water skiing here? 5 You may not get a surfboard from the shop. May I get a surfboard from that shop?

3 Choose ten words from this unit. Record the words using the steps below.

- Tell learners to look at the flowchart. Say *Let's try.* Write *kick* on the board. Ask learners if they can remember what it is and how they can find out if they can't remember. Tell them to look at the 'find the meaning' part of the chart. Say *You can check the meaning in this unit or in a dictionary.*
- Ask the easiest way to show what it is or remember it. *(write a translation or write a definition).* Tell learners to look at the 'record the example' part of the flowchart.
- Look at the next part of the flowchart: 'use it'. Say *You can say the meaning to test a friend.* Say *Now let's do an example.*
- Tell learners to choose three words from the unit and write a sentence for each putting a gap where the word fits. Tell them to follow the flowchart. Learners work alone.
- Monitor and check. Once they have finished, pair learners. Their partner guesses the words from the meaning.

Mission in action!

- Remind learners of their Mission to create a new sport. They look at the pictures on the page and describe what they can see. Share ideas.
- Tell them they will think of a new sport, describe it and get other learners to play it. Ask them what they will need to think about. If you still have the mind maps from Mission Stage 2 show these again. Learners suggest ideas. *(the equipment they need; the rules; how many people play).*
- Learners work in groups and plan their sport.

  Extension If learners want to, they could put a summary with pictures onto a poster.
- Groups present their new sport to the rest of the class. Other learners can ask questions or even try the sport – you might go outside to a sports area or playground.
- Learners vote for the sport they like best.

Activity Book, page 39

See pages TB126–141.

Ending the lesson

- **SA** Complete the self-assessment (see Introduction).

Review

3

1 Rewrite the sentences in the passive. Don't use the underlined word.

1. People hold The Mud Olympics every year.
   The Mud Olympics is held every year.
2. People play lots of different sports.
3. People play football.
4. People sell tickets to raise money for charity.
5. Someone gives prizes to the winners of the competition.
6. People need lots of showers at the event.

2 Write the sentences in the negative and question form.

1. You can play cricket well.
   You can't play cricket well.
   Can you play cricket well?
2. I could hit the ball.
3. You should train every day.
4. We can go water-skiing here.
5. I may get a surfboard from that shop.
6. I will play ice hockey.

3 Choose ten words from this unit. Record the words using the steps below.

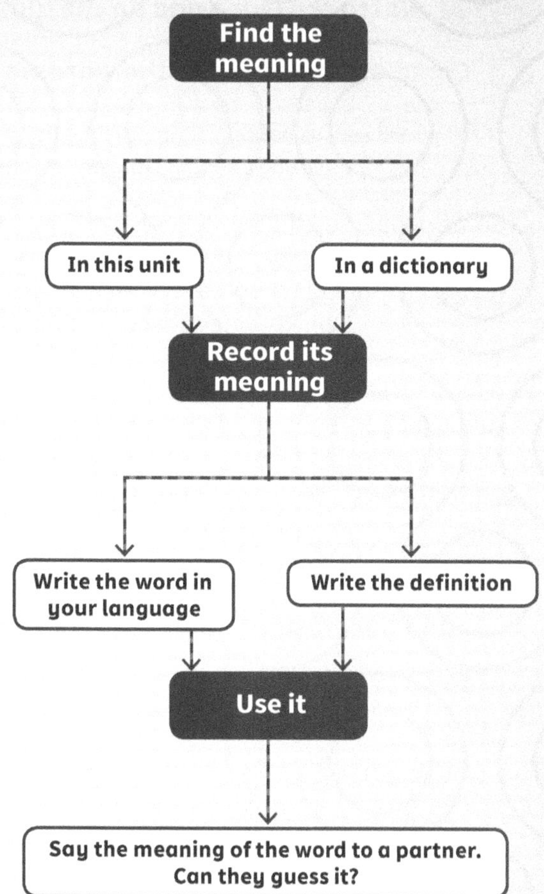

Find the meaning
In this unit
In a dictionary
Record its meaning
Write the word in your language
Write the definition
Use it
Say the meaning of the word to a partner. Can they guess it?

Mission in action!

- Present the new sport.
- Play the sport and give tips.
- Vote for the best!

How to win at my sport:

- Don't forget a helmet! Then you won't be scared.
- You don't need to worry about the other players.

③

Review ••• Units 1–3

1 Watch the video and do the quiz.

2 Complete the text. Use the words in the box.

dull as · as boring · as interesting as · exciting as · as strong and thin · big and strong as

Some people say that athletics isn't **(1)** ________ other sports. They say that watching people run is **(2)** ________ as watching paint dry. But I don't agree! The ends of athletics races are as **(3)** ________ when someone scores a goal in a sport like football or ice hockey. And, when you watch athletics you see lots of different events. Some athletes have to be as **(4)** ________ rugby players or boxers. Other athletes have to be **(5)** ________ as gymnasts. I think the most boring sport is cricket. I don't like golf either – I think that's nearly as **(6)** ________ cricket.

3 Complete the sentences. Use the words in brackets and the present simple with future meaning.

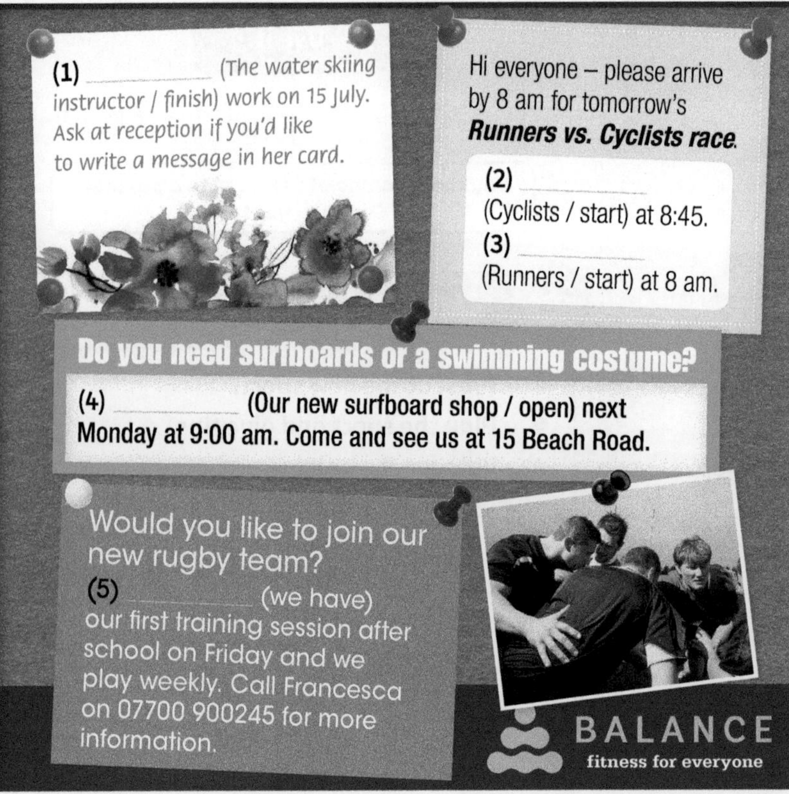
(1) ________ (The water skiing instructor / finish) work on 15 July. Ask at reception if you'd like to write a message in her card.

Hi everyone – please arrive by 8 am for tomorrow's ***Runners vs. Cyclists race.***

(2) ________ (Cyclists / start) at 8:45.

(3) ________ (Runners / start) at 8 am.

Do you need surfboards or a swimming costume?

(4) ________ (Our new surfboard shop / open) next Monday at 9:00 am. Come and see us at 15 Beach Road.

Would you like to join our new rugby team?

(5) ________ (we have) our first training session after school on Friday and we play weekly. Call Francesca on 07700 900245 for more information.

4 Complete the text.

(1) _If_ it's sunny at the weekend, I **(2)** ________ go shopping with my friend, Sue. We'll go to the town centre and look in the shops. There are holes in my jumper's sleeves, so **(3)** ________ there's a sale, I'll buy a new one. **(4)** ________ get one with a cool pattern, **(5)** ________ I can find a pattern I like. Sue wants to buy a leather handbag – I think **(6)** ________ buy one if it's not too expensive.

5 What are you going to do this weekend? Who will you spend time with? Write 25–35 words.

Learning outcomes By the end of the lesson, learners will have consolidated language from Units 1–3.

Recycled language vocabulary to describe clothes, comparative adjectives and adverbs to compare things, present simple to talk about the future, vocabulary to describe technology, first and zero conditional to talk about possibility, verbs connected to computers, vocabulary to describe sports and sports equipment, present simple passive to describe facts and habits, modal verbs to describe possibilities

Materials video, 10 sheets of paper per 3 learners

Warm-up

- Put learners into groups of three.
- Write up on the board a list of vocabulary from Units 1–3.
- Give each group of learners ten slips of paper and tell them to choose ten words to write on them.
- Each group swaps their ten chosen words, face down, with another group. Learners take it in turns to turn over one of the words and give clues to their team who guess the word.
- Learners keep going until all the words are finished.
- When the groups have finished, go through the list on the board checking definitions.

  Fast finishers Learners choose additional words from the board to use as clues.

Pupil's Book, page 40

1 Watch the video and do the quiz.

- Play the video. Learners watch and do the three unit quizzes.
- Check answers.

Key: **Unit 1** 1 A 2 B 3 C 4 A 5 C 6 B 7 A 8 A 9 B 10 A 11 A 12 A
Unit 2 1 A 2 C 3 A 4 A 5 B 6 C 7 B 8 C 9 B 10 B 11 A 12 C
Unit 3 1 B 2 A 3 B 4 C 5 A 6 C 7 C 8 A 9 C 10 B 11 B 12 A

2 Complete the text. Use the words in the box.

- Tell learners to read the text quickly without worrying about the gaps and find out if the writer thinks athletics is interesting or not.
- Check answers. *(Yes, the writer thinks athletics is interesting.)*
- Put the learners into pairs. Ask them to read the paragraph again and decide which words from the box go into the gaps. Check answers.

  Extra support Complete two or three of the answers with the learners and let them complete the rest on their own.

Key: 1 as interesting as 2 as boring 3 fun as 4 big and strong as 5 as strong and thin 6 dull as

3 Complete the sentences. Use the words in brackets and the present simple with future meaning.

- Do number 1 together as an example. Ask them to read the notice quickly. Ask if the event will happen at a planned time. *(yes)*. Ask which tense we use for planned timetables. *(present simple)*. Show them the subject and verb in brackets and ask them to put the verb into the correct form.
- Learners complete the sentences 2–5.
- Put learners into pairs to compare answers.
- Check answers.

Key: 1 The water-skiing instructor finishes 2 Cyclists start 3 Runners start 4 Our new surfboard shop opens 5 We have

4 Complete the text.

- Say *If you remember conditional sentences, you'll answer these questions easily.* Ask them what form you used *(first conditional)* and why *(it is a possibility for the immediate future)*.
- Tell learners to look at the text for 30 seconds and find out what activity it describes *(shopping)*.
- Learners work in pairs to complete the text by putting in the missing words. Check answers.

Key: 2 I'll 3 if 4 I'll 5 if 6 she'll

5 What are you going to do this weekend? Who will you spend time with? Write 25–35 words.

- Put learners into pairs. Give them 1 minute each to talk about their plans for the weekend. Tell them to use their ideas and write their plans down. Remind them of the word limit. Monitor and support.
- Ask learners what they need to include in good writing. Learners offer their ideas (e.g. *good punctuation, spelling, grammar, vocabulary*).
- Put learners into pairs and tell them to swap papers.
- Learners check each other's writing using the checklist of good content. They tell their partner what they have done well and how they can improve their work.

Activity Book, page 40

See pages TB126–141.

Ending the lesson

- Write the beginning of three sentences on the board: *If I have free time tonight, … A sport I enjoy is … For me the most important technology is …*
- Tell learners to complete the sentences so that they are true for them. Ask them to work in groups of four to share and give reasons for their answers.

Learning outcomes By the end of the lesson, learners will have consolidated language from Units 1–3.

Recycled language vocabulary to describe clothes, comparative adjectives and adverbs to compare things, present simple to talk about the future, vocabulary to describe technology, first and zero conditional to talk about possibility, verbs connected to computers, vocabulary to describe sports and sports equipment, present simple passive to describe facts and habits, modal verbs to describe possibilities

Materials pictures of clothes, audio

Warm-up

- Put pictures of a selection of clothing onto the board, e.g. *tracksuit, raincoat, blouse, T-shirt, suit, dress, jewellery, swimming costume, shirt, jumper, shoes, trainers.*
- Write some events on one side of the board: *a party, a sports day, a day at the beach, an important meeting.*
- Put learners into pairs. Tell them to choose clothes for each event. Learners discuss in pairs.
- Put the pairs into larger groups of six. Each pair describes the outfit they have chosen for each event. The other learners point to the pictures.
- Learners vote for the best outfit for each event in their group.

Pupil's Book, page 41

6 Say six sentences.

- Learners work in pairs. Tell them to read the beginnings and ends of the sentences and match them. Check answers.
  Fast finishers Learners think of a different end for two of the sentences.

Key: 1 If you like the tracksuit, you should try it on. 2 If you get brown leather shoes, they'll look good with your brown trousers. 3 If it snows later, my mum will wear her raincoat. 4 If my blouses are dirty, I borrow clean ones from my sister. 5 If my swimming costume is wet, I put it in the garden to dry. 6 If the jewellery isn't expensive, I'll get a new gold chain.

7 Find the mistakes. Write the correct sentences.

- Ask learners what they need to do after they have written something, e.g. in an exam. *(check their work for errors).*
- Tell them they need to check for words, punctuation and grammar errors.
- Tell learners these sentences have grammar errors.
- Put learners into pairs and ask them to spot the errors and write corrections.
- Monitor and support as they work. Check answers.

Extra support Show learners where the error is in the sentence and ask them to focus on correcting it.

Key: 1 My best friend is called Luisina. 2 In my bedroom, there's a bed which is made of wood. 3 My favourite song is called 'One last time'. 4 Last week, we bought some clothes in Santa Fe. 5 The food is chosen by my cousin. 6 They eat special cakes which are made for the wedding.

8 Choose the correct words to complete the sentences.

- Tell learners to read the sentences quickly. Put them into pairs and ask them to choose the correct answer. Check answers.

Key: 1 wouldn't 2 download 3 text 4 might 5 May I 6 Shall I install

9 Choose and complete two of the challenges.

- Tell learners they are going to complete two challenges.
- Ask them to read the three challenges quickly and decide on a title for each one, e.g. *1 clothes, 2 technology, 3 sports.*
- Put learners into pairs and tell them to choose their two favourite challenges. Ask them to complete the challenges and see who can finish successfully first. Check their ideas.
  Fast finishers Learners complete the third challenge.

Key: Sample answers Challenge 1 – things people wear to exercise – trainers, tracksuit, swimming costume; parts of a shirt – sleeves, collar, buttons; things you can wear over a shirt – raincoat, jumper, blouse, tie; things clothes are made from – silk, cotton, leather
Challenge 2 – Learners' own answers
Challenge 3 – Boxing, Instructor, Rugby, Diving, Water-skiing, Athletics, Train, Cycling, Helmet, Extreme ironing, Rackets, Surfing

Activity Book, page 41

See pages TB126–141.

Ending the lesson

- Ask learners to think about the work they have done in Units 1–3. Tell them to think of three things they have learnt that they didn't know before, two things they have got better at and one thing they found difficult.
- Put learners into groups of three. Ask them to compare their ideas. Monitor to understand what learners found useful and challenging.
- Tell learners to make suggestions to their group about how to improve the parts they found difficult.

6 Say six sentences.

If	+	you like the tracksuit you get brown leather shoes it snows later my blouses are dirty my swimming costume is wet the jewellery isn't expensive	+	my mum will wear her raincoat. they'll look good with your brown trousers. I'll get a new gold chain. I borrow clean ones from my sister. you should try it on. I put it in the garden to dry.

7 Find the mistakes. Write the correct sentences.

1 My best friend it is called Luisa.

2 In my bedroom there's a bed which made of wood.

3 My favourite song is call **One Last Time**.

The school discos are organised the teachers.

5 The food is choose by my cousin.

6 They eat special cakes which make for the wedding.

8 Choose the correct words to complete the sentences.

1 I **wouldn't** / **might not** like to chat to my favourite singer. I'm too shy.

2 Can you **download** / **downloading** these pictures for me, please?

3 Could you **texting** / **text** Grandma and ask her what time she's coming?

4 He **shall** / **might** email me after dinner.

5 **I may** / **May I** turn on the TV, please?

6 **Shall I install** / **Install I shall** this software for you?

9 Choose and complete two of the challenges.

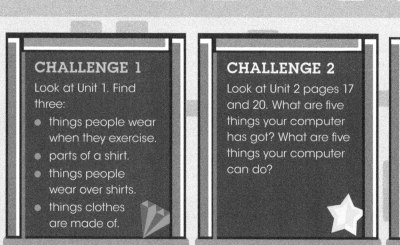

CHALLENGE 1

Look at Unit 1. Find three:

- things people wear when they exercise.
- parts of a shirt.
- things people wear over shirts.
- things clothes are made of.

CHALLENGE 2

Look at Unit 2 pages 17 and 20. What are five things your computer has got? What are five things your computer can do?

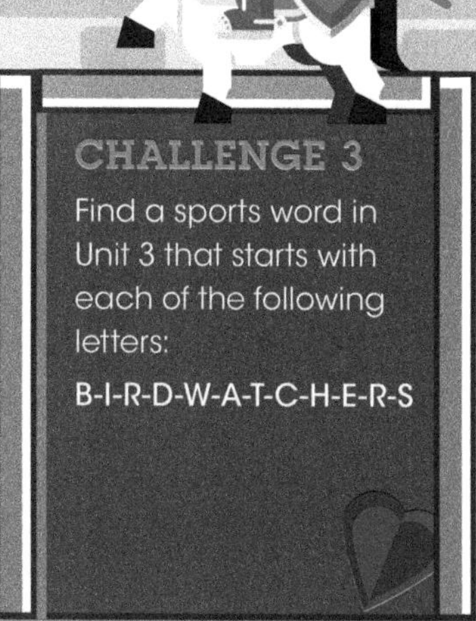

CHALLENGE 3

Find a sports word in Unit 3 that starts with each of the following letters:

B-I-R-D-W-A-T-C-H-E-R-S

4 Be careful!

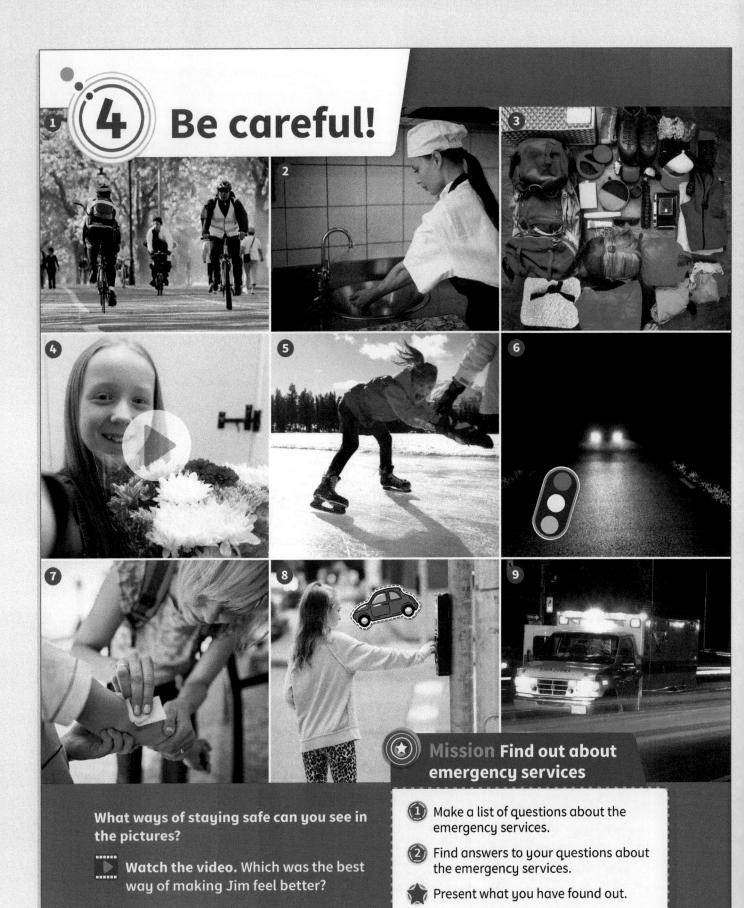

What ways of staying safe can you see in the pictures?

Watch the video. Which was the best way of making Jim feel better?

Mission Find out about emergency services

1. Make a list of questions about the emergency services.
2. Find answers to your questions about the emergency services.
3. Present what you have found out.

Unit 4 learning outcomes

In Unit 4, learners will learn to:

- use vocabulary to describe accidents and illness
- understand and use present perfect simple to talk about unfinished activity
- use present continuous to talk about the future
- read and listen for information and to understand words in context
- develop ideas about medicine and treatments

Materials video, two pictures – a raincoat, a scarf (or real items if possible)

Self-assessment

- **SA** Write *flu, medicine, get better* on the board. Learners look at the words and guess the topic of the unit.
- Read the unit outcomes and clarify. Ask learners to retell them in pairs using their own words. Ask learners to complete self-assessment (see Introduction). Say *Let's learn.*

Pupil's Book, page 42

Warm-up

- In groups of four, learners write on card an activity that can be dangerous, e.g. *crossing a busy road; skiing.* Groups nominate one learner as a 'searcher'. The searchers go outside the classroom. The rest hide their card in the classroom.
- The 'searchers' come back and look for the card for their group. Their group members give clues – if they get close the group say *Be careful.* When they are very close the group say *Danger!* Each group explains the activity and why it is dangerous.

What ways of staying safe can you see in the pictures?

- Learners look at the pictures on page 42 and decide what the people are doing and how they are staying safe.
- Choose a pair to say one thing people are doing to stay safe. The class name the activity and picture, e.g. *This person is staying safe by wearing a helmet and a bright jacket … (She/he is cycling. It's picture 1!).* Go through the pictures again asking *What's the person doing? How are they staying safe?* Check any words that may be challenging.

Key: 1 cycling, wearing a helmet and bright coloured jacket 2 a chef, washing hands and wearing a hat 3 going walking, packing a compass, water, raincoat, warm clothes, sunhat, etc. 4 cutting a flower, wearing gloves 5 walking on the moon, wearing a space suit 6 driving using lights at night, stopping at traffic lights 7 cleaning a cut, wearing gloves 8 crossing the road, looking for cars 9 driving an ambulance, using a warning sound and lights

Watch the video. Which was the best way of making Jim feel better?

- Show a picture of someone ill in bed. Ask learners *Why is he in bed? (He's feeling ill).* Learners repeat. Say *He is very hot.* Mime and say *fever.* Learners repeat. Say *His head and body hurt. What's wrong? (He has the flu).* Learners repeat.
- Ask *What can he do to feel better?* Learners suggest their ideas. Say *He needs to rest, to relax and sleep. Rest.* Learners repeat. Say *Then he'll feel better.* Learners repeat.
- Tell learners to find three things Jenny tries and decide? say? which works best.
- Play the video. Learners watch then discuss in pairs.

Key: The card gets the most stars from Jim.

Extension Learners decide in pairs which of the three things they would like best if they are ill and why.

Mission Find out about emergency services

- Ask *Who can we call for help if we are in danger or need help?* (E.g. *the police, the ambulance service*). Say *They are called the emergency services because they help in an emergency.*
- Say *We're going to make a list of questions about emergency services to find out more. What do you think we'll do after? (We'll answer the questions).*
- Say *Then we'll present what we find. This is our Mission.*

Activity Book, page 42

My unit goals

- Go through the unit goals with the learners. (See suggested techniques in 'Identifying outcomes' in the teachers' in-class guide in Introduction.)
- Go back to these unit goals at the end of each Mission stage during the unit and review them.
- Say *This is our Mission page.*

Ending the lesson

- Put learners into groups of three. Ask when they last felt ill and what happened, e.g. *I had a fever last month. I rested and my mum gave me some cold drinks. Then I felt better.* Learners share their ideas.

  Fast finishers Learners give advice to their partner on other things they could do to feel better.

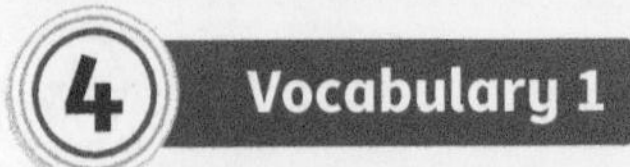

Learning outcomes By the end of the lesson, learners will be able to use vocabulary to talk about injuries and illness and listen and understand words in context.

New language *candle, patient, ankle, break, heart, cut, injure, painful, appointment*

Recycled language *emergency*

Materials audio, pictures (horse riding; a person outside on a snowy day; someone climbing a tree; someone with lots of cakes and sweets; riding a bike, a child skateboarding), sticky tack

Pupil's Book, page 43

Warm-up

- Draw an outline of a person on the board.
- Put learners into groups of four. Say *You have 1 minute. Write as many labels onto the body as you can, e.g. head.*
- Learners label the diagram for 1 minute. Tell the group with the largest number to say their words. Say *Let's check. But if another group has a word you don't have, they will win.* The group read their words. Other groups tick these on their lists. At the end ask the other groups if they have any other words.

1 2.02 Listen and choose the correct answer.

- Learners look at the picture of the video game. Ask what they can see and what they think has happened.
- Say *In this part of the exam, you must choose the correct answer. What can you do first? (read the questions first).* Say *If you read the questions first, you can listen for the answer more easily. You can listen for the important words.*
- Learners look at the questions in pairs. Tell them to find the most important word in the beginning of each question.
- Check their ideas. *(1 shark 2 fire 3 hurt himself).*
- Ask them to read the answers that are possible and think about the most important words in each one. Check ideas. Check they understand the words, e.g. draw a candle on the board and ask learners what it is. Say *candle*. Learners repeat. Show a pair of scissors. Say *scissors.* Learners repeat.
- Say *Let's listen now. Choose the best answer for each.*
- Play the audio. Learners answer. Learners check in pairs.

See audioscripts on pages TB118–123.

Key: 1 C 2 A 3 B

2 2.03 Complete the sentences. Use the words in the box. Then listen and check.

- Write sentences onto the board or put on slides. Tell learners to close their books and read sentences from the audio? *He injured his hand when he was feeding his shark. I've made an appointment for the man to meet the doctor. What's wrong with this patient? He's got a broken heart. That woman's going to the emergency door quickly. Did the monster break the woman's ankle? There was an accident. He cut his hand. It looks very painful.*
- Put the learners into groups of three. Give each group one of the sentences. If possible, give each group a learner dictionary or access to an online dictionary. Ask them to find out the meaning of their word and an example sentence. Monitor and support.
- Ask groups to present their example to the class.
- Play the audio. Learners check their answers.

Key: 1 injured 2 appointment 3 patient, heart 4 emergency door 5 accident 6 break, ankle 7 cut 8 painful

Fast finishers Put learners into pairs. Say *emergency* has four syllables. Listen: *e-mer-gen-cy.* They divide the words into groups with one, two and three syllables.

Key: One syllable: heart, door, break, cut
Two syllables: injured, patient, ankle, painful
Three syllables: appointment

3 In pairs, ask and answer about the picture in Activity 2.

- Put learners into pairs and ask them to look at Activity 2. Say *Can you remember the correct words?* Ask different pairs to say each question and answer to the class.

Key: Learners' own answers

Activity Book, page 43

See pages TB126–141.

Ending the lesson

- Put pictures around the room (*horse riding, a person outside on a snowy day, someone climbing a tree, someone with lots of cakes and sweets, riding a bike, a child skateboarding*).
- Ask learners to look at the pictures. Tell them to think of the dangers and what might happen.
- Put learners into groups. Each learner describes a problem and their group point to the picture, e.g. *I injured my hand when I fell. (You were horse riding!) No, but I was going fast. (You were skateboarding?) Yes!*

1 2.02 Listen and choose the correct answer.

1 The shark bit the man when he was …

A looking for a golf ball. B swimming. C feeding his pet.

2 The fire started because of …

A the monster. B someone cooking. C a candle falling.

3 The man with the big hands hurt himself when he was …

A using scissors. B preparing food. C playing in the park.

EXAM TIP! Read the questions **before** the listening starts.

2 2.03 Complete the sentences. Use the words in the box. Then listen and check.

injured break appointment cut painful heart accident ankle emergency door patient

1 Yes, he ________ his hand when he was feeding his shark.
2 I've made an ________ for the man to meet the doctor.
3 What's wrong with this ________ ? The man who's having his ________ checked.
4 That woman's running to the ________ . Do you know why there's a fire?
5 I think there was an ________ and her pet monster made the fire.
6 Did the monster ________ the woman's ________ , too?
7 While he was making a sandwich, his knife slipped and he ________ his hand.
8 It looks very ________ . It must hurt a lot.

3 In pairs, ask and answer about the picture in Activity 2.

What's wrong with this man?

He's injured his hand.

Language presentation 1

1

VIKTOR, JIM FRIENDLIE

Hi Jim – how are you? 8:27

I haven't been well for a week. 8:27

Jenny told me. Did you get our card? 8:28

Yes – thank you! 8:29

I want to come back soon though to see you all. But I feel awful! 8:29

Yeah, but you need to stay in bed if you want to get better. Drink lots of water! 8:30

I will. 8:31

Can't wait to see you again. 8:31

You too. 8:32

2

ELIZABETH, ALEX

Hi Alex– would you like to come to the park later? 7:04

No, sorry. I need to take my rabbit to the vet. 7:07

Oh no! What's wrong with her? 7:08

She's had a problem with her heart since April. 7:09

7:10

Poor thing! I hope she's better soon. 7:10

Me too! The vet says that she'll be fine. 7:11

3

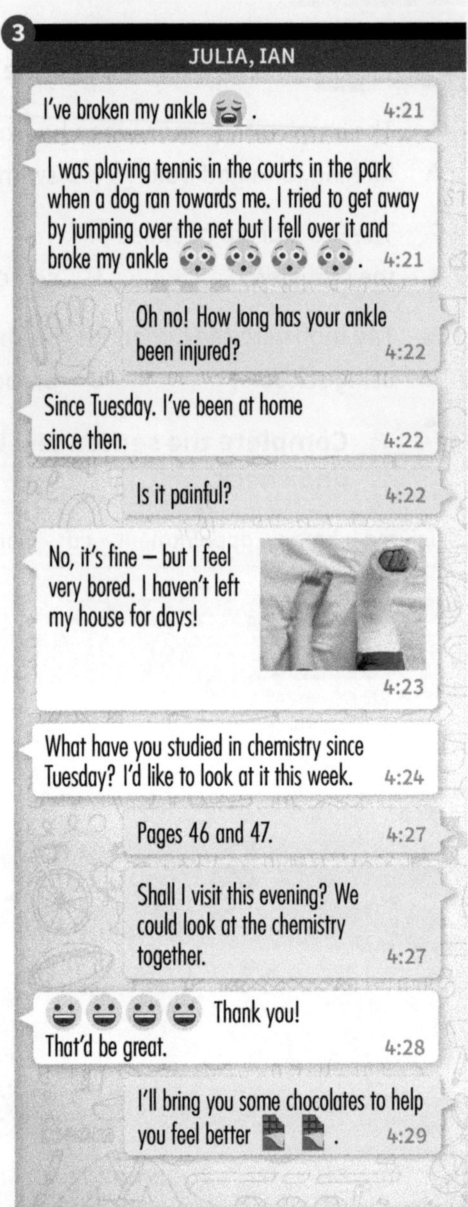

JULIA, IAN

I've broken my ankle. 4:21

I was playing tennis in the courts in the park when a dog ran towards me. I tried to get away by jumping over the net but I fell over it and broke my ankle. 4:21

Oh no! How long has your ankle been injured? 4:22

Since Tuesday. I've been at home since then. 4:22

Is it painful? 4:22

No, it's fine – but I feel very bored. I haven't left my house for days! 4:23

What have you studied in chemistry since Tuesday? I'd like to look at it this week. 4:24

Pages 46 and 47. 4:27

Shall I visit this evening? We could look at the chemistry together. 4:27

Thank you! That'd be great. 4:28

I'll bring you some chocolates to help you feel better. 4:29

1 ☆ Look at the messages again. Choose the correct answer.

1 Why is Viktor writing to Jim?

A He's worried about his friend. B He's going to get Jim a glass of water. C He wants Jim to write a card.

2 Why did Elizabeth write to Alex?

A Her rabbit is unwell. B She's going to go to the vet with him. C She wanted to go to the park with him.

3 What do Julia and Ian agree to do together?

A eat sweets B study chemistry C walk the dog

EXAM TIP! After you've chosen A, B or C, read the text and the question again to **check** that **your answer** is correct.

Learning outcomes By the end of the lesson, learners will be able to read to understand messages and understand strategies for answering questions.

New language *text message, emoticon*, present perfect

Recycled language vocabulary describing illness

Materials access to mobile devices if possible, sticky notes in five different colours

Pupil's Book, page 44

Warm-up

- Draw a smiley face on the board. Ask *Where do we normally see this? (on a phone text message)*. Ask *What do we call these pictures? (emoticons)*.
- Ask learners *Do you send text messages on apps like Messenger or WhatsApp? Do you use emoticons? Which ones do you use most?* Learners suggest answers.
- Say *We're going to send an emoticon message about our day.*
- Draw some emoticons on the board (or project a real phone message). Give an example, e.g. *When I got up I was still tired so I have put a frowning face. I added an egg and a heart because my breakfast was really good. Then I put a walking person because I walked to school.*
- Learners create messages.
- Put learners into pairs and ask them to show each other their drawings and describe their day so far.

Presentation

- Say *We're going to read some messages*. Tell learners to open their books at page 44. Ask *Where would you see this kind of message? (on your phone, online)*.
- Tell learners to look at the three messages quickly and find out which three people are sending a message to Jim, Elizabeth and Julia. Give 1 minute. Check answers. *(Viktor/Alex/Ian)*.
- Tell the learners to read the messages again and decide what they have in common. Ask *Are they about meeting up, pets or being ill?* Ask if they need to read carefully or quickly. *(quickly)*.
- Check answers. *(illness)*.

 **Look at the messages again. Choose the correct answer.**

- Tell learners to look at the questions and read the possible answers A to C. Learners choose answers.
- Tell them to read the text again and check. Say *Often the text will include words from all three choices but you have to find the one with the correct information.*
- Put learners into pairs to compare answers. Check with the class, asking learners to explain their answer.

EXAM TIP! Ask a strong learner to read the exam tip. Say *You should always go back to the text and read again to check answers.*

Key: 1 A (He talks about a card he sent Jim and tells him to drink water, but the reason he is messaging is because he is worried that Jim is OK.) 2 C (Alex talks about taking the rabbit to the vet, but Elizabeth sent a message to ask about going to the park.) 3 B (Julia and Ian are going to do geography – she talks about a dog in the park because that is where she had an accident and Ian offers to bring chocolate when they study.)

Extension Draw a table on the board. Tell learners to copy the table. Ask them to read the messages again and complete the table with the correct information. In pairs, learners compare and check their answers.

	Jim	**Alex's rabbit**	**Julia**
What's wrong?	*he's not well*	*has a problem with her heart*	*has a broken ankle*
When did the problem start?	*a week ago*	*three months ago*	*on Tuesday*
How are they feeling?	*awful*	*quite hot*	*fine but a bit bored*

Activity Book, page 44

See pages TB126–141.

Ending the lesson

- Give out sticky notes using five different colours in equal amounts for five learners in each group. (Or give out squares of different coloured paper and sticky tack.)
- Tell the learners to find their group – all learners with the same colour as them. Explain they will make a message chain. Tell each learner they must reply to the previous message in the chain and include an emoticon in their message.
- Give each learner a number 1 to 5.
- Put a starter message, one for each group, across the top of the board, e.g. *Hi. I'm quite tired and have a headache. Do you want to go to the park for fresh air?* ☺
- Learner 1 from each group comes up and writes a short response on their sticky note, including an emoticon, and sticks it up under the first message.
- Learner 2 then writes a response and so on until all five learners have put up a message. The first group to complete all messages is the winner. Check answers.

Learning outcomes By the end of the lesson, learners will be able to understand and use present perfect simple to describe unfinished actions and use *'for'* and *'since'* to describe durations of actions or states.

New language present perfect for unfinished actions and states, *for, since*

Recycled language vocabulary related to illness

Materials 3 pictures (a foot in a plaster cast, a bandaged hand, a person in bed with flu) Mission worksheets (Teacher's Resource Book page 41)

Pupil's Book, page 45

Warm-up

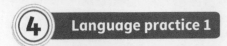

- Put pictures on the board: a foot in a plaster cast, a bandaged hand, a person lying in bed looking feverish. Ask *Which people are injured and which person is ill? (the person in bed is ill, the rest injured themselves).*
- Write on the board *He's had a broken … since last week.* Learners complete the sentence. *(foot).*
- Write up two more sentences with gaps. Learners complete in pairs. *She cut her hand. It's been … (injure) since last week. (injured). He's … (have) flu since last week. (had).*

Fast finishers Learners rewrite the sentences using 'for'.

Presentation

- Point to the picture of a foot in a plaster cast and the sentence *He's had a broken foot since last week.*
- Say *When did he break his foot? (last week). Is it still broken now? (yes). So it started in the past, but it continues … (now).*
- Ask *Which tense is this? (present perfect simple)*
- Underline the verb form and point to the auxiliary verb. Ask *What verb is this? (has).* Point to the main verb and ask *What kind of verb is this? (past participle)*

Grammar look: the present perfect with *how long, for* and *since*

- Learners read the sentences in the left of the **Grammar look** box. In pairs, they choose the correct option in sentences on the right.
- Learners complete the rules 4–6 at the bottom of the **Grammar look** box. Check answers.

Key: 1 a week ago 2 Yes 3 past 4 present 5 I, you, they and we 6 he, she and it

1 2.04 **PRONUNCIATION Listen and repeat.** 
page 119

- Learners listen and repeat. Play the audio. Check learners are pronouncing weak forms /həv/ /bɪn/.
  I haven't been well for a week.
  She's had a problem with her heart for three months.
  I've broken my ankle.
- Learners go to page 118 and do the activity. (See page TB124.)

2 Write six true sentences. Use the phrases in the box or your own ideas.

- Learners look at the box and time phrases. Ask *When do we use 'for' and when do we use 'since' for times?*
- Confirm 'since' gives a point in time and 'for' shows the length of time, e.g. *since Monday (Monday is the starting point); for three days (three days is the length of time).*
- Tell learners to write six sentences using the words in the box or some of their own ideas, e.g. *I've lived here for as long as I can remember. I haven't had a cold for a year.*
- Monitor and support.

3 In pairs, share your sentences from Activity 2 with a small group. Who hasn't felt sick for the longest time?

- Ask learners which sentences are about illness. *(the first and third).* In pairs, they make questions using *'How long has it been since'.* Check answers. *(How long has it been since you had a cold? How long has it been since you felt sick?)*
- In groups of four learners ask and answer the questions to find out who hasn't been ill for the longest time. Groups report back on who hasn't been ill for the longest period.

Complete the Grammar look on page 122. (See pages TB125–126.)

Mission Stage 1

- Write *emergency services* on the board. In pairs, learners think of all the emergency services they can.
- Give each learner a copy of the Mission worksheet (Teacher's Resource Book page 41).
- Tell learners to work individually and do some research about different settings where you could be helped in an emergency, e.g. at school, at a holiday resort, at a sports club, etc. Then they complete a mind map to show the different types of emergencies that these different places treat/encounter, e.g. *Sport coaches treat injuries suffered when people practise sports.*

Activity Book, page 45

See pages TB126–141.

Ending the lesson

- Ask learners which emergency service they would work for and why. Compare ideas.

Grammar look: the present perfect with *how long*, *for* and *since*

'I haven't been well for a week.'
'She's had a problem with her heart since April.'

1 When did Jim start feeling unwell? **a week ago / Monday**

2 Does the rabbit still have a problem? **Yes / No**

We use the present perfect to describe actions that started in the **(3) past / present** and are still happening in the **(4) present / future**.

With **(5) *I, you, they* and *we* / *he, she* and *it*** we use *have* + past participle (e.g. *made, done, eaten* etc.)

With **(6) *I, you, they* and *we* / *he, she* and *it*** we use *has* + past participle.

page 122

1 2.04 PRONUNCIATION **Listen and repeat.** page 118

2 **Write six true sentences.** Use the phrases in the box or your own ideas.

I haven't had a cold I've lived in my house I haven't felt sick I've been at this school	for	a few hours. three weeks. a month. five years. a long time. as long as I can remember.
I've studied geography I haven't eaten chocolate	since	Monday. this morning. 23rd January. yesterday. last winter. I was born.

3 **In pairs, share your sentences from Activity 2.** Who hasn't felt sick for the longest time?

Mission Stage 1

Make a list of questions about the emergency services.

How can I call the emergency services?
Who will come?
What sound does an ambulance make?

Did you know?

A long time ago, when people had sore throats, they tried to get better by putting dirty socks around their necks. Some people put fish on their feet too!

Vocabulary 2

1 Read the diary. What happened to Dizzy at the lake?

4th August

I'm excited because tomorrow I'm going to the hills with my aunt. I'm going to take my dog, Dizzy for a walk and then we're going to go swimming in a lake. We're not going home until after dinner!

My aunt's meeting us tomorrow at 9 am to drive us there – so I should go to sleep now. ☺

5th August

Today something awful happened. We were having a lovely day in the hills – Dizzy was happy and we had a lovely picnic. But when we went to the lake, things started to go wrong.

We were swimming when Dizzy cut her leg badly on a rock. She fell over and started crying. We put a **bandage** round her leg and carried her back to the car.

It looks really painful so we're taking her to the vet this evening. ☹

6th August

The vet gave Dizzy a **prescription** for some **pills**, and she said that Dizzy needs to have a small **operation**.

Also, I think I've got the **flu**. When I got out of the lake, I was so worried about Dizzy that I forgot to get warm and dry. My mum's given me some medicine for my headache. She told me to go to bed and rest. But when I **lie down**, I can't sleep because I'm so worried about Dizzy.

7th August

I've got some great news. Dizzy's operation was a success! Dizzy's **resting** at the vet's at the moment and the vet says she can come home tomorrow. Hooray!

I'm **feeling better** too. So I'll be able to look after Dizzy when she gets home.

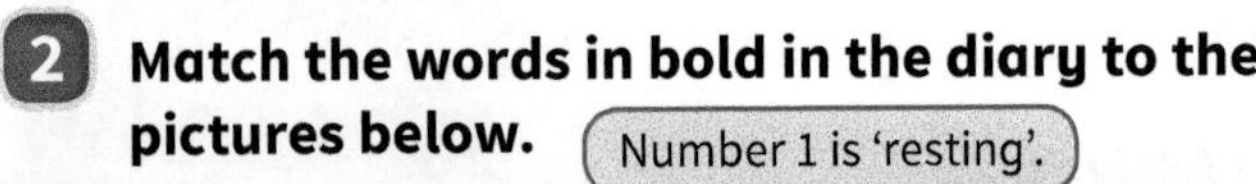

2 Match the words in bold in the diary to the pictures below.

Number 1 is 'resting'.

1 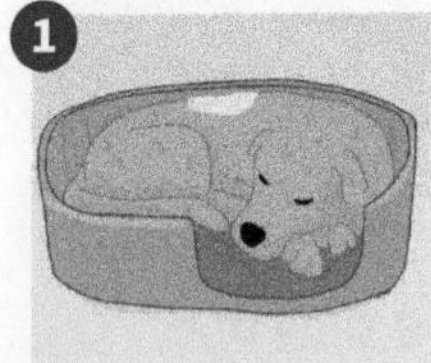

2 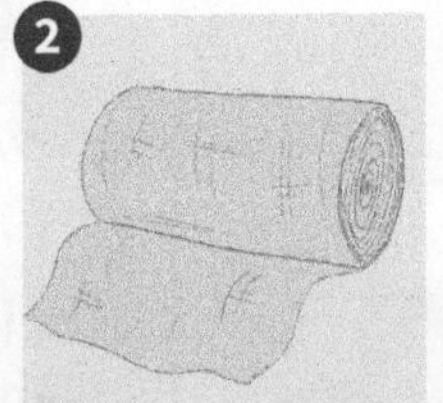

3 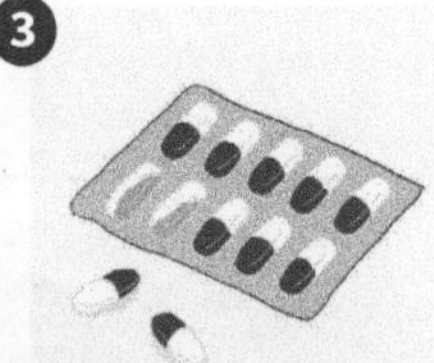

4 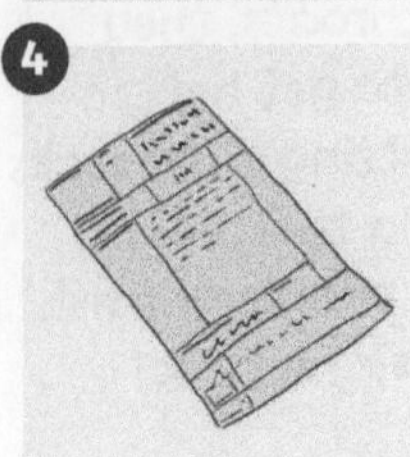

5 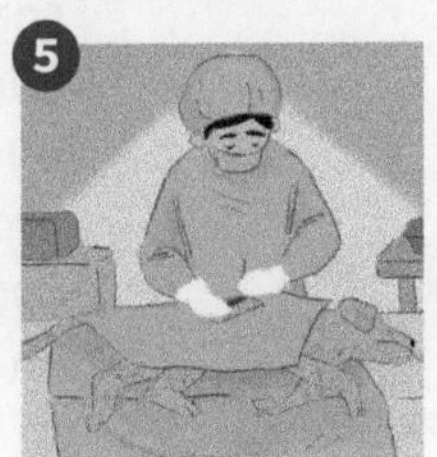

6 

7 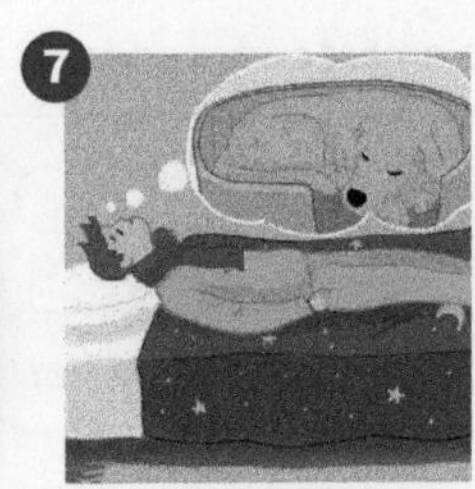

8 

3 Add one sentence (A–D) to the end of each day's diary entry.

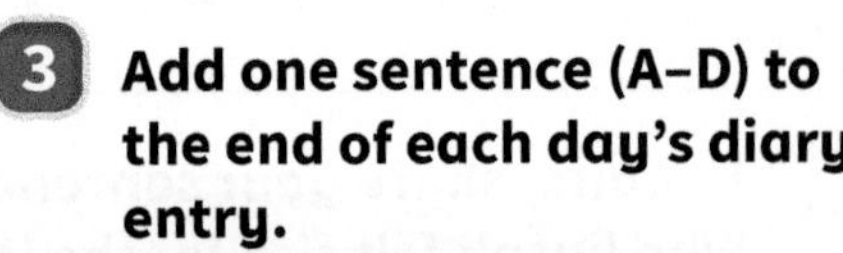

A I wonder what she'll say.

B I can't wait to see her again!

C I hope her operation is OK.

D I'm so excited about the trip.

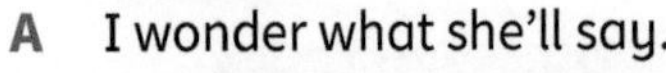

Learning outcomes By the end of the lesson, learners will be able to use vocabulary about medicine and treatments.

New language *bandage, pills/tablets, prescription, operation, lie down*

Recycled language *rest, feel better, flu*

Materials audio

Pupil's Book, page 46

Warm-up

- Tell learners you are going to say three sentences about you and they have to decide which one is not true. Give them three sentences and tell them they can ask questions to find out more, e.g. *I've broken my arm once. I've had flu three times. I was sick two months ago. (P: How did you break your arm? You: When I was skiing. P: How did you break it? You: I fell down on the ski run.*
- Tell learners to think of three sentences about themselves – two that are true and one that isn't.
- Put learners into groups of three or four. Tell them to take it in turns to give their sentences and the rest of the group ask questions. Listen and monitor as learners work.
- The winning students are the ones who give false sentences the group can't spot.

1 Read the diary. What happened to Dizzy at the lake?

- Tell learners to look at the picture and ask who Dizzy is. *(a pet dog)*
- Tell learners to read the diary entry for 4th August only. Ask them about the plans organised for the next day and how the writer is feeling.
- Put them in pairs to check their ideas. *(The plans are to go for a walk and swim in a lake with Dizzy).*
- Tell learners that things don't go to plan and Dizzy has an accident. Ask them to guess what happens. Learners discuss in pairs. Share ideas.
- Learners read the rest of the diary and find the answer.
- Tell them to compare ideas. Check answers with the class.

Key: She cuts her leg on a rock.

2 Match the words in bold in the diary to the pictures below.

- Ask learners to look at the pictures in Activity 2 and guess what they are. Learners suggest ideas.
- Put learners into pairs. Tell them to read the text, find the words in bold and match with the pictures. Monitor and support.
- Check answers with the class. As you ask for each answer, check pronunciation by clapping stress and asking learners to repeat. Check understanding with questions. E.g. *flu: if you have flu how do you feel? (very ill, headache, fever); bandage: what is it made of? (cotton); What kind of medicine have you taken? (pills/tablets); How do you take them? (you usually take them with water); prescription: Who writes a prescription? (doctor); operation: What happens in an operation? (a doctor or vet cuts open a body to fix something); rest: If you rest, what are you doing? (sleeping or trying to relax); lie down: Where can you lie down? (in bed or on a sofa); feel better: if you feel better, is this good or bad? (good).*

Key: 1 resting 2 bandage 3 pills 4 prescription 5 operation 6 flu 7 lie down 8 feel better

3 Add one sentence (A–D) to each day's diary entry.

- Ask learners to read the four sentences. Tell them each one goes at the end of one of the diary entries.
- Put learners into pairs. Ask them to work out which sentence goes with each day. Check answers with the class.

Key: A 5th August B 7th August C 6th August D 4th August

Activity Book, page 46

See pages TB126–141.

Ending the lesson

- Tell learners you are going to do a reverse quiz. Write words on the board: *prescription, rest, flu, bandage, operation, feel better, pills, lie down.*
- Explain these are the answers and their job is to make the clues. Put learners into groups of three and ask them to think of a clue for each word. Do an example together, e.g. *If I am in bed with a cough and a fever, Iwhat illness might I have? (flu).*
- Put the groups together and tell them to take it in turns giving their clues to the other group. The aim is for the clues to be good enough for the other group to get every question correct.
- Groups complete their quizzes. Check which groups were able to give the best clues.

Learning outcomes By the end of the lesson, learners will be able to use present continuous for the future.

New language present continuous for future plans

Recycled language time phrases

Materials pictures with dates and times (cinema labelled Wednesday 7 pm as the example; tennis court labelled Saturday 9.30; shops labelled Saturday 2 pm; park labelled Sunday 1 pm; dinner table labelled Monday 6 pm; TV screen labelled Monday 8pm; coffee cup labelled Tuesday 3 pm)

Warm-up

- Hide the pictures pictures with dates and times around the room.
- Write on the board: Saturday 9.30; *Saturday 2 pm; Sunday 1 pm; Monday 6 pm; Monday 8 pm; Tuesday 3 pm*. Ask learners to say the times aloud.
- Tell learners you have plans for next week at these times. Tell them to find out your plans by looking for the clues. Show them an example: a picture of a cinema labelled *Wednesday 7pm*. Ask what plan this shows. *('On Wednesday I'm watching a film at 7 pm').*
- Put learners into groups of four. Tell them the clues about your plans are hidden in the room. They must find them and make a list. Tell each team to choose one member to write the list. The other group members look for clues. When they find a clue, they put it back, and then run and whisper the day, time and plan to their group writer. The first group to have all the plans is the winner.

Pupil's Book, page 47

Presentation

- Remind learners about the diary on page 46. Ask *Can you remember what time they met Jenny's aunt?* Encourage them to check their books and find the sentence.
- Write on the board: *My aunt's meeting us tomorrow at 9 am.*
- Ask *Is this about now or the future? (the future). Is it a plan? (yes). What tense is it? (present continuous).*

Grammar look: the present continuous for future plans

- Tell learners to read the **Grammar look** box.
- Put learners into pairs. Ask them to choose the correct option in each sentence 1–2, then complete the sentences 1–2 in the bottom part of the box. Check answers.

  Fast finishers Write two more plans using present continuous.

Key: 1 in the future 2 Yes 3 future 4 planned

1 Look at Jenny's calendar. Complete the sentences below using the present continuous.

- Put learners into pairs. Tell them to read the diary and think about Jenny's plans. Look at the example together, e.g. Monday: read the diary entry and show the example sentence. Tell learners to complete the rest of the sentences.
- Monitor and support. Check answers.

Key: 1 At 6 pm today, Jenny's making cookies for her family. 2 Jenny's going to athletics club at lunchtime tomorrow. 3 Jenny's getting Jim a present on Thursday after school. (She's not getting him flowers!) 4 On Friday evening, Jenny's doing her maths homework. 5 At the weekend, Jenny's filming her video diary.

2 In pairs, talk about your plans. How many are the same?

- Put learners into pairs. Tell them to find out about each other's plans and see if any are the same. Read the examples.
- Learners ask and answer questions using the times in Activity 2. Monitor and check for errors.

  Fast finishers Put learners in new pairs and ask them to report to their partner about what they learnt, e.g. *Silvia and I are both playing football on Thursday after school. But on Friday I'm visiting my grandparents and Silvia is visiting her friend.*

  Complete the Grammar look on page 122.
  (See pages TB125–126.)

Mission Stage 2

- Put learners into the same groups as Mission Stage 1 if possible. Ask them which of the emergency services they can remember. Remind them of the question list they created together in Mission Stage 1.
- Put them back into their groups. Learners try to find the information. Assign one or two questions per group. If possible, learners can look up some of the answers on the Internet. If not, the research could be assigned as homework. Share the ideas they have collected.

Activity Book, page 47

See pages TB126–141.

Ending the lesson

- SA Ask learners to complete their self-assessment (see Introduction).

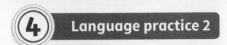

Grammar look: the present continuous for future plans

'We're taking her to the vet this evening.'
'We're not going home until after dinner!'

1 When will Dizzy go to the vet? **In the future** / **now**
2 Will Dizzy definitely go to the vet? **Yes** (they've made the plan) / **No** (they'll make the plan this evening)

1 The present continuous can be used to talk about the present and the **past** / **future**.
2 The present continuous is used to talk about the future when something is **uncertain** / **planned** and we say when it will happen.

page 122

1 **Look at Jenny's calendar.** Complete the sentences below using the present continuous.

My plans!

	Monday	Tuesday	Wednesday	Thursday	Friday	Saturday	Sunday
today	17 6 pm – make cookies for my family	18 lunchtime – go to athletics club	19	20 after school – get Jim a present (not flowers!)	21 evening – do my maths homework	22 film the video diary	23

1 At 6 pm today, Jenny's making ....

At 6 pm today, Jenny's making cookies for her family.

2 .... at lunchtime tomorrow.
3 .... on Thursday after school.
4 On Friday evening, ...
5 At the weekend, ...
6 On Wednesday, ...

2 **In pairs, talk about your plans.** How many are the same?

What are you doing ...

... at 6 pm today?
... tomorrow lunchtime?
... on Thursday after school?
... on Friday evening?
... at the weekend?

What are you doing after school today?

I'm going to watch an ice-hockey match!

Find answers to your questions about the emergency services.

Search Emergency services contact
About 9,397 results (0.21 seconds)
In England, the number you need to call for an ambulance is 999.

Literature

1 **Read the title of the story. What do you think it's going to be about?**

The £20,000 adventure

2.06

Joshua's ill and bored. He has flu, and he has had a fever for several days. But today he's feeling a bit better. His mum says he can go downstairs, lie down on the sofa and watch television with his sister, Chloe.

Joshua and Chloe are watching a programme about crocodiles. There's a knock on the door. It's their cousin, Eddie. He has come to see if Joshua's feeling better. 'How long have you been ill?' he asks. 'For four days,' says Joshua. 'I haven't been to school since last Monday!' 'Lucky you!' says Eddie.

The crocodile programme has finished. The local news programme is starting. 'There was a robbery at Whitton's bank last night. Unfotunately, thieves stole about £20,000 in cash and escaped in a fast car,' the newsreader says. 'The thieves are dangerous criminals.'

'I know that bank,' Chloe says excitedly. 'It's on the High Street.' Joshua's feeling sleepy. His eyes are closing! 'Come on, Joshua,' says Eddie. 'Let's climb some trees.'

★ ★ ★

Outside in the garden Chloe's climbing a tree and the two boys quickly climb up to join her. 'Look at those men!' says Chloe, pointing at two men kneeling on the ground by the river. 'What are they doing?' 'Shhhhhh!' whispers Joshua. 'They'll hear you and they look dangerous!' 'But look!' says Eddie, feeling worried. 'What *are* they doing?'

One of the men is taking a huge pile of papers from a brown bag. 'It's the £20,000!' whispers Chloe. 'You know – the money from the bank on the High Street. Look! They're hiding it in the hole.' 'Yes, and the newsreader said they're dangerous criminals,' whispers Joshua.

The two men look up as if they've heard something. The children freeze – they are terrified.

Learning outcomes By the end of the lesson, learners will be able to read a story to understand main events and understand words in context.

New language *robbery, thieves, criminals, escape, swing, freeze, bleed, rope*

Recycled language present perfect simple, *ill, lie down, feeling better, painful*

Materials audio, 8 large word cards (thieves, criminals, robbery, escape, rope, bleed, swing, freeze), sticky tack

Warm-up

- Tell learners to write some questions. Draw a table on the board and tell the learners to copy it and complete the questions in the left-hand column.

How long have you	A _____	B _____	C _____
_____ *(study) English?*			
_____ *(have) your phone?*			
_____ *(live) in your house?*			
_____ *(be) in this class?*			

- Put learners into pairs to compare questions.
- Check answers. *(studied, had, lived, been)*
- Learners mingle and ask questions. They speak to three other learners and write their names and answers in columns A–C. Give 5–6 minutes to complete the task.
- Ask learners to report back what they found out, e.g. *Sammi has had his phone longer than everyone. Ben has only had his phone for a month.*

Pupil's Book, page 48

1 Read the title of the story. What do you think it's going to be about?

- Write the title on the board. Ask the learners to think about the title and decide what the story is about.
- Learners discuss in pairs. Share their ideas.

2.06 The £20,000 adventure

- Ask learners to read and listen to the story to see if they were right. Remind them they don't need to understand every word.
- Play the audio. Check answers with the class.
- Ask learners if Joshua really hurt his leg. *(No, it was a dream).*

Key: The story describes a dream Joshua has. He thinks he finds some criminals, but it is just a dream.

- Stick some word cards onto the side of the board using sticky tack: *thieves, criminals, robbery, escape, rope, bleed, swing, freeze.*
- Ask learners to think about the meanings and decide what they have in common. Put them in pairs to discuss. Tell them to read parts of the story again to help them.
- While they discuss, put a circular target onto the board.
- Ask learners to decide how well they think they understand each word. Invite a learner up to the board to stick one of the words on the target – near the centre if they are sure and near the edge if they are not sure. Invite learners until all the words are on the target.
- Check the meanings: invite the learners to suggest their definitions or examples. Clarify and check. As you clarify each word ask learners to repeat, checking understanding, e.g. *A criminal is a person who doesn't follow the law.* Say *criminal.* Learners repeat. Highlight the stress on the board.
- Continue with the other words: *A thief is a type of criminal who steals. Robbery is when a thief steals from a place, e.g. from a bank. If a criminal runs away, they escape. If someone doesn't move at all and stays still because they are afraid or surprised, then we can say they freeze. Rope is a kind of strong, thick string. If you hold onto a rope and take your feet off the ground, you can swing. If you cut yourself, you bleed.*

  Extra support Give learners dictionaries to check and help them understand the words.
- Go back to pages 48 and 49. Ask learners to look at the pictures and look for *thieves* and *a rope*. Learners point.
- Tell learners to look at the words again and listen as you give clues. If they know the answer they should raise their hand. Call out clues and select learners as they put their hands up. Clues: *I do this if I run away from something. (escape). If I am making food and cut my hand using a knife, it … (bleeds). A lot of money was stolen from a shop. It was a … (robbery). The people who took the money were very bad … (criminals/thieves). You can use this to tie up a boat or something large (rope). When I am shocked sometimes I can't move, I just do this … (freeze).*
- Ask learners to look at the target again and decide if the words are closer to the centre. Invite them to come up and move the words to a different place on the target if they think they understand them better.

Activity Book, page 48

See pages TB126–141.

Ending the lesson

- Tell learners to work in pairs and talk about their dreams and to describe the last one they remember. Share ideas.

Learning outcomes By the end of the lesson, learners will be able to respond to a text using critical thinking and emotional intelligence and understand how dreams can be affected by real life.

New language adjectives for feelings: *sleepy, excited, worried, terrified, nervous, furious, frightened*

Recycled language *robbery, thieves, criminals, escape, swing, freeze, bleed, rope, bandage, operation, prescription*

Materials audio, paper and pens

Social and Emotional Skill: dealing with fear

- After reading the story, ask learners *Why is Joshua running? (The criminals are running after him). Why can't Joshua run as fast as his friends? (He's hurt his leg). What happens? (He gets to the river, but there are crocodiles). How he control his fear? (He thinks how to get across the river).*
- Give a list of fears you have and encourage the learners to give advice on how to deal with your fear. Say, e.g. *I'm scared of spiders!*
- Point out that in many situations, we feel frightened, but it's important to recognise that, and then do whatever you were going to do anyway.
- Ask *What things frighten you?* Give learners 10 minutes to write down a couple of lines about a situation from their own experience that scared them and one that terrified them. They also write how they dealt with that fear. Learners share their examples.

Warm-up

- Put paper on the floor in the middle of the classroom to make a line. Put a picture of a crocodile on the board. Ask learners what kind of animal it is. *(a crocodile).* Ask learners to stand one side of the paper. Put them into pairs and give each a paper and pen.
- Point to the paper on the floor and say *There is a crocodile in the river, but you can cross here. Answer the questions as fast as you can. If you can spell 'criminal', you can cross.*
- Check the answers of the first five pairs to finish writing and raise their hands. If they are correct let them jump across the river by stepping across the paper. If not go to the next pair. Repeat with *robbery, thieves, escape, swing, freeze, bleed, rope, bandage, operation, prescription.*

  Fast finishers Learners who finish quickly can help read out the next words and check answers.

Pupil's Book, page 49

Presentation

- Tell learners to look at the story on pages 48–49 again.
- Put learners into pairs. Write on the board *Who feels: sleepy, excited, worried, terrified, nervous, furious, frightened?* Ask them to read and find out who feels each emotion and why.
- In pairs, learners discuss when they felt each emotion last. Give them an example, e.g. *The last time I was sleepy I was watching TV. I fell asleep during the film. When I woke up, it was finished.*

Key: Joshua feels sleepy because he is ill. Chloe is excited because she sees the story about the thieves on the news. Eddie is worried because he sees the thieves hiding the money. The children are terrified because the two thieves see them. Joshua is nervous because Chloe and Eddie make too much noise. The thieves look furious because the children have seen them hiding the money. Joshua is frightened when he sees the crocodile in the river.

2 In pairs, talk about the questions.

- Put learners into groups of four. Ask them to look at the three questions and discuss.
- Monitor and support. Ask groups to share their ideas.

  Fast finishers Learners work in pairs. They think of other things that Joshua could do when he sees the crocodiles.

Key: Sample answers 1 Joshua saw crocodiles on TV and then a news programme about a local robbery. 2 He feels frightened. He looks around for a way to escape and sees the rope which could help him swing across.

Activity Book, page 49

See pages TB126–141.

Ending the lesson

- Put learners into groups of three.
- Write some of the key words on the board: *ill, TV, robbery, trees, hiding, noise, cut, run, river, crocodiles, rope.*
- Learners retell the story in groups, using the key words.

The three children watch in complete silence while the men finish hiding the cash and walk away through the wood. 'Let's get it!' says Chloe, climbing down the tree fast. 'Come on, Joshua,' shouts Eddie. 'What are you waiting for? They might come back.' But Joshua isn't feeling well. He thinks he might have a fever again. As he's climbing down the tree he cuts his knee and cries out in pain.

Chloe and Eddie get the bag. They make so much noise that Joshua starts to feel nervous. They don't see the men coming back! Suddenly, the men are standing right behind them and they look furious. 'Hey! Drop that!' they shout. 'Run!' shouts Eddie.

Eddie and Chloe grab the money and run to the bridge as fast as they can. They cross over the river. But Joshua can't run to the bridge. His knee's bleeding. It's too painful to run. 'Hurry up, Joshua, they're going to catch you,' shouts Eddie from the other side of the river.

Joshua decides to swim to the other side. He's just going to jump into the water to cross the river, when he sees crocodiles. He's very frightened now.

'Oh no, crocodiles - how strange!' thinks Joshua for a moment. 'Crocodiles live in Africa, not here!'

Joshua's trapped with the thieves behind him and crocodiles in front of him! Oh no! He can't run to the bridge. He can't swim across the river. What can he do? Then he sees a rope hanging from a tree. Can he swing across?

'Joshua, wake up! You're shouting in your sleep ... something about crocodiles. Are you feeling OK?' asks his mother, coming into the room.

'Oh, Mum. Yes, I'm feeling much better now!' says Joshua.

'Come on. Switch off the television. It's time to eat,' says his mum.

2 In pairs, talk about the questions.

1 Which real-life facts were in Joshua's dream?
2 What do you think of Chloe and Eddie's actions in the story? What would you have done?
3 How do you think Joshua feels when he sees the crocodiles? What does he do to help himself?

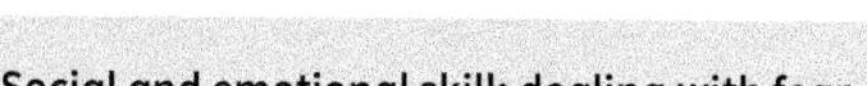

Cross-curricular

1 **Look at the pictures. What do you think they show?**

2 2.07 **Listen and read the text. Check your answers to Activity 1.**

What was life like in the 1700s?

Many poor people didn't eat very well and so when they were ill, they could die. Lots of families had one toilet in the garden and it wasn't very clean. They also didn't have soap (and sometimes no water) to wash their hands. Doctors didn't know very much about what different illnesses were and they didn't have medicines to give people. Children also didn't have vaccinations to prevent them from getting ill and so they got illnesses like measles, chicken pox and flu.

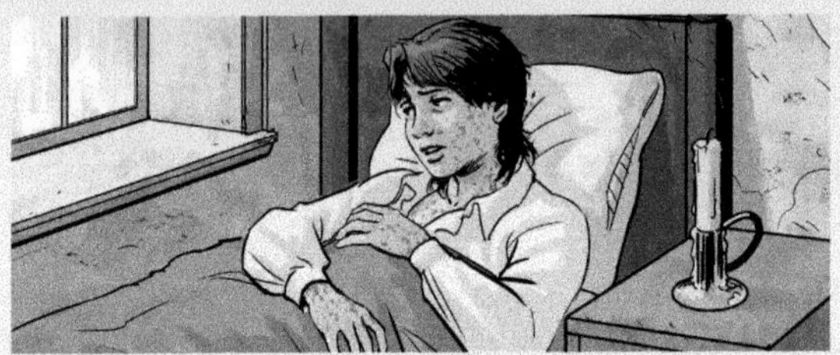

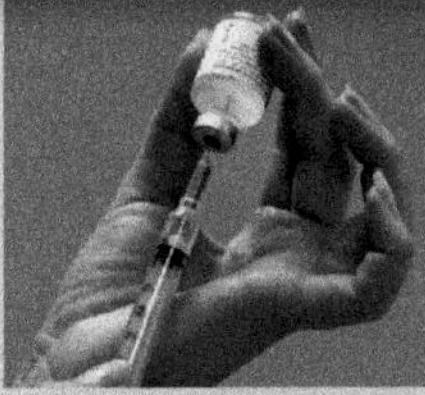

How is life different now?

Doctors have learned a lot about preventing illnesses since the 1940s. We are told to eat a balanced diet and we also know that it's important to wash our hands before we eat or if you cut yourself. Before the 1940s if you cut your finger, bacteria could get into the cut and so lots of people died from a disease called tetanus. Now, we have vaccinations at the doctor. This is an injection to stop us getting the disease. Vaccinations contain a small amount of a virus or bacteria that help the body to fight the disease.

Sir Alexander Fleming (1881–1955): In 1928, Sir Alexander Fleming discovered penicillin and this helped to develop a group of medicines called antibiotics.

During World War I he saw lots of soldiers die from infected cuts.

He started growing germs in dishes to study them.

In 1928 he noticed mould was growing in his dishes and killing the germs.

This was penicillin and it has saved the lives of millions of people.

3 **Read the text again and say *yes* or *no*.**

1 Some people didn't have water in the past.
2 Children had injections to stop them getting ill in the past.
3 In 1928 you could die if you cut your finger.
4 A vaccination gives you a disease.
5 Alexander Fleming died in World War I.
6 He wasn't trying to grow mould.

4 **In pairs, talk about the best treatment for the problems in the box.**

a nosebleed   a cold   a headache   a cut knee

Learning outcomes By the end of the lesson, learners will be able to understand about medicine and treatments throughout history, and read using critical thinking skills (analysis, application, creative thinking).

New language *disease, antibiotics, injection, vaccinations, prevent, virus, balanced diet*

Recycled language vocabulary related to illness

Materials learners' access to Internet if possible

Warm-up

- Ask learners to write down some dates. Remind them to do this using numbers not words. Say *1700s; 1930s; today.*
- Tell them to think about medicines and treatments during these times.
- If possible, learners can use mobile devices to check ideas. If not, they can use their imaginations. Ask them to choose a date and to find out about illness and treatment during that time period.
- Each group writes a description, including what kind of medicines and treatments were used.
- Ask each group to read their description to the class.
- The class guesses which date the group chose. Compare to see if groups who chose the same date had similar ideas.

Pupil's Book, page 50

Presentation

- Write some words on the board: *injection, vaccination, virus, disease.* Ask learners to think about how these relate to the pictures. Put learners into pairs to discuss.
- Check answers. Point to the needle and say *This is used to give an injection.* Ask learners to mime an injection. Say *injection*. Learners repeat. Say *Is there another word for injection? (vaccination).* Learners repeat. Say *Some illnesses can be passed on by viruses. These are diseases*. Learners repeat. Ask for examples of illnesses and disease. If learners can't think of any, give them examples, e.g. *measles, chickenpox.*

1 Look at the pictures. What do you think they show?

- In pairs, learners talk about how the things in the pictures can help people. Check answers.
- Explain how injections can prevent illness. Learners repeat prevent. Explain if a person has an infection, an injection of antibiotics will kill the bacteria. Say *antibiotic*. Learners repeat. Ask if they know the name of an antibiotic. *(penicillin)*.

Key: Sample answers an injection could immunise you against an illness or help you with an illness you already have; washing your hands prevents germs; eating healthily keeps your body heathy

2 2.07 Listen and read the text. Check your answers to Activity 1.

- Learners read and discuss in pairs. Check answers.

Key: an injection contains small amounts of a virus that fight disease; washing your hands prevents germs – in the past people didn't always use soap and water so people weren't clean and got ill; we are now told to eat a balanced diet to stay healthy

3 Read the text again and say *yes* or *no*.

- Tell learners to find the correct part of the text and read it to find the reason for their answer.
- Learners discuss in pairs. Monitor and support.
- Put them into fours and ask them to compare ideas. Check answers with the class.

Key: 1 Yes (Some people in the past didn't have water.) 2 No (People died from infections and injections didn't start until recently.) 3 Yes (You could get tetanus.) 4 No (It stops us getting a disease.) 5 No (He saw soldiers die from infections, so he studied germs after the war. He died in 1955.) 6 Yes (He was trying to study germs and he noticed a mould that killed them. This was penicillin.)

4 In pairs, talk about the best treatment for the problems in the box.

- Put learners into groups of three. Assign each group two of the illnesses. Tell them to discuss how it can be treated.
- Put together groups that have looked at different illnesses. Tell them to report to the other group. They decide if they agree with the suggested treatment.

Activity Book, page 50

See pages TB126–141.

Ending the lesson

- Put learners into pairs: A and B. Tell learner A they work for a newspaper and B they are Alexander Fleming. Learner A should ask B some questions about the discovery of penicillin, e.g. *Why did you want to study germs?* Learners role play.
  Extension Choose one or two pairs to demonstrate their role play to the class.

Learning outcomes By the end of the lesson, learners will be able to understand strategies for reading effectively and understand vocabulary within a text.

New language *century*

Recycled language vocabulary about medicine and treatment

Materials two pictures (a surgery from the past and a surgery today)

Warm-up

- Put up two pictures: a doctor working in the past and a doctor today. Ask learners to describe the differences.
  Extension Learners label as many parts of the pictures as they can.

Pupil's Book, page 51

Presentation

- Tell learners that sometimes words have close meanings. Write *and / so / but* on the board. Ask what these words do in a sentence. *(they link two parts of a sentence).*
- Write *I felt very ill and …* Ask learners to finish the sentence, e.g. *I had a fever.* Say *When we use 'and' we have two similar ideas.* Repeat with 'so' and 'but,' e.g. *I felt very ill, so I went to bed. We use 'so' to show a result; I felt very ill, but I got up anyway. We use 'but' to show a difference.* Ask how it might help them in an exam. *(To choose the correct word, you have to think about what the word does and also the meaning).*

1 Read the words. What are the differences in meaning?

- Do the first one together, e.g. *study/studio/studied: Two of them are verbs; they mean to do school work. But 'studied' is in the past. 'Studio' is a noun; it's a room where an artist works or a TV programme is made.* Learners work in pairs to find the differences. Check answers with the class.

2 Which words in Activity 1 do you use to talk about …

- Put learners into pairs. Tell them to look at Activity 1 to choose the correct words. Check with the class.

Key: century who doctor

3 Complete the sentences with the words from Activity 1.

- Do the first one together, e.g. *We have two sentences and all the verbs and nouns are there. So we need a word that links them. Which word gives a reason for something? (because)* Read the sentence aloud. Ask if it sounds correct. (*yes*).
- Ask learners to complete the questions in pairs. Monitor and support. Check with the class.

Key: 1 Because 2 Where 3 studied 4 bandage 5 months 6 open

4 Read the text. What is it about?

- Say *Look at the title and the picture. What could it be about?* Ask for ideas, e.g. *a woman called Elizabeth from the past.*
- Say *Don't worry about the gaps. Just read the text quickly to find out.* Learners read for 1 minute. Check ideas.

Key: a famous woman in history (one of the first female doctors)

EXAM TIP! Ask a strong learner to read the exam tip aloud. Say *In Part 4 of the Reading and Writing exam, we read the text quickly. Then we need to choose the correct answer. Then we read one more time to check.*

5 Look at the answers to Activity 4. Are any of the answers wrong? Why / Why not?

- Do the first one together. Ask a learner to read the sentence using the answer given (B). Say *Is it the right kind of meaning? (yes). Yes, we need a verb. Is it the right form of the verb? (no, because after 'to' we need an infinitive.) So what's the correct answer? (A study)*
- Say *In this part of the exam, there are usually two questions that check your grammar and the rest check words.*
- Put learners into pairs to check the other answers.

Key: 1 wrong, A is correct, infinitive with 'to'
2 correct 3 wrong, A is correct, 'doctor' is the only job
4 wrong, B is correct, simple past 5 wrong, C is correct, 'and' is the only conjunction that makes sense here
6 wrong, A is correct, nineteenth goes with 'century' to describe the time period

Activity Book, page 51

See pages TB126–141.

Ending the lesson

- In pairs, learners discuss what they found most difficult.

1 **Read the words.** What are the differences in meaning?

study / studio / studied   doctor / medicine / bandage   who / when / where
and / but / because   century / years / months   open / opened / opening

2 **Which words in Activity 1 do you use to talk about …**

- a period of 100 years?
- a question word about a person?
- a person who tells you what medicine to take when you are ill?

3 **Complete the sentences with the words from Activity 1.**

1 Why did Jim cut his arm? ________ he fell off his bike yesterday.
2 ________ was Fred having a rest? In his bedroom.
3 Last week we ________ the heart and brain in biology.
4 Her coach put a ________ around her leg and then she felt better.
5 Julie started rugby lessons in February and she broke her finger two ________ later in April.
6 I'd like to ________ a hospital for sick animals.

4 **Read the text.** What is it about?

Elizabeth Blackwell

Elizabeth was born in the south-west of England but in 1831 she moved to New York with her family. She started to work as a teacher there. She really wanted to **(1)** ______ medicine so she found some books in a library and read those.

(2) ______ she finally went to study medicine, some men in her college didn't believe that she wanted to study. In 1849 she became the first woman in America to pass all the exams she needed to be a **(3)** ______.

In 1868 she **(4)** ______ a college just for women. A year later she went back to England to teach medicine to women in London. Today, you can read a book about her life **(5)** ______ how she helped many women become doctors in the nineteenth **(6)** ______.

EXAM TIP! Read the text **once** to understand what it's about. Read it **again** to choose the best answer. Then, read it **again** to check your answers.

5 **Look at some answers to Activity 4.** Are any of the answers wrong? Why/Why not?

1	A	study	(B)	studied	C	studio
2	A	Who	(B)	When	C	Where
3	A	doctor	B	medicine	(C)	bandage
4	A	open	B	opened	(C)	opening
5	(A)	but	B	because	C	and
6	A	century	B	months	(C)	years

A2 Key for Schools

1 2.08 **Listen. Who's talking?**

1 two friends
2
3
4
5
6

2 2.09 **Read the instructions and the options A, B and C. What do you think the question is? Listen and check.**

You hear a student talking about a film she watched on TV. What ... ?

A an operation
B a king
(C) a queen

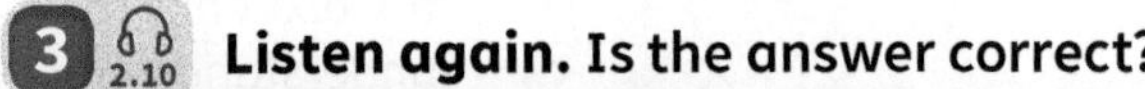

3 2.10 **Listen again. Is the answer correct?**

4 **Read the questions. What are the key words?**

1 Who did the girl watch the film with?
A her mum B her mum and her cousin

2 The film about a magic queen was ...
A a history film. B a cartoon.

3 Which film did the girl want to see?
A the film about an operation B a film about a king

4 Which film did they watch?
A the cartoon B the history film

EXAM TIP! Read the question and options **carefully** before you listen. Think about the situation the person is in and **circle** any **key words**. Then think about similar words you might hear.

5 2.11 **Look again at the questions in Activity 4. Listen and choose the correct answer.**

6 2.12 **Listen and choose the correct answer.**

1 What did the woman buy for her grandson?
A a wallet B a football C a scooter

Learning outcomes By the end of the lesson, learners will be able to understand strategies for listening effectively to find the correct structural words to complete sentences.

New language *the sun goes down, poor*

Recycled language *feel sick, operation, field, club, knee*

Materials pictures (a teacher, children in a playground, a businesswoman in an office, a father and son in a kitchen, a doctor in a hospital, a customer in a shop), phrase cards (Check your homework, Let's play football, I have a meeting, Help clear the table, Take this medicine, How much is it?)

Warm-up

- Put the pictures of different people around the walls of the classroom.
- Put learners into six groups. Say *Let's think about the words people say in different situations.* Give each group a large phrase card with sticky tack. Ask the group to decide which person from the picture they think said the words and to stick the card up on that picture. Learners discuss and stick up the pictures. Check answers.

Pupil's Book, page 52

Presentation

- Say *In Part 4 of the Listening exam, you will hear different people speaking. You need to think about who they are.*

1 2.08 Listen. Who's talking?

- Play the first example from the audio. Show the answer: 1 two friends. Ask how they knew *(they were talking about their first day at school)*. Play the rest of the audio.
- Put learners into pairs to say why they decided on their answers.

See audioscripts on pages TB118–123.

Key: 1 mum and daughter, birthday present
2 farmer, their cows 3 customer (to waiter), food
4 two boys, football 5 teacher (to students), a lunch break

2 2.09 Read the instructions and the options A, B and C. What do you think the question is? Listen and check.

- Tell learners to work in pairs and predict what the question might be. Share ideas but don't confirm. Play the audio.
- Put learners into pairs to compare ideas. Check answers.

See audioscripts on pages TB118–123.

Key: What was the film about?

EXAM TIP! Ask a strong learner to read the exam tip aloud. Say *So in Listening Part 4, you will see some questions with different choices for answers. How many options do you have? (two).* Say *If you read the questions and answers carefully, you can find clues about the person and their situation. This will help you answer.*

3 2.10 Listen again. Is the answer correct?

- Play the audio again. Learners listen again; this time they check if the answer shown in Activity 2 is correct. *(It is!)* Point out that there are distractors in each of the five extracts in this part of the exam, but learners always hear each speaker twice.

4 Read the questions. What are the key words?

- Keep learners in the same pairs. Ask them to underline the key words that give clues. Check their answers.

Key: Sample answers 1 who, watch, with 2 film, magic, cartoon 3 film, girl want to see 4 film, they watch

5 2.11 Look again at the questions in Activity 4. Listen and choose the correct answer.

- Tell learners they shouldn't choose an answer just because they hear the words in the answer. They need to listen carefully and think about the meaning too.
- Play the audio. Put learners into pairs to compare ideas.

Key: 1 B 2 B 3 A 4 A

6 2.12 Listen and choose the correct answer.

- Play the audio. Put learners into pairs to compare ideas. Check answers with the class. *See audioscripts on pages TB118–123.*

Key: B

Activity Book, page 52

See pages TB126–141.

Ending the lesson

- Learners look at the pictures from the Warm-up. Put them into pairs to create a short dialogue for their picture, using the phrase card is in the dialogue. Each pair says their dialogue. The others guess the picture.

Learning outcomes By the end of the lesson, learners will have used language from the unit to talk about illness, medicine and treatments and revised the language and skills.

Recycled language unit language

Materials list of 20 words from Units 1–4, paper and colouring pens

Warm-up

- Make a list of approximately 20 words taken from this unit and units previously studied. Write them onto the board or put them onto a slide.
- Show learners the list and check understanding quickly.
- Now cover the words (with paper or hide the slide). Give learners 1 minute to write down as many words as they can remember. Ask how many each pair have found.
- Check by asking those with the highest number to say the words they have and tick them off.
- Now ask learners to sit face to face, one of them with their back to the board. Cover half the words again but leave half visible. (Stick paper over the board or show a slide with only half the words.)
- Tell each learner who can see the words to give clues to her/his partner who can't see, e.g. a definition / mime / examples, until the partner says the word. Say they can do the words in any order. After 5 minutes, pairs swap positions. Cover the words just done and reveal the second half of the words. Learners repeat the task. This variation on 'hot seat' is to get learners thinking more deeply about the meaning of the words.

  Fast finishers Learners choose five words and write a sentence with each as an example.

Pupil's Book, page 53

1 Choose the correct answer.

- Ask learners to look at the sentences.
- Look at the first sentence together. Ask which answer they think is correct. *(A)*. Ask why. *(The question is in the present perfect and talks about the amount of time the person has felt ill. 'For' shows a duration; 'since' shows the start time. The person started to feel ill when the accident happened).*
- Put learners into pairs. Ask them to complete the sentences.
- Monitor and support. Check answers.

Key: 1 A 2 B 3 A 4 B 5 B

2 ★ Read the diary entry. Choose the correct answer.

- Ask learners to look at the question quickly and see what they have to do. Ask if they can remember the best way to do this kind of question.
- Note their ideas onto the board: *Look at the title and picture to understand the type of text. Read it quickly to get a general idea of what it is about. Read carefully and choose the correct answer. Think about the meaning of the word and a little about grammar. Read again with the answer to check it is correct.*
- Put learners into pairs. They say the correct word.
- Check answers.

Key: 1 B 2 A 3 C 4 B 5 C

3 Choose ten words from this unit. Record the words using the steps below.

- Say to learners *Well done. You've learnt a lot of new language. But once you have learnt something what do you need to do? (revise/review it).*
- Tell learners to look at the flowchart. Ask *What do you think this can help you do? (revise new language).*
- Say *Let's try.* Write the word *medicine* on the board. Ask learners if they can remember what it is. Learners suggest answers. Show them how to use a dictionary to check.
- Look at the next part of the flowchart: 'record its meaning'. Ask learners to decide what they should write in their notebooks, e.g. definition, word class, translation and perhaps an example.
- Say *Now I can show a friend and test them. This helps me learn and my friend learn.*
- Tell learners to choose three words from the unit or from previous units. Tell them to follow the flowchart and check and record the meanings.
- Learners work alone. Monitor and check. Once they have finished, pair learners and ask them to show the meaning of their words to their partner who guesses it.

Mission in action!

- Put learners into the same groups as earlier in the Mission.
- Learners review the questions they asked and what they found out about the emergency services.
- Tell each group to choose one emergency service or a particular topic to present.
- Give out paper and colouring pens. Ask learners to create a presentation about their chosen service/topic.
- Learners work in groups and present their information.

Activity Book, page 53

See pages TB126–141.

Ending the lesson

- **SA** Complete the self-assessment (see Introduction).

1 Choose the correct answer.

1 How long have you felt ill for?
A Since the accident. B For the accident.

2 What's wrong?
A I'm injuring my ankle. B I've injured my ankle.

3 Is your arm broken?
A I don't know. It's been painful since I fell off my bike.
B I don't know. It is painful since I fell off my bike.

4 How long have you had that cut?
A Three days ago. B For three days.

5 How long have you been a patient here?
A Last Tuesday. B Since last Tuesday.

2 ★ Read the diary entry. Choose the correct answer.

15th August

Dear Diary,

Dizzy and I are feeling better now. We're having a special day together tomorrow to celebrate. In the morning I'm (1) ______ Dizzy for a haircut and a bath at the pet shop. I might buy her a new toy too. At 1 pm, (2) ______ meeting Carl and his dog, Floppy. Carl is my best friend and Floppy is Dizzy's best friend! Then, in the afternoon, my (3) ______ driving us to the hills again. We're (4) ______ walking and swimming – but I hope we (5) ______ going to the vet again!

	A		B		C	
1	A	take	B	taking	C	took
2	A	we're	B	we	C	we'll
3	A	aunt	B	aunt are	C	aunt's
4	A	go	B	going	C	to go
5	A	don't	B	not	C	aren't

3 Choose ten words from this unit. Record the words using the steps below.

Find the meaning
→ In this unit / In a dictionary
→ Record its meaning
→ Copy the definition / Write a translation of the word
→ Use it
→ Show the meaning to a friend and ask them to guess the word.

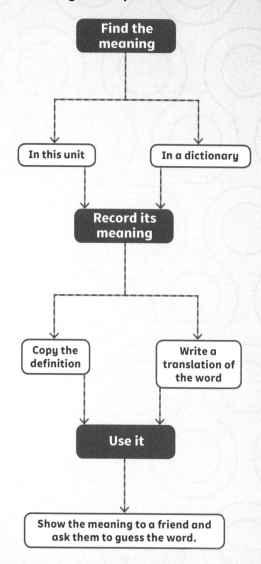

Mission in action!

Present what you have found out about emergency services.

In England, if you call 999, someone will probably answer the phone in five seconds.

5 Fun foods

1 What food can you see? Choose three things that you'd like to eat.

Watch the video. How many chillies does Jim eat?

Mission Take part in a cooking competition

1. Find out about food in different countries.
2. Choose a country and food. Plan how to make it.
3. Present your country and food. Choose a winner.

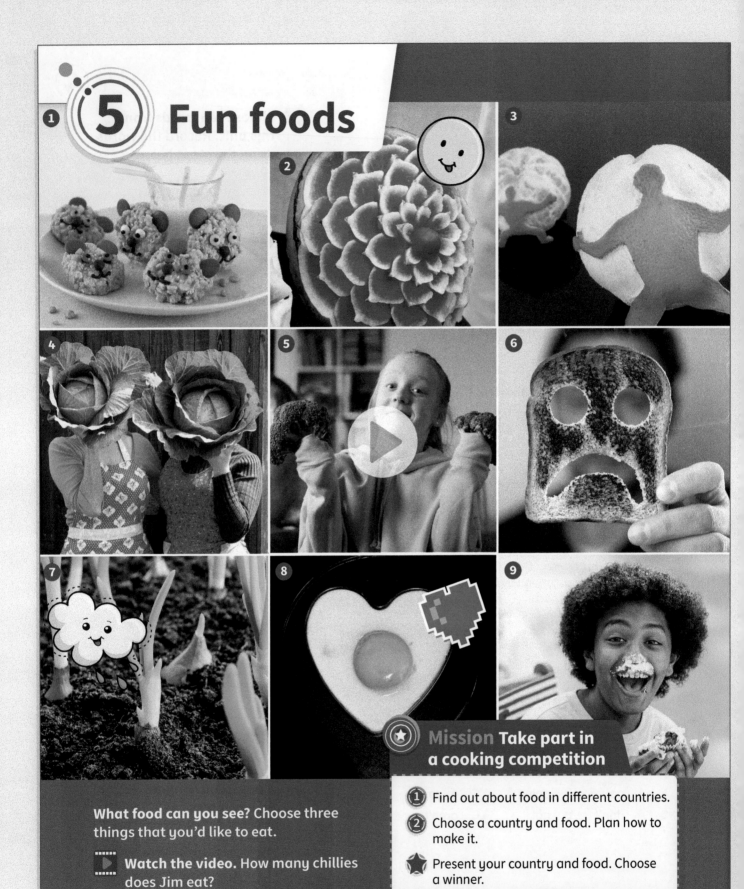

Unit 5 learning outcomes

In Unit 5, learners will learn to:

- use vocabulary to describe food and cooking
- understand and use the past simple passive
- understand and use *prefer* and *would rather*
- read and listen for information
- understand empathy and apologising
- understand the idea of nutrition and food groups

Materials video, pictures of chillies, mushrooms and salmon

Self-assessment

- **SA** Write or project the unit outcomes on the board.
- Ask learners to decide what the key words are in each outcome. Rub out or delete the other words.
- Put learners into pairs. Tell learners to rebuild the unit outcomes using the key words.
- Ask learners to clarify each one in their own words. Tell them to complete their self-assessment (see Introduction).
- Say *Let's learn*.

Pupil's Book, page 54

Warm-up

- Write *food* on the board.
- In pairs, learners tell their partner the food they hate most.

  Fast finishers Learners talk to a new partner. They write down the three foods they which the learners they spoke to dislike the most.

What food can you see? Choose three things that you'd like to eat.

- Say. *What food can you see in the pictures?* Learners work in groups of three and say as many foods as they can in 3 minutes. Point to each picture. Ask the name for each.
- Say the name of each food clearly. Clap the stress for the words with more than one syllable, e.g. *biscuits, cake, orange, cabbage, watermelon, toast, onions, eggs, broccoli*. Learners repeat. Go through each picture again and write the words randomly onto the board.
- Put learners into pairs. Tell pairs to test each other by taking it in turns to say a word. Their partner points to the correct picture.

Watch the video. How many chillies does Jim eat?

- Show learners pictures of chillies, a mushroom and a salmon. Ask the names. Say *chillies* and clap on the stress. Learners repeat. Continue with *mushrooms* and *salmon*.
- Ask *Which one is spicy? (chillies are spicy)*. Say *Yes, spicy food tastes hot*. Ask learners if they know any other foods that are spicy. Learners offer ideas.
- Ask learners how many chillies they think Jim eats in Jenny's vlog.
- Say *Watch and check*.
- Play the video. Check answers.
- Ask if learners can remember the game *Choosing between three strange options!* Tell learners to watch again to find out what the three options are. Play the video.
- Put learners in pairs. Ask them to decide on what the three questions were and answer the questions themselves. *(Options: broccoli as hands or a salmon as a head; mushrooms in your shoes or growing in your hair; eat five cabbages or five chillies.)*

  Extension Learners play the same game with their partner. They decide which one they would choose and why.

Key: Jim eats a small bite of one chilli and then he stops.

 Mission Take part in a cooking competition

- Write on the board: *food/country/competition*.
- Tell leraners to read the Mission statement to match the key word with the correct part of the statement. Check their ideas.
- Say *This is our Mission.*

Activity Book, page 54

See pages TB126–141.

My unit goals

- Go through the unit goals with the learners. (See suggested techniques in 'Identifying outcomes' in Introduction.)
- Go back to these unit goals at the end of each Mission stage during the unit and review them.
- Say *This is our Mission page.*

Ending the lesson

- Play hangman. Write lines on the board to represent the letters of a word. Ask learners to call out letters. If they are correct, write them into the gap where they. If they are not correct, draw a line on a hanging stickman. List the letters covered on the board so learners don't repeat them. Learners try to guess the word before the stickman is complete.
- Tell learners to play hangman in their groups using their favourite foods. Monitor and check.

Learning outcomes By the end of the lesson, learners will be able to use vocabulary to describe foods.

New language *oil, garlic, lamb, herbs, steak, fruit, vegetable, meat*

Recycled language *biscuits, cake, orange, cabbage, watermelon, pancakes, onions, eggs, broccoli, mushrooms, chilli, salmon*

Materials audio, pieces of card/paper or mini-whiteboards

Pupil's Book, page 55

Warm-up

- Give a card (or mini-whiteboard) to each learner. Ask them to write down a food item they like and one they hate – meat, a vegetable or fruit.
- Tell learners to mingle and talk to each other to find out what they like and don't like. Demonstrate how to do it. Write *cabbage* and *carrots*. Show learners your words.
- Say *I like this food because it is sweet and has a nice colour. I hate this food because it is soft when you cook it and I don't like that. It tastes horrible. (You hate cabbage and you like carrots!). Yes. That's right.*
- Learners mingle and talk to other learners. They take it in turns to guess which foods their partner likes or hates.

1 Match the shopping lists (A–C) to the correct shopping baskets below. Then say the food that is in each basket.

- Ask learners to look at the baskets of food. Put them in pairs. Tell them to read the shopping lists A to C. Ask them to match the shopping list with the correct basket.
- Check answers. Read shopping list A. Ask learners which basket it is. Read each item. Learners point. Repeat with B and C.
- Point to each item and ask learners to say the words. Correct pronunciation as necessary.

  Extension Ask learners *Can you see any meat?* Learners point to lamb and steak. Ask *Can you see any vegetables?* Learners point to cabbage, onions, broccoli, mushrooms. Ask *Can you see any fruit? (no).*

Key: A red basket B blue basket C green basket

2 2.13 Listen, point and say the numbers.

- Tell learners to listen to the word and say the number of the food they hear, e.g. say *If I hear oil, which number is it? (11).*
- Play the audio. Learners listen and say the number.

Track 2.13

broccoli, chilli, garlic, herbs, lamb, cabbage, mushroom, oil, onion, salmon, steak

Key: 1 mushroom 2 lamb 3 herbs 4 garlic 5 broccoli 6 salmon 7 chilli 8 steak 9 cabbage 10 onion 11 oil

3  Draw three foods from Activity 1 and hide your pictures. Then guess which food your partner has.

- Give a card (or mini-whiteboard) to each learner. Ask them to draw three food items quickly using the items in Activity 1.
- Tell learners to talk to their partner. Demonstrate how to do it. Use a picture of a cabbage but don't show it to the learners. Say *Ask me questions. I can answer yes or no. Encourage learners to ask questions, e.g. Is it meat? (no). Is it a vegetable? (yes). Is it orange? (no). Is it green? (yes). Is it broccoli? (no). Is it cabbage? (yes!).*
- Learners take turns to ask and answer questions and try to guess what pictures their partner has drawn.

4 Play 'I went to the supermarket and bought … '

- Show learners how to play the game. Start by saying *I went to the supermarket and bought an onion.* Choose a learner and encourage them to repeat your sentence and add a new item. *I went to the supermarket and bought an onion and some salmon.* Repeat with the next learner, e.g. *I went to the supermarket and bought an onion, some salmon and ten mushrooms.*
- Put learners into groups of six or seven to play the game.

  Extension When groups have finished, play the game with the whole class. Support learners if they get stuck.

Activity Book, page 55

See pages TB126–141.

Ending the lesson

- Use a ball. Ask learners to stand in two lines. Ask a learner to throw it to a partner and say *meat, vegetable* or *fruit*.
- The person who catches the ball says a food that fits the category, e.g. for *meat* the learner can say *lamb*. They throw the ball again giving a new category.
- Keep going until the ball has circulated between all the learners.

  Extra support Learners keep a word list in front of them to help them find words.

1 **Match the shopping lists (A–C) to the correct shopping baskets below.** Then say the food that is in each basket.

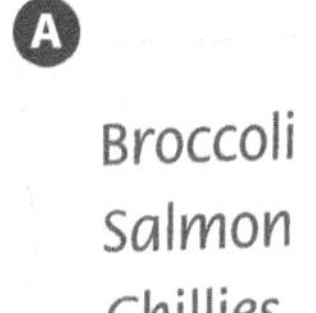

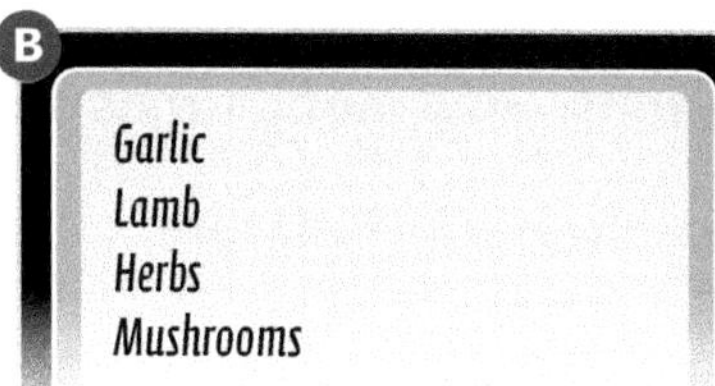

C
Cabbage
Steak
Onions
Oil

2 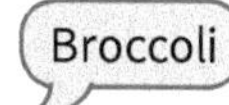 **Listen, point and say the numbers.**

Broccoli

Number 5

3 **Draw three foods from Activity 1 and hide your pictures.** Then guess which food your partner has.

Have you got something green?

Yes, I have.

Is it a vegetable?

Yes, it is.

You've got broccoli!

4 **Play 'I went to the supermarket and bought …'.**

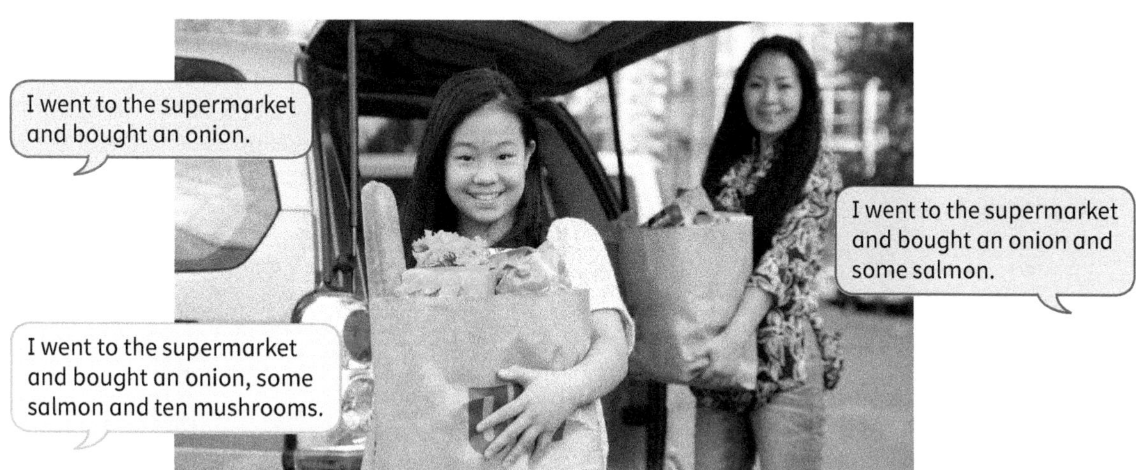

⑤

Language presentation 1

1 **Look at the pictures in Activity 3. Answer the questions.**

- Which food can you see in the pictures?
- What's your favourite vegetable?

2 2.14 **Listen to five conversations. How many times do you hear the word 'broccoli'?**

3 2.15 **Listen again. Choose the correct picture.**

1 What's Claire's favourite dinner? ____

2 What would Mum like to have for dinner? ____

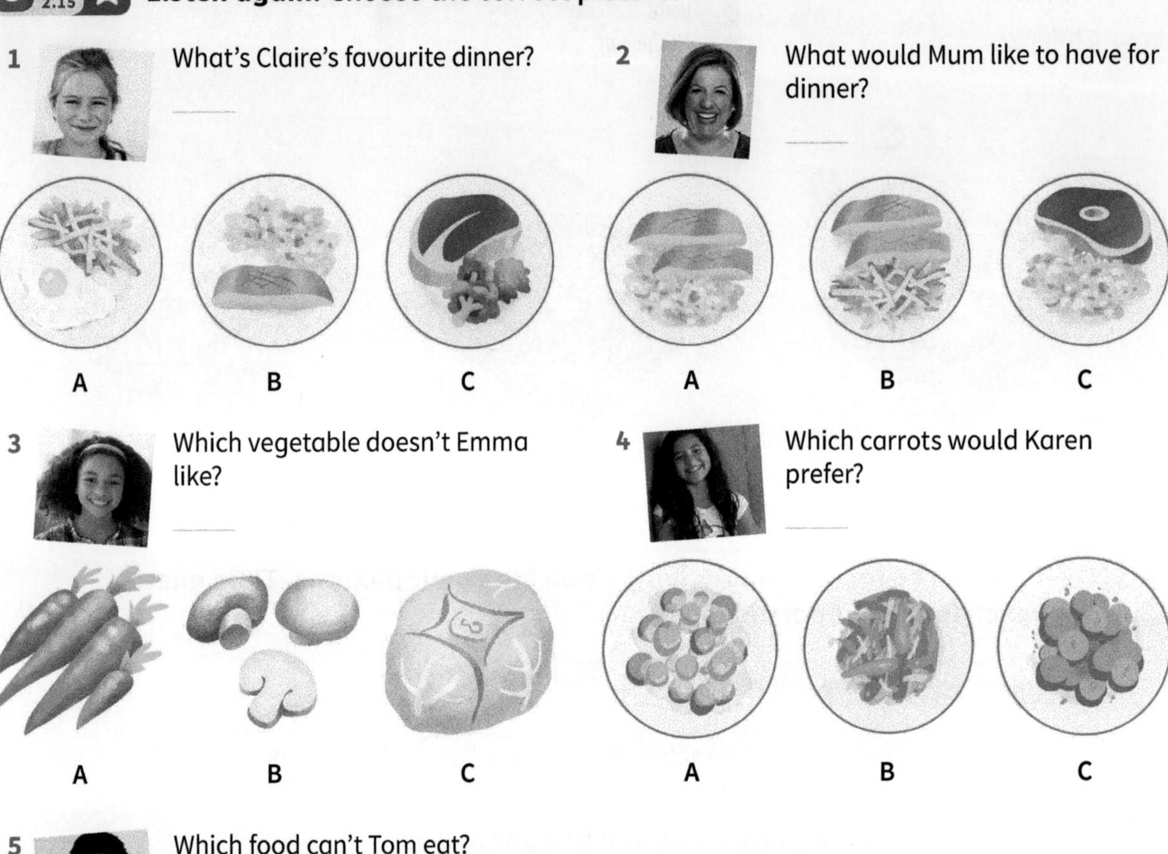

3 Which vegetable doesn't Emma like? ____

4 Which carrots would Karen prefer? ____

5 Which food can't Tom eat? ____

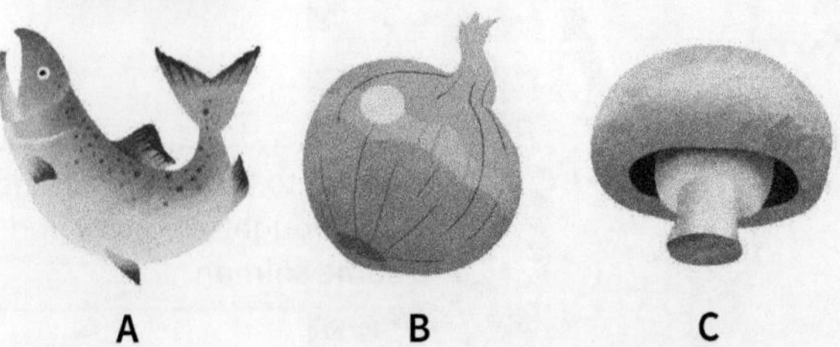

A B C

EXAM TIP! Try to answer as many questions as you can the first time you listen. **Check your answers** and do any missing answers when you listen to it the second time.

4 **Can you solve Claire's problem?** Think of a meal everyone at Claire's party can eat and write a menu.

Learning outcomes By the end of the lesson, learners will be able to listen for specific information and understand preferences in spoken English.

New language *sauce, carrots, would rather* + verb to show preference

Recycled language *oil, garlic, lamb, herbs, steak, fruit, vegetable, meat, broccoli, salmon, chillies, cabbage, onions, mushrooms*

Materials pictures (steak, fish, chicken, lamb, hamburger; chocolate, cake, apples, colae, milk), sticky tack, paper and pencils

Pupil's Book, page 56

Warm-up

- Put learners into groups of three or four.
- Put the food pictures on the board face down so that learners can't see them. Write numbers 1 to 10 under them.
- Tell learners to pick two numbers, one between 1–5 and one between 6–10 and write them down.
- Turn over the food pictures. Say *You need to use the two foods to make a strange meal. For example, if I have fish and chocolate, I'll make a chocolate and chilli sauce to go on the fish. Let's see who can make the most interesting meal.*
- Learners decide how to use their two food items.
- Go around and ask learners to describe their meal. The class votes for the strangest meal idea.

  Extension Ask learners to describe the most unusual food they have eaten and if they liked it or not.

1 Look at the pictures in Activity 3. Answer the questions.

- Put learners into pairs. Tell learners to look at the pictures in Activity 3 and say the names of the food.
- Check their answers. Give the food names for any items they don't know. Ask learners which food they would like to eat the most and the least. Share ideas.

2 2.14 Listen to five conversations. How many times do you hear the word 'broccoli'?

- Say *Let's listen to Claire planning a birthday dinner for her mum. Listen and put up your hand when you hear 'broccoli'.*
- Say *Show me what you'll do. Broccoli!* Learners raise their hands. Play the audio.
- Learners put up their hands when they hear the word.

EXAM TIP! Ask a stronger learner to read the exam tip. Say *If you have a lot of questions to answer, try to do all of them. But if you miss one don't panic. Complete any missing answers when you listen again. And check the ones you have completed if you can.*

See audioscripts on pages TB118–123.

3 2.15 Listen again. Choose the correct picture.

- Look at the pictures 1–5. Tell learners they have to choose the meal discussed by each person as they listen.
- Ask *How many people are there? (five) And how many answers are there to choose from? (three)* Say *So remember there are two answers you don't need but some of the words might be the same so you need to listen carefully.*
- Play the audio again. Learners complete the task.
- Put them into pairs to compare answers. Check answers.

Key: 1 C 2 A 3 C 4 B 5 A

4  Can you solve Claire's problem? Think of a meal everyone at Claire's party can eat and write a menu.

- Tell learners to work in groups of three. They think about the different ideas and what Claire's mum likes. *(healthy food).* Say *What meal would everyone like?*
- Compare ideas.

Activity Book, page 56

See pages TB126–141.

Ending the lesson

- Put learners into groups of six. Give out paper. Ask learners to draw a circle onto the paper. Tell them to draw three straight lines across the circle to create six segments in the circle.
- Learners each write one food item in one of the segments.
- Tell each group to use a pencil as a spinner. They put the pencil on top of the paper and spin it to see where the tip of the pencil points.
- Each learner takes it in turns to spin the pencil. They read the name of the food it lands on. The learner talks about if they like or don't like the food, the last time they ate it and where they ate it. Learners play and talk in groups.

  Fast finishers Learners all spin a second time. When they land on a word their team mates cover it and they see if they can spell it.

Language practice 1

Learning outcomes By the end of the lesson, learners will be able to express preferences using *would rather* and *prefer*.

New language *prefer, rather*

Recycled language food vocabulary

Materials 2 large cards (healthy; unhealthy), sticky tack, Mission worksheets (Teacher's Resource Book page 50).

Pupil's Book, page 57

Warm-up

- Ask learners to stand in the centre of the classroom. Stick up two cards ('healthy' and 'unhealthy') on each side of the room. Tell learners to go to the correct side of the room depending on the food you call out. Say *carrots*. Learners move to the 'healthy' side. Say *cake*. Learners move to the 'unhealthy' side.
- Choose a learner to call out a word. The others move to the correct side. The learner who said the word sits down. Continue until only one learner is left standing. The final learner can choose their own word and point to the answer.

  Fast finishers Choose learners who need extra support first and fast finishers last. Remind them not to repeat words. The last learners have to work harder to find words.

Presentation

- Say *I prefer healthy food. I prefer chicken to steak. And I'd rather have fruit than cake after lunch.* Ask *Do I generally prefer healthy food? Always or just today?* (*always*). Ask *Do I want fruit or cake after lunch? (fruit).* Ask *If I am comparing two things, will I use 'prefer' or 'rather'? (rather).*

Grammar look: *rather* and *prefer*

- Invite a learner to read out the sentences in the left of the **Grammar look** box. In pairs learners choose the correct option for questions 1–6. Check answers.

Key: 1 carrots 2 always 3 salmon 4 at the party 5 prefer 6 rather

1 In pairs, ask and answer the questions. Use your own ideas.

- Show the first sentence and complete it together. Ask learners *Do you prefer steak or salmon?* Learners suggest answers.
- Tell learners to complete the sentences with their own ideas.
- When they have completed their questions, put learners into new pairs. Tell them to ask and answer their questions.
- Ask some pairs to share their questions and answers with the class.

EXAM TIP! Ask a learner to read out the exam tip. Say *When we are speaking it is sometimes difficult to understand questions. In the exam, it can be worrying. But don't worry. Ask the person to repeat what they said.*
Tell learners to listen and repeat. Say *Could you repeat that please?* Learners repeat. Correct pronunciation as necessary. Repeat the sequence with *Pardon* and *I'm sorry. I don't understand.*

2  Choose one question from Activity 1 and ask your class. Draw and write about the results.

- Tell learners to choose one of the questions they wrote in Activity 1. Tell learners they are going to do a survey and find out what the class thinks. Learners choose a question.
- Learners mingle and ask classmates their question. Check they have paper and pen to write the answers. Tell them to think about how to collect answers, e.g. ticks or words so they can count up the choices to tell the class.
- Monitor and support as necessary.
- Tell learners to present their question and the results.

  Complete the Grammar look on page 123.
  See pages TB125–126.

Mission Stage 1

- Ask learners to think about food in different countries. Say *What food is famous in this country?* Learners suggest ideas.
- Put learners in small groups to research and categorise cooking ingredients and food in different countries, depending on where they come from. Give each group a copy of the Mission worksheets (Teacher's Resource Book page 50) Then learners get in pairs with learners of a different group to tell each other what food they have in their maps and talk about what they like the most. *Salmon is eaten in Norway. I prefer Chinese food.*

Activity Book, page 57

See pages TB126–141.

Ending the lesson

- Write up the questions: *Would you rather have a salmon's head or hands made of broccoli? Would you rather grow mushrooms in your socks or in your hair? Would you rather eat five chillies or five cabbages?*
- Put learners into pairs and ask them to answer each question. Now ask each pair to ask their own strange questions. Monitor and check.

Grammar look: *rather* and *prefer*

Karen: 'I prefer carrots to broccoli.'

1 What does Karen like more? **carrots / broccoli**

2 Which of the words could you add to the first sentence? **at the party / always**

Mum: 'I'd rather have salmon.'

3 What would Mum prefer to eat? **salmon / broccoli**

4 Which of the words can you add to Mum's answer? **at the party / always**

Tom: 'I'd prefer to have mushrooms.'

5 Which word is followed by the *to*-infinitive verb form (e.g. *to go, to have, to eat*)? **rather / prefer**

6 Which word is followed by the infinitive verb form without *to* (e.g. *go, have, eat*)? **rather / prefer**

We use *would rather* and *prefer* to say that we want or like one thing more than another thing.

page 123

1 **In pairs, ask and answer the questions.** Use your own ideas.

1 Do you prefer steak or salmon?
2 Do you prefer … or …?
3 For lunch tomorrow, would you prefer to … or …?
4 Do … or …?
5 …, would you …?
6 For dinner tonight, would you rather have broccoli or mushrooms?

2 **Choose one question from Activity 1 and ask your class.** Draw and write about the results.

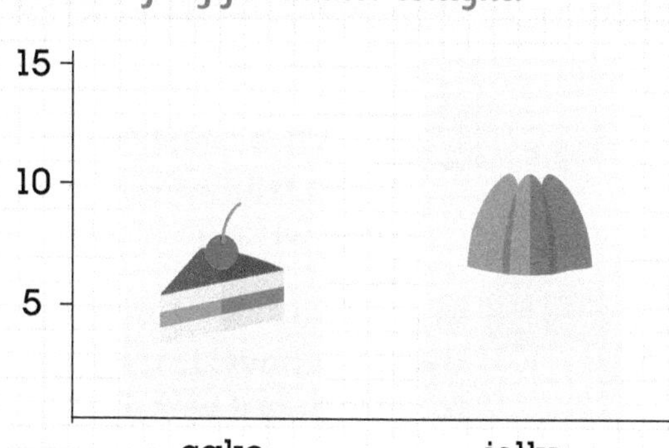

I asked my class: 'Would you prefer cake or jelly for dinner tonight?' 12 people said they'd prefer cake. 15 people said they'd prefer jelly.

EXAM TIP! If you don't understand something remember to use these useful phrases:

Could you repeat that, please?

Pardon?

I'm sorry, I don't understand.

Mission Stage 1

Find out about food in different countries.

⑤

Vocabulary 2

1 **Read Jim's blog quickly. Which ingredients do you need for each dish?**

Jim's Big Blog

From ***roast*** *chicken to* ***boiled*** *potatoes, Jenny and I love food (maybe because our dad's a chef.) Last week we asked three of our dad's friends how to make some awesome dishes. Enjoy!*

How was it made?!?

How was this ice cream sandwich made?

This sandwich wasn't made from bread! It was made from two cookies and some ice cream. It's an awesome dessert.

First, I got a round pot of ice cream and **cut** it into four pieces. Then I put each slice of ice cream onto a big cookie. Finally, I put another cookie on top. It was soooooooooooooo delicious!

(If you REALLY love sugar, you can melt some chocolate in a bowl over a **saucepan** and pour it onto your finished sandwich!)

– LittleLolz

How was this egg made?

Well, I think everyone knows how to **fry** an egg. You just break it and put it into a hot **frying pan** with some oil. This egg was fried like all others. But I used one little trick.

Before I put the egg in the pan, I **sliced** a large onion with a knife. Then, I took the largest ring of the onion and added it to the frying pan. Next, I put the egg into the onion ring to cook. That's how the egg was cooked in a circle. The last thing I did was make sure the egg looked happy!

– CookEggcellent

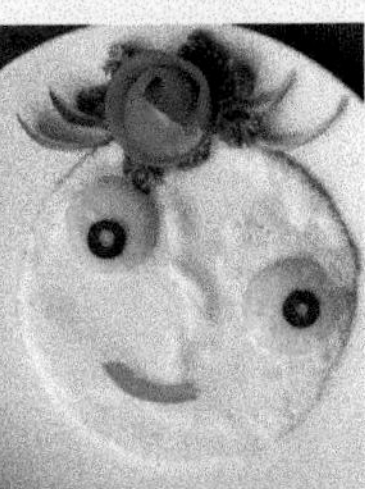

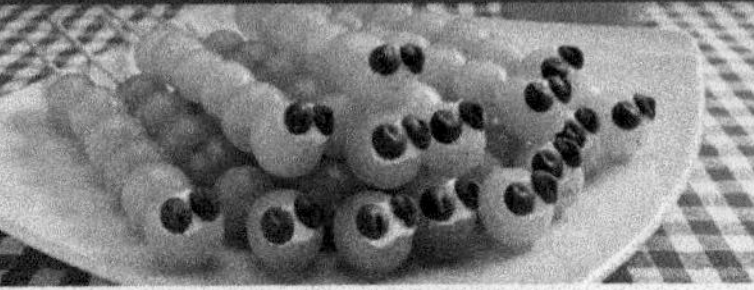

How were these caterpillars made?

Don't worry, these aren't real caterpillars! And they're very easy to make too, so they're perfect if you like healthy snacks.

To make a caterpillar, first, put six grapes on a stick and add eyes. Then, put the caterpillars in a **dish** in the freezer. I waited for about an hour (I put on the **kettle** and made myself a cup of tea) and the caterpillars were ready!

I took the caterpillars to a picnic and my friends said they were delicious. In fact, they were so popular that they were finished before I tried one!

– Pocco911

2 **Match the pictures to the words in bold in the blog.**

Number 1 is 'slice'.

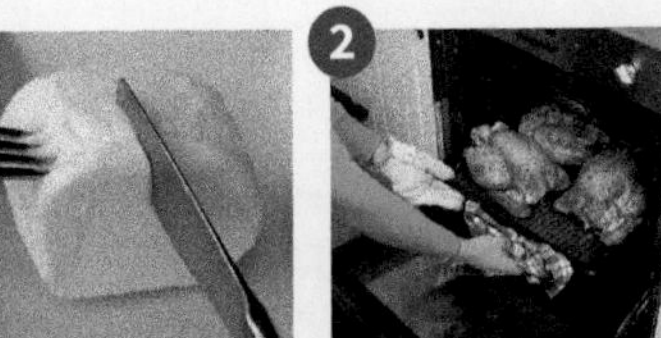

1 2 3

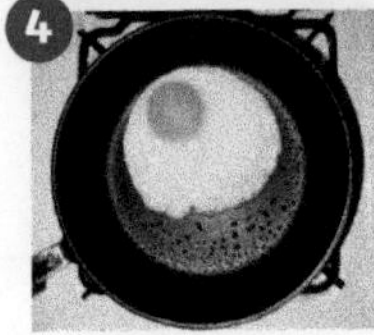

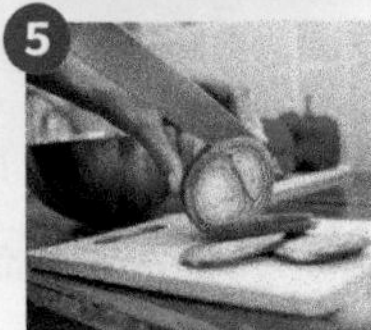

4 5 6 7 8 9

3  2.16 **What are the answers to the riddles?** Listen. Then write your own.

4  **Choose one of the dishes from the text above. Draw pictures to show how it was made.**

Learning outcomes By the end of the lesson, learners will be able to read to understand specific information.

New language *roast, boiled, slice, melt, pour, fry, break, cut, cook, knife, frying pan, kettle, dish*

Recycled language food vocabulary

Materials audio, pictures (a chef, spaghetti Bolognese, roast chicken, hamburger and chips, ice cream sundae), sticky tack, word cards (minced meat, tomato sauce, spaghetti, chicken, oil, bread roll, burger, meat, salad, potatoes, ice cream, fruit sauce)

Pupil's Book, page 58

Warm-up

- Show pictures of well-known foods, e.g. spaghetti Bolognese, roast chicken, hamburger and chips, ice cream sundae. Put up a picture of a chef, e.g. wearing a chef's hat. Write the key ingredients on cards (minced meat, tomato sauce, spaghetti, chicken, oil, bread roll, burger meat, salad, potatoes, ice cream, fruit sauce).
- Point to the picture of the chef. Ask *What's his job? (chef).* Learners repeat. Say *Here are some famous dishes. What are they?* Write the names under the pictures.
- Ask *What is an ingredient? (the food used to make a dish).*
- Put learnersv in pairs to choose a runner and a writer. Put the ingredient cards out on a table at the front of the room. The runner goes back and forward, reading each ingredient then whispering to his/her partner to write down.
- Once pairs have collected all 11 ingredients, they list them under the correct dish. The pair who finish first and have written the ingredients under the correct dish win.

  Fast finishers Learners try to describe how the dishes are made.

1 Read Jim's blog quickly. Which ingredients do you need for each dish?

- Ask learners to look at the blog text on page 58. Ask *What is the blog about? Read the title*. Learners suggest ideas. (*it describes how to make different dishes).*
- Learners read the questions above each section and decide which ingredients are needed for each dish in pairs.
- Ask the learners to read the blog again and find out if they were correct. Ask *Will you read carefully or quickly? (quickly).*
- Learners compare answers in pairs. Check answers.

Key: 1 ice cream, cookies, (optional sugar) 2 egg, onion 3 grapes

2 Match the pictures to the words in bold in the blog.

- Tell learners to look at the pictures. Do the first one together as an example. *(slice)*. Learners read the text again to try to understand the words better in pairs.
- Check answers. As you do this check learners understand each item, e.g. *slice:* mime the action.
- Ask learners to repeat each word.

Key: 1 slice 2 roast 3 boiled 4 fry 5 cut 6 saucepan 7 dish 8 kettle 9 frying pan

3 2.16 What are the answers to the riddles? Then write your own.

- Ask learners to listen to some riddles. Play the first riddle and pause the audio. Ask learners if they know the answer. Learners guess. Play the answer.
- Now tell learners to listen to the other riddles and give the answer. Play the audio pausing between each one so learners can guess. Learners listen and give their ideas.
- Put learners into groups of three. Ask them to write their own riddles. Monitor and support.
- Once they have finished, ask learners to read out their riddles. The rest of the class try to guess the answer. (If you have a large class put the learners into groups of six to eight to work in groups.)

See audioscripts on pages TB118–123.

Key: 1 a knife 2 a frying pan 3 a dish 4 a saucepan 5 a kettle

4 Choose one of the dishes from the text above. Draw pictures to show how it was made.

- Put learners into groups of three. Learners choose a dish, read the text again carefully and draw and label pictures showing how the dish was made.
- Regroup learners to work with learners who did a different recipe. Learners explain their recipe to the group.

Activity Book, page 58

See pages TB126–141.

Ending the lesson

- Put learners into groups of four. Show the pictures from the Warm-up again. Ask each learner to choose one of the dishes and describe how they think it is made. The other learners guess the dish. Monitor and support.

5 Language practice 2

Learning outcomes By the end of the lesson, learners will be able to use past simple passive accurately.

New language past simple passive

Recycled language food vocabulary, verbs for cooking, nouns for cooking equipment

Materials paper and colouring pens

Warm-up

- Tell learners about a sandwich filling you like, e.g *ham with salad*. Ask them to think of the most interesting filling they can, e.g. *banana and chocolate spread*.
- Learners sketch and label their sandwich with colouring pens.
- Put learners into groups of six. Each learner shows their sandwich. The group votes for their favourite. They can't vote for their own sandwich. The winner from each group comes to the front and describes their sandwich to the class. Learners vote for their favourite.

Pupil's Book, page 59

Presentation

- Use the winning sandwich recipe from the Warm-up. E.g. *A banana and chocolate spread sandwich.* Say *The banana was cut into slices. It was put in the bread and then chocolate spread was added.*
- Ask learners *Do we know who made the sandwich? (no). So what kind of sentences did I use to describe making it? (passive).*

Grammar look: the passive (past simple)

- Learners read the sentences in the left of the **Grammar look** box then choose the correct option in each question 1–3 in pairs. Check answers.

  Fast finishers Tell learners to copy the sentences changing them to active sentences and using 'I', e.g. *I didn't make the sandwich from bread …*

Key: 1 They're passive. 2 the past 3 was or wasn't + past participle (e.g. made, written, had)

Complete the Grammar look on page 124.
See pages TB125–126.

1 2.17 PRONUNCIATION Listen and repeat.

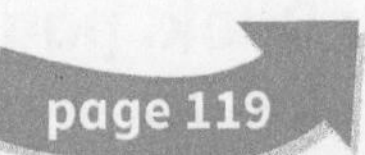

- Say *Let's listen and say the words.* Play the audio. Learners repeat. Correct if necessary.
- Say *Listen to the ends of the words. Cooked, fried. Can you hear any difference?* Learners suggest ideas. *(cooked has a /t/ sound, but fried has a /d/ sound)*. Say *melted. What is the sound at the end?* Learners suggest ideas. *(it has an /ɪd/ sound).*

Track 2.17
That's how the egg was cooked in a circle!
This egg was fried.
They were finished before I tried one.

- Learners go to page 119 to complete the Unit 5 Activity (see page TB124).

2 How were the chocolate dishes made? Write a sentence for each picture (1–8).

- Point to the final picture. Say *What kind of bowl is the fruit in? (a chocolate one).* Ask *What did the chef use to make the bowls? (balloons).*
- Tell learners to complete the sentences in pairs.

Key: 1 Some chocolate was melted in a bowl over a saucepan. 2 Chocolate circles were made on a plate. 3 Some balloons were filled with air. 4 The balloons were dipped into the chocolate. 5 The balloons were placed on the chocolate circles. 6 The balloons were left until they were hard. 7 Holes were made in the balloons. 8 The chocolate dishes were filled with fruit.

3 Cover the sentences in Activity 2. Try to remember each one.

- Put learners into pairs. Tell them to cover each sentence but use the pictures to help them say the sentences.

  Extra support Learners can use the original question stems to help them reform the sentences.

Mission Stage 2

- Put learners into the same groups as Mission Stage 1.
- Tell them to decide on a famous dish from one country.
- Ask them to draw the stages and make sentences using passive forms. Give out paper and colouring pens to create a recipe poster showing how to make the dish.
- When they finish, collect the posters for the final stage.

Activity Book, page 59

See pages TB126–141.

Ending the lesson

- Put learners into groups of four. Each learner describes what they have eaten that day. Each group decide who has eaten the healthiest food and why. Share ideas.
- **SA** Ask learners to complete their self-assessment (see Introduction).

Grammar look: the passive (past simple)

'This sandwich wasn't made from bread. It was made from two cookies and some ice cream.'

1 Are the sentences active or passive? **active** / **passive**
2 When is the sentence talking about? **the past** / **the present**
3 How is the passive made (in the past simple)?
was **or** ***wasn't*** **+ past participle** (e.g. *made, written, had*) /
was **or** ***wasn't*** **+ infinitive** (e.g. *to make, to write, to have*)

We use the passive when we don't know who does something or when it isn't important who does it.

page 123

1 2.17 PRONUNCIATION **Listen and repeat.** page 119

2 **How were the chocolate dishes made? Write a sentence for each picture (1–8).**

1 
Some chocolate | melt | in a bowl over a saucepan

2 
Chocolate circles | make | on a tray

3 
Some balloons | fill | with air

4 
The balloons | dip | into chocolate

5 
The balloons | put | on the chocolate circles

6 
The balloons | leave | until they were hard

7 
Holes | made | in the balloons

8 
The chocolate dishes | fill | with fruit

3 **Cover the sentences in Activity 2. Try to remember each one.**

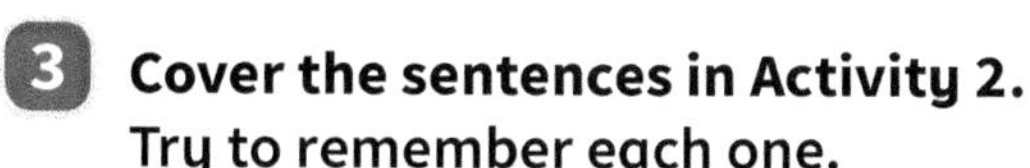
Some chocolate was melted in a bowl!

Mission Stage 2

Choose a country and food. Plan how to make it.

Pizza * Cheese *
Tomato * Olive

Literature

1 **Have you read any diaries? What did you think of them? Do you write, or would you like to write, a diary of your own?**

2.19

The very, very interesting diary of Juana Sánchez

Monday

My parents think the show is brilliant. It's the only thing they talk about. 'Oh, Juana,' Mum said at breakfast. 'Your brother's got 63,000 subscribers to his channel!' 'Oh, Juana,' Dad said at dinner. 'Your brother's going to be world famous.' 'My last video was watched 1,000,000 times, Juana,' Carlos said. 'Have you seen the show yet?' No, I haven't. I'd rather clean my granddad's shoes with an old toothbrush.

The show's on YouTube. It's the only thing he talks about. 'Oh, Juana,' he said after dinner when I was washing up his dirty plate. 'I made chilli today. My fans loved it!'

Wednesday

Before dinner, I asked Carlos to help me lay the table. 'Well, Juana,' he said, 'I'm an Internet star now, you know, and I haven't got time to lay the table. I've got my next show to think about.'

I'm going to ask Mum if we can change him for a cat.

Learning outcomes By the end of the lesson, learners will be able to read a diary entry and understand empathy and apologising.
New language *worms, show, fan, views*
Recycled language food vocabulary, verbs describing cooking, *would rather*
Materials audio, 10 squares of paper for each pair of learners

Warm-up

- Put learners into pairs. Give each pair ten squares of paper. Tell them you will dictate some words and they need to write one word per square. They can take it in turns to write.
- Say *frying pan, roast, apple, lamb, cake, steak, banana, ice cream, pour, kettle.*
- Put pairs into fours and ask them to check their spelling.
- Now ask the learners to put the words in alphabetical order as quickly as possible. The first to finish will be the winners.
- Learners group the words. Check which pair is quickest. *(apple, banana, cake, frying pan, ice cream, kettle, lamb, pour, roast, steak).*
- Now ask learners to find any words that are food. *(apple, banana, cake, ice cream, lamb, steak).*
- Ask learners to find any words that are equipment. *(frying pan, kettle).*
- Ask learners to find any words that are ways of cooking. *(roast, pour).*
- Check which pair is quickest in each case.
- Finally tell learners to turn over the papers and see if they can remember the ten words.

Pupil's Book, page 60

1 Have you read any diaries? What did you think of them? Do you write, or would you like to write, a diary of your own?

- Ask learners to look at the text on pages 60–61. Ask them what kind of text it is. *(a diary).*
- Put learners into pairs. Ask learners if they have ever read any diaries and what they thought about them.
- Learners share their ideas.
- Ask if they have written or would like to write a diary of their own. Learners discuss.

Presentation

- Ask learners to look at the pictures on pages 60–61. Ask them to guess what is in Juana's diary. Learners suggest ideas.
- Point to the picture of a worm and ask what it is. Learners suggest answers. Say *worm.* Learners repeat.
- Point to the picture of Carlos. Say *Carlos is Juana's brother. What do you think he does on YouTube? (presents a cooking programme).* Say *Yes, he presents a cookery show.* Say *show.* Learners repeat.
- Tell learners *Carlos has lots of fans. People who like him.* Say *fans.* Learners repeat.
- Ask how you can understand if something is popular on YouTube. *(from the number of views).* Tell learners views are when people watch your programme. Say *views.* Learners repeat.

2.19 The very, very interesting diary of Juana Sánchez

- Tell learners they will read and listen to the first part of the story. Ask *What do Juana and Carlos's mum and dad think about his show? What does Carlos think? What does Juana think? How do we know?*
- Tell learners to read and listen to the diary entries for Monday and Wednesday. Play the audio for Monday and Wednesday then stop.
- Put learners into pairs and ask them to compare their ideas.
- Check answers. *(his mum and dad think it is brilliant because he has 63,000 fans; Carlos is proud because his last video was watched a million times; Juana is annoyed because she says she would rather clean her grandad's shoes with a toothbrush).*
- Put learners into pairs. Tell them to look at the pictures. Ask *What do you think happens when Carlos does his cookery show?* Learners predict. Tell them to listen and check.
- Play the rest of the audio while learners read.
- Check answers. *(Carlos does his show but it goes wrong because Juana has put worms in the pot instead of spaghetti).*
- Put learners into groups of five. Ask each learner to read the diary entry for one day. Assign one person to Monday, one to Wednesday, one to Friday and Saturday and one to Sunday.
- Tell each learner to read the entry for that day in detail.
- Learners close their books and try to remember what happened on the day of their diary entry. They retell the story.

  Extension Choose a confident group to retell the story to the class.

Activity Book, page 60

See pages TB126–141.

Ending the lesson

- Put learners into small groups.
- Ask if they watch cookery shows on TV or the Internet and if they like them. Why or why not?
- Learners discuss and share ideas.

Learning outcomes By the end of the lesson, learners will have read a diary entry and understood empathy and apologising.

New language *apologise, empathy, play a trick*

Recycled language *worms, show, fan, views*, food vocabulary, verbs describing cooking, *would rather*

Materials access to the Internet if possible

Social and Emotional Skill: apologising and empathy

- After reading the diary entry, point out that when there's a problem, it is good to talk and try to understand how the other person feels. If you can feel empathy towards that person, it is easier to talk to them.
- In groups of four, learners make an empathy poster. They think of four situations and then the best thing to say to a person to show empathy. It can be things like not being invited to the cinema or someone being rude to someone. They can illustrate their work. Each group presents their poster to the class.

Warm-up

- Put learners into groups of three or four. Ask if they watch YouTube, what kind of show or videos they watch and if they have a favourite personality on YouTube.
- Learners discuss in groups. Ask them what makes people good YouTube personalities, e.g. *being funny*.
- Share ideas. If possible, invite learners to show the clips they like best and explain why.

Pupil's Book, page 61

Presentation

- Ask learners to read the diary entries again. Write on the board: *63,000, 1,000,000, 4*. Ask learners what the numbers show.
- Learners work in pairs. Check answers. *(63,000 – people who follow Carlos on YouTube; 1,000,000 – views for his last video; 4 – the age Juana thinks Carlos behaves on the day of his show).*
- Keep learners in the same pairs. Ask learners to talk about why Juana was annoyed with Carlos.
- Ask learners if Juana is right to feel annoyed. Share their ideas.
- Now ask learners to think about why Carlos might feel upset and if he's right to feel upset. Learners discuss.
- Ask them to share their ideas. *(he has a lot of fans and his show didn't go well because of the worms).*

2 In pairs, role play a conversation. Imagine you are Juana and Carlos.

- Tell learners that when they have a problem it is good to talk about it and try to understand the other person's feelings.
- Write *empathy* on the board. Say *Empathy is when we try to … (understand how other people feel).*
- Put learners into pairs and ask *How can we show empathy to people?* Learners discuss in pairs.
- Share answers, e.g. *We can say things like 'I understand'; we can ask if we can help.*
- Ask *How can we tell someone about our feelings?* Learners suggest ideas. Say *We can explain how we feel. We can say 'I'm angry with you because …'* Say *I'm angry because …* Learners repeat.
- Ask *How can we apologise?* Learners suggest ideas. Say *We can say 'I'm very sorry, but …'* Say *I'm very sorry, but …* Learners repeat.
- Put learners into pairs. Tell them they are going to role play what happened after the show.
- Give each learner a role: Carlos or Juana.
- Ask them to read the information about their role in Activity 2. Learners work in pairs and role play. Monitor and support.
- Choose some confident learners to perform their dialogue for the class.
- Ask learners to think about a time they argued with someone or someone upset them. Ask if they can understand how the other person felt.

Activity Book, page 61

See pages TB126–141.

Ending the lesson

- Write on the board: *I feel happy when … ; I feel sad when … ; I feel angry when …* Tell learners to think about each phrase and how to finish the sentences. Ask them to draw pictures that represent their sentence endings.
- Put learners into groups of three and ask them to show their pictures. Their partners guess what the pictures represent. When they have guessed the endings, ask learners to find out if they have anything in common or if all their answers are different.

  Fast finishers Learners complete additional sentences with feelings from the text, e.g. *I am sorry when …*

Friday

I was tired after school and wanted to relax on the sofa, but Carlos kept talking about his next show. 'On Sunday morning I'm going to do my new recipe for spaghetti bolognese. All I need is ... .' The only way I could get him to stop talking was to say, 'Carlos, on Sunday, I'm going to watch your show.'

Saturday

I had to help Dad in the garden this morning. I hate gardening. There are worms everywhere – long, thin worms. I don't like worms, but they gave me an idea ...

Sunday

Carlos was like a four-year-old at a birthday party today. 'I'm so happy you're going to watch my show,' he said. 'I've got everything ready – the onions, the garlic, the herbs, the spaghetti. Now, time for my shower.' Carlos always has a shower before his shows. 'I must look my best for my fans!' he says. When he was in the bathroom, I went into the kitchen, took the spaghetti out of the pot, and put something else in.

'Right, let's go!' said Carlos when he came back into the kitchen. 'Mum and Dad usually turn the camera on for me, Juana, but you can do it today. Are you ready? Let me get in position. OK. Press the button ... now. Good morning, friends!. Today I'm going to show you how to make spaghetti bolognese. Now, in this pot I've already put the ... worms! Arghhhhhhhhhhhhh!'

OK, it wasn't the nicest thing to do. But more people have watched this video than any of his other ones! And I'm sure he'll talk to me again – one day.

2 **In pairs, role play a conversation. Imagine you are Juana and Carlos.**

STUDENT A You are Carlos. You are very angry with Juana. You don't understand why she played a trick on you.

STUDENT B You are Juana. You want to say sorry to Carlos. You know you did the wrong thing, but you'd like him to understand that he shouldn't talk about himself all the time and that he should ask other people about their interests.

I'm very angry with you, Juana. My show is very important to me. Why did you put worms in my pot?

I'm very sorry, Carlos. But why do you talk about your show all the time?

Cross-curricular

1 **Read the text and look at the photos. What food groups do the foods belong to? Which nutrients do they give us? Use the words in the boxes.**

Food groups: grains, cereals and potatoes | meat, fish, nuts and beans | dairy | fruits and vegetables | fats and oils

Nutrients: calcium | vitamins and minerals | fats | proteins | carbohydrates

Superfoods?

It's important to eat a balanced diet and different foods give us different nutrients. Proteins make our muscles strong. Calcium is good for our teeth and bones and carbohydrates give us energy to exercise and play in the day.

Some foods have more nutrients than others but does this make them superfoods? Most doctors think that we shouldn't call them 'superfoods' but 'super diets' – this means we should eat a healthy, balanced diet with lots of fruit, vegetables and wholegrain foods.

Here are some foods that aren't super, but have lots of vitamins that are very good for you:

Blueberries have got vitamins K and C in them as well as other nutrients. Some people think that blueberries can protect us from heart problems and improve our memory. Try adding them to your breakfast cereal or have them for a snack.

Blueberries

Oily fish like salmon or sardines have got vitamin D, protein and some B vitamins. Oily fish has also got good fat in it. If you eat oily fish two or more times a week it keeps your eyes and your bones healthy.

Oily fish

Broccoli has got lots of vitamins, calcium and fibre in it! It's a vegetable that you can eat in salads, soups and with meat and fish.

Broccoli

Some people think that dark chocolate is good for us, but like any food, you shouldn't eat lots of it. A little bit of dark chocolate is better than milk chocolate, but if you eat it too much, it's an unhealthy choice.

Chocolate

2 2.20 **Listen and read the text again.** Match the sentence halves.

1 Proteins are good for
2 Calcium is good for
3 We should eat
4 Blueberries have got
5 Oily fish
6 Broccoli
7 You shouldn't eat

A has got vitamin D in it.
B has lots of fibre in it.
C too much chocolate.
D vitamin K in them.
E a healthy balanced diet.
F your teeth and bones.
G your muscles.

3 **In pairs, talk about food you prefer.** Do you eat any 'superfoods'?

I'd rather eat cereal for breakfast than toast.

I prefer blueberries to strawberries.

Learning outcomes By the end of the lesson, learners will be able to respond to a text using critical thinking and emotional intelligence and understand nutrition and food groups.

New language *grains, cereals, dairy, calcium, vitamins and minerals, fats, proteins, carbohydrates*

Recycled language *balanced diet*, food vocabulary, *prefer*

Materials 6 pictures (a field of wheat, a plate of beef, a bowl of nuts, some milk, cabbage and butter)

Warm-up

- Draw a large bar chart on the board with the categories 'meat' 'dairy' 'vegetables' 'fruit' on the bottom axis.
- Show learners four sticky notes with the words *chicken, strawberries, butter* and *carrots* on them. Say *Where shall I put these on the chart?* Learners suggest answers. Stick 'chicken' on the axis above 'meat', 'strawberries' above 'fruit', 'butter' above 'dairy' and 'carrots' above vegetables.
- Check learners understand the categories. Say *We're going to build up the bars on the chart. Let's think of examples for each food category and see which one has the most.* Ask learners to predict which category they think they will find the most examples for.
- Give out sticky notes. Tell each learner they need to write at least one word and add it to the correct 'bar' of the chart. Learners write words on the sticky notes and come up and stick them onto the board in the correct category.
- Monitor and check.
- Review and see which 'bar' on the chart has the most examples. See if the learners predicted correctly.

  Fast finishers can add more than one sticky note.

Pupil's Book, page 62

Presentation

- Put some pictures on the board of a field of wheat, a plate of beef, a bowl of nuts, some milk, cabbage and butter.
- Write on the board: *cereals, nuts, fats, vegetables, dairy, meat.*
- Put learners into pairs and tell them to match the food to the category. Check answers.
- Explain foods fit into different categories and each category gives us different nutrients. Ask what nutrients do for us. *(help our bodies to work)*. Say *nutrients.* Learners repeat.

1 Read the text and look at the photos. What food groups do the foods belong to? Which nutrients do they give us? Use the words in the boxes.

- Ask learners to read the food groups and nutrients in the boxes. Tell them to look at the pictures and predict which food group they belong to and which nutrients they give us. Learners suggest answers, then read the text to check their ideas.
- Put learners into pairs to compare answers. Check answers.
- Learners discuss which of the superfoods they like.

  Fast finishers Learners try to add an additional food to each food category.

Key: tomatoes: fruits and vegetables, vitamins and minerals
avocado: fruits and vegetables, proteins
nuts: nuts and beans, fats
spinach: fruits and vegetables, vitamins and minerals
bread: grains, carbohydrates cheese: dairy, calcium

2 2.20 Listen and read the text again. Match the sentence halves.

- Ask learners to read the sentences and think about which ending fits with the beginning of each sentence 1–7.
- Tell learners to read the text again carefully and match the sentence halves. Put learners into pairs to compare answers. Check answers with the class.

Key: 1 G 2 F 3 E 4 D 5 A 6 B 7 C

3 In pairs, talk about the food you prefer eating. Do you eat any 'superfoods'?

- Ask learners to work in pairs and discuss which foods they usually eat and which of the superfoods they prefer eating.
- Their partner should give them advice on what they could do to improve their diet or make it more balanced.

Activity Book, page 62

See pages TB126–141.

Ending the lesson

- Put learners into groups of three to five. Ask them what we have learnt about healthy eating. Learners discuss.
- Share ideas. Draw out the idea of a balanced diet. Ask if it is OK to eat small amounts of foods like chocolate.
- Tell learners to design a 'superfood' dinner. Tell them to think of each nutrient and decide what to include on the menu to provide each one.
- Learners work in groups. Monitor and support.
- Groups share their ideas. The class says whether they would like each dinner or not.

Learning outcomes By the end of the lesson, learners will be able to listen and read to find key words and read using critical thinking skills (analysis, application, creative thinking).

Recycled language vocabulary related to food and cooking

Materials word cards (one per learner)

Warm-up

- Create pairs of word cards in advance for each pair of learners.
- Give out the cards randomly, one per learner. Tell learners they need to find a partner with a synonym – a word that means the same or nearly the same as their word. Ask learners what a synonym is. *(a word with the same meaning as another word).*
- Learners mingle, saying their word until they find their partner, then stand with them. Monitor and support.
- Once all the learners have found their partner, ask them to stand in a circle next to their partner. Each pair reads out their words. Other learners decide if it is a match.

  Alternative To make the task easier make sure each pair of word cards is a different colour, e.g. blue and red, so that learners only have to look for people with a different colour.

  Word pairs: come/arrive, steal/rob, injure/hurt, fast/quick, happy/pleased, horrible/terrible, sad/unhappy, afraid/frightened, like/love, good/excellent, speak/talk, look/see, nobody/no-one, noisy/loud.

Pupil's Book, page 63

1 Read and answer the questions.

- Learners look at the pictures on page 63 in pairs and guess where the food might be cooked. Learners discuss.
- In the same pairs, learners read and discuss the questions.
- Share their ideas.

Key: Sample answer 1 You can visit new places and learn how to cook local dishes.

2 Read the questions. Think of some places Tim visited.

- Ask *Why is it important to listen to the instructions? (because it tells us about the situation, the topic and people that we will hear and that helps us understand. It also helps us to understand exactly what to do).*
- Learners read the rubric and brainstorm eight places Tim visited.
- In pairs, learners predict eight places they think Tim might visit. Ask some pairs to share their ideas with the class.

3 2.21 Listen to the conversation. Write two places you hear for each day.

- Remind learners of the instruction they read: *What day did he visit the places?* Ask what two pieces of information they need to find. *(the days and the places).* Ask learners what key words they might need to listen for so they can answer the question. *(days of the week, names of places).*
- Ask learners to read and listen to the example.
- Play the audio.
- Learners choose the key words in the answer in pairs. Check answers.

See audioscripts on pages TB118–123.

Key: 1 Tuesday – hotel, apartment 2 Wednesday – castle, Museum of Food and Drink 3 Thursday – TV studio, Town Hall 4 Friday – train station, famous park 5 Saturday – a café, a farm

EXAM TIP! Ask a strong learner to read the exam tip. Say *Sometimes you will hear different words from the ones written down, but they have the same meaning. So it is good to think of similar words when you look at the questions.*

4 2.22 Listen again and choose the correct place.

- Repeat previous audio. Check answers with the class.

Key: 1 A 2 D 3 F 4 G 5 H

Activity Book, page 63

See pages TB126–141.

Ending the lesson

- Show learners a map of the world. Put this up on the board or project a map. Put learners in groups of four and tell them they are going to plan a tour. Tell them it can be a cookery tour or a different type of tour, e.g. a sports tour or a tour of famous trains.
- Tell learners to decide on the type of tour they want to do. Once they have decided they should decide on where they want to go. They can visit four countries. They choose a route, making sure they have a reason for visiting each place.
- Learners plan their tour topic and routes in their groups. If possible they can look for information on the Internet to get additional information.

  Extension Choose one or two groups to present their route and the reason they chose it.

1 **Read and answer the questions.**

1 What can you do on a cooking tour?

2 Would you like to go on one? Why/Why not?

2 **Read the question.** Think of some places Tim may have visited.

You will hear Tim talking to a friend about a cooking tour with his dad. What day did he visit the places?

Where did Tim go?
The museum.
A shopping centre.

3 2.21 **Listen to the conversation.** Write two places you hear for each day.

1 Tuesday ______ ______
2 Wednesday ______ ______
3 Thursday ______ ______
4 Friday ______ ______
5 Saturday ______ ______

4 2.22 **Listen again and choose the correct answer.**

Days

1 Tuesday ______
2 Wednesday ______
3 Thursday ______
4 Friday ______
5 Saturday ______

Places

A apartment
B train station
C café
D museum
E TV studio
F town hall
G park
H farm

EXAM TIP!
Remember, sometimes you hear **two options**. Listen carefully for words that might mean that one option isn't correct. For example:

- no
- didn't
- weren't

1 **Which phrases in the box are useful for starting a story?**

One day … Finally, Dear Sally, Then, Lots of love, After that, Last week Thanks for your email, Next, Because of this, In the end, Yesterday,

2 **Look at picture A and write a sentence. Use a phrase from the box in Activity 1.**

A

3 **Which of the sentences is the best first line for this story? Why?**

1 One day a man drinks an orange juice. ________________

2 Tony likes cooking. ________________

3 Last week John went to have dinner at a restaurant. ________________

4 **Look at the rest of the story.** Choose a phrase and finish the sentences.

Then/Next ________________

Finally/In the end ________________

5 **Read two students' answers. In pairs, talk about which story is better and why.**

In the second story, the people have names.

1

a man one day goes to eat in ristorant. He's look his phone. A girl enters. She is with woman. The girls present is beutifull People is happy.

2

One day, John went to have dinner at Tony's restaurant. He was waiting for someone and he felt worried. Then his daughter Betty arrived with her mum. Betty opened her beautiful present and Tony gave her a necklace. It was a really fun evening.

EXAM TIP! Remember to write about **all three** pictures. Your story should have a beginning, a middle and an end.

Learning outcomes By the end of the lesson, learners will be able to understand strategies for writing a story effectively.

New language *one day, finally, in the end, after that*

Materials examples of story books or readers if possible (alternatively pictures of book covers)

Warm-up

- Show pictures of four or five book covers. Ask learners which ones are interesting. (If possible bring in a selection of story books or readers and put them out on a table. Invite the learners to come and look at the different books.) Learners choose the book they think they would like to read and discuss why in pairs.
- Ask a few learners to explain their choice to the group.

  Extension/alternative Learners describe one of their own books and show it to their partner. They explain what it is about, if they are enjoying it and why they think it is good or not.

Pupil's Book, page 64

Presentation

- Say *In Part 7 of the Reading and Writing exam, you will write a short story. It can help if you know some of the words we often use in stories.*

1 Which phrases in the box are useful for starting a story?

- Ask learners if they know any famous stories. Ask if there are any phrases or words that are often found in stories. Learners suggest ideas. They look at the box in Activity 1 to see if any of their suggested phrases are included.
- Learners decide which phrases might be found in a story in pairs. Check answers. Encourage learners to say why they decided on their answers.

Key: One day … Finally, Then, After that, Next, Because of this, In the end, Yesterday, Last week (These all show the time and order of the stories' events, whereas the other phrases are more typical in a letter or email.)

2 Look at picture A and write a sentence. Use a phrase from the box in Activity 1.

- Learners look at the first picture and describe it. Ask them to choose one of the phrases from Activity 1 and write a sentence in their own words.
- Put learners into pairs to compare ideas. Check answers.

  Fast finishers Learners discuss how the story might continue.

3 Which of these sentences is the best first line for this story? Why?

- Keep learners in the same pairs.
- Ask for their ideas and clarify which is best, discussing why.

Key: 'Last week John went to have dinner at Tony's restaurant.' This gives the character a name and introduces an action that could lead to a story. 'Tony likes cooking' is very basic and not interesting. We don't know if Tony is the main character. 'One day a man drinks an orange juice' is just descriptive and not very engaging; also in a story characters tend to have names.

4 Look at the rest of the story. Choose a phrase and finish the sentences.

- Tell learners to look at the rest of the pictures in pairs and work out why the man is happy. Check ideas.

Key: Sample answer He's happy because the girl likes her present.

5 Read two students' answers. In pairs, talk about which story is better and why.

- Ask learners to read the two stories and think about which one is better. Learners read then work in pairs to decide which is better and give reasons.

EXAM TIP! Ask a strong learner to read the exam tip aloud. Say *Make sure you write about each picture. This will help you write a beginning, middle and end for the story. You can write about something in the past or the present.*

Key: A and B both describe the story but B is better. A has punctuation, spelling and grammar mistakes; it uses simple and short sentences. It only has 28 words and the characters are not named. B has better grammar, spelling and punctuation. It names the characters and there is a clear beginning, middle and end.

Activity Book, page 64

See pages TB126–141.

Ending the lesson

- Ask learners to look at the pictures and tell the story in pairs.

Learning outcome By the end of the lesson, learners will have used language from the unit to talk about food, cooking and nutrients and revised the unit language and skills.

Recycled language unit language

Materials pictures of food (any from the unit), posters from Mission Stages 1 and 2

Warm-up

- Put 10–15 pictures of food up on the board. Include items from different food groups.
- Point to two of the pictures. Ask, e.g. *Would you prefer to eat the chicken or the spaghetti?* Learners respond.
- Invite different learners up to select two pictures and ask which food the other learners prefer. Continue until all the pictures have been selected.
- Now put learners into pairs and say *Can you put the pictures into groups? For example, the salmon and the chicken both give us protein.*
- Learners discuss and create categories. Check ideas.
- Finally ask them to choose two or three of the foods and think of a meal they can make. Tell them to describe how they will make it using passive forms. E.g. *We are using the potatoes, salmon and broccoli. First the salmon is cooked with some herbs. The potatoes are roasted in the oven and the broccoli is boiled for 2 minutes.*

  Fast finishers Learners draw and label three pictures showing how they make their meal.

Pupil's Book, page 65

1 Choose the correct words to complete the sentences.

- Ask learners which phrases we can use to talk about our preferences. *(prefer, would rather)*. Ask which phrase is followed by 'to'. *(prefer: e.g. I prefer to do …)*.
- Ask which one we use when we compare two things. *(would rather: I'd rather have this)*. Ask if we say *prefer* or *would prefer* when we are talking about what we like generally.
- Put learners into pairs to look at the sentences and decide which of the words is correct. Check answers.

Key: 1 prefer 2 rather 3 have 4 to eat 5 I'd 6 We

2 Complete the text. Use the words in brackets and the past passive.

- Ask learners to look at the question quickly and see what they have to do.
- Tell them to think about how we make a past passive. *(was/were and past participle)*.
- Ask the best way to do the question. *(Look at the picture and read the text quickly to get a general idea of what it is about. Don't worry about the gaps. Then go through and fill in the gaps thinking about how to use the verb correctly. Finally read it again to check that the answers are correct).*
- Put learners into pairs. They say the correct word.
- Check answers.

Key: 1 were decorated 2 were dressed 3 was cooked 4 was roasted 5 were fried 6 was sliced

3 Choose ten words from this unit. Record the words using the steps below.

- Say *Well done. You've learnt a lot of new language. Now let's think about interesting ways to remember the words.*
- Tell learners to look at the flowchart. Say *Let's try.* Write the word *roast* on the board. Ask learners if they can remember what it is and how they can find out if they can't remember. Tell them to look at the 'find the meaning' part of the chart. (You can check the meaning in this unit or in an online recipe.)
- Ask the easiest way to show what it is or remember it. (Use a picture or use an example with a gap to help you revise, e.g. *I _____ chicken in the oven.*) Tell learners to look at the 'record the example' part of the flowchart.
- Look at the next part of the flowchart: 'use it'. Say *You can use your sentence to test a friend.*
- Say *Now let's do an example.* Tell learners to choose three words from the unit and write a sentence for each putting a gap where the word fits. Tell them to follow the flowchart.
- Learners work alone. Monitor and check.
- Once they have finished, pair learners. Ask them to show their sentences to their partner and ask them to try to fill in the gaps.

Mission in action!

- Put learners into the same groups as earlier in the Mission.
- Give back to each group the poster they created for a national dish. Learners review the plans they made.
- Tell each group to practise presenting their information. They should talk about the country they have chosen, the name of the dish and describe how it is made.
- Learners practise their presentations.
- Invite each group to present their information.
- Ask the class to choose the best dish. Announce the winner.

Activity Book, page 65

See pages TB126–141.

Ending the lesson

- SA Complete the self-assessment (see Introduction).

1 Choose the correct words to complete the sentences.

1 I always **prefer** / **rather** broccoli to mushrooms.

2 At the picnic, I'd **prefer** / **rather** have sandwiches than lamb and cabbage.

3 I'd rather **have** / **to have** onion sauce, please.

4 I'd prefer **to eat** / **eat** garlic than onion.

5 For lunch today, **I'd** / **I** prefer to have steak than salmon.

6 **We'd** / **We** always prefer food with lots of chilli in it.

2 Complete the text. Use the words in brackets and the past passive.

Last week, I went to a restaurant for my grandma's birthday. The restaurant was very strange. The walls **(1)** ____________ (decorate) with vegetables and the waiters **(2)** ____________ (dress) as carrots!

First, I had broccoli soup. It **(3)** ____________ (cook) with chilli and onion so it was delicious – but very spicy. Next, I had lamb with vegetables. The lamb **(4)** ____________ (roast) perfectly and the vegetables were brilliant too. They **(5)** ____________ (fry) with some lovely herbs. Finally, for dessert, I had an apple that **(6)** ____________ (slice) so it looked like a bird!

3 Choose ten words from this unit. Record the words using the steps below.

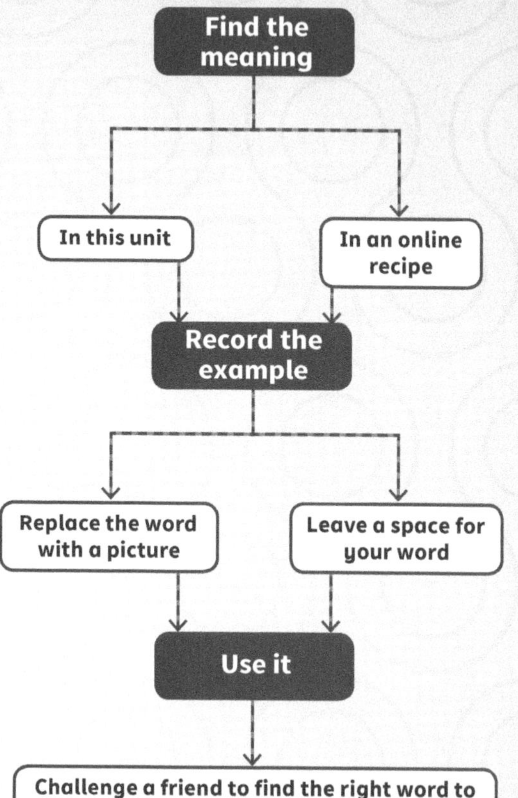

Replace the word with a picture
Leave a space for your word

Challenge a friend to find the right word to complete your sentence.

Mission in action!

Present your country and food. Choose a winner!

I've made a main course that's popular in Portugal.
I can't wait to try it!

6 Environmentally friendly

1 2  3  4  5  6  7  8  9

WOW

Mission Share ideas to protect the environment

1. Find environmentally friendly items at home.
2. Find out about how your items are environmentally friendly. Interview each other.
3. Present your ideas to protect your environment.

What can you see in the pictures? Which objects have been recycled?

Watch the video. What does Jenny make from her old jeans?

Unit 6 learning outcomes

In Unit 6, learners will learn to:

- use vocabulary to describe the environment
- understand and use phrases of quantity
- understand and use tag questions
- read and listen for information
- understand reasons and ways to look after the environment
- understand ecosystems

Materials video, picture of the Earth taken from space, (optional: pictures of the natural world, e.g. waterfalls, animals)

Self-assessment

- **SA** Show pictures from the unit. Hold a copy up and point or ask them to look through the pages in their book quickly. Learners discuss what they will learn.
- Show the outcomes on the board.
- Ask learners if they guessed any of them.
- Choose a few pairs and ask each to explain one of the learning outcomes. Clarify if necessary.
- Ask learners to complete self-assessment (see Introduction). Say *Let's learn.*

Pupil's Book, page 66

Warm-up

- Show a picture of the Earth taken from space. Ask *What is it?*
- In pairs, learners decide what the most beautiful or interesting thing in the world is. Give examples, e.g. a waterfall, an unusual animal. Share ideas.
- Show a picture of plastic and rubbish, e.g. on a beach. Ask *What can you see? (rubbish).* Ask *Why is this a problem? (it is bad for the environment and dangerous for wildlife).* Ask what we can do to prevent this. Learners suggest ideas. If they don't mention it, add *recycling*. Learners repeat.

  Fast finishers Learners think of three things people do that are bad for the environment.

What can you see in the pictures? Which objects have been recycled?

- Show pictures of objects: a dustbin, lightbulb and a curtain. Learners repeat the words.
- In pairs learners say how the objects could be used for a new purpose, e.g. *A dustbin could be used as a table.*
- Say *Open your books at page 66. What can you see in the pictures? And what do you think the objects were before they were changed?* Put the learners into groups of three to say as many things as they can.
- Learners say the names of the original objects and the rest of the class say what the object is now. E.g. *It was a frying pan. (it's the picture on the wall!).*
- Say the name of each object. Learners repeat.

Watch the video. What does Jenny make from her old jeans?

- Show a picture of jeans. Tell them Jenny, recycles jeans to make two new things. Ask *How could you recycle jeans?* Learners discuss in pairs.
- Say *If your house is cold, what do you need? (heating). And if your house is too hot, what do you need? (air conditioning).* Tell learners one of Jenny's ideas is about heating and air conditioning. Say *Watch and check.*
- Play the video. Learners watch. Check answers.
- Divide learners into two groups. Tell one group to think about the bag and the second to think about the snake. Tell them to work with a partner from the same group and say how to make their item. Learners watch again and check.

  Extension Learners think of another use for the jeans and explain how they would make their idea.

Key: Jenny makes a bag and a snake from her jeans. The snake can be used at the bottom of a door to keep your heating in during winter and the air conditioning in during summer.

Mission Share ideas to protect the environment

- Say *We're going to learn about how we protect the environment.*
- Ask learners to read the Mission statement in pairs and write one question about the Mission.
- Write the statements on the board in random order while they do this. Tell learners to close their books. Ask learners to look at the statements on the board and decide the correct order. Check their answers. Number the statements 1 to 3.
- Put learners into threes. They ask and answer each other's questions, e.g. *Where will we look for things that protect the environment? (at home).* Say *This is our Mission.*

Activity Book, page 66

See pages TB126–141.

My unit goals

- Go through the unit goals with the learners. (See suggested techniques in 'Identifying outcomes' in the teachers' in-class guide in Introduction.)
- Go back to these unit goals at the end of each Mission stage and review them. Say *This is our Mission page.*

Ending the lesson

- In groups of four, learners discuss if they have ever recycled something at home and what it was. Share ideas.

Learning outcomes By the end of the lesson, learners will be able to use vocabulary to describe foods.

New language *tap, sink, dishwasher, plug, bulb*

Recycled language *curtain, dustbin, rubbish, air conditioning, heating*

Materials audio, large pictures of household objects, sticky notes

Pupil's Book, page 67

Warm-up

- Find some large pictures of household furniture or objects, e.g. a cupboard, a TV, a cup, knives and forks and so on. Cover each picture with sticky notes or paper.
- Put the first picture up on the board. Remove one sticky note or part of the paper to show a small section of the picture underneath. Ask learners to guess what it is. If they can't guess, remove a second sticky note / section of paper.
- Continue until the object is identified or revealed. The learner who guesses the object first is the winner of the round.
- Repeat with other pictures.
- Once all the pictures are revealed hold them up and ask learners to repeat what the object is and then the room where it is usually found, e.g. *It's a cup. We usually keep it in the kitchen.*

  Alternative If possible, use a projector and use a reveal tool to show the pictures bit by bit.

1 (2.23) Listen and point to the things in Ela's house. Say the numbers.

- Ask learners to look at the diagram in pairs. Ask what it shows. *(a house).*
- Tell them to look at the pictures of objects 1–12 and name them. Don't check at this stage but monitor to see how much they know.
- Read the instruction for Activity 1 with the learners. Ask *What kinds of words will be important to do the task? (the names of the objects).* Tell learners to listen out for these words to help them.
- Play the audio. Pause it after each item for learners to discuss in pairs. Ask them for their answers.
- If a section is difficult, play the section again.

  Extension Once the task is complete, play the audio without pauses and encourage the learners to call out the items.

See audioscripts on pages TB118–123.

Key: bulb – 2, plug – 8, sink – 9, tap – 10, candles – 3, curtains – 1, dishwasher – 5, dustbin – 6, rubbish – 12, heating – 4, air conditioning – 7, electricity – 11

2 In pairs, use the words in the box to check the things (1–12) in the picture.

- Demonstrate with a strong learner. Ask *What's number 1? (curtains).* Encourage the learner to ask you a question.
- Learners work in pairs. Monitor and correct.

  Fast finishers Learners repeat the task but this time give the words and their partner gives the number of the object.

3 Complete the diagram with the words from Activity 1.

- Ask learners to look at the diagram. Draw the Venn diagram onto the board. Tell learners to copy it.
- Once they have a copy, show an example on the board. Say *I've touched a candle today. Which circle?* Learners point. Add the word to the diagram. Say *If it is in the kitchen and I have touched it where will I write it? (in the middle section). And if it isn't in any of the spaces, you can write it outside the circle.*
- Learners complete the task. Monitor and support.

4 In pairs, share your diagrams. What are three differences?

- Learners compare their diagrams in pairs. Show the example. Tell learners to find three differences.
- Learners complete the task.
- Ask a few pairs to report back on what they found.

Activity Book, page 67

See pages TB126–141.

Ending the lesson

- Show learners a paper plate. Ask what it is and where it is normally found. *(a plate; in the kitchen)*
- Ask learners to think of other items that can be found in a kitchen. Encourage them to include ideas from the lesson but other items too. As they suggest ideas, write a list onto the board. Give out paper plates. Learners draw and label five items from the list.
- Learners mingle with their plates and ask other learners what they have in their kitchen. Tell them they can only ask for one thing each time, e.g. *What do you have in your kitchen? I have a sink. What do you have? A dustbin.* If the learner they ask says one of the objects on their own plate, they can cross it out. The first learner to cross out all their items is the winner. Once the winner has finished, the others can continue to complete the task.

  Fast finishers Learners work together. They show their plate to a partner for 30 seconds then cover it up. Their partner tries to remember the five objects.

1 2.23 **Listen and point to the things in Ela's house.** Say the numbers.

Above the stairs is a cool bulb.

Number 2

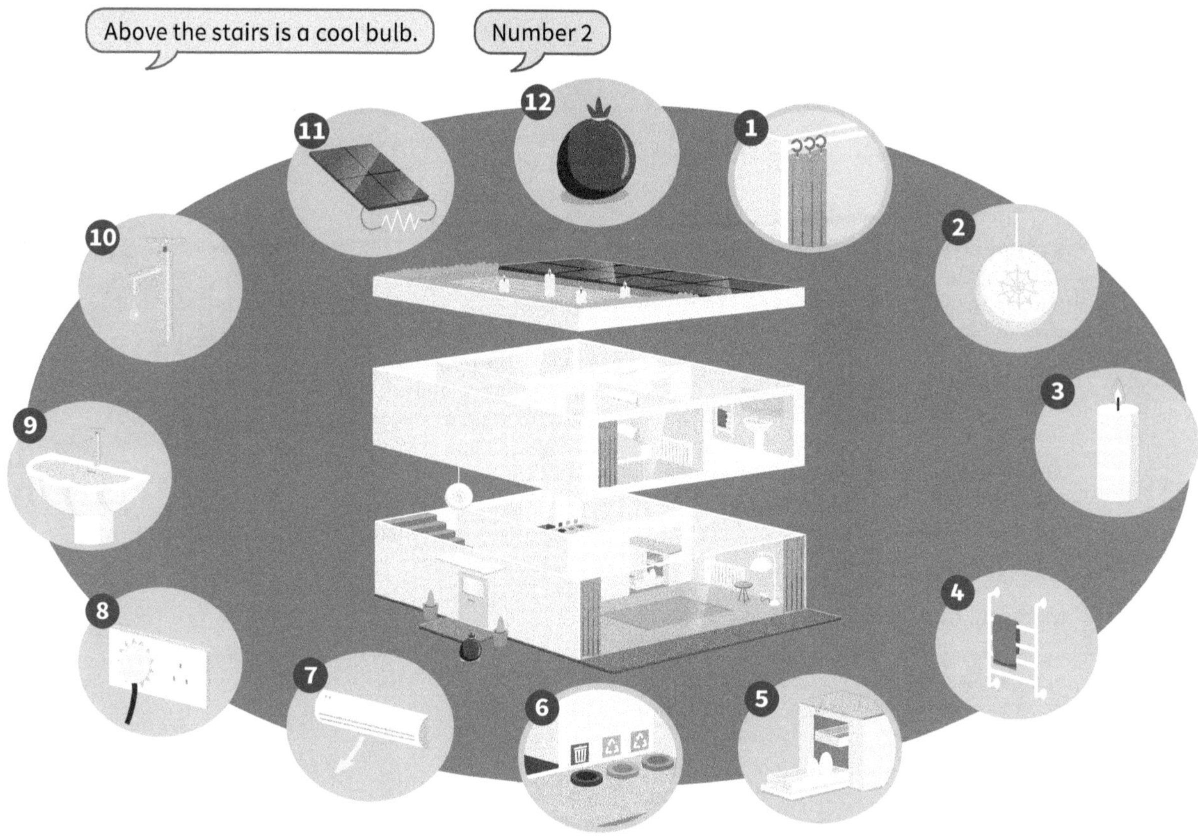

2 **In pairs, use the words in the box to check the things (1–12) in the picture.**

curtain dustbin tap electricity rubbish sink air conditioning dishwasher candle plug bulb heating

What's number 1?

Curtain.

3 **Complete the diagram with the words from Activity 2.**

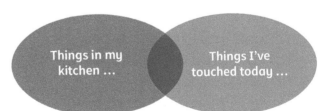

Things in my kitchen …

Things I've touched today …

4 **In pairs, share your diagrams.** What are three differences?

I've touched a dustbin today but Clara hasn't.

Language presentation 1

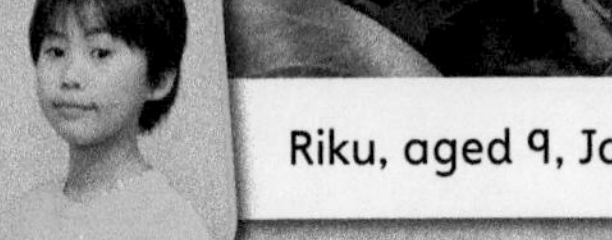

Riku, aged 9, Japan

Most people aren't surprised that I don't have a dishwasher. But when I say that fish clean my dishes for me, many people don't believe me!

In my garden there's a small room, called the kabata. In the room, there's a lot of water from our town's river. My family use the water to clean vegetables and wash dishes. A little food falls off the bowls that we wash – but that's OK because there are lots of fish living in the water, and the fish eat the food. The fish keep the water clean!

After the water comes to my kabata, it goes into the river or onto farms. A kabata is a great way to save water!

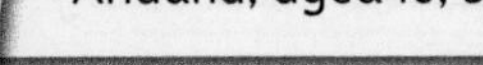

Ariadna, aged 10, Spain

There isn't heating or air conditioning in my house.

I live in a traditional cave house – a house that's built inside a hill. The ground around the house keeps the house cool when the weather is hot, and warm when the weather is cold. My house is great because it doesn't use much electricity.

People think that I don't have Wi-Fi, electricity or even water in my cave house – but I do!

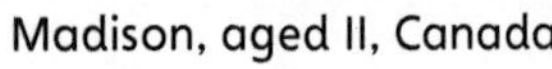

Madison, aged 11, Canada

In my house there isn't a dustbin. My family don't need one because we don't throw away much rubbish. In fact, we only throw away a few bags each year.

How do we do it? Well, we're careful when we go shopping – we take our own bags to put our food in. Some things are always wrapped in plastic, but we try not to buy them. Instead, we buy lots of fresh fruit and vegetables.

Finally, when we have a little rubbish, we try to use it. I've made a lot of cool things from plastic bottles!

1 Read the article for 60 seconds. Which item *doesn't* each child have in their house?

2 Read the article again and say *yes* or *no*.

1 Riku's kabata is in the kitchen of their home.
2 The kabata is used to do the washing up.
3 The water that's in the kabata is dirty.
4 Ariadna's home was built a long time ago.
5 Her house is on top of a hill.
6 She can't use the Internet in her house.
7 Madison's family throw away less rubbish than most people.
8 Her family don't buy things in plastic bottles, boxes or bags.
9 She often recycles things by using them in a new way.

3 Why is each house better for the environment than normal houses? Which would you like to live in?

In Riku's house they save water. It's bad for the environment to use too much water because …

Learning outcomes By the end of the lesson, learners will be able to read for specific information and understand expressions of quantity.

New language *cave, throw away, plastic, kabata*

Recycled language *dishwasher, dustbin, rubbish, heating, air conditioning, electricity, environment*

Materials a plastic bottle, paper and colouring pens

Pupil's Book, page 68

Warm-up

- Put learners into groups of three or four. Write *Japan, Canada, Spain* on the board.
- Assign a different country to each group and ask them to think about houses in that country. Add a list to the board: *house or flat? / size? / garden or balcony? / type of furniture*.
- Tell learners to discuss what houses might be like in each country. (If one is your country ask learners for a description using the list as an example, then assign the other two countries).
- Learners discuss in groups. Check if learners think houses will be similar or different.
  Extension Ask learners why they think there might be differences in houses in the world, e.g. weather / habits in lifestyle.

1 Read the article for 60 seconds. Which item *doesn't* each child have in their house?

- Tell learners they are going to read about three homes: one from each country. Say *Each house doesn't have one important thing. Let's find out what is missing in each house.*
- Tell learners they will read very quickly to get the information – just 1 minute. Remind them when getting a general idea, we don't need to understand every word in detail.
- Ask them to open their books at page 69 and read the text. Say *You have 1 minute.*
- Learners read. After a minute tell learners to stop and close their books. Put them into pairs to compare ideas. Check answers.

Key: dishwasher, dustbin, heating and air conditioning

2 Read the article again and say *yes* or *no*.

- Say *The houses all help the environment in different ways. One doesn't have a dustbin because they don't throw away much rubbish.* Mime *throw away*. Learners repeat. Say *For example, they try not to use plastic*. Show something made of plastic or plastic wrapping. Learners repeat.
- Tell learners to look at the instruction for Activity 2. Ask them the best way to check the information. *(Read the questions. Then read the text quickly to find the right part and read that part in detail).*
- Learners read and answer the questions then compare answers in pairs. Check answers.
  Alternative Divide learners into three groups: 1, 2 and 3. Tell group 1 to read the Japan text and answer questions 1–3; ask group 2 to read the Canada text and answer questions 4–6; ask group 3 to read the Spain text and answer questions 7–9. Learners can be paired within their groups to check answers. Then regroup the learners into threes: one learner from each group. The three learners swap information so that they have the answers for all nine questions. Finally ask learners to read the two texts they haven't looked at to check they agree with the answers.

Key: 1 Yes 2 No 3 No 4 Yes 5 Yes 6 No 7 Yes 8 No 9 No

3 Why is each house better for the environment than normal houses? Which would you like to live in?

- Put learners into groups of four or five. They discuss why each house is good for the environment. Share ideas.
- Learners go back into groups to decide which house they would like to live in. Check answers.

Key: 1 Riku's house: Because they don't use a dishwasher, they save electricity and use natural water for cleaning. The water they use is kept clean by fish so it can be used again on farms. The food helps feed fish.
2 Madison's house: The family produces very little rubbish; they try not to use plastic packaging and they recycle things; they use their own bags for shopping.
3 Ariadna's house: Because the cave stays warm in winter and cool in summer, they don't use electricity for heating and air conditioning.

Activity Book, page 68

See pages TB126–141.

Ending the lesson

- Ask learners to read the final paragraph of the Canada text again. Ask what the family do with plastic bottles. *(make a lot of cool things)*
- Put learners into groups of three. Ask them to think of an interesting way to re-use a plastic bottle. Learners work together and plan an idea. Invite groups to share their ideas.
  Fast finishers Learners draw and label a diagram showing how they would use the bottle and present the plan.

6 Language practice 1

Learning outcomes By the end of the lesson, learners will be able to express quantities accurately.

New language *a lot of, lots of, a little, a few, many, much*

Recycled language *environment*

Materials pictures (two or three bottles; many plastic bottles), two real plastic bottles if possible: one with a little water and one that is full, Mission worksheets (Teacher's Resource Book page 59)

Pupil's Book, page 69

Warm-up

- Draw a suitcase on the board. Say *We're going on a trip to find out about the environment in different places.* Put learners into groups of five. Assign each group a location, e.g. the jungle, Antarctica, the desert, the Atlantic Ocean.
- Tell learners to think about what they would pack in their suitcase, e.g. *I'm going to the desert, so I'm taking a lot of sun cream. I'm taking five T-shirts.*
- Pair learners from different groups to guess what is in their partner's suitcase, e.g. *I think you've taken a lot of warm clothes and some gloves. Yes, but I'm taking five pairs of gloves because they are easy to lose.*

Presentation

- Draw a glass on the board. Draw a line near the top to represent water. Say *Is there a lot of water or just a little? (a lot of water). What's another way to say this? (lots of water).* Learners repeat. Check they say the weak form for 'of' /əv/.
- Rub out the line and draw a second one near the bottom of the glass. Say *And now? (a little water).*
- Show learners a picture of lots of bottles. Say *How many plastic bottles? (a lot).* Show a picture of two or three bottles. Say *And now? (a few).*

Grammar look: *a lot of, lots of, a few, a little, many, much*

- Ask a learner to read out the sentences at the top of the **Grammar look** box. Tell learners to choose the correct options in pairs.

Key: 1 lots of and a lot of 2 many 3 much 4 a little 5 a few

Complete the Grammar look on page 124.
See pages TB125–126.

1 2.24 **PRONUNCIATION Listen and repeat.**

- Play the audio. Check pronunciation. Make sure they use a weak form of 'a' /ə/, 'of' /əv/ and the final syllable of water /wɔːtə/.

Track 2.24
There's a lot of water. We only throw away a few bags each year.

- Learners complete the activity on page 119 (see page TB124).

2 Look at the three pictures and write the story. Write 35 words or more, using some of the words in the box.

- Learners review how to do the question. *(First look at each picture carefully to understand what is happening. Write about each picture. Check the story has a beginning, middle and end. Include language found in stories).*
- Learners tell the story in pairs, using words from the box. Learners write the story.

EXAM TIP! Ask a stronger learner to read the exam tip. Say *Now you have finished your story, read it again and check it.*

3 Read your story to a small group. Whose story do you like best?

- Learners read their stories in small groups.
- Ask each group to choose the story they like best.

Did you know?

- Read out the fact. Ask learners how many bottles they use in a week and how they can recycle them.

Mission Stage 1

- Give each learner a photocopy of the Mission worksheet (Teacher's Resource Book page 59). Say *What can you find in your home that is good for the environment?*
- Learners can mark the appliances using a red-green code, e.g. in the bathroom they could mark a bath as red and a shower as green. Then they work in pairs and tell each other what they have in their list.

Activity Book, page 69

See pages TB126–141.

Ending the lesson

- Learners play a guessing game. Say *I see something beginning with … b.* Learners guess the object, e.g. *Is it a book? (no). Is it the board? (yes).*

Grammar look: *a lot of, lots of, a few, a little, many, much*

'There's a lot of water from our town's river.'
'There are lots of fish living in the water.'
'Many people don't believe me.'

'My house doesn't use much electricity.'
'When we have a little rubbish, we try to use it.'
'We only throw away a few bags each year.'

1. ***Lots of* and *a lot of* / *A little*** means 'a large amount of' something (e.g. money, time, food) or number of something (e.g. clothes, people, cars).
2. ***Many* / *Much*** means 'a large amount of' something (e.g. money, time, food). It's usually used in negative sentences and questions.
3. ***Many* / *Much*** means 'a large number of' something (e.g. clothes, people, cars). It's usually used in negative sentences and questions.
4. ***Lots of* and *a lot of* / *A little*** means 'a small amount of something' (e.g. money, time, food).
5. ***A few* / *Many*** means 'a small number of' something (e.g. clothes, people, cars).

page 124

1 2.24 **PRONUNCIATION Listen and repeat.** page 119

2 **Look at the three pictures and write the story.** Write 35 words or more, using some of the words in the box.

a lot of	lots	a few	a little	many	much

EXAM TIP! When you've finished writing, **read your text again** and check the grammar and spelling.

Did you know?

We use more than 100,000,000* bottles every day. That's the same weight as six Statues of Liberty. Many of these bottles aren't recycled and cause problems for the environment.

*one-hundred million

3 **Read your story to a small group.** Whose story do you like best?

Mission Stage 1

Find environmentally friendly items at home.

Vocabulary 2

1 2.27 **Listen to the podcast.** Who always uses recycled paper? ....

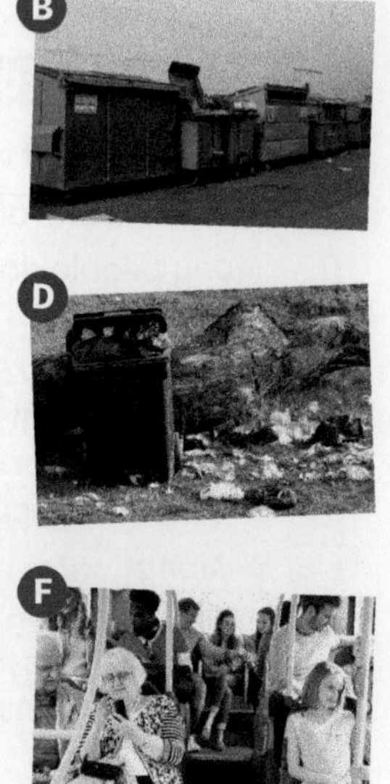

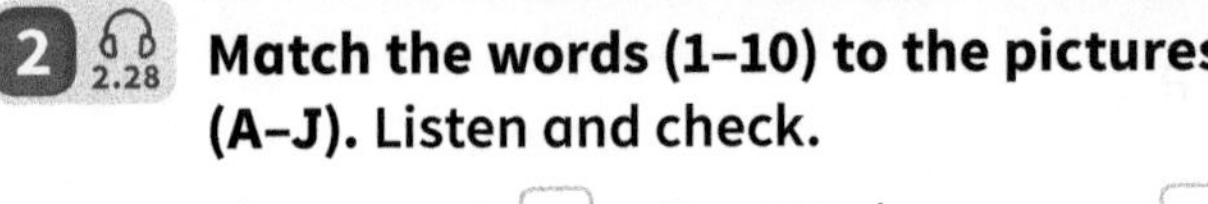

2 2.28 **Match the words (1–10) to the pictures (A–J). Listen and check.**

1	recycle	☐	6	petrol	☐
2	area	☐	7	path	☐
3	litter	☐	8	pollution	☐
4	traffic jams	☐	9	gas	☐
5	public transport	☐	10	rainforest	☐

3 2.29 **Listen again.** Which time was better for the sentences (1–6)?

	Now	When Grandma was young
1 People are better at recycling.	✓	
2 People make less rubbish.		
3 People are better at throwing away their litter.		
4 The air is cleaner.		
5 People use less gas and electricity.		
6 People save gas and electricity.		
TOTAL:		

4 **When do you think life was better for the environment?** Discuss and vote.

Learning outcomes By the end of the lesson, learners will be able to listen to and understand opinions.

New language *area, litter, pollution, traffic jam, public transport, petrol, path, gas, rainforest*

Recycled language *recycle, environment, electricity*

Materials audio, poster paper and colouring pens

Pupil's Book, page 70

Warm-up

- Write *recycle* on the board. Show learners a piece of paper.
- Put learners into fours. Tell them to find as many uses for old paper as they can, e.g. *We can colour it and use it to wrap presents!*
- Give 3 minutes then check which group has the most ideas. Ask learners if they think we use more paper now or in the past and why. Share ideas.

1 2.27 Listen to the podcast. Who always uses recycled paper?

- Tell learners they will listen to a podcast. Ask them to look at the pictures in Activity 1 and ask *What kind of people are talking in the podcast? What are they talking about? (an old lady and a young boy; recycling).*
- Ask learners to predict which person they think always uses recycled paper. Learners suggest answers. Don't confirm. Check. Play the audio.
- Put learners into pairs to compare answers.
- Check with the class.

See audioscripts on pages TB118–122.

Key: the brother

2 2.28 Match the words (1–10) to the pictures (A–J). Listen and check.

- Tell learners to look at the pictures in pairs to say what each picture shows. Point to each picture and ask learners for words. If they are unsure, tell them they will find out soon.
- Tell learners to read through the words in pairs to match them to the letters. Tell them to listen and check.
- Play the audio. Check answers repeating any difficult words.

Key: 1 B 2 H 3 D 4 E 5 I 6 F 7 J 8 A 9 C 10 G

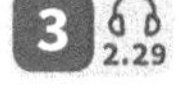

3 2.29 Listen again. Which time was better for the sentences (1–6)?

- Ask learners to look at the table and read the sentences 1–6 in pairs. Ask them to try to remember from the podcast which time things were better – now or in the past. Encourage them to give details. Monitor and support.
- Play the audio again to check. Check answers.

Key: 1 Now 2 When Grandma was young 3 Now 4 When Grandma was young 5 When Grandma was young 6 Now

4 When do you think life was better for the environment? Discuss and vote.

- Ask learners to vote by putting their hands up. Ask *Is life better for the environment now or when Grandma was young?*
- Divide the class into two teams based on their opinions. Put undecided students in either team to make teams roughly the same size.
- Pair learners within their teams to decide the three most important reasons their side of the debate is correct.
- Tell learners to stand facing each other in two lines in the middle of the room, each team on one side of the room. Ask them to try to persuade their partner (from the opposing team) to change their minds.
- Ask one team to move along one place (one learner will need to join the other end of their line). Repeat several times. Ask learners to return to their seats. Ask if anyone changed their opinion, and if so, why.

Activity Book, page 70

See pages TB126–141.

Ending the lesson

- Tell learners to think about life 100 years ago. Ask them to think about transport, food, work, shopping and entertainment and compare now with that time.
- Learners discuss in pairs.
- Put the pairs into groups of four. Give out poster paper and pens. Ask the groups to create a mind map including the five categories. They write notes about today in one colour and the past in a different colour.
- Once they have finished creating their mind maps, ask them to discuss each category and compare the past with now and say? which is better for the environment, e.g. *Now we play video games and use mobiles all the time. In the past people played instruments or played games outside. So the past was probably better for the environment.*
- Once learners have finished, share key ideas.

  Fast finishers Learners write five sentences – one for each of the categories – comparing the past with the present.

Learning outcomes By the end of the lesson, learners will be able to use tag questions accurately.

New language tag questions (auxiliary verb and pronoun)

Recycled language vocabulary related to recycling

Materials paper and colouring pens

Warm-up

- Write sentences on the board. Learners decide in pairs if they are true or false now compared to the past.
  1 *People are better at recycling.*
  2 *People make less litter.*
  3 *People are better at throwing away their litter.*
  4 *The air is cleaner.*
  5 *People use less gas and electricity.*
- Check answers, reminding learners the sentences are from the podcast in the last lesson. *(1 T 2 F 3 T 4 F 5 F).*
- Learners correct the sentences that are wrong by adding to them, e.g. for the second sentence they could add 'don't'.
  Extra support Learners can refer to the table they copied in the previous lesson to help remember.

Pupil's Book, page 71

Presentation

- Leave sentences 1 and 2 on the board from the Warm-up.
- Point to each as you say them, adding a question tag. Say *People are better at recycling, aren't they?* Learners agree.
- Say *People make less litter now, don't they?* Learners disagree.
- Repeat the questions, but write the question tag at the end in a different colour. Ask *What are these? (question tags).* Say *We can add these to make a question.*
- Look at the first sentence again. Point to the main clause of the sentence and ask *Is this part of the sentence positive or negative? (positive). And the verb? (to be). So is the question tag positive or negative? (negative). Yes – we use the opposite and the right verb.* Repeat with the other example.
  Extension Say the examples with a rising intonation and a falling question. Say *Sometimes we use tag questions because we don't know something. Sometimes we just want to check something we think is true. We show this in the way we say it.* Ask learners to repeat the two intonations.

Grammar look: tag questions

- Learners read the sentences in the box. Highlight the auxiliary verbs and their repetition.
- Learners choose the correct option in each question 1–4 in pairs. Check answers.

Key: 1 negative 2 positive 3 the same 4 do, does or did

1 Match the sentences (1–6) to the correct tag questions (A–F).

- In pairs, learners match and say the sentences with the question tags. Check answers.

Key: 1 B 2 E 3 A 4 F 5 D 6 C

Complete the Grammar look on page 124.
See pages TB125–126.

2 Invent a character. Ask and answer the questions from Activity 1.

- Say *Imagine you are a different person in the podcast and answer the questions. Try to think of some funny answers.*
- Demonstrate the task. Ask a strong learner to ask the questions using the tag questions, e.g. *Your name's Margret, isn't it? No, my name's Grandma Recycle! You live in London, don't you? No, I don't! I live on the moon!*
- Put learners into pairs to ask and answer.
  Fast finishers Learners repeat the questions in pairs but give answers that are true for themselves.

Mission Stage 2

- Remind learners of the Mission worksheets they completed in Stage 1 for things in their house that are environmentally friendly.
- Create a mind map on the board. Write *my home* in the middle of the board. Add the names of different rooms: *kitchen, bathroom, living room, bedrooms, hall, dining room.*
- Learners add names of items they think are good for the environment onto the rooms.
- Learners interview each other in pairs and find out what items their partner has and how they help the environment. Monitor and support.
- Ask some pairs to repeat their dialogue in front of the class.

Activity Book, page 71

See pages TB126–141.

Ending the lesson

- Put learners into groups of six. Ask them to sit in a circle.
- Demonstrate how to do the activity in one circle. Give a sentence to the learner on your right that is either true or false, e.g. *Your name is Albert, isn't it?* Encourage the learner to respond, e.g. *No it isn't, it's Julia!* Learners ask and answer questions.
- **SA** Ask learners to complete their self-assessment (see Introduction).

Grammar look: tag questions

\+ − − +

'Everyone recycles a lot, don't they?' 'You couldn't recycle, could you?'

'Since you started school you've travelled by car, haven't you?'

'The air was cleaner then, wasn't it?'

Tag questions change statements into questions. They're often used to check that someone agrees with us.

1 When the first part of the sentence is positive, the tag question is **positive / negative**.
2 When the first part of the sentence is negative, the tag question is **positive / negative**.
3 If the first part of the sentence has an auxiliary verb (e.g. *be*, *have*, *can* etc.), you use the **the same / a different** auxiliary verb in the tag question.
4 If the first part of the sentence doesn't have an auxiliary verb, we use ***is, are*** **or** ***was*** / ***do, does*** **or** ***did*** in the tag question.

page 124

1 Match the sentences (1–6) to the correct tag questions (A–F).

1 Your name's Glenda,
2 You live in London,
3 Your house was built a long time ago,
4 You don't have a dishwasher,
5 You haven't been to the rainforest,
6 You can't use public transport,

A wasn't it?
B isn't it?
C can you?
D have you?
E don't you?
F do you?

2 **Invent a character.** Ask and answer the questions from Activity 1.

Your name's Glenda, isn't it?

No, my name's Holly Wood. And I love American films!

What things in your house help the environment?

Mission Stage 2

Find out about how your items are environmentally friendly. Interview each other.

We use lots of blankets so we don't need to put the heating on very often.

Literature

1 **Look at the pictures. Where do you think the story takes place? What animals can you see?**

The fall of a Mayan city

2.30

The Mayan king looked down at the city from his palace. He felt very sad. He could remember the brightly coloured pyramids and temples; the exotic gardens full of jaguars, pumas and parrots and the buzzing street markets with delicious food from all over his empire. It was one of the great wonders of the world. But now the city was silent and empty. And why was this …?

Many years before, when the king was looking for somewhere to live, he saw a big beautiful ceiba tree in the heart of the tropical rainforest. He decided that it was the perfect place to make his home. Just as he was about to leave an old man appeared from behind the tree.

'We have always looked after the rainforest and you must too,' he said. 'Don't chop down the trees! Build your city somewhere else!' And he disappeared into the forest again.

But the king ignored the old man's advice. 'He's just a crazy old man,' he thought to himself. And he built his city nearby.

As the king and his people became richer and more powerful the city grew and grew. People needed more space to build their houses and grow their corn. So they chopped down more and more trees from the rainforest. Everything seemed perfect, until one day things started to change. At first it didn't rain as much as it usually did and the rivers became smaller and smaller. Then it stopped raining and the rivers dried up. The corn in the fields and the vegetables in the gardens dried up, too. With little food and water, the people started to leave the city. The king was very worried.

'What can I do?' he asked his advisors.

None of them could give him an answer. Then he remembered the old man he met in the forest. He went back and looked for the tall ceiba tree. Eventually he found it but now it was standing alone in the middle of a desert. He sat under its branches in the shade.

Suddenly, the same old man came out from behind the tree.

Learning outcomes By the end of the lesson, learners will be able to read a story and understand the importance of looking after the environment.

New language *pyramid, temple, jaguar, puma, parrot, dry up*

Recycled language *rainforest*, quantities

Materials audio, rainforest sounds, (audio from Internet), 6 pictures (a rainforest, jaguar, puma, parrot, a Mayan pyramid and a Mayan temple), sticky tape, a map

Warm-up

- If possible, search for 'rainforest sounds' on the Internet and play the audio to learners. Tell learners to close their eyes and listen. Let the audio continue to play and ask learners to imagine where they might be.
- Ask them to imagine what they can feel (is it warm or cold, wet or dry?). Ask them what they see if they turn around, if there are any people or animals near them, what they can smell.
- Tell learners to open their eyes and work with a partner. They discuss what they imagined. Share their ideas.

  Alternative If audio is not possible, write the word *rainforest* on the board and ask learners to imagine they are in a rainforest.

Pupil's Book, page 72

1 Look at the pictures. Where do you think the story takes place? What animals can you see?

- Ask learners to look at the text on pages 72–73. Ask them what kind of text it is. *(a story)*
- Put learners into pairs. Ask learners to look at the pictures and think about where the story happens and which animals they can see. Check their ideas.

Presentation

- Put some pictures on the board: a rainforest, jaguar, puma, parrot, a Mayan pyramid and a Mayan temple.
- Point to the first picture of the rainforest. Ask what it is. *(a rainforest)*. Ask where these are found. *(in South America)*. Show learners on a map if necessary.
- Say *Let's look at some of the animals we can find in a rainforest.* Point to the pictures of the jaguar, puma and parrot. Ask learners if they know any of the animals. Say the names. Learners repeat.
- Ask learners if they know who lived in the rainforests in the past. *(Mayans)* Say *The Mayans built great cities in the past …* Point to the pyramid and ask what it is. Say *For example, they built pyramids.* Learners repeat *pyramid.* Say *And they built temples.* Point to the picture. Learners repeat *temple.*

  Extension Ask learners to discuss whether they think a Mayan city was a good place to live and why.

2.30 The fall of a Mayan city

- Point to the first picture on page 72 of the Mayan King looking at his city. Ask *Who do you think he is? (a king).*
- Ask *How does the city look? (empty).* Ask *Why is it empty and what is the king thinking?* Learners discuss in pairs.
- Tell learners to listen and read the story on page 72 and find out if their ideas are correct.
- Play the first part of the audio to the end of page 72.
- Learners read and listen. Learners compare ideas in pairs.
- Check answers. *(the king feels sad because he remembers when the city was full of animals, plants and people; he built a city in the rainforest and cut down the trees. He didn't look after the rainforest and slowly the place became a desert).*
- Ask *What happens next?* Learners discuss in pairs.
- Share their predictions.
- Tell learners to look at page 73. Play the second part of the audio to the end.
- Learners read page 73 and listen to the audio then check in pairs.
- Check answers. *(the king understands that he has damaged the rainforest, he starts to plant trees and the city gradually comes back to life).*

Activity Book, page 72

See pages TB126–141.

Ending the lesson

- Put learners into pairs: A and B. Tell learner A they are a visitor to the Mayan city. Tell learner B they have lived in the city for many years.
- Learner A will ask learner B about life in the city.
- Put learner As into pairs and ask them to think of some questions to ask, e.g. *Where was the city built first of all? What did they do to build the city? What was it like when it was first built?*
- Put learner Bs into pairs and ask them to check the story again – how it started, what happened and what a person living in the city might be like.
- Put learners A and B back into their original pairs.
- Learner A interviews learner B. Learner B retells the story of the city, explaining what they saw and how they felt.
- Learners role play. Monitor and support.

  Fast finishers Learners practise their interview again and demonstrate at the front of the class at the end of the activity.

Learning outcomes By the end of the lesson, learners will have read a story for detail and understood the importance of looking after the environment.

New language *apologise*

Recycled language *pyramid, temple, jaguar, puma, parrot, rainforest,* quantities

Materials pictures of different types of trees, sticky tack

Social and Emotional Skill: learning from your mistakes

- After reading the story, ask *Why did things go wrong in the Mayan city? (The king didn't look after the rainforest and nature). Why didn't the king listen? (He was too arrogant). Do you think the king realised he had made a mistake? (yes).*
- Say, e.g. *I didn't recycle paper every day last week. I'll do it every day from now on. I came to school by car today, but I'll walk tomorrow. I had a bath last night, but I'll have a shower tomorrow.*
- Learners think of mistakes they have made because they didn't listen to their parents, friends or teachers.
- Learners create a comic of four to six scenes describing what happened. They present it to the class and say why they won't make the same mistake again and what they have learnt.

Warm-up

- Stick pictures of different types of trees around the room.
- Ask learners why trees are important for the environment. Put them in pairs to discuss. Share their ideas.
- Ask learners to look at the pictures. Tell them to choose the tree they like the best and stand next to it. Learners speak to those standing at the same picture and explain why they like the picture best.

Pupil's Book, page 73

Presentation

- Give each learner a number: 1, 2 or 3, and two slips of paper. Tell learners they will each write down two sentences on their pieces of paper. Tell them to write the sentence when they hear their number.
- Complete a dictation saying each sentence slowly and clearly twice so that learners can write.
  Learner 1: *This means plants can't grow and also the water doesn't go back into clouds.*
  Learner 2: *When there isn't much rain, nothing can grow.*
  Learner 3: *Trees are important because they stop water going into the ground.*
  Learner 1: *If there are no clouds, there isn't much rain.*
  Learner 2: *When there is no water and nothing grows, animals die.*
  Learner 3: *If there is too much water on the ground, it washes away the nutrients.*
- Put learners into groups of three and ask them to put their six sentences on the table and put them into the correct order. Learners work in groups. Show the correct order on the board.
- Now ask learners to read the sentences and find three ways that trees help the environment. Share ideas.

  Fast finishers Learners draw a diagram of how trees help protect the environment.

2 In pairs, talk about the questions.

- Ask learners to think about the story again and look at the pictures. Tell them to find a paragraph that describes the place where the king decided to build his city. Learners point, *(paragraph 2)*. Ask them to find a paragraph describing what happened to the environment. *(paragraph 5)*. Tell them to read the paragraph again.
- Put learners in pairs and ask them to find sentences in the story that help them find the answers. Check their answers.

  Fast finishers Learners draw a diagram with labels showing what happens when trees are cut down.

Key: 1 When the trees were cut down, there wasn't as much rain, the rivers became smaller, it stopped raining and the water dried up. The vegetables stopped growing and the people started to leave. 2 They stopped cutting down trees and started planting new ones.

Activity Book, page 73

See pages TB126–141.

Ending the lesson

- Put learners in pairs. Ask who they think the old man is and why the king didn't listen to him. Learners share ideas.

'Look what you've done,' said the old man.

The king fell to his knees and asked, 'Please tell me – what should I do?'

'Well there is a solution but it will take many, many years,'the old man said. This time, the king listened carefully to every word.

'If you plant two trees for every one you chopped down then maybe the rain will return and maybe the rivers, the plants, the birds and the animals will come back,' the old man said, and suddenly disappeared, just like before.

Quickly, the king ordered his people to plant trees where there was now desert. Slowly but surely, as the years passed, the trees grew, the rain came back and the rainforest filled with life again. First the animals and birds returned and then the people. The king was delighted. Before he died he made sure that the ceiba tree was always protected, so that his people would look after the rainforest.

2 In pairs, talk about the questions.

1. What happened in the story when the people cut down too many trees in the rainforest? Why did this happen?
2. How did they fix the problem?
3. Do you think the king was responsible for what happened?

Cross-curricular

1 **Look at the pictures. What living and non-living things can you see in them?**

2 2.31 **Listen and read the text about urban ecosystems. Find the animals – do you know them all?**

Where we live

An ecosystem is all of the living and non-living things that are in an area. Living things include all of the plants and animals and non-living things are the rocks, water, soil and sand. Examples of ecosystems are an ocean, a rainforest, a pond, a desert, a river, grassland or an urban ecosystem.

As cities and towns get bigger, other ecosystems get smaller. This means that a lot of animals don't have anywhere to live and so they start to come into cities and towns to look for food and somewhere to sleep. Usually these are small animals like mice, rats and foxes, but in some cities there are some very unusual animals:

Leopards in Mumbai

Mumbai is a very big city and about 24 million people live there. It also has a big park called the Gandhi National Park and this is where leopards and other animals live. But as the city gets bigger, the leopards are losing their homes. So, the leopards often come into town to look for food. Some people are trying to find a different place for the leopards but the animals don't like moving to different places. So for now, people and leopards have to try and live together.

Peregrine falcons in New York

Peregrine falcons usually live near the beach but when they started to die, people in New York decided to help them live in the city. Now New York has more peregrine falcons than any other city in the world. That's amazing, isn't it? They like living in the city because there are lots of high places to make their nests where they are safe and there is a lot of food to eat too. The people of New York and the birds live happily together.

Did you know?

Birds sing louder in cities. This is so that they can be heard by other birds – they are talking!

3 **Read the text again and in pairs, answer the questions.**

1 How have humans changed natural ecosystems?
2 Should the leopards move to a different home?
3 What problems do you think wild animals have when they live in a city?
4 What problems do you think people have when wild animals come into a city?

Learning outcomes By the end of the lesson, learners will be able to respond to a text using critical thinking and emotional intelligence, and understand ecosystems in the city.

New language *ecosystem, leopard, peregrine falcon, urban, wild, soil*

Materials 8 pictures (rocks, sand, ocean, soil, city buildings, streets, a fox, dustbins), sticky tack

Warm-up

- Put up eight pictures on the board (rocks, sand, ocean, soil, city buildings, streets, a fox, dustbins).
- Write *urban* on the board. Say to learners *What kind of place is urban? (a city or town is urban).*
- Ask *What is good about living in an urban area*? Share ideas (e.g. *lots of things to do; shops are easy to find; there are a lot of people around if you want to meet people; you can find jobs and schools easily*). Ask what is not so good about it, (e.g. *it is very crowded and there isn't much space; there can be a lot of traffic; there is a lot of pollution*).
- Put learners into pairs and show the pictures on the board. Ask them to decide which pictures relate to an urban environment. Go through their answers. As you check them ask the word for each picture. Say the words for new items for learners to repeat: *rocks, sand, ocean, soil, fox.*

  Fast finishers Learners make a list of other things you might see in an urban area.

Pupil's Book, page 74

1 Look at the pictures. What living and non-living things can you see in them?

- Ask learners to look at the pictures on the page in pairs and make a list of all the things they can see.
- Learners discuss. Check answers. Ask them to point to: ocean, soil, dustbins, city buildings, streets, a fox.
- Ask learners if there is anything about the pictures that is surprising. *(animals in the city).*

Key: Living: fish, squirrel, mouse, fox, plants, trees, deer
Non-living: tree trunk, rocks, sand

2 2.31 Listen and read the text about urban ecosystems. Find the animals – do you know them all?

- Write the word *ecosystem* on the board.
- Ask *What is an ecosystem?* Learners suggest answers. Don't confirm or correct at this stage. Tell learners to read the first part of the text 'Where we live' and find out.
- Check answers. *(an ecosystem is all the living and non-living things in an area).*
- Tell learners to read the whole text and find any animals. Put learners into pairs to check answers. Ask them if they know what the animals are.
- Check answers. Ask learners to point to the leopard and the peregrine falcon.

  Extension Ask learners why the leopard and the falcon have started living in cities. Learners discuss in pairs. Share answers. *(the leopards are looking for food; the falcons can build nests high up and find food).*

Key: mice, rats, foxes, leopards, birds, peregrine falcons

3 Read the text again and, in pairs, answer the questions.

- Ask learners to work in pairs. Tell them to read the questions and then look back at the text and information to help them answer. Learners discuss in pairs. Share answers.

Key: Sample answers 1 Humans have built over natural areas so there is less space for animals to live in and the food they eat has gone. 2 It would be better for leopards to be in a natural place to live, but it is difficult if they don't want to move. 3 In the city, people might be afraid if they see animals and try to kill them. They could be hurt by traffic. They might eat things that are not good for them. 4 If animals come into the city, they could hurt people or their pets.

Activity Book, page 74

See pages TB126–141.

Ending the lesson

- Put learners into groups of three to five. Ask *What have we learnt about ecosystems?* Learners discuss. Share ideas.
- Tell learners to design a new special park for the leopards. Ask them to work in groups to plan the park. They should make it as good enough for leopards to want to live there. Learners work in groups of three and plan their park.
- Ask each learner to work with another learner from a different group. Each learner compares their plans.
- Learners go back to their original group and report what they learnt from their partner. The group adapts their plan to include any new ideas they have heard.
- Ask a few groups to present their plans to the class.

Learning outcomes By the end of the lesson, learners will be able to speak about homes and places to live and speak effectively giving extended answers.

New language *beach hut, houseboat, tree house, castle*

Recycled language vocabulary related to homes and environment

Materials word cards (one per learner)

Warm-up

- Put learners into pairs: A and B. Tell A they have 1 minute to describe their home to their partner and B should just listen. Start the time. Learners talk. After 1 minute say *Stop.* Tell B to ask a question about what they heard, e.g. *Is your bedroom big or small?*
- Tell B they have 1 minute to describe their ideal house. Start the time. After 1 minute say *Stop*. Tell A to ask something about what they heard, e.g. *Do you want your swimming pool inside or outside?*

Pupil's Book, page 75

Presentation

- Tell learners *In the Speaking exam, you need to answer some questions. It is important to speak as much as possible.*

1 Watch the video to see an example of Speaking Part 2.

- Tell learners to watch the video and to pay attention to the examiner's questions and the pupils' answers. Play the video.

2 Read the question and two answers. Which answer is better? Why?

- Ask two learners to read the dialogue bubbles.
- Ask which answer is better. Tell learners it is fine to answer *'no'* in the exam so long as they give reasons. They must show their English, but their opinion isn't tested. Remind them that this is a warm-up question and they only get one, so they need to speak as much as they can.

Key: The second answer is better because the learner has given reasons to explain their opinion.

3 Look at these pictures. Think of one thing to say about each home.

- Learners look at the pictures.
- Learners discuss each picture in pairs. Monitor and support.
- On the board, write *flat, tree house, castle, houseboat, beach hut.* Learners match the words with the correct pictures in pairs.
- Check answers with the class. *(1 beach hut, 2 houseboat, 3 treehouse, 4 castle, 5 flat).* Remind learners if they don't know the correct word for something they should find a different way to say it, e.g. *the house in the tree.*

4 Choose an adjective and make a question. Ask and answer the questions.

- Ask learners to look at the adjectives in the box. Say *In the exam, you need to speak well together and show interest in what your partner says. Let's make some questions.*
- Tell learners to work in pairs and use the adjectives to make more questions. Ask learners for ideas so the class hear a range of possible follow-up questions.
- Learners ask and answer questions.

  Fast finishers Pair learners with new partners and ask them to ask and answer more questions together.

Key: Sample answers Do you think a beach hut? is fun? Do you think a boat is boring? Do you think a treehouse is interesting? Do you think a castle is expensive?

5 Look at the pictures in Activity 3 again. Ask and answer.

- Ask learners to read the examiner's question. Remind them that in the exam they must speak for at least 1 minute.
- Put them into pairs to discuss. Check answers with the class.

EXAM TIP! Ask a strong learner to read the exam tip. Say *You will be asked to give an opinion. There isn't a right or wrong answer, but you must give a reason. Let's practise.*

6 Look at the questions. Choose an answer and finish the sentences with your own ideas.

- Tell learners to look at the questions and the beginning of the answers. Tell them the examiner will ask two questions at the end of the exam and they should give their opinion. Put them into pairs to take turns to be the examiner and ask the questions while their partner answers.
- Monitor and check for extended answers.

Activity Book, page 75

See pages TB126–141.

Ending the lesson

- Ask learners to think about a house they know and really like which isn't theirs, e.g. a friend's house.
- Put them into groups of three. Tell them to describe the house to their group and explain why they liked it so much.
- The group choose which house they think is the best.

1 **Watch the video to see an example of Speaking Part 2.**

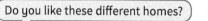

2 **Read the question and two answers.** Which answer is better? Why?

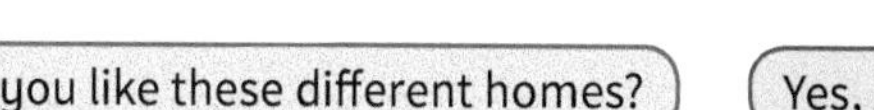
Do you like these different homes?

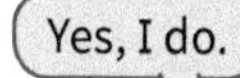
Yes, I do.

No, I don't because this one is very small and this one hasn't got any curtains.

3 **Look at these pictures.** Think of one thing to say about each home.

4 **Choose an adjective and make a question.** Ask and answer the questions.

Do you think a beach house is … ?

Do you think a tree house is … ?

Do you think a castle is … ?

Do you think a flat is … ?

fun boring interesting expensive noisy

Do you think a beach house is fun?

Yes, I do. It's fun because …

5 **Look at the pictures in Activity 3 again.** Ask and answer.

Which of these homes do you like best? Why?

I like the beach houses best because …

6 **Look at the questions.** Choose an answer and finish the sentences with your own ideas.

Now, would you prefer to live in the town or the countryside? Why?

I think … because …

I prefer … because …

Which is more important? Living with heating or living with electricity?

It's more important to … because …

EXAM TIP! Practise giving your opinion to a friend. Remember to use **full sentences**.

A2 Key for Schools

1 **Read the two example exam questions below.** What does each person want to know?

Read the email from your British friend Emily.
Write an email to Emily and answer the questions.

From: Emily **To:**

It's my party on Friday but I need some help. Can you come to my garden after school finishes at 4:30 pm? Which food can you bring? What shall we tidy up?

Emily

Write 25–35 words.
Write the email on your answer sheet.

You recently joined a new afternoon club. Write a note to your English-speaking friend Linda. In your note:

- Tell her what you do at the club
- Say how much it costs
- Ask if your friend wants to go with you

Write 25–35 words.
Write the email on your answer sheet.

2 **Look at the answers below.** What can Costas and Federica do to improve their writing? Use the checklist.

Dear Emily,
Thanks for your message. I'm fine thanks. I know about your party and I can come at 4:30 on Friday. I can make and bring a very good Greek salad. I think we could tidy up the kitchen and the play area.
Bye,
Costas

Hi Sam,
I go to a nature club every Tuesday after school. We make instruments from wood. It's fun! It's only costs 2 euros every week.
See you tomorow,
Federica

EXAM TIP! To get a good mark, your writing must have **all three** things being asked for in the exam.

CHECKLIST

- [ ] Write to the person in the question.
- [ ] Write about the 3 things in the question.
- [ ] Write 25–35 words.
- [ ] Write on the answer sheet.

Learning outcomes By the end of the lesson, learners will be able to understand strategies for writing a message effectively.

New language *email, note*

Materials sentences cut up into individual word cards on different colours (*My house has a garden where we grow lots of vegetables. Your family recycle all your plastic bottles, don't they? If we want to protect the environment, we shouldn't cut down trees.*)

Warm-up

- Create a set of word cards in advance. First write each sentence with the words spaced out. Use different coloured card or paper for each one. Blue cards: *My house has a garden where we grow lots of vegetables*. Red cards: *Your family recycle all your plastic bottles, don't they?* Green cards: *If we want to protect the environment, we shouldn't cut down trees.* Now cut up the sentences to create single word cards. Duplicate the sentences if you have a large class, but use different colours for each sentence set.
- Give out the cards in random order. Tell learners to stand in colour groups (all learners with red cards in one group and so on). Explain that each group has a complete sentence and they need to stand in the correct order holding up their word cards to make a sentence. The first group to rebuild their sentence is the winner.
- When they have finished, ask learners to say their sentence by having each learner say their word.

Pupil's Book, page 76

Presentation

- Say to learners *In Part 6 of the Reading and Writing exam, you will write a short message. It's useful to think about what type of message it is.*
- Ask learners to look at the two messages and decide what type of message they are. *(an email; a note)*.

1 Read the two example exam questions below. What does each person want to know?

- Ask learners to find out what each person wants to know.
- Put learners into pairs to discuss. Check answers. Ask *How many things do you have to put in each answer? (three)*.

Key: Emily: Can you meet her at 4.30 / which lights you can bring / what to tidy. Linda: what you do at the club / how much it costs (You will also ask her to go with you.)

EXAM TIP! Ask a learner to read out the exam tip. Remind learners to look out for three things they must write about in this part of the exam.

2 Look at the answers below. What can Costas and Federica do to improve their writing? Use the checklist.

- Tell learners to follow the list to create a good answer.
  Fast finishers Learners discuss what else they need to do to ensure a good answer. *(good grammar and punctuation; appropriate words)*.
- Tell learners to decide how the two answers can be improved. Learners discuss in pairs. Check answers.

Key: Costas writes Emily's name and he answers two of the questions, but he doesn't talk about lights, he talks about food. He could end the message better, e.g. *See you.* He writes too many words, so his answer needs to be shorter.
Federica writes her message to Sam, not Linda, so she needs to check she has written to the correct person. She answers the two questions, but she doesn't invite Linda to come with her, so she should include this.

Activity Book, page 76

See pages TB126–141.

Ending the lesson

- Put learners into pairs. Ask them to plan an activity, e.g. a party, a football game, a visit to the park. Tell them to think of three things they want their friends to tell you, e.g. *1 can they come to the activity / 2 can they bring something / 3 can they choose something – e.g. drinks to have.*
- Learners work in pairs and plan. They note down the activity and the three pieces of information they want to know.
- Give out large sheets of paper and ask them to note down the information. Once they have finished, tell each pair to pass their page to the pair next to them. Learners circulate their paper.
- Tell each pair to read about the activity they have been passed and the three things the other pair want to know.
- Tell them to write a short answer giving the information and then to pass the paper back to the original pair.
- Ask the original pairs, using to check the answer the checklist from Activity 2 to see if everything is included.
- Choose one or two good examples and show them to the class, identifying why the answer is successful.

Learning outcome By the end of the lesson, learners will have used language from the unit to talk about the environment and ecosystems and revised the language and skills from the unit.

Recycled language unit language

Materials pictures of places (e.g. a city, a forest, a beach, a mountain, a house), learners' Mission worksheets from Stage 2

Warm-up

- Put five or six pictures of places around the room on the walls, e.g. a city centre, a forest, a beach, a mountain, a house.
- Learners work in groups doing a 'gallery walk' around the room and stop in front of each picture.
- Learners describe what they can see in each picture, the problems each environment might have and how it can be prevented, e.g. *There are lots of trees in the forest. It would be bad for the environment if the trees were cut down, so we shouldn't do this.*

  Fast finishers Learners use sticky notes to add labels to one of the pictures showing their ideas.

Pupil's Book, page 77

Read the text and choose the correct words.

- Ask learners which phrases we can use to talk about quantities. *(much, many, a lot of, lots of, a little, a few).*
- Ask which words are used with negatives and questions usually. *(much, many).* Ask which words are used with things we can count *(a few)* and things we can't count *(a few).*
- Ask learners how to do the question. *(read the text to get a general idea; look at the possible answers and choose one; read again to check).*
- Learners work in pairs to decide which words are correct. Check answers.

Key: 1 many 2 a few 3 lots of 4 a lot of 5 a little 6 much

2 Say a tag question for each sentence. Then match the questions and answers (A–F).

- Do the first one together as an example. Point out the verb in the main clause – 'is'. Ask if it is positive or negative. *(positive).* Ask *So what should the question tag be? (negative).* Ask for the correct question tag. *(isn't it?).*
- Learners complete the rest of the sentences.
- Learners look through the answers and decide which one matches each question.
- Learners work in pairs and take it in turns to ask and answer the questions. Monitor and check to make sure they are matching the questions and answers accurately.

Key: 1 isn't it 2 can't we 3 is there 4 should I 5 aren't we 6 wasn't it
1 B 2 E 3 A 4 F 5 C 6 D

3 Choose ten words from this unit. Record the words using the steps below.

- Say to learners *Well done. You've learnt a lot of new language. Now let's think about another interesting way to remember the words.*
- Tell learners to look at the flowchart. Say *Let's try.* Write the word *bulb* on the board. Ask learners if they can remember what it is and how they can find out if they can't remember. Tell them to look at the 'find the meaning' part of the chart. (You can check the meaning in this unit or in a dictionary.)
- Ask the easiest way to show what it is or remember it. *(use a picture or similar words).* Tell learners to look at the 'record the example' part of the flowchart. Say *In this case, a drawing will help.* Draw a sketch of a bulb on the board.
- Look at the next part of the flowchart: 'use it'. Say *You can use your sentence to test a friend. For example, I can show my drawing and see if you can say the word.*
- Tell learners to choose three words from the unit and find similar words or do a drawing for each. Tell them to follow the flowchart. Learners work alone. Monitor and check.
- Once they have finished, pair learners. Ask them to show their meanings to their partner for them to guess the word.

Mission in action!

- Put learners into the same pairs as Mission Stage 2.
- Give back the Mission worksheets. Learners review their ideas. Put pairs together into groups of four. Tell each group to share their ideas and create a poster demonstrating ideas for protecting the environment.
- Learners practise presenting the information then present to the class. As each group presents, make a list of the ideas, adding to it if any new ones are suggested.
- Review the class list for protecting our environment.

Activity Book, page 77

See pages TB126–141.

Ending the lesson

- **SA** Complete the self-assessment (see Introduction).

1 Read the text and choose the correct words.

Last week, our art class's project was to make something using recycled materials. At first, we didn't have **(1)** ______ ideas so we did some research on the Internet. Then I made a bag with **(2)** ______ old T-shirts. It's big so I can put **(3)** ______ my things in it. My friend, Anna, wanted to use **(4)** ______ old cardboard boxes. So she made a cool bookcase.

You can make amazing things with **(5)** ______ rubbish and it doesn't take **(6)** ______ time if you plan carefully and use your imagination.

1	A	a lot of	B	many	C	a little
2	A	much	B	a little	C	a few
3	A	lots of	B	much	C	many
4	A	many	B	a lot of	C	a little
5	A	a little	B	much	C	a few
6	A	many	B	a few	C	much

3 Choose ten words from this unit. Record the words using the steps below.

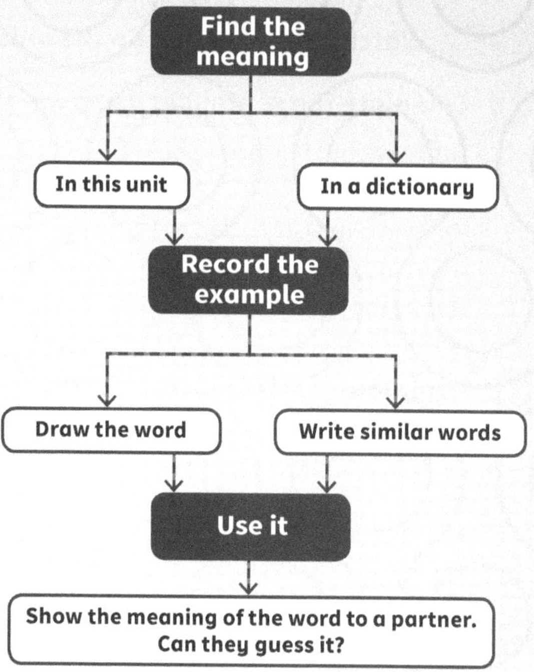

2 Say a tag question for each sentence. Then match the questions (1–6) to the answers (A–F).

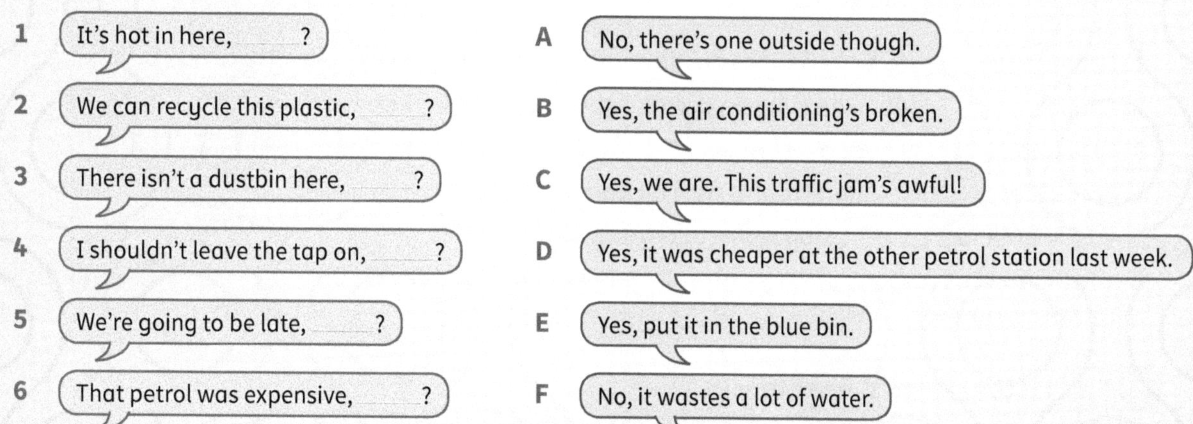

1 It's hot in here, ______ ?
2 We can recycle this plastic, ______ ?
3 There isn't a dustbin here, ______ ?
4 I shouldn't leave the tap on, ______ ?
5 We're going to be late, ______ ?
6 That petrol was expensive, ______ ?
A No, there's one outside though.
B Yes, the air conditioning's broken.
C Yes, we are. This traffic jam's awful!
D Yes, it was cheaper at the other petrol station last week.
E Yes, put it in the blue bin.
F No, it wastes a lot of water.

If my family and I put new bins in our house, we can recycle more plastic.

Mission in action!

Present your ideas to protect your environment.

Review • • • Units 4–6

1 **Watch the video and do the quiz.**

2 **Complete the sentences using *for* or *since*.**

1 The new path has been open ______ three weeks.
2 My family have recycled everything ______ we moved to our new house.
3 This traffic jam has stopped us ______ an hour!
4 I've picked up the litter in the picnic area every day ______ a month.
5 I've been worried about the rainforest ______ I watched a TV program about it.
6 I've taken public transport to school ______ I started going there.

3 **Complete the sentences. Use the words in brackets and the present continuous.**

Next Monday, I'm not going to work. At 9 am, **(1)** ______ (**I/get up**) and boiling myself an egg for breakfast. At 10 am, **(2)** ______ (**I/drive**) to the mountains and going fishing. **(3)** ______ (**I/take**) a frying pan. If I catch a fish, I'll make a fire and fry it for my lunch. After lunch, **(4)** ______ (**I/not/answer**) the phone because I want to lie down and rest. Then, at 8 pm, I'm going to the cinema with my son. **(5)** ______ (**We/watch**) *Spiderman*.

4 **Write about your day tomorrow.** **Write 25–35 words.**

5 **Complete the sentences.** **Use the words in the box.**

turn on | prefers (x2) | to drink | would rather (x2)

1 John ______ to have candles on his hamster's birthday cake.
2 Jane ______ get blue penguin curtains than get ones with aliens.
3 My dad ______ use a dishwasher than wash up in the sink.
4 My sister ______ hotel rooms with air-conditioning.
5 Judy prefers ______ tap water to bottled water.
6 Joshua would rather ______ the air conditioning than take off his favourite jumper.

6 2.32 **Listen.** **Write the sentences.**

1 

2 

3 

4 

Learning outcomes By the end of the lesson, learners will have consolidated language from Units 4–6.

Recycled language vocabulary to describe accidents and illness, present perfect simple to talk about unfinished events, present continuous to talk about the future, past simple passive, vocabulary to describe the environment

Materials video, audio

Warm-up

- Put learners into pairs. Tell learners to look at Units 4–6 and pick out six new words they learnt in the units.
- Put the pairs into groups of four. Tell each pair to act out the word they have chosen. The other pair try to guess.
  Fast finishers Choose additional words from the units.

Pupil's Book, page 78

1 Watch the video and do the quiz.

- Play the video. Learners watch and do the three unit quizzes.
- Check answers.

Key: **Unit 4** 1 B 2 C 3 B 4 B 5 B 6 A 7 A 8 A 9 B 10 C 11 B 12 A
Unit 5 1 A 2 C 3 B 4 A 5 C 6 B 7 C 8 A 9 C 10 B 11 B 12 B
Unit 6 1 C 2 A 3 B 4 C 5 B 6 B 7 B 8 C 9 A 10 A 11 C 12 B

2 Complete the sentences using *for* or *since*.

- Ask *How long have we worked on English today?* Learners answer – encourage them to use two different forms, e.g. *since 9.30 / for 15 minutes*.
- Put learners into pairs to read the sentences and choose either *for* or *since*.
- Learners work in pairs. Check answers.
  Fast finishers Learners write two sentences about their day so far using *for* and *since*.

Key: 1 for 2 since 3 for 4 for 5 since 6 since

3 Complete the sentences. Use the words in brackets and the present continuous.

- Tell learners what you are doing this weekend (e.g. *On Saturday, I'm meeting my friend and going to the cinema*).
- Put learners into groups of three and ask them to tell their group a plan for the weekend. Share answers.
- Clarify which tense is used and why. *(present continuous to talk about plans).* Tell learners to look at the paragraph of the man's plans. Complete 1 together. Learners complete 2–5.

Key: 1 I'm getting up 2 I'm driving 3 I'm taking 4 I'm not answering 5 We're watching

4  Write about your day tomorrow. Write 25–35 words.

- Tell learners to write about their plans for tomorrow. Show how to complete a quick mind map on the board. Write *tomorrow* in the middle of the board and add on a few activities. Ask *Why can this help? (Planning helps you find ideas and then organise your writing).*
- Learners complete their own mind maps. Tell them to use the mind maps to help them write about their day. Remind them of the word limit.
- Ask learners to review their writing and see if they can spot one error in spelling, grammar or punctuation to correct.

5 Complete the sentences. Use the words in the box.

- Remind learners of the plans they made for the weekend. Choose two of the plans and ask *Which plan would you rather have?* Learners answer. Write the activities onto the board, e.g. *films, sport*. Ask *Do you prefer films or sport?* Learners answer.
- Tell learners to look at the sentences and the words in the box.
- Do the first example together.
- Learners complete numbers 2–6 in pairs. Check answers.

Key: 1 prefers 2 would rather 3 would rather 4 prefers 5 drinking 6 turn on

6 2.32 Listen. Write the sentences.

- Tell learners they will listen to a story and write it. Explain they will hear the sentence several times so they should write what they can each time leaving space for words they can't hear.
- Play the audio. Learners listen and write. Repeat the audio two more times encouraging learners to add more words each time. Put learners into groups of three to compare what they have written. Play the audio again so learners can add final words.
- Check answers, writing each sentence onto the board.

See audioscripts on pages TB118–123.

Key: 1 The cyclist was hit while she was going to school. 2 Her leg was injured and her bike was damaged. 3 The girl was taken to hospital. 4 She was kept at the hospital until she felt better.

Activity Book, page 78

See pages TB126–141.

Ending the lesson

- Learners work in pairs and tell their partner about a time they had an accident or injury.

Learning outcomes By the end of the lesson, learners will have consolidated language from Units 4–6.

Recycled language vocabulary to describe food and cooking, tag questions, *prefer* and *would rather* for preference, phrases to describe quantity

Materials pictures of food, audio, sticky notes, red, green and orange board pens or cards

Warm-up

- Put pictures of food on the board, e.g. hamburger, steak, broccoli, mushrooms, carrots, salmon, cake, ice cream.
- Point to different foods and ask, e.g. *Do you prefer a hamburger or steak? (I prefer …).*
- Put learners into groups of three. Tell them to ask each other about the pictures, e.g. *You like carrots, don't you? Yes, I do.*

Pupil's Book, page 79

7 Find the exam mistakes. Write the correct sentences.

- Tell learners *When we write answers what can we do at the end to make the writing better? (check for mistakes).*
- Ask learners to look at the sentences. Say *Let's check the sentences. Each one has a mistake.* Do the first example together. Remind them 'much' is usually in negatives and questions.
- Learners work in pairs. They correct sentences 2–6.
- Check answers.

  Extra support Show learners the error for correction in each sentence.

Key: 1 I spend ~~much~~ **a lot of** money on clothes.
2 In my town you can go to the museum, the beach and a lot **of** other beautiful places. 3 I like it ~~alot~~ **a lot**.
4 I haven't got ~~much~~ **many** DVDs. 5 I don't have ~~much~~ **many** things to do today. 6 People spend **a** lot of time in front of the TV.

8 Read the situations and complete the tag questions.

- Tell learners to read the sentences in the box and find out what the topic is. *(food).*
- Look at the example given. Put learners into pairs. They complete the answers for 2–5.
- Monitor and support.
- Ask a few pairs to say their sentences for the class – one student says the sentence, a second gives the response.

  Extension Learners choose one of the examples and continue creating a mini-dialogue.

Key: 2 You haven't got a spare onion, have you?
3 You don't like broccoli, do you? 4 My uncle can eat mushrooms, can't he? 5 You travel to school by bus, don't you?

9 Choose and complete two of the challenges.

- Tell learners they are going to complete two challenges. Write three topics on the board: *health, home, cooking.*
- Ask them to read the three challenges quickly and match the challenges 1–3 with the topics. *(1 cooking, 2 health, 3 home).*
- Put learners into pairs and tell them to choose their two favourite challenges.
- Ask them to complete the challenges and see who can finish successfully first.
- Learners work in pairs.
- Check their ideas.

  Fast finishers Learners complete the third challenge.

Activity Book, page 79

See pages TB126–141.

Ending the lesson

- Draw three columns on the board. Add a red circle to the top of one column, an orange to the middle column and a green to the third column.
- Tell learners these are traffic lights (green is for things they are confident about, red is for things they don't know properly, orange is for things they think they know).
- Put learners into pairs. Give out three sticky notes to each pair. Ask them to look at the vocabulary and language from Units 4 to 6 and find one thing they are confident about, one they aren't sure about and one they don't understand. Each pair adds their sticky note to the board.
- Monitor as they work.
- Look at the items listed in the red column and call them out. Check if any of the pairs put the same item in the green column. If they have done, ask them to explain to the other learners. If they haven't, clarify yourself.
- Now repeat with the orange column.
- Finally, go to the green column. Ask learners to give examples of each item.

7 Find the mistakes. Write the correct sentences.

1 I spend much money on clothes.

2 In my town you can go to the museum, the beach and a lot other beautiful places.

3 I like it alot.

4 I haven't got much DVDs.

5 I don't have much things to do today.

6 People spend lot of time in front of the TV.

8 Read the situations and complete the tag questions.

1 You are at a restaurant with your family. The salmon is very expensive. What do you say?
The salmon is very expensive, isn't it?

2 You don't have enough onions for your recipe. You want to know if your friend has a spare one. What do you say?
You haven't ______

3 Your friend is coming to your house for dinner. You think she doesn't like broccoli but you want to check. What do you say?
You don't like ______

4 You think your uncle can eat mushrooms but you want to check with your mum. What do you say?
My uncle can ______

5 You think your friend goes to school by bus. What do you say?
You travel ______

9 Choose and complete two of the challenges.

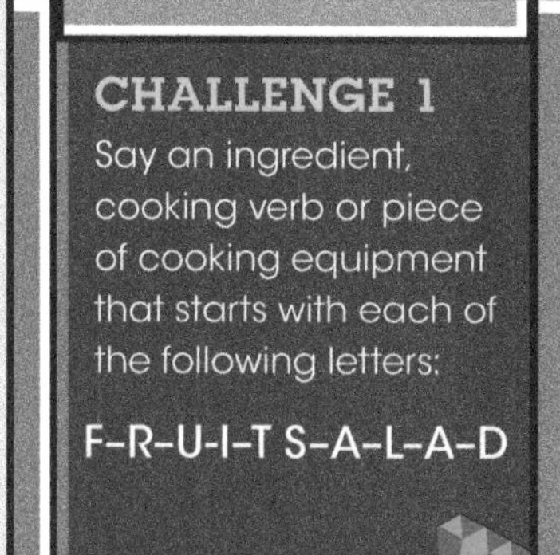

CHALLENGE 1
Say an ingredient, cooking verb or piece of cooking equipment that starts with each of the following letters:

F-R-U-I-T S-A-L-A-D

CHALLENGE 2
Look at Unit 4. Find:

- seven things that can make you feel bad.
- three things that can make you feel better.
- a part of your body.

CHALLENGE 3
Look at the pictures of objects on pages 67 and 70. Write a list of 10 objects that you have in your home and 5 objects that you don't have.

7 Feeling it

1 2 3 4 5 6 7 8 9

How would you feel in each picture? When have you felt like this?

 **Watch the video.** What makes Jim feel annoyed?

Mission Make a 'feelings wheel'

1. Brainstorm different emotions you feel.
2. Make a list of tips for feeling better.

 Make a feelings wheel with real suggestions.

Unit 7 learning outcomes

In Unit 7, learners will learn to:

- use vocabulary to describe feelings and emotions
- understand and use modal verbs to describe obligation and necessity
- understand and use *such* and *so*
- read and listen for information
- understand empathy and showing emotions

Materials video, 3 pictures (someone jogging, someone sitting on the sofa watching TV, a person standing on a busy train)

Self-assessment

- **SA** Write the unit topic on the board. Add a list: *amazed, advice, relax, understand.* Ask learners to work in groups of three and discuss what they will learn. Share ideas.
- Look at the unit outcomes (write/project them on the board) and ask learners to check if they guessed correctly.
- Ask learners to complete self-assessment (see Introduction). Say *Let's learn.*

Pupil's Book, page 80

Warm-up

- Draw a smiley face on the board. Ask *What is it? (a smiley face emoticon).* Ask learners what other emoticons we use. Encourage them to describe the emotions that each represents. Learners can draw the emoticon as they explain it.
- Write *Right now I feel …* Tell learners to work in pairs and describe how they are feeling right now. Share ideas.

  Fast finishers Learners discuss *'Yesterday I felt … '.*

How would you feel in each picture? When have you felt like this?

- Ask learners to look at the pictures in pairs and describe what people are doing in each picture. Ask how the person in each picture is feeling.
- Ask for their ideas. Give the correct word in each case.
- Now ask learners to work in pairs and mime the emotion. Their partner tries to guess which emotion they are showing.

Watch the video. What makes Jim feel annoyed?

- Stick up the three pictures on the board. Say *Here are some activities I've done this week. What have I done?* If necessary, prompt or give the correct words and learners repeat, e.g. *jogging.*
- Say *I went jogging – it was hard work but afterwards I felt satisfied. Happy with what I did. Satisfied.* Learners repeat. Say *I also watched TV, but the film wasn't good. In fact I felt …* mime boredom … *bored.* Learners repeat. Say *I also travelled on the train. But it wasn't very nice because there were too many people. I couldn't sit down. I felt … (annoyed).* Learners repeat.
- Tell learners *At the beginning of the vlog, Jim feels bored. Jenny does three things to stop him being bored. But it doesn't always work.* Ask them to find out what makes Jim feel annoyed. Play the video. Check answers.
- Write numbers 1, 2 and 3 on the board. Say *Can you remember the three things Jenny did to stop Jim feeling bored? (showed a cat video, took him jogging, made pizza).*
- Tell learners to watch again and check how Jim felt after each activity. Play the video.
- Check answers and clarify or repeat any new words, e.g. *embarrassed. (happy but still bored after the cat video; annoyed and embarrassed after jogging; great after the pizza).*

  Extension Learners discuss how each of the three activities in the vlog would make them feel.

Mission Make a 'feelings wheel'

- Tell learners *First we'll need to think about different feelings or … (emotions).* Learners repeat. Say *But some emotions are not good, so we'll think about ways to feel … (better).* Ask *What do you think will go on the feelings wheel? (feelings and suggestions to feel better).*
- Put learners into threes. Tell them to repeat the Mission, saying one part each. Say *This is our Mission.*

Activity Book, page 80

See pages TB126–141.

My unit goals

- Go through the unit goals with the learners. Either read these or put them onto the board or a poster (See suggested techniques in 'Identifying outcomes' in the teachers' in-class guide in Introduction.)
- Go back to these unit goals at the end of each Mission stage during the unit and review them.
- Say *This is our Mission page.*

Ending the lesson

- Say *I feel bored. Do you have any good ideas for me? I don't want to eat pizza or go jogging.*
- Tell them to make a list of five things you could do that would stop you feeling bored in groups of five. Say *Let's see who can suggest the best idea.*
- Invite each group to suggest their best ideas to you.
- Choose one idea you like from each group.

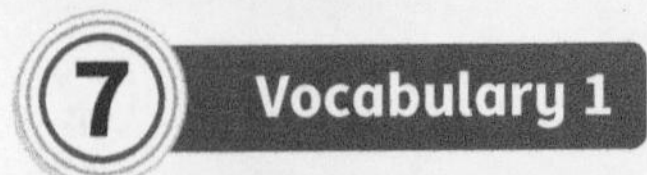

Learning outcomes By the end of the lesson, learners will be able to use vocabulary to describe emotions.

New language *relaxed, amazed, miserable, interested, positive, negative, worried*

Recycled language *annoyed, bored, embarrassed, satisfied*

Materials audio, squares of paper (11 per three learners)

Pupil's Book, page 81

Warm-up

- Tell learners they are going to draw a happiness graph. Ask learners to think of three activities. Give examples, e.g. *playing football, watching a film, reading a book*.
- Demonstrate drawing a line graph on the board. Draw two axes on the board. Write three activities along the bottom axis. Draw a frowning face at the bottom of the vertical axis and a smiley face at the top of it.
- Draw a line on the graph that demonstrates how you feel about the activities. E.g. Draw the line low at the beginning. Say *I don't like football so I feel annoyed if I have to go to a football match.* Draw the line upwards for the second activity. Say *I like seeing films so I feel satisfied when I see a film.* Draw the line to a high peak on the third activity – say *I love reading so I feel very positive when I am reading.*
- Learners choose activities and draw their own line graph.
- Ask learners to show and explain their graph to their partner, then find out how their partner feels about the same activities. As their partner tells them how they feel, they draw a second line onto the graph in a different colour to represent their partner.
- Invite a few learners to show their graphs to the class and explain how they and their partner feel.

  Fast finishers Learners write sentences onto the graph for their own line and their partner's line.

1 Read the poster. Match the definitions (1–11) to the words in bold.

- Ask learners to look at the poster. Tell them it is an 'ideas wall' where people have put sentences to show how they are feeling. Ask them *How many feelings does it show? (11).*
- Write up some words: *fireworks, dolphins, pizza, the dentist.* Say *What kind of feelings are connected to each one?* Learners suggest ideas.
- Tell learners to read the posters and see if their ideas are correct, then compare in pairs. In pairs, learners look at the definitions 1–11 and match to one of the feelings in bold.
- Check answers. As you go through the answers, say each word clearly. Learners repeat.

  Extension Learners divide the adjectives that describe positive feelings and words that describe negative feelings.

Key: 1 negative 2 positive 3 relaxed 4 satisfied 5 miserable 6 bored 7 amazed 8 worried 9 annoyed 10 embarrassed 11 interested

2 Complete five of the *I feel* … sentences from Activity 1 so that they are true for you.

- Look at the first example together and read the two things that make people feel relaxed. Say *I feel relaxed when I go for a walk in the park.* Tell learners to choose five of the emotions and write sentences that are true for them.
- Learners work in pairs and tell each other their five sentences. Monitor and correct as they work.

  Fast finishers Learners compare their sentences with a new partner and find out if they chose similar adjectives.

3  PRONUNCIATION Listen and repeat.

- Ask learners to listen and repeat the words.
- Play the audio. Learners listen and repeat.
- Learners complete the task. Monitor and support.

  Track 3.02
  bored
  worried
  positive
- Learners complete the activity on page 119 (see page TB124).

Activity Book, page 81

See pages TB126–141.

Ending the lesson

- Write the adjectives of feeling onto the board: *relaxed, bored, annoyed, miserable, amazed, positive, embarrassed, negative, interested, satisfied, worried.*
- Learners work in groups of three. Give out 11 squares of paper to each group and tell them to copy the words onto the squares of paper – one word per paper. Tell them to check the spelling as they write.
- Tell learners to put the adjectives in alphabetical order. Learners complete the task as quickly as possible. See which group finishes first.
- Tell learners to divide the words into three groups – words that have one syllable (or sound), words that have two syllables and words that have three syllables. Remind them the sound and spelling of the words can be different.
- Tell learners to divide the words into two groups: positive and negative emotions.

  Extension Learners turn the papers face down. They take it in turns to pick up a word and try to remember the definition.

1 **Read the poster.** Match the definitions (1–11) to the words in bold.

A I feel **relaxed** …
- when I'm at home with my cats.
- at school when I'm with my friends.

B I feel **miserable** …
- when I'm ill.
- when it rains for days and days. I like sunny weather!

C I feel **annoyed** …
- with Sam for telling Marie my secret.
- about the rain today. I want to ride my bike.

D I feel **amazed** …
- when I go to watch fireworks.
- when I see rainbows.

E I feel **positive** …
- about my team this season. (I think we'll win the league!)
- about my friends. I love you all!

F I feel **worried** …
- because I don't have a T-shirt for P.E. Can anyone lend me one?
- about going to the dentist next week.

G I feel **negative** …
- about my project – I need to try harder.
- when I can't answer a question in maths.

H I feel **satisfied** …
- when I finish some work at school and I know I've tried my best.
- after I've eaten a huge pizza!

I I feel **embarrassed** …
- when I speak in front of other people.
- when my phone rings in the library!!!!

J I feel **interested** …
- in dolphins. Did you know that some dolphins only have eight teeth but others have 250?
- in recycling old clothes. Who wants to learn sewing with me?

K I feel **bored** …
- when my friends play computer games.
- when I'm sitting in the car. But it's great to arrive at the beach or my cousin's house!

1 only thinking of the bad side of something ☐
2 full of hope ☐
3 free of worries ☐
4 pleased because you have what you wanted ☐
5 very unhappy ☐
6 unhappy and tired because something isn't interesting ☐
7 very surprised ☐
8 unhappy and thinking about your problems ☐
9 a bit angry ☐
10 shy ☐
11 wanting to read about, talk about or learn more about something ☐

2 **Complete five of the *I feel …* sentences from Activity 1 so that they are true for you.**

I feel relaxed when I'm at home watching TV.

3 3.02 **PRONUNCIATION**
Listen and repeat.

page 119

1 **Read Jim's blog quickly. What problems do you think the people have?**

Jim's Big Blog

This week we asked our friends if we could help with any of their problems. Here's what we wrote!

Helping our friends

Hello,

I love your blog! You always have interesting ideas to write about.

How can I think of ideas for my blog? I often sit in my room thinking until I feel miserable. Please help!

Thanks, Kyo_hearts

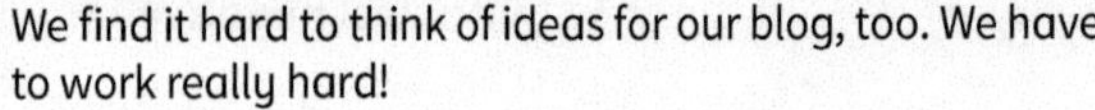

We find it hard to think of ideas for our blog, too. We have to work really hard!

The best way to have a few good ideas is to have lots of ideas. You should write a long list of things you're interested in. You needn't worry if some of your ideas aren't very good and you don't have to spend more than five or ten minutes writing either. When you've finished the list you can use the best ideas in your blog.

Jim

Hi Kyo_hearts,

You ought to write about something you love. It doesn't matter if your blog's popular or not. If you're blogging about what you love, then you'll love blogging.

Jenny

Hi,

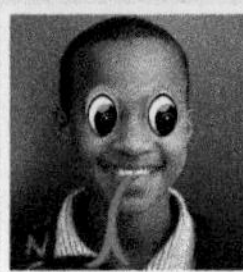

I'd like a pet snake to love and look after, but my parents say that I can't. I ask them but they always say I have to wait until I'm older. I'm so annoyed with them. Do you think I should get one without telling them?

Florenville2025

I think you ought to understand your parents. Why don't they want you to have a snake? Maybe they're worried about how much it costs? Or maybe they're annoyed with you because you often ask them about it?

You shouldn't get a snake without telling your parents. You'll be too worried about them finding it.

Jim

Hi Florenville2025,

No! NO! NO! You **MUSTN'T** get a snake without telling your parents. You should try to be satisfied with what you have. You ought to get a plant if you want something to love and look after.

If your parents say you can't have a snake, you must listen to them!

Jenny

2 ☆ **Read the blog again. Say which person ...**

1 enjoyed reading Jim and Jenny's blog.
 A Kyo_hearts B Florenville2025

2 thinks it is hard to have ideas to write about.
 A Jim B Jenny

3 feels a bit angry with his parents.
 A Jenny B Florenville2025

4 thinks that Florenville2025 won't feel relaxed if he gets a snake.
 A Jim B Jenny

EXAM TIP! Make sure you know exactly which part of the text gives you the answer to the question. If it helps you, **underline the sentences** in the text which are useful.

3 **Who do you think gave the most useful advice? What advice would you give?**

Learning outcomes By the end of the lesson, learners will be able to read for specific information and understand modal verbs of necessity and obligation.

New language *should, ought to, have to, needn't, must, mustn't*

Recycled language adjectives describing emotions

Materials paper and pens

Warm-up

- Tell learners to think about taking an exam. Ask them what is difficult about an exam and how they feel about it.
- Learners discuss in pairs. Share their ideas.
- Say to learners *Let's think of some advice, some ideas to help.* Write on the board *If you are taking an exam, you should …*
- Put learners in groups of four. Tell them to think of at least three ways to end the sentence. Give an example, e.g. … *you should do all your homework to get ready.*
- Learners work in groups of three and discuss. Share ideas.

  Extension Learners make a poster for the classroom wall on exam advice.

Pupil's Book, page 82

1 Read Jim's blog quickly. What problems do you think the people have?

- Tell learners to look at the pictures. Ask them to guess the problems that the people have.
- Learners discuss in pairs.
- Tell learners to read quickly and see if any of the ideas listed on the board were correct.
- Learners read quickly and answer the questions.
- Put learners into pairs to compare ideas.
- Check answers. Go through their predictions on the board and tick or cross them out. Confirm the final answers.

Key: Kyo_hearts can't think of ideas for a blog. Florenville2025 would like a pet snake, but isn't allowed.

2 ★ Read the blog again. Say which person …

- Put learners into pairs. Tell them to read the questions in Activity 2 carefully to think about the information they need to find. Ask them to underline key words in the questions.
- Share ideas. *(1 enjoyed reading, 2 hard to have ideas, 3 angry, 4 won't feel relaxed).*
- Tell them to read again. This time they look for the specific information, so they need to read carefully. Remind them the words may not be exactly the same as the question but have a similar meaning. Learners read carefully.
- Put learners into pairs to compare ideas.
- Check answers. In each case ask them to find the words that helped them answer. *(1 I love your blog = enjoyed reading; 2 how can I think of ideas = hard to have ideas; 3 annoyed = angry; 4 be too worried = won't feel relaxed).*

Key: 1 A 2 A 3 B 4 A

EXAM TIP! Ask a stronger learner to read the exam tip. Say *So we read the article once to get a general idea of the content. Then we read some parts more carefully to find answers.*

3 Who do you think gave the most useful advice? What advice would you give?

- Ask learners to think about the advice Jim and Jenny have given and think about whether they agree with it or not. Do they have any other advice they can add?
- Learners discuss in pairs. Share their ideas.

Key: Learners' own answers.

Activity Book, page 82

See pages TB126–141.

Ending the lesson

- Tell learners to close their books. Put learners into pairs. Give each pair a sheet of paper.
- Write two lists on the board: *1: unhappy, difficult, should write about what you enjoy; 2: angry, happy, not a good idea to get a snake without telling your parents*
- Ask learners to copy the words onto the paper.
- Tell learners that the blogs all contain words with the same meanings. Tell them list 1 comes from the first blog and list 2 comes from the second.
- Tell learners to find words or phrases with the same meaning in the blogs and write them next to the items on the list. The first pair to finish are the winners.
- Learners open their books at page 82 and check. See which pair finishes first.
- Check answers. *(1: unhappy – miserable, difficult – hard, should write about what you enjoy – ought to write about something you love; 2: angry – annoyed, happy – satisfied, not a good idea to get a snake without telling your parents – you shouldn't* (alternative *you mustn't) get a snake without telling your parents).*

  Fast finishers Learners draw and label a diagram showing how they would use the bottle and present the plan.

7 Language practice 1

Learning outcomes By the end of the lesson, learners will be able to use modal verbs of necessity and obligation.

New language *should, ought to, have to, needn't, must, mustn't*

Recycled language adjectives of emotion

Materials cards with problems written on them (e.g. *I forgot my homework*).

Pupil's Book, page 83

Warm-up

- Put learners into pairs. Ask them to think of a problem they had, who they talked to and what they did.

Presentation

- Ask learners to look at the blogs on page 82 again in pairs and find any words or expressions used to give advice.
  Extra support Give learners a list of words and ask them to find them in sentences in the blog: *needn't, have to, should, ought to, must, mustn't*. Check answers, highlighting the sentences where the words appear.
- Ask learners *Which advice sounds the strongest? (mustn't get a snake; must listen; have to wait).*
- Ask *Which advice is saying 'it's a good idea'? (should / ought to).* Ask *Which advice sounds like you can choose? (needn't worry; don't have to spend).*

Grammar look: *needn't, have to, should, ought to, must, mustn't*

- Look at the title of the box. Ask learners *What kind of verbs are these? (modal verbs).*
- Ask a strong learner to read out the first three sentences. Ask which modal verbs are used. *(have to / must / mustn't).* Say *Is this something we can choose or is it something another person is telling us? (another person is telling us).* Say *'you have to wait' and 'you must listen' means I can't choose. And 'you mustn't get a snake' is the same. I can't choose to get a snake.*
- Say *Be careful. 'Must' is positive and the same as 'have to'. 'Mustn't' is negative. But 'don't have to' is different.* Say *If you don't have to do something can you choose? (yes). Which other word is similar? (needn't).*
- Read out the final two sentences. Say *Are these sentences letting you choose? (yes). But they are saying this is a good idea? (yes).*
- Draw a table on the board. Tell learners to copy it. They work in pairs and write the correct modal verbs in the boxes.

	positive	*negative*
Someone tells me – no choice	*must* *have to*	*mustn't*
It's up to me		*needn't* *don't/doesn't have to*
Someone tells me it's a good idea / not a good idea	*should* *ought to*	*shouldn't*

- Ask learners to work in pairs to do questions 1–3 in the **Grammar look** box. Check answers.

Key: 1 must 2 Needn't 3 ought to

Complete the Grammar look on page 125.
See pages TB125–126.

1 Read two more messages to Jim and Jenny. Write three sentences to reply to each message. Use *needn't, have to, should, ought to, must* or *mustn't*.

- Learners read the two messages.
- Learners check in pairs then think of three pieces of advice they can give. Tell them to write three sentences using the modal verbs. Monitor and support as they work.
  Extra support Give learners some sentence stems for each picture to help them start the story.

2 In pairs, share your ideas. Which letter would you like to reply to?

- Tell learners to compare their ideas and sentences in pairs and choose which letter they would like to reply to.
- Ask learners to read out sentences giving the best advice.

Mission Stage 1

- Ask *What do you do each day at school?* Learners list some of the different activities they do at school. Compare ideas. Ask learners to look at their activities and think about how they feel. They can make a mind map.
- Share ideas asking why they feel the different emotions.

Activity Book, page 83

See pages TB126–141.

Ending the lesson

- Tell learners to stand in two lines in front of you. Explain that the first learner to answer will gain a point for their team.
- Show a card with a problem to the two learners at the front of the line, e.g. *I forgot my homework.* The two learners at the front try to answer by giving advice, e.g. *You must tell the teacher; you should write a note so you don't forget again.* Award a point to the team which gives the fastest advice correctly. Repeat for other problems.

Grammar look: *needn't, have to, should, ought to, must, mustn't*

'I have to wait until I'm older.'

'If your parents say you can't have a snake, you must listen to them!'

'You mustn't get a snake without telling your parents.'

'You needn't worry if some of your ideas aren't very good.'

'You don't have to spend more than five or ten minutes writing either.'

'You should try to be satisfied with what you have.'

'You ought to write about something you love.'

1 *Have to* and **must** / **should** have similar meanings. They're used when we don't choose to do something and someone else (like a parent, teacher or the police) chooses for us.

2 ***Ought to*** / ***Needn't*** and *don't have to* have similar meanings. They are used when we do not need to do something. Their meaning is different to *mustn't*. *Mustn't* is used when there is a rule about something you cannot do.

3 *Should* and ***ought to*** / ***mustn't*** have similar meanings. They are used when something is correct or a good thing to do. We can choose if we want to do these things.

page 125

1 **Read two more messages to Jim and Jenny.** Write three sentences to reply to each message. Use *needn't, have to, should, ought to, must* or *mustn't*.

1

I forgot my best friend's birthday last week and I didn't get him a card or say 'Happy Birthday'. I feel really miserable because of it. What should I do?

SnakeGoat

2

My friends want to go swimming in the river after school, but I'm worried about it. There's a big sign that says it's dangerous to swim. What should I do?

Lunchtime_Tam

2 **In pairs, share your ideas.** Which letter would you like to reply to?

I'd like to reply to Letter 1. I forgot my cousin's birthday once, so I know what SnakeGoat should do.

Mission Stage 1

Brainstorm different emotions you feel.

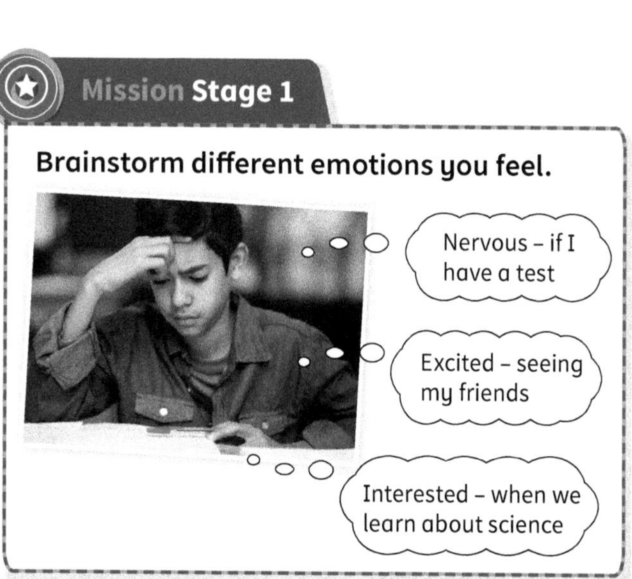

Nervous – if I have a test
Excited – seeing my friends
Interested – when we learn about science

Vocabulary 2

1 3.04 **Listen. Where did the boy fall asleep?** ______________________

2 3.05 **Listen again and point to pictures 1–6.**

3 3.06 **Complete the sentences.** Use the words in the box. Listen and check.

breathe deeply   do exercise   go jogging
goes to the gym   look after her health
keep fit   reduce stress   recover   aching   diet

1 My mum said she was feeling worried because we're moving house so she wanted a way to __________ .
2 We go to the sports centre together to relax and __________ .
3 You can __________ there, like running or swimming.
4 When we __________ we wear special glasses. It feels like we're running away from a monster!
5 While my mum __________ to lift weights, there's a big swimming pool where I go to swim with sharks.
6 After we exercise, there are lovely places to sit and __________ .
7 There's a little pool that we sit in when we've got tired, __________ legs.
8 There's a garden on the roof. You can just sit, __________ and listen to the river.
9 They've only got healthy food. A good __________ is important – so they haven't got cake or ice cream.
10 My mum always says she wants to __________ better.

4 ★ **In pairs, ask and answer the questions.**

1 What kinds of exercise do you like doing?
2 What do you do to look after your health?
3 What do you think are the best ways to reduce stress?

EXAM TIP! When you answer questions, use **full sentences** and try to say four things.

Learning outcomes By the end of the lesson, learners will be able to listen to understand opinions.

New language *breathe, exercise, keep fit, reduce stress, recover, aching*

Recycled language modal verbs of necessity and obligation

Materials audio, picture of a gym, 3 pictures (junk food, a sofa, someone looking very stressed)

Pupil's Book, page 84

Warm-up

- Ask learners to suggest ways of keeping healthy. Pick up on the idea of exercise. Say *Exercise is important. It helps us to keep fit.* Say *exercise* and *keep fit.* Learners repeat.
- Say *Exercise also helps us relax. If we are stressed or worried it helps us. It reduces stress.* Learners repeat. Say *We can also reduce stress by breathing deeply.* Take a deep breath. Say *breath deeply.* Learners repeat.
- Ask learners how they feel after exercise. Say *Sometimes our bodies are aching …* (mime aching). Learners repeat. Say *And we need time to recover, to feel stronger and less tired again.* Say *recover.* Learners repeat.
- Show learners a picture of a sports centre. Ask *What is it?* Ask what they can find (e.g. *running machines, weights, swimming pool, showers, café*).
- Tell them that they are going to plan a visit to a gym. They should think about what they will do for exercise and what they will do to recover after.
- Put learners into groups of three or four to plan.
- Learners share ideas.

1 3.04 Listen. Where did the boy fall asleep?

- Tell learners they will listen to a conversation between two friends about going to a sports centre. Ask them to listen and find out where the boy fell asleep.
- Play the audio. Learners check in pairs. Check answers.

See audioscripts on pages TB118–123.

Key: On the roof of the sports centre, listening to the river.

2 3.05 Listen again and point to pictures 1–6.

- Tell learners to read through the activities 1 to 6 in pairs and try to remember which ones the boy did.
- Tell them to listen and check. Play the audio. Check answers.
- Track 3.05 Repeat previous track.

Key: 1 go jogging 2 swim in the big pool 3 recover in the small pool 4 relax in the roof garden

3 3.06 Complete the sentences. Use the words in the box. Listen and check.

- Ask learners to read the sentences 1–10 and think about which words go into the gaps.
- Learners work in pairs to complete the gaps.
- Monitor and support as they work.
- Tell them to listen to the audio one more time and choose their final answers. Play the audio.
- Check answers with the class.
- Track 3.06 Repeat previous track.

Key: 1 keep fit 2 reduce stress 3 do exercise 4 go jogging 5 goes to the gym 6 recover 7 aching 8 breathe deeply 9 diet 10 look after her health

EXAM TIP! Ask a stronger learner to read the exam tip. Say *In the speaking part of the exam, we know it is important to give long answers. How can we do it?* Learners suggest ideas. Say *Remember to use complete sentences. Give lots of examples and try to say four things not just one.*

4 In pairs, ask and answer the questions.

- Ask learners to read the questions in pairs and answer as fully as possible.
- Monitor and support as they talk. Share ideas with the class.

Activity Book, page 84

See pages TB126–141.

Ending the lesson

- Act being tired. Tell learners *I've been working hard recently. And I don't feel good. I have a few problems.* Show pictures of junk food, a sofa and a stressed face. Ask learners for the problems. *(unhealthy eating; sitting and not exercising; stress).*
- Say *I need some advice. I have a day to myself. I think I should try to do something to feel better. What kind of things do you think I should do?* Tell learners to plan a day, e.g. activities/food/places.
- Learners discuss and plan in groups of five. Each group presents a plan for the day. Choose the one you like best.

  Fast finishers Learners write five sentences giving advice to someone who is working too much.

Learning outcomes By the end of the lesson, learners will be able to use *so* and *such* to describe unusual or surprising things.

New language *so … that, such a … that*

Recycled language adjectives of emotion

Materials playing cards (or 9 large cards with symbols and the numbers 2–10 written on them), pictures (a huge dinner, e.g. an oversized hamburger or sandwich, a beautiful view)

Warm-up

- Show learners some playing cards (or make a few by drawing symbols and writing numbers onto nine large cards – ensure you have the numbers 2 to 10. Ask learners the names of the symbols. *(hearts, diamonds, clubs and spades).*
- Ask them which one they like best. Learners answer.
- Say *Let's play a guessing game.* Divide the class into groups of four. Show them nine cards (numbered 2 to 10). Mix the cards up then put them face down.
- Hold up the first card. Ask *What number is it?* Learners say. Tell them *Guess if the next card is higher or lower. Choose an answer for your group.* Learners discuss quickly and choose. Groups call out their guess.
- Hold up the next card and award a point to groups that guessed correctly. Continue going through the rest of the cards. (The last one should be easy to guess!)
- Ask learners *How did you feel when we played the game?* Learners suggest ideas. Encourage them to use a range of words, e.g. *stressed/excited/satisfied*.
- Put learners into pairs. Tell them to discuss with their partner how they felt at different parts of the game. They find out if they felt the same way.

  Extra support Learners have a list of adjectives to refer to.

Pupil's Book, page 85

Presentation

- Put up on the board a picture of a huge meal, e.g. an oversized hamburger. Ask learners if they would like to eat it. Learners respond. Ask *Do you think most people could eat all that food? (no).* Say *It's so big that I couldn't eat it.* Learners repeat. Say *It's such a big meal that I couldn't eat it.* Learners repeat.
- Now show a picture of a beautiful view. Ask if learners think it is a nice place. Learners respond. Say *It's so beautiful that I took a photo.* Learners repeat. Say *It's such a beautiful place that I took a photo.* Learners repeat.

Grammar look: *such … that / so … that*

- Ask learners to read the sentences in the top of the **Grammar look** box from the listening text.
- Put the learners into pairs. Ask them to choose the correct option in each question 1–3. Check answers clarifying where necessary.

Key: 1 surprising, strange or unusual 2 so 3 such

Complete the Grammar look on page 125.
See pages TB125–126.

1 Complete the sentences. Use *so … that* or *such … that*.

- Tell learners they will complete the sentences using *so … that* or *such … that*. Ask them to read the first example and say why the answer is 'such'. *(because it is a noun: 'big sandwich').*
- Learners complete the sentences in pairs. Check answers.

Key: 2 so, that 3 so, that 4 such, that 5 so, that 6 such, that

2 Complete the sentences with your own ideas.

- Learners complete the sentences in pairs. Check answers.

3 Work in small groups. Talk about when three of the sentences in Activity 1 described your life.

- Read the example together.
- Put learners into groups of three. Tell them to take it in turns to say sentences that are true for them.

Key: Learners' own answers.

Mission Stage 2

- In pairs learners think of emotions that are negative, e.g. bored/stressed, and why people feel them.
- Ask for ideas and create a list on the board. In pairs learners think of some tips or advice to help the person feel better for each emotion. Remind them of language they can use, e.g. *should / ought to / needn't*, etc.
- Once learners have finished, put pairs together to create groups of six. Ask them to share their ideas.
- Check suggestions with the whole group. Go through the list on the board and ask each group what tips they can give.

Activity Book, page 85

See pages TB126–141.

Ending the lesson

- **SA** Ask learners to complete their self-assessment (see Introduction).

Grammar look: *such … that / so … that*

'It's so fun that my mum and I always laugh a lot!'
'It's such a relaxing place that I once fell asleep there!'

1 *So … that* and *such … that* are used for **surprising, strange or unusual / boring, uninteresting or normal** situations.

2 We use ***so / such*** with adjectives (e.g. *good, bad, boring*) or adverbs (e.g. *quickly, tiny*).

3 We use ***so / such*** with noun phrases (e.g. *an interesting person, a great cook*).

page 125

1 **Complete the sentences.** Use *so … that* or *such … that.*

1 I exercised for such a long time that my legs ached!
2 I felt ______ stressed ______ I couldn't sleep!
3 I was ______ embarrassed ______ my face was red!
4 I thought it was ______ a boring book ______ I didn't finish it!
5 I felt ______ annoyed ______ I walked away!
6 It was ______ a big sandwich ______ I couldn't eat it all!

2 **Complete the sentences with your own ideas.**

1 It was such a delicious cake that ______
2 The weather was so ______
3 The test was so difficult that ______
4 It was such a hot day that ______

3 **Work in small groups.** Talk about when three of the sentences in Activity 1 described your life.

When I went to the mountains with my grandpa, I exercised for so long that my legs ached.

When I went swimming last Monday, I swam for such a long time that my arms ached.

Mission Stage 2

Make a list of tips for feeling better. Share your list with your friend. Do they have any good ideas you missed?

How to feel better!!
☺ Play some sport
☺ Call your friend
☺ Look at photographs of your family

1 In pairs, talk about the questions.

1 What does a cowboy do?

2 Where do wolves live? What do they eat?

3.07 The cowboy who cried wolf

Life on the ranch was quiet. Everyone worked hard to grow plants and look after the animals, and they fell asleep straight away when night came. But one night, a noise woke them all up. AHR-WOOOOO! They knew that noise! It was a wolf, and there were a lot of calves on the ranch. Somebody would need to make sure that no wolves got into the fields.

Buck was the youngest cowboy on the ranch and he was always looking for excitement. Early the next morning Cody, one of the older cowboys, said to Buck, 'You have to stay here today and look after the calves. There are wolves about! If you see one you should shout, "Wolf!" The people on the ranch will come and help you.' Buck was annoyed. He wanted to ride with the others! But he had to do what Cody said. So, the cowboys rode off to the west and Buck stayed in the field to look after the calves.

Buck was so bored! He had no one to talk to, and no wolves came. Buck stared so hard that his eyes hurt. Hours passed and Buck was miserable. Finally, he had an idea. 'The ranch workers will come and talk to me if a wolf comes,' he thought. He jumped up and shouted, 'Wolf!' At once men came running from the ranch. His little sister, Blossom, came too.

'Where's the wolf?' shouted the men. 'It was over there,' said Buck. 'But it went away when I shouted.' The men waited for a few minutes, but when they didn't see a wolf, they went back to their work.

'Did you really see a wolf?' Blossom asked Buck. 'Of course, I did,' he said. Blossom gave him a strange look. Buck felt embarrassed, but Blossom didn't say anything.

Learning outcomes By the end of the lesson, learners will have read a story and be able to understand the importance of telling the truth.

New language *calves, wolf, truth, lie*

Recycled language adjectives of emotion, *should, have to, must, mustn't*

Materials audio, picture of a ranch in America

Warm-up

- Put learners into groups of four.
- Show them a picture of a ranch in America (ideally from the past).
- Ask *What is it? (a ranch: like a big farm).* Ask *Which country has ranches? (America: If learners suggest other countries, e.g. Australia, accept the answer but say this one is in America).*
- Ask what they think life was like for the first ranchers. *(they had to work hard).*
- Tell learners to discuss what kind of problems they think the people on the ranches had to deal with.
- Learners discuss in pairs.
- Share their ideas. *(they had to build everything themselves; they had to grow and make their own food because there were no shops; there were dangerous animals around).*

  Extension Ask learners if they would like to have worked on a ranch in the past or not. If not what would they miss from their life now? Share ideas.

Pupil's Book, page 86

1 In pairs, talk about the questions.

- Ask learners to look at the title of the story on page 86 and the pictures on pages 86–87. Ask them what kind of text it is. *(a story).*
- Put learners into groups of three. Ask learners to imagine a typical day for the cowboys in the pictures and describe it. Learners discuss.
- Put two pairs together to make groups of four and ask them to compare their ideas and see if they are similar.
- Put learners back into pairs. Ask learners to think about the title and the pictures and answer the questions.
- Check their ideas.

Presentation

- Ask learners to look at the pictures on page 86 and point to: a calf, a wolf, a cowboy, the ranch. Ask learners *What is the plural for calf? (calves). And for wolf? (wolves).*
- Ask them to look at the first picture on page 87 and point to the characters. Say *This is Buck, this is his sister Blossom and this is Curly, an older cowboy.* Ask them how they think each person is feeling in the picture. Learners share ideas.

  Extension Ask learners to guess what happens in the story from the pictures. Put them into pairs to discuss and share their ideas. Make a note of their predictions to check off when they have read the story.

3.07 The cowboy who cried wolf

- Tell learners to listen and read the story on page 86 and find out if their ideas for the first part of the story are correct.
- Play the first part of the audio to the end of page 86.
- Learners read and listen.
- Ask learners to compare their ideas in pairs.
- Check their answers.
- Ask *Which lie did Buck tell? (He said a wolf had come). Why did he tell the lie? (Because he was annoyed and bored and wanted the men to come and talk to him).*
- Ask learners what they think happens next. Learners discuss in pairs.
- Share their predictions.
- Tell learners to look at page 87. Play the second part of the audio to the end.
- Learners read page 87 and listen to the audio.
- Learners compare ideas in pairs.
- Check answers. Ask *Did Buck tell more lies? (Yes, he said the wolves had come back). Was it a good thing or bad thing? (bad thing). Why? (Because when the wolves came later no one believed him).*

Activity Book, page 86

See pages TB126–141.

Ending the lesson

- Put learners into pairs.
- Ask them to think about the story and think of five sentences that describe the story. Tell them to change two of the sentences so that they are not true, e.g. *The youngest cowboy Cody had to look after the calves.*
- Put the pairs of students into groups of four.
- Tell each pair to give their sentences to the other pair. They listen and spot the sentence which is incorrect, e.g. *No that's not true. The youngest cowboy is Buck, not Cody!*
- Monitor and support as they work.

  Fast finishers Learners pair with a new set of partners and try again.

Learning outcomes By the end of the lesson, learners will have read a story to understand description and understand the importance of telling the truth.

New language *ashamed*

Recycled language *ranch, cowboy, calf, wolf,* adjectives of emotion, *so, such*

Materials audio pictures of places with different activities (busy street, park, sports centre)

Social and Emotional Skill: telling the truth

- After reading the story, ask learners *Are there situations when it is OK to tell a lie?* Say *We sometimes tell 'white' lies so we don't hurt someone's feelings, e.g. your friend asks if you like their new trousers. You don't like them, but say you do to avoid hurting their feelings.*
- In pairs, learners make a short story with two possible outcomes: one where people in the story tell the truth and one where they tell a lie. Learners read the story to the class, explaining why it's better not to lie.

Warm-up

- Tell them to look at each picture and describe what is happening to remind them of the story. When they have finished, ask *How many times did Buck lie about the wolves? (twice). What happened when he didn't lie? (no one came).*
- Give each learner a role: Buck, Blossom, a cowboy (Curly), a ranch worker (Jeb), a calf, a wolf. They act out the story.

  Extension Choose a group to act out their role play for the class.

Pupil's Book, page 87

Presentation

- Put learners in groups of three and ask them to imagine how each character felt during the story.
- On the board write: *excitement, annoyed, bored, miserable, embarrassed, worried, bored and lonely, amazed, furious, annoyed.* Check understanding quickly. Tell learners these words are in the same order as the story. Ask them to try to guess what or who each adjective is about and why.
- Ask learners to read quickly to find the words. Tell them to read these parts of the story again to check their ideas.
- Ask learners to describe how Buck feels at the end of the story, e.g. *embarrassed because everyone knew he lied.* Ask why the calves were killed. *(no one believed Buck any more).*

  Fast finishers Learners read the adjectives to a partner. Their partner gives the meaning of the adjective.

Key: excitement – Buck always looks for excitement. annoyed – Buck is annoyed when he has to look after the calves. bored – Buck feels bored when he is left alone. miserable – After a few hours, Buck feels miserable. embarrassed – Buck feels embarrassed when he tells Blossom a lie.
worried – Cody was worried about the wolves.
bored and lonely – Buck was bored and lonely on the fourth day. amazed – How the ranch workers felt when they went to help a second time and there were still no wolves. furious – Blossom has guessed her brother is lying and is very angry with him. annoyed – Blossom tells him everyone is annoyed with him because there have been no wolves.

2 In pairs, talk about the questions.

- Put learners in pairs and ask them to discuss the questions. Tell them to find parts of the story that help them find the first answer. Ask them to share ideas about telling lies.

Key: Sample answer 1 Buck is responsible because if he hadn't lied, the workers would have come to save the calves.

Activity Book, page 87

See pages TB126–141.

Ending the lesson

- Give groups of three a picture, e.g. a busy street, activities in a park, a sports centre with lots of activities. Learners write ten sentences describing the picture: five are true and five are incorrect. Then put each group of three with another group which has a different picture.
- The first group shows their picture to the second for a minutes, then hides it. They read their sentences. The second group says if the sentence is true or false. They get a point for each sentence they get right plus an extra point if they can correct the information.
- The second group give the first group their picture to repeat the sequence.

7

The next day Buck wanted to go with the other cowboys, but Cody was worried about wolves. 'You must stay and look after the calves again,' he said. So, Buck stayed! Day after day, it was the same thing, looking at a dull field of cows. By the fourth day, he was so bored and lonely that he shouted, 'Wolf!' again. Once more the men from the ranch ran to help him. They were amazed when they didn't see a wolf attacking the calves. 'Where's the wolf?' they called to Buck. 'It was over there,' said Buck. 'But it ran away when I shouted.' 'Are you sure you saw a wolf?' asked a man called Jeb. 'I definitely saw one!' said Buck. 'That's why I shouted.' The men from the ranch went away again, complaining.

Blossom was furious with her brother. 'There was NO wolf,' she said to Buck. 'You mustn't shout "wolf" again. Everybody is very annoyed with you!'

The next day Buck suddenly heard AHR-WOOOOOO! He jumped up. It wasn't one wolf! It was 3 … 4 … 5 … a pack of wolves! 'Wolves! Wolves! Wolves!' screamed Buck. But nobody came. They didn't believe him anymore! Buck ran at the wolves, shouting. But it was too late. All the calves were dead and Buck knew he would be in BIG trouble …

2 In pairs, talk about the questions.

1 Who or what is responsible for the death of the calves? Why?

2 Do you ever tell lies? Why?/Why not? When might you tell a lie?

3 How do you think Buck feels when he realises he's made a mistake? Do you think he feels bad for telling lies?

Cross-curricular

1 **Look at the pictures below. What different emotions can you see?**

2 3.08 **Listen and read the text. Why is it good to understand how other people feel?**

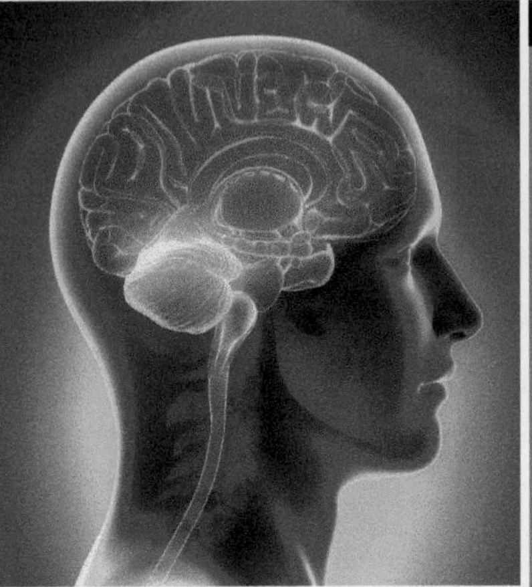

Emotional awareness

We can feel different things on different days. Sometimes we feel miserable because we had an argument with a friend and sometimes we feel worried about something. It's important to understand our feelings and learn how to show them so that we don't make our friends, our family and ourselves sad.

Babies and children show their emotions by laughing or crying because they can't say what they feel and why. As we grow up, we learn how to understand how we are feeling. This is called emotional awareness. It also helps us have good relationships with other people.

When we feel strong emotions or we are stressed there are chemicals in our brains that can make us feel happy, annoyed or sad. This chemical is called cortisol. It can be good for us because it gives us energy. However, if we feel too stressed then we have too much cortisol in our brains and it's difficult to sleep.

When you see your friends, you might be able to work out what they are feeling by their faces. How do you think these people feel?

It's good to think about how other people are feeling too. For example, if your friend is sad that he didn't get onto the football team and you are sad with him, you are sharing his sadness – this is called empathy. Have you ever seen that your dad is annoyed when he has to tidy your things? If you think about how your dad feels and understand that he's doing extra work and why he might feel annoyed … that's also empathy.

Empathy and emotional awareness are important for all relationships – at home, at school and at work when we are older. It helps you to understand more about the people and the world around you.

3 **Read the text again and say *yes* or *no*.**

1 We need to understand our own feelings before we can understand other peoples'.

2 Cortisol helps us sleep.

3 We can sometimes understand how friends feel by looking at them.

4 Adults often feel empathy when they have to tidy things.

5 You should think about how other people feel in all situations.

4 **In pairs, talk about things you can do when you are feeling stressed or sad.**

When I feel stressed, I like to go outside for a walk.

I like playing my guitar.

Learning outcomes By the end of the lesson, learners will be able to respond to a text using critical thinking and emotional intelligence, and will have developed their emotional awareness.

New language *emotional awareness, chemicals, brain*

Recycled language adjectives of emotion

Materials paper, two boxes

Warm-up

- Ask learners to think of two emotions that they have talked about in the lessons so far.
- In pairs, learners mime their emotions using their faces and bodies. Their partner guesses the emotions.
- Ask learners *How easy was it to guess the emotion?*

  Fast finishers Learners test each other on the spelling of the two adjectives they chose.

Pupil's Book, page 88

1 Look at the pictures below. What different emotions can you see?

- Ask learners to look at the pictures on the page in pairs and decide what each emotion is. Check answers.
- Check understanding of *amazed* and *upset*. Say *If I am amazed do I feel surprised? (yes). Is it because something is really good or really bad? (really good). If I am upset do I feel happy or sad and worried? (sad and worried). What kind of things might make me feel upset?* (E.g. *if I argue with my friend or break my favourite game*).
- Now ask them to look at the picture on the left and the title of the text. Ask *Is this a story or an article? (an article)*

Key: annoyed, amazed, upset, worried, tired, stressed

2 3.08 Listen and read the text. Why is it good to understand how other people feel?

- Write the title *emotional awareness* on the board.
- Ask *What do we do when we have emotional awareness?* Learners suggest answers. *(awareness is when you think about something and try to understand it)*.
- Ask learners why it is good to be aware of emotions and how other people feel. Check their ideas but don't confirm.
- Learners read the text and find out if their predictions are correct. Check answers with the class. *(It helps us have good relationships with other people and stops us making them feel sad)*.
- Tell learners that the article is also about empathy. Ask learners to read the paragraph under the pictures of faces again and check the meaning of *empathy*. Check answers.

  Extension Ask learners to look at the text again and find as many feeling words as they can. (*miserable, worried, stressed, sad, annoyed)*.

3 Read the text again and say *yes* or *no*.

- In pairs, learners read the sentences then look back at the text to help them answer. Learners say *yes* or *no* to the sentences.
- Share answers. Ask learners to explain their answers.

Key: 1 yes (if we learn how we feel, it helps us understand how other people feel) 2 no (cortisol gives us energy and too much stops us sleeping) 3 yes (we can work out how people feel by looking at their face) 4 no (adults feel empathy when they understand what other people feel) 5 yes (if you try to understand how other people are feeling, you can understand why they do things and it is important at home, at school and at work)

4 In pairs, talk about things you can do when you are feeling stressed or sad.

- Ask learners to think about things that can make them feel stressed or sad. Give learners 2 minutes to think of situations that can be stressful or sad in pairs. Share ideas. (Make sure learners only talk about things they feel comfortable sharing.)
- Give an example, e.g. *If I feel sad, going out and getting some fresh air and exercise relaxes me.*

Activity Book, page 88

See pages TB126–141.

Ending the lesson

- Give learners a sheet of paper each. Put two boxes at the front of the class, one labelled 'positive' and the other 'negative'.
- Ask learners to go through the lesson pages and choose one of the words that describes feelings. Tell them to write it onto their paper. Now divide the class into three or four groups and stand in circles.
- Each learner gives their word to their group. The others say when they might feel that emotion. If it is a negative emotion, they also give some advice on what the person could do, e.g. *If you are annoyed, you should talk to someone and explain your problem. That can help you feel better.* Then the learner screws up their paper and throws it into the correct box depending on whether the adjective is positive or negative.
- Pull a few of the adjectives out from each box, show the class and ask them to describe their examples.

Learning outcomes By the end of the lesson, learners will be able to read to understand the main ideas in paragraphs and find details in a text.

New language *company, business, invent, jewellery, popular*

Recycled language adjectives of emotion

Materials paper

Warm-up

- Ask learners to write down some words. Read out the words: *ought to, must, annoyed, unhappy, worried.*
- Put learners into pairs and ask them to check their spelling.
- Tell them to think of another word or phrase that has the same meaning. Learners work in pairs. Check answers.

Pupil's Book, page 89

Presentation

- Tell learners *In the Reading and Writing exam Part 2, you have to read a lot. What advice would you give someone if they have to do the reading test?*
- Learners work in pairs and suggest ideas.

1 Look at the title and the picture and answer the questions.

- Put learners into pairs to decide why they think the club is amazing and what the boy's dream is.
- Remind them to read quickly and find the answers without worrying about every word. Learners work in pairs.

Key: Learner's own answers

2 Read the text and check your ideas.

- Remind them to read quickly to find the answers without worrying about every word. Put them into pairs to compare answers.

Key: 1 The club helps school children who are bored or worried and lonely 2 He dreams about having a club in every school.

3 Read the text again. Match the main ideas (A–E) to the title and paragraphs (1–5).

- Ask learners to look at the text again and tell you how many paragraphs it has. *(five)*. Ask why we have different paragraphs in a text. *(Each paragraph has its own main point)*. Ask *What does the first paragraph usually do? (explains what the text is about).*
- Tell learners to look at the example – matched to paragraph 1. Say *Let's read the rest of the main ideas.* Tell learners to read the other four sentences.
- Put learners into pairs to say the paragraph numbers.

Key: A boy's interest in starting a club - 2 The boy's future plans - 4 The boy's advice - 5 What you can do in the club - 3

4 Where does the writer or Ben say this? Find the sentences in the text.

- Say *You need to find the information in the text, but it might not be in the same words.* Put learners in pairs and ask them to find the sentences in the text. Check answers but ask the learners to identify the words in the text that helped them.

Key: The money I get helps kids in our areas. You don't need to know lots of facts or be good at science in my club. Ben would like his own business soon. It's important to talk to someone when you feel unhappy at school.

5 Read the question and choose the correct answer.

- Ask learners to read the question. Put learners in pairs to answer it.

Key: B

EXAM TIP! Ask a stronger learner to read out the exam tip. Tell learners *In general, it is a good idea to read quickly the first time and carefully the second time.*

Activity Book, page 89

See pages TB126–141.

Ending the lesson

- Put learners into groups of three. Tell them to think of a school club that they think could be used to help people. Ask them to decide what they do in the club, who can join and how it will help people.
- Learners present their clubs to the class.
- The class choose which club they would like to join.

1 **Look at the title and the picture and answer the questions.**

1 Why do you think the club in this text is so amazing?

2 What could the boy's dream be?

2 **Read the text and check your ideas.**

1 An amazing club!!

2 Ben Bampton's just started a school club called 'Helping Dreams'. He became interested after reading about a company that helps schoolchildren who feel bored or worried. I told my dad, 'I'd like to do something like that too.' 'Let's call that company now!' he answered. 'That's how I learned about finding pieces of machines or clothes and inventing something new with them. I sell the new objects during the lunch break. The money I get helps kids in our area who feel alone. I now understand that if you want to help people, you should do it as a team.'

3 'You don't need to know lots of facts or be good at science in my club. You can make a new game from an old CD player or some jewellery from used handbags.'

4 Ben's simple idea has grown and his town thinks his club is fantastic! Ben would like to start his own business soon. He's finding ways to make his helpful ideas cost less. He plans to have 'Helping Dreams' clubs in every school, so any child who wants to build something can join the team for free.

5 Ben feels amazed because his club is so popular and says, 'It's important to talk to someone when you feel unhappy at school. You should try to have fun with friends, and my club helps with that, too! Anything is possible! Look at me and my dream!'

3 **Read the text again.** Match the ideas (A–E) to the title and paragraphs (1–5).

A This tells me what the text is about. 1

B A boy's interest in starting a club. ____

C The boy's future plans. ____

D The boy's advice. ____

E What you can do in the club. ____

4 **Where does the writer or Ben say this?** Find the sentences in the text.

- The money helps other children who live near the school.
- You don't need to get good marks if you want to be in the club.
- The boy's next project is to have his own business.
- Share your problems at school with someone.

5 **Read the question and choose the correct answer.**

Ben plans to …

A be more popular.

B have clubs like his in more schools.

C be healthier at school.

EXAM TIP! Practise reading texts **quickly** for **main ideas** and then **more carefully** to find **details**.

A2 Key for Schools

1 **In groups, talk about what you do to relax before a school exam or test.**

I go to my friend's house.

I eat a snack with my sister. She's so funny!

I read my favourite book.

2 **Read the start of the conversation and complete the instructions.**

You will hear (1) __________ talking to her friend (2) __________ about (3) __________ .

Sophie Hi Yuri, what's the matter? Have you got a cold?

Yuri I'm very tired actually. I'm not sleeping enough at the moment.

Sophie Are you worried about your science test?

Yuri Yes, I had a maths test yesterday and history today. If I don't sleep well, I won't get a good mark …

3 3.09 **Listen and check. What advice could you give to Yuri?**

4 **Look at the example answer. Why is A the best answer?**

Example: 0 What's wrong with Yuri at the moment?

(A) He's tired. **B** He's got a temperature. **C** He's got a cold.

5 **What are the questions about? Put them in the right group.**

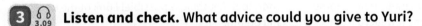

Who feels tired at the moment? Which test did Yuri do yesterday?
What does Yuri do to stop feeling worried? Which two things shouldn't he use late at night?
Who believes that good sleep helps memory? Who feels better now?

Facts	Opinions	Feelings
		Who feels tired at the moment?

6 3.10 **Listen to the conversation. Answer the questions from Activity 5.**

EXAM TIP! Before you listen, look at the questions. Do they ask you for a fact, opinion or feeling? Think of phrases we use for these things. For example:
In fact … **I'm sure …** **I'm worried …**

Learning outcomes By the end of the lesson, learners will be able to understand strategies for listening effectively.

New language *actually, in fact*

Recycled language adjectives of emotion, modal verbs, language related to illness

Materials audio

Warm-up

- Put learners into pairs: A and B. Tell learners to describe what they did yesterday evening to their partner.
- Put pairs together in fours. Ask each learner to tell the group what their partner told them. They say how they think their partner felt. Their partner confirms.

Pupil's Book, page 90

Presentation

- Say *In Listening Part 2, you have to listen for information. What kind of words can you listen for? (adjectives of feeling).*

1 In groups, talk about what you do to relax before a school exam or test.

- Read the examples together. Put learners into pairs to discuss. Ask *Which ideas would help you relax best?*

2 Read the start of the conversation and say the complete the instructions.

- Ask learners what kind of information they think will go into each gap. *(names, a topic).* Put them into pairs and ask them to answer the questions.

  Fast finishers Learners discuss what else they need to do to ensure a good answer. *(think about the type of words you are looking for before you listen).*

3 3.09 Listen and check. What advice could you give to Yuri?

- Tell learners to listen and think about Yuri's problem.
- Play the audio. Put learners into pairs to discuss.

Track 3.09

Narrator: For these questions, choose the correct answer. You will hear Sophie talking to her friend Yuri about sleeping.
Sophie: Hi Yuri, what's the matter? You don't look very well. Have you got a cold?
Yuri: Hi Sophie, I'm very tired actually. I'm not sleeping enough at the moment.
Sophie: Oh! Why not? Are you worried about your science test?
Yuri: Yes, it's tomorrow. I had a maths test yesterday and history today. If I don't sleep well I won't get a good mark …

Key: Learners' own answers

4 Look at the example answer. Why is A the best answer?

- Put learners into pairs to decide why A is best.

Key: He says he is tired and not sleeping.

EXAM TIP! Ask a strong learner to read the exam tip. Say *It's important in this part of the exam to think about the questions and answers. Do you need a fact or an opinion or to think about how someone is feeling? You will have 20 seconds to read through the questions before you listen to think about what the question is asking.*

5 What are the questions about? Put them in the right group.

- Tell learners to copy the table. Put learners into pairs to put the questions into the table. Check answers.

Key: Facts: What test did Yuri do yesterday? What does Yuri do to stop feeling worried? Opinions: Who believes that good sleep helps memory? Which two things shouldn't he use late at night? Feelings: Who feels tired at the moment? Who feels better now?

6 3.10 Listen to the conversation. Answer the questions from Activity 5.

- Put learners into pairs. Now ask to put the words into the correct category. Play the audio. Learners listen. Check answers.

See audioscripts on pages TB118–123.

Key: Facts: In fact, because Opinions: I think, I'm not so sure Feelings: I'm worried, I feel better already

Activity Book, page 90

See pages TB126–141.

Ending the lesson

- Put learners into pairs. Ask them to think of a problem they have at school. Tell them to make a dialogue. They should include a fact beginning 'In fact', an opinion and a feeling. Then put pairs together. Tell each pair to say their dialogue. The listeners raise their hands when they hear the fact, the opinion and the feeling.

Review

Learning outcomes By the end of the lesson, learners will have used language from the unit to talk about feelings and obligation and revised the unit language and skills.

Recycled language unit language

Materials paper and scissors (or circles of paper), colouring pens, Mission worksheets (Teacher's Resource Book page 68)

Warm-up

- Tell learners to choose five words from the unit and copy them.
- Put learners into groups of three. Ask them to test each other by saying the words. Their partners spell the words out.

Fast finishers Learners create five sentences using their words.

Pupil's Book, page 91

1 Look at the signs and choose the correct words to complete the sentences.

- Ask learners to look at the signs in pairs and decide what they think each sign is telling them.
- Keep learners in the same pairs. Tell them to read the sentences under each sign then choose which one is correct.
- Check answers, clarifying as necessary.

Key: 1 needn't 2 shouldn't 3 should 4 mustn't 5 must 6 shouldn't

2 Write one sentence using *so ... that* or *such ... that*.

- Ask learners to look at the beginnings of the sentences and think about how to write them using *so* or *such*. Look at the example. Point out that 'bored' is an adjective and 'so' not 'such' is used.
- Learners complete the rest of the sentences 2 to 6 then compare in pairs. Monitor and check.

Key: 2 I think it's such a fun gym that I go after school every day. 3 She does exercise so carefully that she never gets injured. 4 I think painting is such fun that I tell all my friends to try it. 5 I had such a bad headache that I couldn't stand up. 6 I played football for such a long time that I had to lie down to recover.

3 Choose ten words from this unit. Record the words using the steps below.

- Say to learners *Well done. You've learnt a lot of new language. Now let's think about another interesting way to remember the words.*
- Tell learners to look at the flowchart. Say *Let's try.* Write the word *stressed* on the board. Ask learners if they can remember what it is and how they can find out if they can't remember. Tell them to look at the 'find the meaning' part of the chart. Say *You can check the meaning in this unit or in a dictionary*.
- Ask the easiest way to show what it is or remember it. *(write a definition and the opposite word).* Tell learners to look at the 'record the example' part of the flowchart. Say *What is the opposite of 'stressed'? (relaxed).*
- Look at the next part of the flowchart: 'use it'. Say *You can say your meaning or the opposite to test a friend. For example, I can say 'this is the opposite of relaxed and means I am worried and upset'.* Say *Now let's do an example.*
- Tell learners to choose ten words from the unit and find the meanings and opposite words. Tell them to follow the flowchart. Learners work alone. Monitor and check.
- Once they have finished, pair learners. Ask them to show their meanings to their partner and ask them to try to guess the word.

Mission in action!

- Put learners into pairs. Give each pair a copy of the Mission worksheet (Teacher's Resource Book page 68).
- They have to review all stages of the Mission using their completed Mission stages. They use the feelings wheel to show their initiatives to deal with different emotions at school. They could make it part of a PowerPoint or video presentation, or whatever they decide supports their ideas.
- Learners mention the emotions they have identified as the most important to pay attention to with this project, e.g. *When we are tired we can feel annoyed.* *Feeling worried makea us feel a lack of confidence.*
- Next, they present their suggestions for those emotions. *If you have a rest you won't feel tired.* *If you plan your homework, you reduce stress and you will improve your self-confidence.*
- Learners give a list of wellbeing actions for the class to follow.
- For the final outcome, put the feelings wheel on the class wall to remember.

Activity Book, page 91

See pages TB126–141.

Ending the lesson

- SA Complete the self-assessment (see Introduction).

1 Look at the signs and choose the correct words to complete the sentences.

1

You **needn't** / **must** worry. It's OK to drink this water.

2

You **don't have to** / **shouldn't** swim here. It's dangerous!

3

You **should** / **mustn't** walk here. You oughtn't to run.

4
CAUTION
This sign has sharp edges.

You **have to** / **mustn't** touch this sign. You might cut yourself.

5

You **must** / **needn't** turn off your phone here. People are studying.

6

You **shouldn't** / **have to** put food in this bin. It's only for paper.

2 Write one sentence using *so … that* or *such … that*.

1 I felt bored during the film. I fell asleep.
I felt so bored during the film that I fell asleep.

2 I think it's a fun gym. I go after school every day.

3 She does exercise carefully. She never gets injured.

4 I think painting is fun. I tell all my friends to try it.

5 I had a bad headache. I couldn't stand up.

6 I played football for a long time. I had to lie down to recover.

3 Choose ten words from this unit. Record the words using the steps below.

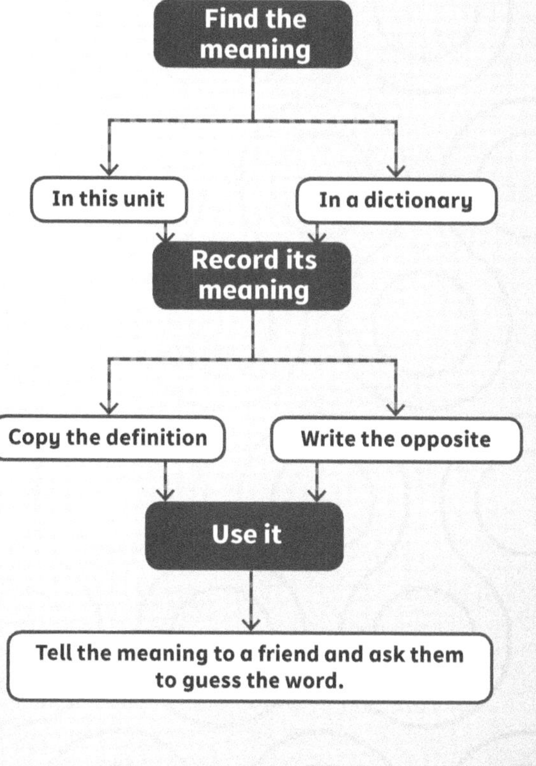

Mission in action!

Make a feelings wheel with real suggestions.

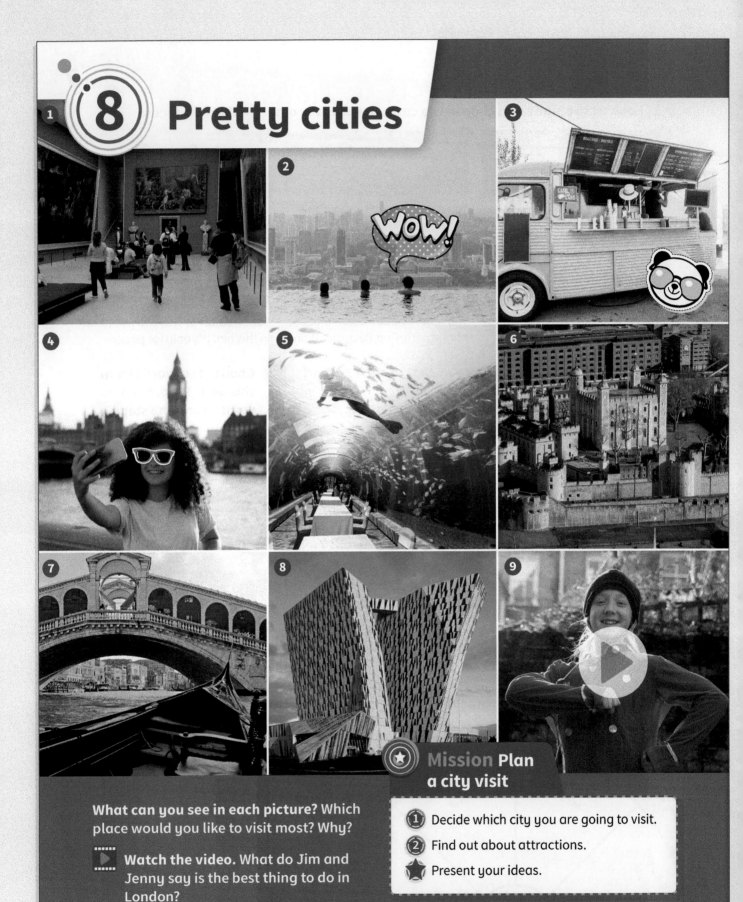

8 Pretty cities

Mission Plan a city visit

1. Decide which city you are going to visit.
2. Find out about attractions.
3. Present your ideas.

What can you see in each picture? Which place would you like to visit most? Why?

Watch the video. What do Jim and Jenny say is the best thing to do in London?

Unit 8 learning outcomes

In Unit 8, learners will learn to:

- use vocabulary to describe cities
- understand and use indirect questions
- understand and use 'used to' to talk about past habits and states
- read and listen for information
- understand responsible tourism and looking after places you visit

Materials video, pictures: Paris (Eiffel Tower); London (London Bridge); Rio de Janeiro (Christ the Redeemer statue); China (Great Wall of China); USA (Empire State Building), Russia (Red Square, Moscow)

Self-assessment

- **SA** Write the unit topic on the board. Underneath write a list: *city, tour, museum, ecotourism*. Put learners into groups of three. Ask them to think about what they will learn in the unit.
- Now show the unit outcomes. Ask learners if they guessed correctly.
- Ask learners to complete self-assessment (see Introduction).
- Say *Let's learn.*

Pupil's Book, page 92

Warm-up

- Put up pictures of some famous landmarks, e.g. Eiffel Tower; London Bridge; Christ the Redeemer statue; Great Wall of China; Empire State Building, Red Square, Moscow.
- Put learners into groups of three and tell them to decide which countries are shown. Check answers.
- Ask learners if they have been to any of the places in the pictures. Learners compare ideas in groups.

What can you see in each picture? Which place would you like to visit most? Why?

- Put learners into pairs and ask them to discuss what they can see in each picture.
- Write some words on the board: *gallery, skyscraper, zoo, tower, palace, bridge, hotel*. Ask learners to decide which pictures the words go with.
- Go through the pictures again in order. For each ask *What can you see?* Check any words that may be challenging asking learners to point to the picture and repeat.

Watch the video. What do Jim and Jenny say is the best thing to do in London?

- Show a picture of London. Ask learners *Where is this? (London).*
- Ask *Do you know any places to visit in London?*
- Tell learners Jenny and Jim will describe interesting things to do in London. Ask them to watch and find out what they think is the best thing to do. Play the video.
- Put learners into pairs to discuss their ideas.
- Check answers with the group. Ask learners if they can remember any other activities Jenny and Jim enjoyed doing in London. Learners suggest ideas.
- Write up the activities on the board in random order: *sleeping in the museum; looking at London (from the London Eye); river-bus tour; watch London's street entertainers; shopping in London.*
- Tell learners to watch again and write down the order of the activities. *(river-bus tour; shopping; street entertainers; looking at London; sleeping in the museum).*

Key: sleeping under a dinosaur at night in the museum

Extension Ask learners to decide if they would like to sleep in the museum for a night and which of the five activities they would like best.

Mission Plan a city visit

- Tell learners they are going to choose a city to visit.
- Say *We're going to choose a city to visit. How can you choose best? (find out what there is to do).*
- Confirm this stage of the Mission. *(Yes, we'll find out about the good things to do – these are the attractions).* Learners repeat *attractions*. Say *Then we'll present what we find.*
- Ask learners to retell you the three parts of the mission.
- Say *This is our Mission.*

Activity Book, page 92

See pages TB126–141.

My unit goals

- Go through the unit goals with the learners. Either read these or put them onto the board or a poster. (See suggested techniques in 'Identifying outcomes' in the teachers' in-class guide in Introduction.)
- Go back to these unit goals at the end of each Mission stage during the unit and review them. Say *This is our Mission page.*

Ending the lesson

- Put learners into pairs. Ask them the last time they visited a different place. Tell them to think about something they liked and something they didn't enjoy.
- Share their ideas and find out if any learners have visited the same places.

Fast finishers Learners discuss if they enjoy visiting other cities. Why or why not?

Learning outcomes By the end of the lesson, learners will be able to use vocabulary to describe tours and listen and understand words in context.

New language *sightseeing, department store, festival, collection, sculpture, monument, (bus) tour, gallery*

Recycled language *cruise, tower, palace*

Materials audio, sticky notes

Pupil's Book, page 93

Warm-up

- Write the name of your town or city on the board.
- Put learners into groups of four. Say *Welcome to our city/town of (name)! We are here to give you a tour!*
- Ask learners what happens on a tour. *(you visit different places in a city or area and learn about it).*
- Tell learners to think about what interesting things they would include on a tour of their home city/town.
- Learners discuss in groups. Share ideas.

1  Look at the adverts for city tours. Match the pictures (1–10) to the words in bold in the advert. Then listen and check.

- Learners discuss what people are doing in the pictures on page 93. *(tours).*
- Say *On a tour you can see lots of different things. Let's find out.*
- Learners look at the descriptions quickly and find out which three cities are in the tours. Give them 30 seconds.
- Check answers. *(Toronto in Canada, London in the UK, New York in the USA).*
- Learners look at the words in bold and match to the photos in pairs. Do the first one together as an example. E.g. *The first picture shows people on a boat. If you are doing a tour on a boat we call it a cruise.*
- Tell learners to listen and check. Play the audio.
- Check their ideas. As you do this check that they understand the words, e.g. *Why do we have monuments? (to remember a famous person or event). Is a tower low or high? (high).* As you check each word ask learners to repeat them.

Key: 1 cruise 2 monument 3 tower 4 palace 5 sculpture 6 gallery 7 festival 8 collection 9 sightseeing 10 department store

Track 3.11

1 cruise
2 monument
3 tower
4 palace
5 sculpture
6 gallery
7 festival
8 collection
9 sightseeing
10 department store

2 Write sentences about which places your class would like to visit.

- Write the three sentence stems on the board (and draw the face emoticons if possible).
- Put learners into pairs and ask them to think about the three tours. Ask them to tell their partner which activities they would like to do and which places they would like to visit. Learners discuss in pairs.
- Ask learners to vote by putting up their hands. Go through each place and ask learners to vote for their favourite. Count the number of votes and write the place and the number of votes each one scored.
- Tell learners to look at the scores and decide which place the class would love to visit, which one they wouldn't mind visiting and which one they wouldn't like.
- Ask a few learners to give reasons for their votes.

Alternative Instead of using hands to vote, give each learner a sticky note. Ask them to write their name on it. Write the places on the board. Tell learners to choose their favourite, come up and stick their name next to it. This will help you see which learners like which place.

EXAM TIP! Ask a strong learner to read the exam tip. Ask learners what they can say to show they are giving an opinion, e.g. *I think.* Say *In the Speaking exam, you might need to give an opinion. You can say what you think people will like or not like.*

3 A teacher is going to take some students on one of the tours. In pairs, talk about the tours and say which the students would find most interesting.

- Ask learners which tour they think the students would enjoy the most and why.
- Read the examples together. Learners discuss their ideas in pairs. Share their ideas.

Activity Book, page 93

See pages TB126–141.

Ending the lesson

- Put learners into pairs. Ask learners to look at the pictures on the page and test each other, e.g. *What's in picture 3? (a tower).*

1 3.11 **Look at the adverts for city tours.** Match the pictures (1–10) to the words in bold in the advert. Then listen and check.

Boat tour of Toronto

Only $19!!

- See the city from the water on our one-hour **cruise**.
- Learn about Toronto's history and **monuments**.
- Take photos of some of Canada's most famous buildings and **towers**.

Art tour of New York

- Visit a **gallery** and see one of the U.S.A.'s best art collections.
- See amazing **sculptures** as we walk through New York's streets.
- The tour ends at a music **festival** in a park – so bring your dance shoes!

London sports tour

Call 020 7946 0949 for more information

- Take a **sightseeing** bus tour of London's most famous sports stadiums.
- Look round the Wimbledon Lawn Tennis museum and it's amazing **collection** of tennis prizes.
- The tour goes past Buckingham **Palace** and finishes at London's famous sports **department store**.

2 Write sentences about which places your class would like to visit.

We'd love ....

We wouldn't mind ....

We wouldn't like ....

3 ☆ **A teacher is going to take some students on one of the tours.** In pairs, talk about the tours and say which the students would find most interesting.

I think her class would love to visit a gallery and look at the sculptures.

Me too! And I think they wouldn't mind going on a river cruise because they could take lots of amazing photos.

EXAM TIP! To give opinions, say what would or wouldn't be a good option and **why**.

Language presentation 1

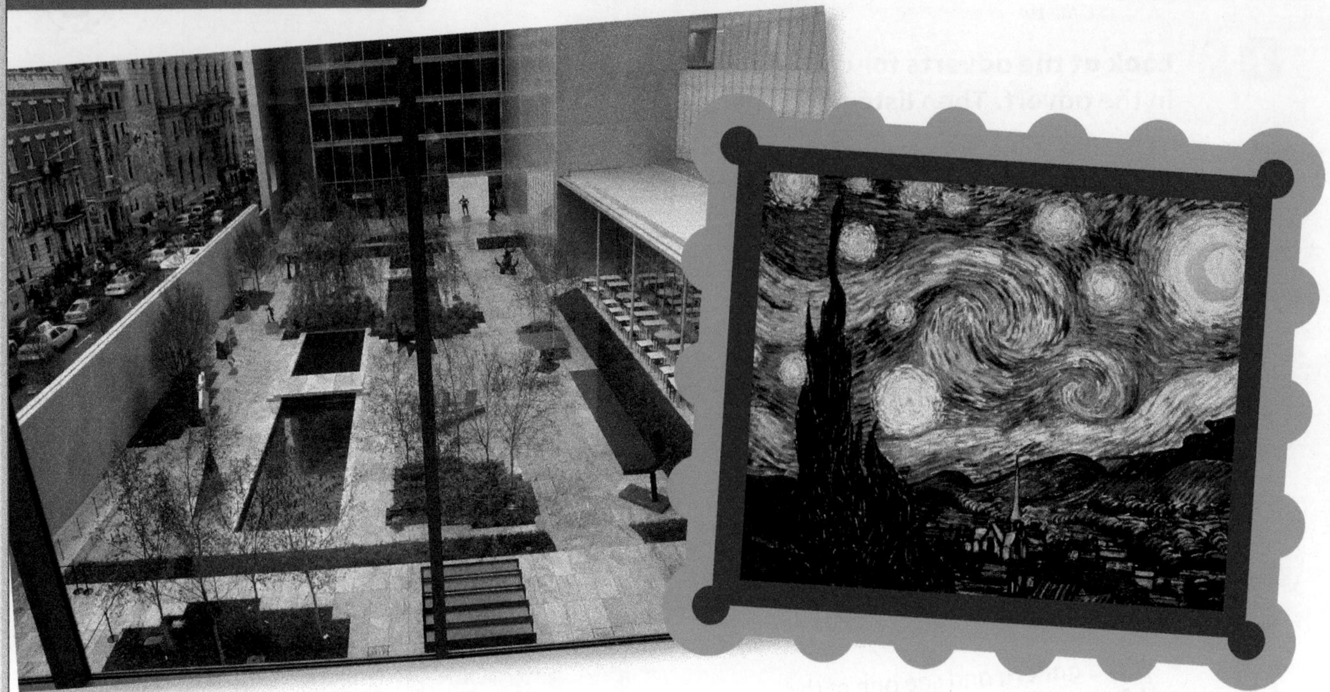

1 **Look at the pictures and choose the correct words to complete the sentences.**

1 I think the building is probably in **London** / **New York** / **Toronto**.
2 I think the building is probably a **department store** / **monument** / **gallery**.
3 I think the painting might be by **Da Vinci** / **Van Gogh** / **Monet**.

2 3.12 **Listen to a radio show called Charlies' Challenge and check your answers to Activity 1.**

3 3.13 ★ **Listen again, and write the correct answers.**

Charlies' Challenge
About
The gallery has around (1) ________ paintings.
Tickets are: (2) ________ for children
Has amazing pictures like Van Gogh's (3) *The* ________ *Night*
Information
Website: (4) www.________.org
Phone number: (5) ________

EXAM TIP!
Make sure you **read the notes and question** before the recording starts. Can you think of any possible answers before you listen?

4 **In pairs, answer the questions.**

1 Is there a gallery like this where you live?
2 Would you like to go on a school trip to this gallery?

Learning outcomes By the end of the lesson, learners will be able to listen to complete notes accurately.

New language *probably, might, Da Vinci, Van Gogh, Monet, challenge*

Recycled language *tour, cruise, monument, gallery, museum, department store*

Materials audio, paper and pens

Pupil's Book, page 94

Warm-up

- Tell learners to get out a pen and paper. Ask them to write down what they hear. Tell them you will repeat the sentences three times. Read the sentences slowly.
- *Yesterday I did a BANANA of the city to see interesting places. We saw pictures in the art BANANA. We took photos at the BANANA in the park. Then we went on a BANANA up the river.*
- Ask learners to work in pairs and compare what they have written, making corrections if necessary.
- Ask learners *What is strange about the text? (the word banana).* Now ask learners to think about some of the new words they learnt in the previous lesson and replace the word 'banana' with a more appropriate word.
- Learners work in pairs. Check their answers. *(tour; gallery; monument; cruise).*

  Extension Put learners into pairs. Learners write a sentence using one of the new words. They say their sentence to their partner replacing the word with 'banana'. Their partner guesses the word.

1 Look at the pictures and choose the correct words to complete the sentences.

- Tell learners to look at the pictures and think about what they can see. Learners suggest ideas. Tell them to read the three sentences below. Ask them to guess the answers in pairs.
- Share ideas and note the most popular answers onto the board. Don't confirm the answers at this stage.

2 3.12 Listen to a radio show called Charlie's Challenge and check your answers to Activity 1.

- Tell learners to listen and check their predictions. Play the audio.
- Learners listen. Put them into pairs to compare ideas.
- Check answers. Go through their predictions on the board and tick or cross them out. Confirm the final answers.

  See audioscripts on pages 118–123.

Key: 1 gallery 2 New York 3 Van Gogh

EXAM TIP! Ask a strong learner to read the exam tip. Say *If we think about what is in the notes we can listen better.*

Ask learners *If you hear numbers will you write them as numbers or words? (numbers). And if you have a difficult name you might hear what? (spelling).*

3 3.13 Listen again and write the correct answers.

- Ask learners what they will need to do. *(fill the gaps).* Tell them to read each sentence to think about what might be in the gap, e.g. a number, a name or other information. Put them in pairs to discuss.
- Share answers. *(1 probably a number as it says 'around', 2 may be a price, 3 the name of the picture, 4 a website address).* Remind learners that thinking about the gaps will help them understand what to listen for. Play the audio again. Learners listen carefully. Check answers.

Key: 1 2,300 2 free / nothing 3 Starry 4 MoMA 5 212 708 9400

4 In pairs, answer the questions.

- Put learners into pairs to compare ideas. Ask some pairs to share their answers with the class. Check answers.

Key: Learners' own answers

Activity Book, page 94

See pages TB126–141.

Ending the lesson

- Tell learners to look at page 94 and pick three words from the page. Put learners into pairs. Give each learner a sheet of paper. Tell learners to write their three words out, but mix up the letters to create an anagram. E.g. *y l l g r e a = gallery.* Ask learners to give their paper to their partner.
- Each learner tries to solve the anagram and rewrite the words into the correct order. Tell learners to choose two anagrams they think are the best.
- Put pairs into groups of four. Each pair dictates the letters of their first anagram to the other pair. They try to solve the anagram. Repeat with the second anagram.

  Extra support Learners keep their books open to check the letters of the anagrams.

Learning outcomes By the end of the lesson, learners will be able to understand and use indirect questions accurately.

New language indirect questions (*Do you know how many paintings there are?*)

Recycled language *museum*

Materials paper, access to the Internet if possible

Pupil's Book, page 95

Warm-up

- Write on the board *Toys, Sport, Films, Fashion*.
- In groups of three, learners decide what kind of museum they would like to open.
- On the board, write: *Opens … / Closes … / Tickets $… / You can see …* Tell learners to make notes about the organisation of their museum, e.g. opening and closing? times, price of tickets, what people can see. Ask learners to mingle and talk about the museum their group designed.
- Groups report back on which museum they liked best.

Presentation

- Tell learners *My museum is very interesting. Ask me a question.* Write on the board *Can you tell me what … .*
- Put learners into pairs and ask them to finish the sentence. Check ideas.
- Write up the correct form: *Can you tell me what you can see?*
- Underline 'what you can see' and ask *What would we normally say in a question? (What can you see?)* Say *So here, is this normal sentence order or question order? (normal sentence order).* Underline the first part of the sentence in a different colour ('Can you tell me …'). Say *The question part is here at the beginning so the second half is in normal order.*

Extra support Give learners the full question but mix the words up and ask them to find the correct order.

Grammar look: *indirect questions*

- Put learners into pairs. Look at the title of the box. Ask learners *What kind of questions are these? (indirect questions).*
- Learners complete sentences 1 and 2. Check answers.

Key: 1 more 2 changes

Complete the Grammar look on page 126.
See pages TB125–126.

1  **PRONUNCIATION**
Listen and repeat. 

- Play the audio. Correct learners pronunciation as necessary.

Track 3.14
Girl: Do you know how many paintings there are?
Boy: Could you tell us how old the National Gallery is?

- Learners complete the activity on page 119 (see page TB124).

2 Put the words in order to make questions.

- Learners look at the jumbled sentences in pairs and put them into the correct order. Remind them to look for clues, e.g. *The capital letter comes at the start of the sentence and the question mark comes at the end.*
- Do the first one together as an example. Learners complete the remaining sentences. Check answers. Ask learners to read out sentences in the correct order.

Key: 1 Could you tell me what I can see at the museum, please?
2 Do you know what time the museum closes?
3 Do you know where the museum is?
4 Could you tell me how much tickets are, please?
5 Could you tell me the museum's phone number, please?
6 Do you know if I can take photos at the museum?

3 Answer the questions from Activity 2 about one of the museums below.

- In pairs, learners choose one museum each, then take turns to answer the questions about one of them.

 Mission Stage 1

- In pairs, learners make a list of the things they think make a city interesting to visit. Share ideas.
- Tell learners the first stage of the Mission is to choose a city to visit. If possible, learners look up different cities on the Internet or prepare at home and bring in their ideas.
- In groups of five, learners share ideas and choose a city to visit. Tell them to think of reasons for their choice. Learners discuss and research.
- Ask each group to say which city they have chosen and a sentence about why they think it might be interesting.

Alternative Choose a selection of cities and provide some information and pictures in paper format and ask the learners to look at the different options and choose their favourite.

Activity Book, page 95

See pages TB126–141.

Ending the lesson

- Ask learners to find their notes from the Warm-up about their museum idea. Put the pairs together.
- Each pair asks their partners questions about their museum, using indirect questions.

Grammar look: indirect questions

'How many paintings are there?'

'Do you know how many paintings there are?'

1 Indirect questions are usually **more / less** polite then normal questions.
2 When we use indirect questions, the word order **changes / stays the same.**

page 126

1 3.14 **PRONUNCIATION Listen and repeat.** page 119

2 Put the words in order to make questions.

1 what I can see / please? / Could you tell me / at the museum,

2 what / Do you know / time / closes? / the museum

3 the museum / where / please? / Could you tell me / is,

4 how / tickets / please? / much / Could you tell me / are

5 the / please? / Could you tell me / museum's / phone number,

6 if / Do you know / take photos / I can / at the museum?

3 Answer the questions from Activity 2 about one of the museums below.

BATA SHOE MUSEUM

Tickets:
Adults, $14,
Children (aged 5–17), $5

What you can see:
Old shoes, famous people's shoes and much more!

Opening times: 10 am–5 pm
(10 am–8 pm on Thursdays)

Finding us:
We're on 327 Bloor Street West, in Toronto

Call us on: 0523 6498 213

Photos: You can take photos anywhere in the museum.

LONDON TRANSPORT MUSEUM

Tickets:
Adult £17.50;
Free for children (under 18)

You can see:
Old buses, trains, taxis and many other things

Opening hours:
10:00 am–6:00 pm
on Monday – Thursday, Saturday and Sunday
Fridays 10:00 am–8:00 pm

Address:
Covent Garden Piazza, near the River Thames

Phone number:
0625 9587 31

Bring a camera because you can take photos in the museum!

Mission Stage 1

Decide which city you are going to visit.

I really want to go to Istanbul. It looks so cool!
That sounds great! Let's look for river cruises there.

Vocabulary 2

1 **Read Jim's blog.** Do you think these places are boring or beautiful?

Jim's Big Blog

Last week, Jenny and I visited London. While Jenny took photos of the famous places in London, I took photos of things that might look boring – but that I think are amazing.

Boring or beautiful? My photos of London

Jenny said, 'Oh Jim! You're not taking a photo of that, are you?'

Some people say that this is London's most beautiful roundabout! That's because of the amazing glass building in the middle of the **roundabout**. In the building is a **booking office** where you can buy tickets and a cinema with the largest screen in Britain!

Jenny said, 'That's just a car park, Jim!'

This **car park** was built in 1928 – and, with 1,000 spaces, it used to be the biggest car park in the country! It used to have two different restaurants inside, too. When it was built, there was even a plan to put a golf course on the top of it. Today, the building's still a car park but sometimes events like fashion or film shows happen there.

Jenny said, 'This is the ugliest place we've been all day!'

I think this station's amazing. It opened in 1863 – that's more than 150 years ago! In fact, London had the first **underground** stations in the world. Today the trains are electric, but they didn't use to be. They used to make the air very dirty!

Jenny said, 'Really Jim? ANOTHER photo?!'

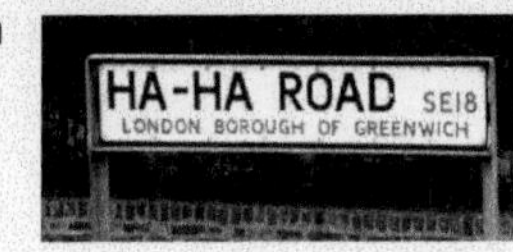

This **signpost** made me laugh a lot. It was on a normal **pavement** in London! There are lots of interesting street names in London, like Brick Lane and Pie Corner. Can you guess what used to be made on those streets?

Jenny said, 'Can't we get a map and go?'

This is the **tourist information** centre in London. Jenny went there to get a map and find out the **opening hours** for a gallery. While Jenny was chatting and Mum was getting some money from a **cash machine**, I took this photo. I love this building because it's very new, but looks amazing next to the old buildings nearby. The building is also good for the environment – its roof collects water to use in its toilets and for its gardens.

2 **Match the definitions (A–I) to the words in bold in Jim's blog.**

- **A** Something that you walk on, next to a road
- **B** Somewhere that you get money
- **C** The times that a place is open
- **D** Somewhere people leave cars
- **E** Something next to a road that gives you information
- **F** A train that travels under the streets
- **G** Somewhere where you can buy tickets
- **H** Somewhere you can ask questions about a new city
- **I** Somewhere roads meet and that cars drive around

3 **Look at the pictures in Jim's blog.** Which words in bold in the blog can you see? Which words can't you see?

Learning outcomes By the end of the lesson, learners will be able to listen to understand opinions and understand *used to* to describe past habits and states.

New language *roundabout, car park, station, signpost, tourist information centre, used* to + verb

Recycled language words describing places in the city

Materials audio, 8 pictures (a historical monument, a palace, a park, a museum; on the other side a roundabout, a car park, a signpost and a tourist information centre), sticky tack

Pupil's Book, page 96

Warm-up

- Ask learners to think about the city or town where they live. Put them in pairs and ask them to think of five pieces of information about their home town/city. E.g. *There are two parks here. There is a car park next to the library.* Tell them to make questions from their facts, e.g. *How many parks are there? Do you know what is next to the library?*
- Put three of the pairs together to make groups of six. Learners take it in turns to ask and answer questions about their home. Any of the four learners not in the pair who ask the question can answer.
- Learners ask and answer questions. The learner who answers the most questions is the winner.

Presentation

- Tell learners they are going to read a blog about the city.
- Put up some pictures on the board: on one side a historical monument, a palace, a park, a museum; on the other side a roundabout, a car park, a signpost and a tourist information centre.
- Ask them to look at the pictures and decide what they can see in each. Learners discuss in pairs.
- Check their ideas. Go over the pictures on the left. Check the words for the pictures on the right. *(roundabout, car park, signpost, tourist information centre).* After each one say the word again for learners to repeat.
- Tell learners they are going on a city tour. Ask them which things they would like to see – the pictures on the left or the right. Learners discuss. Share their ideas.
- Ask learners if they would be surprised to find out that Jim liked the places on the right more. Learners respond.
- Ask learners why they think Jim is interested in the places on the right. Learners discuss.
- Tell learners they are going to read the blog and find out.

1 Read Jim's blog. Do you think these places are boring or beautiful?

- Ask learners to read the blog and decide if the places are boring or beautiful. Learners read.
- Put learners into pairs and ask them to compare ideas.

2 Match the definitions (A–I) to the words in bold in Jim's blog.

- Learners look at the definitions and check if they know the correct words.
- In pairs, learners match the words in bold with the definitions.
- Check answers.

Key: A pavement B cash machine C opening hours D car park E signpost F underground G booking office H tourist information centre I roundabout

3 Look at the pictures in Jim's blog. Which words in bold can you see? Which words can't you see?

- Tell learners to look at the words they chose for A to I. Ask them to look at the photos again and divide the words into two lists: words for things they can see in the photos and words for things they can't see.
- Learners work in pairs to try to decide. Monitor and support.
- Learners check by going through the list of words they can see and pointing. Check answers with the class.

Key: Can see: a car park, signpost, tourist information centre? roundabout
Can't see: a pavement, cash machine, opening hours, underground, booking office

Activity Book, page 96

See pages TB126–141.

Ending the lesson

- Ask learners to think of places in the city they can see. As they suggest ideas write a list of them onto the board.
- Put learners in groups of three.
- Ask them to choose at least five of the things on the list.
- Give out paper and colouring pens. Tell the learners to create a mini-map of a city centre including the five things they have chosen from the list.
- Learners draw and label their map.
- Invite learners to present their maps and explain what the different places on the map are.
- The class chooses the map they like the best and give reasons for their choice, e.g. *That city has a tower in the park. I think it is beautiful. But it has a car park so it is easy to drive there.*

  Fast finishers Learners write two to three sentences describing their city or town.

Learning outcomes By the end of the lesson, learners will be able to use *used to* and *didn't use to* to talk about things that happened and facts that were true in the past.

New language *used to* + verb, *didn't use to* + verb

Recycled language words to describe cities

Materials pictures of a city in the past and the same city now, Mission worksheets (Teacher's Resource Book page 77)

Warm-up

- Find a picture of a city in the past and the same city now.
- Put the pictures on the board side by side. Ask learners what the pictures have in common. *(they are the same city at different times).*
- Put learners into pairs and ask them to find five differences, e.g. *In the first picture there are some horses in the street, but in the second picture there are a lot of cars.*
- Share their ideas.

  Alternative If you are able to copy pictures, put the learners into pairs. Give one of the pair a picture of the city now and give the second learner a picture of the city in the past. Tell them to speak and try to find five differences without looking at their partner's picture.

Pupil's Book, page 97

Presentation

- Remind learners of the pictures from Jim's blog on page 96. Point to the picture of the car park. Ask *Why was the car park important in the past? (it used to be the biggest car park in the country).*
- Repeat the sentence. Say *Is it the biggest car park now? (no).* Repeat *'it used to be but it isn't now'.*

Grammar look: *used to and didn't use to*

- Ask learners to read the sentences in the top left of the **Grammar look** box from the text.
- Put the learners into pairs. Ask them to find the words 'used to' and 'use to' in each sentence and look at them carefully to see if there are any differences.
- Ask them what they notice *(no -d on the negative form).*
- Tell learners to read questions 1–3 on the right of the **Grammar look** box and choose the correct option in each.
- Check answers, clarifying where necessary.

Key: 1 Yes 2 Often 3 No 4 often 5 don't

1 Guess which of the facts (1–4) is false.

- Learners read the short text and find out which place the person visited.
- Share answers. *(Shakespeare's Theatre).*
- Tell learners to read the facts about the theatre again and decide in pairs which one is not true.
- Check answers.

Key: 3 is false – football was invented more than 200 years after Shakespeare died.

Complete the Grammar look on page 126. See pages TB125–126.

2 Write three true sentences and one false sentence about yourself. Use *used to* or *didn't use to*. In groups, guess the false sentences.

- Ask learners to work in groups of four.
- Tell learners *Think about when you were younger and write four sentences.* Tell them each sentence must use 'used to' or 'didn't use to', but one of them should be false.
- Tell learners to take it in turns saying their sentences. Their group should try to find out which sentences are false.

  Fast finishers Learners rewrite the sentence that is false so that it is true.

Mission Stage 2

- Put learners into the same groups as Mission Stage 1. Remind them of the city they chose. Give each learner a copy of the Mission worksheet (Teacher's Resource Book page 77).
- Ask learners to talk together and say what they know about the city.
- Learners discuss in groups and compare ideas.
- Ask learners to research the places they could visit. In their research, they can read about the places they want to visit and discuss the history of the buildings.
- When they have decided what places they are going to visit, they draw the itinerary they are going to follow. Then they look at their itinerary in pairs and ask each other questions to go to different places, e.g.

  This sculpture used to be at the Prado Museum.

  There's a river cruise at 9.00 am.

Activity Book, page 97

See pages TB126–141.

Ending the lesson

- **SA** Ask learners to complete their self-assessment (see Introduction).

Grammar look: *used to / didn't use to*

'They used to make the air very dirty.'
'Today the trains are electric, but they didn't use to be.'
'Can you guess what used to be made on those streets?'

1 Did trains make the air dirty in the past? **Yes / No**
2 How many times did this happen? **Often / Only once**
3 Does it happen now? **Yes / No**

Used to means that things happened **(4) often / once** in the past. They **(5) still / don't** happen now. It's also used for facts that were true, but aren't now.

page 126

1 Guess which of the facts (1–4) is false.

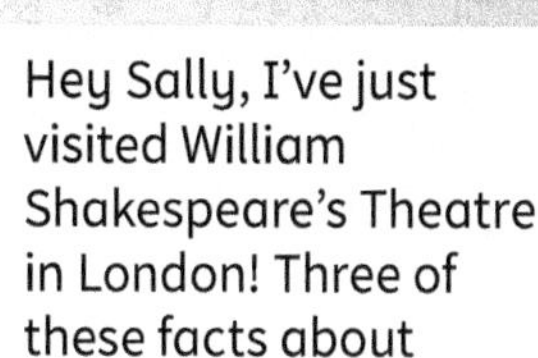

Hey Sally, I've just visited William Shakespeare's Theatre in London! Three of these facts about Shakespeare are true. Can you guess which one is false?

1 Shakespeare used to live in London.
2 Women didn't use to act in Shakespeare's plays.
3 Shakespeare used to like watching football.
4 Shakespeare's brother Edmund Shakespeare also used to write plays.

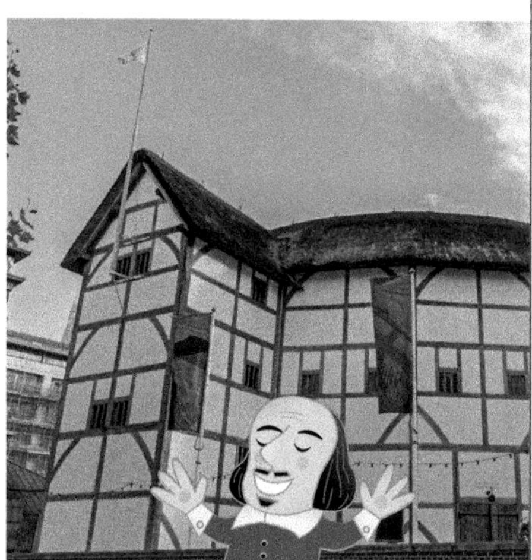

2 Write three true sentences and one false sentence about yourself. Use *used to* or *didn't use to*. In groups, guess the false sentences.

Mission Stage 2

Find out more about the attractions in the city.

Search
All Maps Images Settings Tools
About 1,200 results (0.36 seconds)
You can see the whole of the city from the top of the fairground!

Literature

1 **What can you see in the pictures? What do you think the novel is about?**

3.16

Chapter One
The case of the Butterfly Diamond

He got the message at midnight. 'Bad news. Arabella Von Thursday's stolen The Butterfly Diamond. Can you help?' Of course he could help! He was Johnny Ming after all, and helping was what he did. From Monday to Friday he was a successful businessman, the manager of Ming's Marvels, a three-storey furniture shop in Old Shanghai. But at the weekend, he did something a little different – and what could be more different than being 'China's Number 1 Secret Detective'?

'We think she's going to sell it somewhere in England,' said Huxley on the phone. 'Do you know when the exhibition starts?' asked Johnny Ming. 'Next Tuesday,' said Huxley, sounding worried. 'You must get here right away!' Yes, thought Johnny Ming as he packed his suitcase. I must get there right away, and you must reduce your stress. Huxley used to be a relaxed and happy man, but there was so much to worry about these days, especially Countess Arabella Von Thursday. She was a dangerous criminal who stole paintings, sculptures and now diamonds. If she wasn't stopped, the great museums of the world would soon be empty.

In the full-length mirror next to the front door, Johnny Ming looked at himself one more time. His white suit was perfectly clean and his black tie was just right. The brown and white leather shoes he was wearing were so shiny that you could see your face in them. He checked the time on his pocket watch, then tied it to his belt by a chain. Before locking his suitcase, he checked that he had everything – red and white toothbrush, clothes for various climates, a wooden tennis racket, a big box of milk chocolates and enough apple juice for seventy-two hours. He pushed up his Panama hat and tapped his walking stick on the floorboard. He was ready to go. Blowing out the long line of candles in the hall, he said to the dark, 'You won't win this time, Arabella Von Thursday!'

Learning outcomes By the end of the lesson, learners will have read a part of a novel.

New language *novel, detective, exhibition, diamonds, suitcase, hot-air balloon*

Recycled language *stress, relaxed, sculptures, paintings, museums,* clothes vocabulary, *criminal, candle, rubbish, traffic jam*

Materials audio, picture of diamonds

Warm-up

- Ask learners what kind of book a novel is. *(a story).*
- Put learners into groups of four. Ask them *What kinds of novels can you think of?* Learners discuss their ideas.
- Share ideas, e.g. *romantic, drama, detective stories.*
- Ask learners to tell their group the kind of novels they like reading best and why, then the kind of novels they hate reading and why.

  Extension Ask learners to tell their group about a novel they read which they loved. They can describe the story, the characters and why it is good.

Pupil's Book, page 98

1 What can you see in the pictures? What do you think the novel is about?

- Ask learners to look at the title of the story on page 98 and the pictures on pages 97–98. Ask them what kind of text it is. *(part of a novel).* Put learners into pairs. Ask learners to look at the pictures and say what they can see and if they think the story will be interesting. Learners discuss in pairs.
- Write on the board: *suit, diamonds, Panama hat, detective, suitcase, hot-air balloon, exhibition.*
- Tell learners they can see some of these things in the picture, but others are not.
- Ask learners to decide which they can see. Learners work in pairs.
- Check their ideas. Ask learners to point to a suit, Panama hat, suitcase, hot-air balloon. Ask them if they think they can see a detective. *(yes).* Tell them the man in the suit is a detective. Ask *What does a detective do? (find criminals and solve crimes).*
- Go back to the board and tick off the words they can see.
- Ask learners to think about the other words. Show them a picture of diamonds and ask them which word it is. Say *diamonds.* Learners repeat.
- Ask learners what happens at an exhibition. *(you can see paintings or historical things).* Say *exhibition.* Learners repeat.

Presentation

- Ask learners to look at the title and pictures again and decide what kind of story it is.
- Learners discuss in pairs.

  Extension Ask learners to guess what happens in the story from the pictures. Put them into pairs to discuss and share their ideas. Make a note of their predictions to check off when they have read the story.

3.16 Chapter One The case of the Butterfly Diamond

- Tell learners to listen and read the story on pages 98 and 99 to find out if they are right about the kind of story it is.
- Play the first part of the audio to the end of page 98.
- Learners read and listen. Ask learners to compare their ideas in pairs. Check their answers.
- Tell learners they are going to read and listen to the story again in more detail.
- Write some questions on the board: *Who are the characters in the story? What does Johnny do Monday to Friday? Who has stolen the diamonds? What does Johnny pack for his journey? Who does he find in the hot-air balloon?*
- Ask learners to read and listen again and find the answers to the questions. Check answers. *(Johnny Ming, Countess Arabella, Mia, Sami; Johnny has a furniture shop from Monday to Friday but is a detective the rest of the time; Countess Arabella Von Thursday stole the diamonds – she is a dangerous criminal; Johnny packs a red and white toothbrush, a tennis racket, clothes, a box of chocolates and apple juice; he finds Mia and Sami in the hot-air balloon).*

Activity Book, page 98

See pages TB126–141.

Ending the lesson

- Divide the class into two groups: A and B. Put learners into pairs within their groups.
- Tell the pairs in group A to think about Countess Arabella Von Thursday and why she is a dangerous criminal. Ask them to imagine how she stole the diamonds. Tell group B to think about Johnny Ming and what he does every day. Ask them to imagine how he became a detective.
- Learners work in pairs and discuss their character.
- Regroup students into new pairs so that each pair has one person from each group. Tell them to share their ideas about the characters.
- Monitor and support as they work.
- Share ideas with the class.

  Fast finishers Learners decide who they think Huxley is and how he knows Johnny.

Learning outcomes By the end of the lesson, learners will have read part of a novel to understand details.

New language *ashamed*

Recycled language *detective, exhibition, diamonds, suitcase, hot-air balloon*

Materials paper and pen for dictation

Social and Emotional Skill: keeping calm under stress

- After reading the story, ask learners *What qualities does Johnny Ming need to be a secret detective? (he has to be brave, adventurous, daring). Say He needs to keep calm in stressful situations to think clearly. Ask When does he do this? (when he meets Sami and Mia). What does Johnny say about Huxley? (he gets worried and very stressed).*
- Put learners in groups of four. Suggest stressful situations to each group or they can invent their own.
- Each group says how they would keep calm in their situation. Share ideas as a class and discuss if they did the right thing.

Warm-up

- Put learners into pairs. to write down some words. Dictate the words: *message, diamonds, suitcase, flying, girls.*
- Ask learners to check their words and the spellings. Tell learners the words all appear in the story in the same order. Tell them to think about the story and use the key words to retell the story without looking. Check their ideas.
- Ask them to go back to pages 98–99 and find the words in the story to check if they are correct.

Pupil's Book, page 99

Presentation

- Ask learners to look at the picture on page 99 and describe each girl, thinking about what they look like. Ask them to guess what kind of character each girl has. Share their ideas.
- Put the learners into groups of three.
- On the board write: *Why are Mia and Sami in the balloon? What is their family like? What do they want to do?*
- Learners discuss in groups. Build up a story for who the girls are and why they are there, using learners' ideas.

  Fast finishers Learners decide what kind of family Mia and Sami have.

2 In pairs, role play a conversation. Imagine you are Sami and Mia waiting in the hot-air balloon for Johnny Ming.

- Ask learners to read the question and the example speech bubbles.
- Divide the class into two. Tell half the class they will be Sami. Tell half the class they are Mia. Tell them to read the information about their character again.
- Put learners into pairs with another learner who has the same role as them. Ask them to discuss with their partner.
- Pair learners with a new partner. One should be Mia and one should be Sami. Tell them to role play their dialogue as they wait in the hot-air balloon.
- Learners work together in pairs. Monitor and support.
- Choose some pairs to demonstrate their dialogues.
- Ask learners to decide what Johnny says to the girls. Ask what he will do.
- Learners work in their pairs again. Monitor and support as they discuss. Share ideas with the class.

  Extension Put learners into threes to think about what happens next in the novel. Tell them to decide if Johnny and the girls stay in the balloon and if they catch Countess Arabella Von Thursday. Learners discuss. Invite learners to share ideas. The class choose the idea they like best for the rest of the story.

Activity Book, page 99

See pages TB126–141.

Ending the lesson

- Put learners into pairs. Ask them to look at the picture of Johnny Ming. Tell them to describe what he is wearing. Invite one of the pairs to give their description. Ask them to read the third paragraph and check their answers.
- Now tell them to imagine the character of Arabella Von Thursday and what she looks like. Learners discuss in pairs.
- Tell learners to share their ideas and find out if other pairs have a similar idea.

  Extension Tell learners to draw a picture of Countess Arabella Von Thursday and label her clothes. Put learners into pairs and ask them to choose one character from the story. They describe to their partner what they are wearing. Their partner says which character they are, e.g. *I'm wearing a white suit and a hat. You are Johnny Ming!*

Minutes later Johnny Ming was flying above the rubbish and traffic jams of the city. He smiled to himself. Alone in Blue Wonder, his beloved hot-air balloon, he had time to ... what was that? Something was moving near his feet.

Looking down, he saw two pairs of eyes. 'Stand up immediately!' he said. The girls were no more than eleven years old. Johnny Ming breathed in deeply. China's Number One Secret Detective mustn't be too annoyed. 'What is the meaning of this?' he asked as calmly as he could. 'I'm Mia,' said the one with the black hair. 'And I'm Sami,' said the one with the red hair. 'And we know where the Butterfly Diamond is,' they said together. Johnny Ming's mouth was open, but he couldn't speak. 'If you let us help you,' said Sami. 'We won't tell anyone who you really are.' 'Well,' said Mia as she crossed her arms. 'What do you say, Mr Ming?'

2 **In pairs, role play a conversation.** Imagine you are Sami and Mia waiting in the hot-air balloon for Johnny Ming.

STUDENT A You are Sami. You are worried. You think you and Mia have done the wrong thing. You think Johnny Ming will be angry with you.

But we don't know where the Butterfly Diamond is, Mia! What will Johnny Ming say when we tell him?

STUDENT B You are Mia. You aren't worried. You think you and Sami have done the right thing. You think Johnny Ming will be excited to have two helpers.

It's OK, Sami. If we help Johnny Ming, we'll become secret detectives like him!

8

Cross-curricular

1 **Look at the pictures and match them to the headings (1–4).**

1 Don't feed the animals
2 Respect local customs and traditions
3 Protect the environment
4 Support local communities

A 

B 

C 

D 

2 3.17 **Listen and read the text. What ideas from Activity 1 are good for Uluru?**

When you visit another country, do you think about where you put your rubbish? Do you look at the signposts and do what they say? Do you learn about the people that live there and do the same things that they do? If the answer is yes to these questions, then you are an ecotourist!

A good example of ecotourism is in Australia. This is Uluru (Ayers Rock) in Australia. Lots of tourists used to visit the rock and climb it. But they were damaging it and they weren't respecting local customs. Uluru used to belong to the Aboriginal people of Australia and they didn't use to climb it because it was an important place for them. So, in 1985 the Australian government gave it back to the Aboriginal people and now most tourists don't climb it.

Did you know?

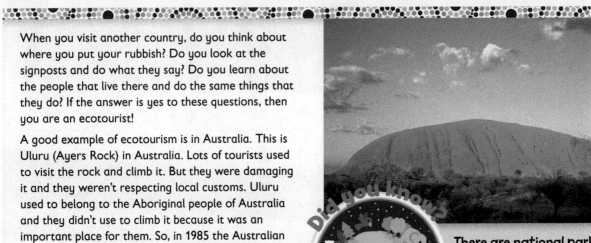

There are national parks all around the world. They cover about 6% of the Earth's surface.

3 3.18 **Listen and write the correct answers.**

Timanfaya National Park

Location: Lanzarote, the Canary Islands, Spain
Size: (1) ____________
Popular name of the park: (2) ____________
Transport: (3) ____________
Interesting activity: (4) ____________
Type of food: (5) ____________

4 **Choose a holiday location in your country. Make a list of ways that people can be responsible tourists there.**

Learning outcomes By the end of the lesson, learners will be able to respond to a text using critical thinking and emotional intelligence and understand responsible tourism.

New language *ecotourist, damage, customs*

Recycled language *rubbish, signposts, rock*

Materials marker pens, poster paper, sticky tack

Warm-up

- Ask learners to think about tourism. Put them into groups of five. Give out large sheets of poster paper and marker pens. Tell half the groups to think about the good things about tourism and half the groups to think about the problems. Groups make a mind map or list.
- Ask groups who have discussed the same thing to look at each other's mind maps or lists. Tell them to add extra ideas onto their mind map. Put the posters onto the wall with sticky tack so learners can refer to them.
- Put learners into pairs: one learner who thought about the benefits and one learner who thought about the problems of tourism. Tell them to share their ideas.

  Fast finishers Learners think of a place they have visited and decide if tourism has been good or bad or both for the place they visited.

Pupil's Book, page 100

Presentation

- Remind learners of some of the problems of tourism.
- Ask learners *If we damage something do we look after it or cause problems? (cause problems)*. Ask for examples of how tourists can damage a place, e.g. *leave rubbish.*
- Say *If we visit a new place we should understand local customs – the habits people have in that place.* Give an example, e.g. *In some countries people take off their shoes when they go inside but in others they don't. Why could this cause problems?* (e.g. *you might upset someone if you don't take off your shoes*).
- Tell learners that tourism can also be good. Say *Do tourists like to see local customs? (Yes, because they learn about the place they are visiting).*
- Ask *Do tourists spend money? (yes).* Say *The money can be used to help protect the environment.*

1 Look at the pictures and match them to the headings (1–4).

- Ask learners to match the headings to the pictures. Learners discuss in pairs. Check answers.

Key: 1 C 2 D 3 A 4 B

2 3.17 Listen and read the text. What ideas from Activity 1 are good for Uluru?

- Learners listen and read to find out where it is and if tourism has been good for the place. Learners compare answers in pairs.
- Check answers. *(it's in Australia; tourism was a problem to start with, but now it isn't).*
- Tell learners to read again and decide in pairs which ideas from Activity 1 are good for Uluru. Check answers.
- Ask learners what we call tourism that is good for the place and looks after the environment. *(ecotourism).* Learners repeat.

Key: respect local customs and protect the environment

3 3.18 Listen and write the correct answers.

- Tell learners to read the question and look quickly at the text in Activity 3.
- Ask them the best way to complete the task. *(read the notes and think about the type of information in the gaps).*
- Learners read the notes in pairs and talk about the types of words they think might be in the gaps, e.g. a number or name. Tell learners to listen and write notes. Play the audio.
- Learners compare answers in pairs. Check answers.

See audioscripts on pages TB118–122.

Key: 1 square kilometres 2 Fire mountains 3 bus or camel ride 4 the camel ride 5 traditional food

4 Choose a holiday location in your country. Make a list of ways that people can be responsible tourists there.

- Put learners into groups of four. Ask them to think about a place in their country which might be popular with tourists.
- Tell learners to think of what could be bad for that place and how it can be protected. Ask learners to make a list of things people can do. Monitor and support as they work.

Activity Book, page 100

See pages TB126–141.

Ending the lesson

- Put two groups of four from Activity 4 together to make a group of eight. Ask them to share their ideas from the activity.
- Tell them to make a list of dos and don'ts for tourists visiting your country.

Learning outcomes By the end of the lesson, learners will be able to read to understand the vocabulary in a text.

New language *trip, travel, tour*

Recycled language vocabulary related to tourism

Materials paper

Warm-up

- Ask learners to tell you some different word types. Give them an example, e.g. *verbs.* Put learners into pairs and ask them for different word classes. Share ideas (e.g. *nouns, adjectives, prepositions, pronouns, adverbs*).
- Write up the word *start* and ask learners *What kind of word is this?* Share their ideas.
- Tell them to listen to two sentences. *What time does the film start? The start of the film was really good.* Ask which form the word has in each sentence. *(a verb and a noun).* Tell learners it is important to think about the type of word to use them correctly.

Pupil's Book, page 101

1 Read and write the words in a sentence. What are the different meanings?

- Tell learners to write a sentence for each word.
- In pairs, learners explain the different meanings.
- Check answers.

Key: Sample answer *Travel* is mainly used as a verb, e.g. *We often travel by train. Trip* is a noun and we usually use it to talk about a short journey to a place and back, e.g. *I went on a trip to the zoo today. Tour* is a noun or verb and usually describes a visit where you learn about a place, e.g. *We went on a tour of the city. We toured the city.*

2 Read the text below. Can you guess the words you don't know?

- Tell learners to look at the title of the text and the picture.
- Put learners into pairs. Ask them to decide what they think the text is about. Share their ideas.
- Tell them to read quickly and find out if they are correct. Remind them to read quickly and find the answers without worrying about the gaps. Put them into pairs to compare answers.
- Tell learners to think about the gaps. Look at the example together. Ask learners why 'are' is correct. *We need a positive noun so it isn't B; cities is a plural so it can't be A and must be C.* Ask learners if this checks their grammar or their vocabulary. *(grammar).* Tell them four sentences will test the correct vocabulary and two test grammar.
- Put learners into pairs to decide which of the questions test vocabulary. Learners look at the questions in pairs and decide. Check answers.

Key: Numbers 2, 4, 5 and 6 test vocabulary.

3 Read the text again. For each question, choose the correct answer. Why are the other choices incorrect?

- Tell learners to read the sentences and the text again, read the three options for each one and decide on the answer.
- Remind them that in the exam they will need to colour in an answer key like the example.
- Put learners in pairs to choose the correct options.
- Monitor and support. Check answers.

Key: 2 A (*wants* is the only grammatically correct answer after 'our company' B is wrong because it can't go with 'to') 3 A (C is plural B is the wrong meaning because it only describes the actual travel) 4 B (*with* is the only correct answer grammatically) 5 B (*visitor* is singular and *passenger* describes someone travelling rather than someone on holiday) 6 A (*after* is the only grammatically correct answer look after) 7 C (*busy* is the only adjective with the correct meaning)

EXAM TIP! Ask a strong learner to read the exam tip. Say *Remember to read the text first to get a general idea then think about the kind of words that go into thegaps.*

Activity Book, page 101

See pages TB126–141.

Ending the lesson

- Put learners into groups of three. If possible, bring in some books or show pictures of book covers.
- Ask learners to look at the books and decide which one they would read and why. Learners discuss in groups.
  Alternative Learners find a book that they would like to read. Encourage them learners to take a book out of the library. At a later point put learners into groups of five and ask them to talk about what they have read and if it is interesting.

1 **Read and write the words in a sentence.** What are the different meanings?

travel trip tour

2 **Read the text below.** Can you guess the words you don't know?

A modern travel company

Cities **(1)** ______ important places and our company, City Tourism, **(2)** ______ to help visitors explore and have fun.

Choose a **(3)** ______ with us and you'll be really surprised at how many different activities there are. The people you stay **(4)** ______ teach you something new and then you go sightseeing. For example, learn about garden bees or make bright costumes for a festival. Afterwards, you can go on a tour of the colourful street art. It's our most popular activity, so book early!

Many **(5)** ______ come back every year. This year we are going to build little houses to look **(6)** ______ the animals that live in the city. We will keep you **(7)** ______ so it doesn't matter how old you are, you'll never be bored!

3 **Read the text again.** For each question, choose the correct answer. Why are the other choices incorrect?

2	**A** wants	**B** can	**C** need
3	**A** holiday	**B** journey	**C** trips
4	**A** by	**B** with	**C** at
5	**A** passengers	**B** families	**C** visitor
6	**A** after	**B** for	**C** to
7	**A** noisy	**B** tired	**C** busy

Example:

1 **A** is **B** isn't **C** are

Answer: **A B C**

EXAM TIP! **Practise reading** all kinds of short texts and guess words you don't know.

B1 Preliminary for Schools

1 **In pairs, talk about the types of holidays you enjoy.**

I like going to visit my family at the beach, because it's sunny. What about you?

I prefer to go to the city. My brother and I love shopping!

2 **Look at the title. Read the text quickly. What is the text about?**

Our unusual holidays

We **(1)** used to have boring, sightseeing holidays. My dad always wanted to go to museums! But **(2)** ________ days my family and I travel around the world visiting strange places. Before, we used to stay in hotels, but now we normally go camping.

We decided to go to the mountains because I love **(3)** ________ photos of wild animals with my digital camera. The **(4)** ________ exciting thing is where we sleep – our tent is high on the side of the mountain! I love it, but my sister feels **(5)** ________ worried that she can't sleep.

There are lots of animals there, and it can be dangerous. If you decide to go, you **(6)** ________ hide your food so a bear doesn't look for some in your tent!

3 **Read the text above. Look at the first answer. Why is it correct?**

4 **Look at the text below. What kinds of words are missing?**

On the river in Copenhagen

I think the best way **(1)** ________ visitors to see Copenhagen is by going on a different kind of river cruise. It's not very expensive and it's even a good way to **(2)** ________ some exercise!

In December, lots of people go to the river and take a kayak to celebrate the end of **(3)** ________ year. There are lots of lights **(4)** ________ it gets very dark in the winter! Everyone starts singing and then they travel along the river. You can pass by the parks and gardens, as well **(5)** ________ the most famous monuments.

The city looks beautiful but it can get very cold, so make sure you bring a big coat! **(6)** ________ favourite part is having a delicious hot chocolate with my family afterwards.

5 **Read and write the correct answer.**

EXAM TIP! Remember to think about the **type of word** you need in the space.

Learning outcomes By the end of the lesson, learners will be able to understand strategies for reading effectively.

New language *camping, bear, tent, kayak*

Recycled language *sightseeing, travel, visitors, river cruise*

Materials 3 pictures (a campsite, a bear, a kayak)

Warm-up

- Put learners into pairs: A and B. Tell learner A to speak for 1 minute about their last holiday.
- Stop them after 1 minute. Tell learner B to summarise what they can remember, saying *'You said … '*
- Swap learners over. This time learner B speaks for 1 minute and learner A summarises.
- Ask learners if their partner remembered what they said.

Pupil's Book, page 102

Presentation

- Show learners three pictures: a campsite, a bear and a kayak on a river. Point to the campsite and ask *What are the people doing? (camping).* Show a tent and ask *What is it? (a tent).* Learners repeat. Say *So this is a camping holiday.*
- Point to the kayak and ask *What kind of boat is this? (a kayak).* Learners repeat. Say *So this is a kind of river cruise holiday.* Point to the bear. Ask *What kind of animal is this? (a bear). Is it dangerous? (yes).* Ask *Would you see this on a camping holiday or a river cruise holiday? (possibly both).*

1 In pairs, talk about the types of holidays you enjoy.

- Ask learners if they have ever been on a camping holiday or a river cruise holiday before. Learners share ideas.
- Put them into pairs. Ask them to think about the types of holiday they enjoy. Ask them to read the dialogues.
- Learners discuss in pairs. Remind them to give reasons why they enjoy each type of holiday and ask questions to find out about their partner's choices. Share their ideas.

  Extension Ask learners what kind of holiday they would not enjoy, e.g. *I don't like sports so I wouldn't enjoy a skiing holiday.*

2 Look at the title. Read the text quickly. What is the text about?

- Tell learners to look at the title of the first text and look at the picture. Ask them what the text is about. Learners suggest ideas.
- Ask them to read very quickly and check if they were correct.
- Put learners into pairs to compare answers.

3 Read the text above. Look at the first answer. Why is it correct?

- Tell learners to read the text again and look at the gaps. Ask them to think about the type of words that go into the gaps and look at the example.
- Tell them to decide why the example is correct. Check answers.

Key: The sentence describes their past habits.

4 Look at the text below. What kinds of words are missing?

- Tell learners to look at the title and picture of the second text to decide why the holiday is unusual.
- Learners discuss in pairs. Tell them to read the text quickly and see if they were correct.
- Ask them to read again and this time decide what kinds of words go into the gaps. Share answers.

5 Read and write the correct answer.

- Put learners into two groups. Pair them within their groups. In pairs, they read the text again and decide which words go into the gaps.
- When they have finished, pair learners again with someone from the opposite group and ask them to compare answers. Check answers.

Key: 1 do 2 of 3 the 4 when 5 as 6 My

EXAM TIP! Ask a strong learner to read the exam tip. Say *Remember to read the text first to get a general idea then think about the kind of words that go into the gaps.*

Activity Book, page 102

See pages TB126–141.

Ending the lesson

- Put learners into groups of three. Ask them to think about an unusual holiday they would like to go on. They should think about the place, what they would do there and why it is unusual.
- Ask each group to present their idea for an unusual holiday. The class votes for the most interesting idea.

Learning outcomes By the end of the lesson, learners will have used language from the unit to talk about tourism and places to see in a city and revised the unit language and skills.

Recycled language unit language

Materials poster paper, colouring pens (optional: computer access)

Warm-up

- Tell learners to think about a visit or a holiday they did when they were younger.
- Put learners into pairs to discuss. Say *Tell your partner what you used to do and where you used to go.*

  Fast finishers Learners check if any of the places or activities they did in the past are similar.

Pupil's Book, page 103

1 Choose the correct indirect questions.

- Tell learners you need to find out where the tourist information centre? is. Write *Could you tell me …* and ask learners to finish the sentence. *(where the tourist information centre? is).*
- Rub out the first part of the sentence and ask learners what else you could write. *(Do you know …).*
- Put learners into pairs.
- Ask learners to look at the two options in sentence sets 1 to 6 in pairs. Tell them to decide which question in each case is correct. Check answers, clarifying as necessary.

Key: 1 A 2 B 3 B 4 A 5 B 6 A

2 Complete the sentences with *used to* and a verb.

- Tell learners to look at the sentences and think about how to complete the sentences using *used to*.
- Look at number 1 together as an example.
- Tell learners to complete the rest of the sentences 2 to 6 in pairs. Check answers.

Key: 1 used to travel 2 used to have 3 used to live 4 used to go 5 used to be 6 used to open

3 Choose ten words from this unit. Record the words using the steps below.

- Say *Well done. You've learnt a lot of new language. Now let's think about another interesting way to remember the words.*
- Tell learners to look at the flowchart. Ask if they can remember where to find an example. Tell them to look at the 'find an example' part of the chart. (You can check the meaning in this unit or in a dictionary.)
- Ask them to think of an interesting way to record it. *(Write an example sentence, but put a gap instead of the word then choose an extra word to include so that you have to choose between the correct word and the extra word).* Tell learners to look at the 'record the example' part of the flowchart.
- Look at the next part of the flowchart: 'use it'. Say *You can test a friend with your sentence. Ask them to choose the correct word for the gap.* Say *Now let's do an example.*
- Tell learners to choose a word from the unit and write an example sentence. Tell them to choose an additional word as an option. Tell them to follow the flowchart.
- Learners work alone. Monitor and check.
- Once they have finished, pair learners. Ask them to show their sentences and the two words to their partner and ask them to try to guess the word.

Mission in action!

- Put learners back into the same groups as Mission Stage 2.
- If possible, give back the mind maps or lists they made at Stage 2 and tell them to look at the city they chose and the top three attractions.
- Invite each group to create a presentation. Give out poster paper and colouring pens or, if possible, give learners access to computers so they can create a slide show or presentation.
- Remind learners to include the name of the city and to explain what their top three activities are and why.
- Learners work in groups. Monitor and support.
- Invite each group to present their city and what you can do in the city. Then invite the class to ask questions.
- Take a on asking which city each learner would like to visit.

  Alternative Instead of presenting to the whole class, ask each group to choose two learners to present their ideas and space each group presentation around the classroom. Learners who are not presenting circulate and look at the presentations. They can ask questions as they look at the presentations. Only the learners who have circulated vote for the best city.

Activity Book, page 103

See Teacher's Book pages TB126–141.

Ending the lesson

- **SA** Complete the self-assessment (see Introduction).

1 Choose the correct indirect questions.

1 A Do you know where Buckingham Palace is?
B Do you know where is Buckingham Palace?

2 A Could you tell me what time does the cinema open, please?
B Could you tell me what time the cinema opens, please?

3 A Do you remember how much were the cruise tickets?
B Do you remember how much the cruise tickets were?

4 A Would you mind explaining how I can get to the National Gallery?
B Would you mind explaining how can I get to the National Gallery?

5 A Do you know who is that?
B Do you know who that is?

6 A Could you explain why the building is good for the environment, please?
B Could you explain why is the building good for the environment, please?

2 Complete the sentences with *used to* and a verb.

1 Five years ago, I __________ on the underground a lot, but now I usually travel by bus.

2 I __________ a stamp collection. But I gave it to my friend last year.

3 I __________ in London. But I moved last year and now I live in a small village.

4 I usually go shopping at a department store. But I __________ shopping at the market.

5 The building in the town centre __________ a palace, but now it's a gallery.

6 The tourist information centre __________ at 9:30. But these days it opens at 11:00.

Mission in action!

Present ideas about the city you chose and what you can do there.

3 Choose ten words from this unit. Record the words using the steps below.

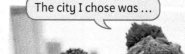

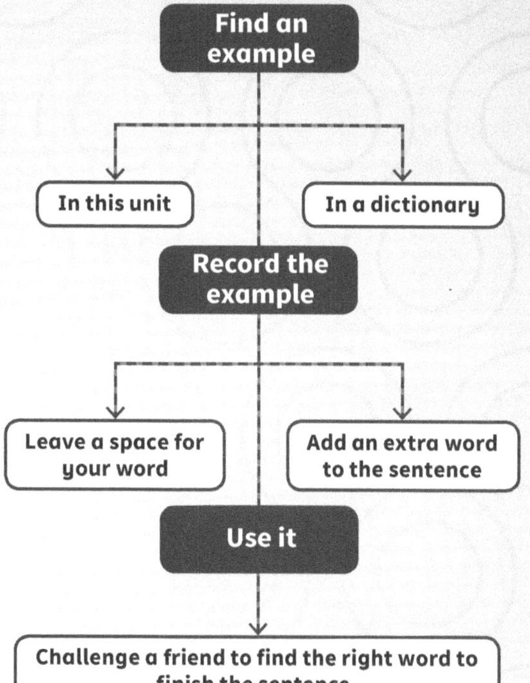
Find an example
In this unit
In a dictionary
Record the example
Leave a space for your word
Add an extra word to the sentence
Use it
Challenge a friend to find the right word to finish the sentence.

The city I chose was …
A trip to Paris!

9 Lights, camera, action!

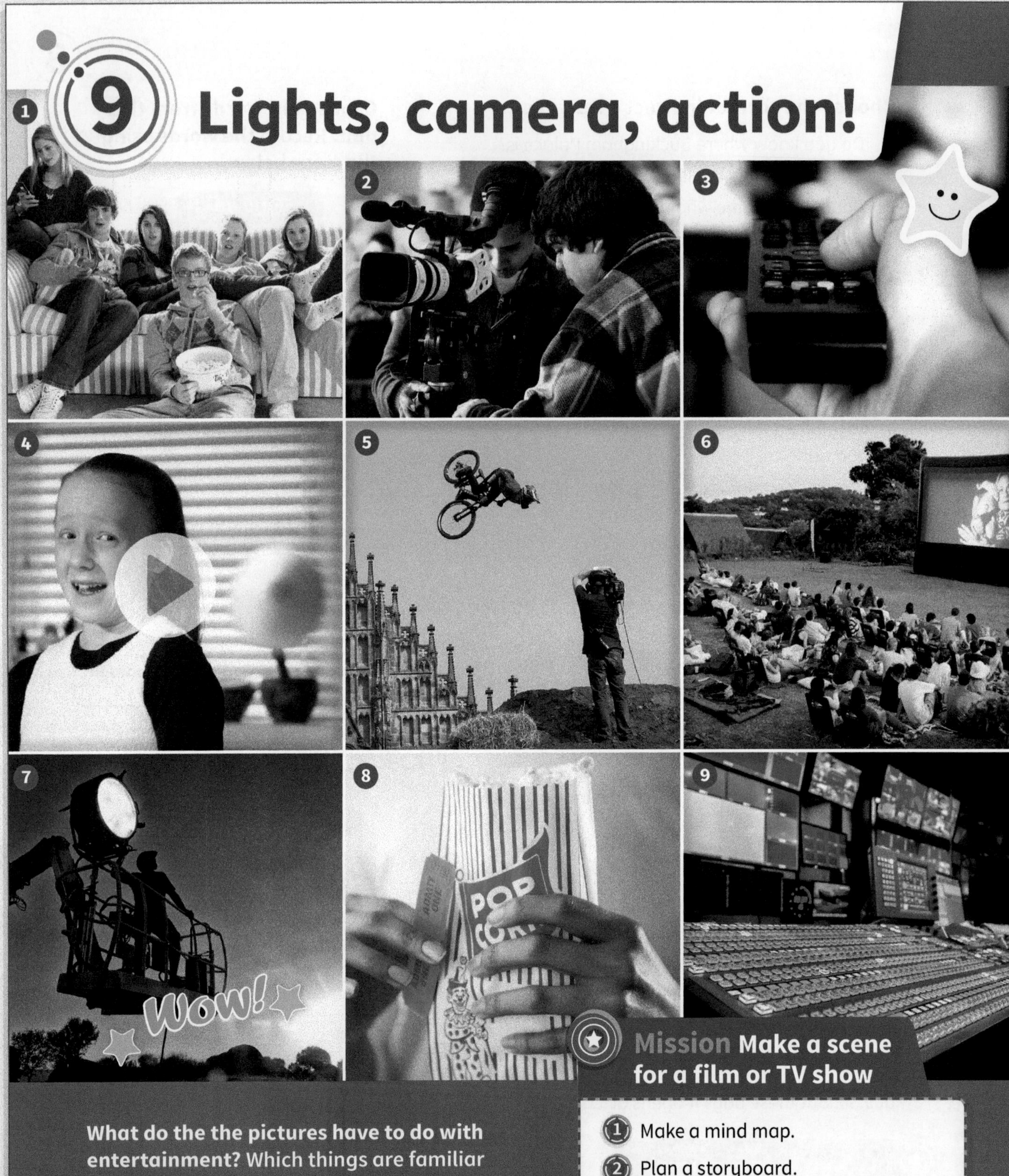

Mission Make a scene for a film or TV show

1. Make a mind map.
2. Plan a storyboard.
★ Present your scene. Choose the best ones!

What do the the pictures have to do with entertainment? Which things are familiar to you?

Watch the video. Why does the lemon hate Jenny?

Unit 9 learning outcomes

In Unit 9, learners will learn to:

- use vocabulary about TV and film
- understand and use the causative 'have/got'
- understand and use the second conditional
- read and listen for information and opinion
- identify and express opinions
- understand how special effects are used in films

Materials video; 4 or 5 pictures (stills from films that learners might know, e.g. *Frozen, Charlie and the Chocolate Factory, Finding Nemo, High School Musical, Mulan*)

Self-assessment

- SA Write the unit topic on the board.
- Ask learners to decide what the key words are in each outcome. Rub out or delete the other words.
- Put learners into pairs to rebuild the unit outcomes using the key words. Ask learners to clarify each one and write the full sentence back onto the board.
- Ask the learners to complete self-assessment (see Introduction).
- Say *We'll look at these again at the end of the unit.*

Pupil's Book, page 104

Warm-up

- Put up pictures of stills from some famous films that learners might know.
- Put learners into pairs and tell them to discuss if they know the films and if they have seen them. Check answers.
- Learners compare ideas in groups. Share learners' ideas.

What do the pictures have to do with entertainment? Which things are familiar to you?

- Put learners into pairs and ask them to discuss what is happening in each picture and what they can see.
- Go through the pictures again in order. For each ask *What can you see?* Check any words that may be challenging asking learners to point at the picture and repeat

Watch the video. Why does the lemon hate Jenny?

- Tell learners they are going to watch a vlog and Jenny and Jim describe a film they have made. Say *In the film they use some special effects.* Ask them what special effects do *(they are tricks in filming that make something look real).* Ask them for examples of special effects they know.
- Ask them *What kind of film do you think they made?* Learners suggest ideas. If they don't suggest it, add *horror – a scary film* and *comedy – a film that makes us laugh.* Ask learners for examples of horror films and comedy films.
- Ask *Who do you think is filming and who gives a performance?* Check 'performance' *(acting)* Learners suggest ideas.
- Ask them to watch and find out what kind of film it is and who acts in it. Tell them to find out why the lemon hates Jenny.
- Play the video. Put learners into pairs to discuss their ideas.
- Check answers with the group.

Key: It's a 'horror' film for Jenny (comedy for Jim). Jenny acts while Jim films. The lemon hates Jenny because she cut up his brother and turned him into lemonade.

Extension Ask learners to find out which special effects Jim and Jenny used in the film.

Key: They used curtains to make it seem like night, they put the lemon on a string to make it float, they filmed sideways to make it look like she was walking up a wall.

Mission Make a scene for a film or TV show

- Tell learners they are going to choose a city to visit.
- Say *We're going to make a scene for a film or TV show. What do you think you need to do first? (plan ideas).*
- Ask learners to read the Mission statement. Say *You can plan using a mind map then plan a storyboard.* Ask what a storyboard is. Learners suggest ideas. Say *They are drawings that show what the film will show.* Say *Finally, you will present your scene and we'll choose the best one.*
- Ask learners to retell you the three parts of the Mission.
- Say *This is our Mission.*

Activity Book, page 104

My unit goals

- Go through the unit goals with the learners. Either read these or put them onto the board or a poster (see suggested techniques in 'Identifying outcomes' in the teachers' in-class guide in Introduction).
- Go back to these unit goals at the end of each Mission stage during the unit and review them.
- Say *This is our Mission page.*

Ending the lesson

- Put learners into pairs. Ask them who their favourite actor is and which films they have been in.
- Learners discuss in pairs. Share their ideas.

Learning outcomes By the end of the lesson, learners will be able to use vocabulary to describe TV programmes and listen and understand words in context.

New language *news, cartoon, drama, documentary, quiz show, chat show*

Recycled language *comedy, news, horror, action*

Materials audio; if possible, examples of TV listings

Pupil's Book, page 105

Warm-up

- If possible, show learners some examples of real TV listings. Ask *What is it? (a TV guide).*
- Ask learners which kinds of programmes they watch on TV.
- Share ideas.
- Write on the board the name of TV channels, e.g. *Channel 1, Channel 2, Channel 3,* etc. and clarify.
- Ask learners to think of a TV show for each channel, e.g. Say *There is a horror film on Channel 1.* Make a note on the board under that channel. Say *There's a football match on Channel 2 …* Write under the channel.
- Learners plan a programme for each TV channel and create a TV guide in pairs.
- Monitor and support while they work.
- Tell learners they are going to find out which of their programmes is most popular.
- Ask learners to mingle. Each pair shows their TV guide to another pair who choose which programme they would like to watch. Remind learners to keep count of the number of votes each programme gets. Learners talk to as many other pairs as possible.
- Once the activity is over, choose some of the pairs to say which of their programmes was the most popular.

1 Look at the TV guide. Match the words in the box to the pictures (1–9).

- Learners look at the pictures on page 105 and think about the kind of programme shown.
- Learners guess in pairs.
- Tell learners to look at the programme names in the box.
- Look at the first picture together and ask what kind of film it is. *(action).*
- Tell learners to work in pairs and match the type of programme with the pictures.

2 3.19 Listen and check.

- Tell learners to listen and check their answers.
- Play the audio.
- Check their ideas and understanding.
- After you have checked, tell learners to listen to your clue and point to the correct picture. Say sentences. Learners point to the correct picture.

This programme makes us laugh. (comedy)
This programme tells us what is happening in the world today. (news)
In this programme, you can win a prize. (quiz show)
Children will love watching this. (cartoon)
You can learn about your favourite film star in this programme. (chat show)
If you want to learn facts about the world around us, you can watch this. (a documentary)
This type of film will make you feel afraid. (horror film)
If you want to watch a programme about events in people's lives you can watch this. (drama)

Key: 1 a cartoon 2 a chat show 3 a comedy 4 a documentary 5 a drama 6 the news 7 a horror film 8 a quiz show

Track 3.19

1 an action film
2 a cartoon
3 a chat show
4 a comedy
5 a documentary
6 a drama
7 the news
8 a horror film
9 a quiz show

3 3.20 PRONUNCIATION Listen and repeat.

- Tell learners they are going to say the words correctly.
- Play the audio again, but pause after each item for learners to repeat.
- Monitor and listen, correcting pronunciation as necessary.
- Learners complete the task on page 119 (see page TB124).

Activity Book, page 105

See pages TB126–141.

Ending the lesson

- Put learners into groups of three.
- Tell them to choose one person to guess answers.
- Tell the other two to look quickly at the different types of programmes and choose one. They think about what they might see if they are watching that kind of programme. They mime a scene or situation from the programme.
- The third learner guesses what it is.
- Learners swap roles so that a different person guesses and repeat.
- They swap roles a final time so the last learner guesses.
- Invite a few learners to repeat their mimes for the whole class to guess.

1 **Look at the TV guide.** Match the words in the box to the pictures (1–9).

the news	a cartoon	a chat show	a comedy	a drama
a horror film	a documentary	an action film	a quiz show	

What's picture number 1?

It's an action film.

This week on TV ...

Popular now | Recommended for you | Watch it again

1

Evil men have taken Doug's dog – but he'll do anything to get it back.

2

Nemo is lost and his dad goes on a long journey to find him.

3

Interviews with top stars.

4

Join us for more lunchtime laughs!

5

Learn about the life of turtles near the beaches of Mexico.

6

Clara tells Tony the truth about the broken table.

7

The latest stories from around the world.

8

Lost. Scared. Alone. And there's something terrible in the forest ...

9

We ask families what they know. Let's find out!

2  3.19 **Listen and check.**

3  3.20 **PRONUNCIATION**
Listen and repeat.  page 119

PHOTOS BLOG LINKS CHATS

A 

Question from:

Eiffel_64

Hey guys,

You're all coming to my birthday party next weekend, aren't you? I'm really excited about it. Mum's having a special superhero cake made for me and we're going to watch a film. But I want to ask you something. Can you all dress up as your favourite film character? I think that would be so cool! I'm going to dress up as Batman, of course.

B 

CatGirl_22

Hey Eiffel_64. Cool! I'd LOVE to dress up as my favourite film character. Can you guess who it is? Spiderman, of course! I think Spiderman's cooler than Batman because he's part spider and part man. My dad has had a spider costume made for me so I'll wear that.

C 

FriendlyJ

Hey, that's such a great idea! My favourite film is *Finding Nemo*. Have you seen it? It's a cartoon and a comedy about a fish called Nemo and his dad. One day Nemo gets caught by a boat and is sent to live in a dentist's office. I'd like to dress as Nemo but I don't have time to make a fish costume. So I think I'll come as a clown instead because Nemo's a clown fish! Do you think that's OK? I could have my face painted too!

D 

Sharky_McMarky

Can I dress up as a penguin? My favourite film is a documentary called *March of the Penguins* – you should watch it. I love it so much that last year I had penguin-shaped ice creams made for my birthday. Did you know that father penguins look after the eggs while the mothers are looking for food? When the eggs become baby penguins, they have to wait a long time for their mothers to feed them. Will there be lots of food at your party?

1 **Read the posts quickly.** Who will each child dress as? Match the posts (A–D) to pictures (1–4).

1 

2 

3 

4 

2 **Read Eiffel_64's post again.** Say *yes* or *no*.

1 Eiffel_64's birthday party is next Monday.

2 Eiffel_64 will watch a film at the party.

3 Eiffel_64 thinks his friends should all wear suits to the party.

4 Batman is Eiffel_64's favourite film character.

3  **Write two yes/no sentences about one of the posts.** In pairs, say your sentences.

Catgirl_22 wants to dress up as Batman.

No, she wants to dress up as Spiderman.

Learning outcomes By the end of the lesson, learners will be able to read to find detailed information and understand causative *have/get* in a text.

New language *dress up*

Recycled language *film, documentary, cartoon*

Materials audio, paper and pens

Pupil's Book, page 106

Warm-up

- Ask if any of the learners have had their birthday recently or will have their birthday soon. Learners respond. Ask the class what we say to someone when it is their birthday. *(Happy birthday!)*
- Ask learners to think about birthday parties and what happens, e.g. games, cake, doing an activity, dressing up.
- Tell them to imagine the best birthday party ever. Ask them to think about what activities they would do / what they could wear / the food they would eat / cake and so on. Tell them to plan what they would like best.
- Put learners into pairs to discuss their ideas and plan the best birthday party.
- Share ideas and ask the class if they like the different ideas.

  Extension Learners vote for the best party idea.

1 Read the posts quickly. Who will each child dress as? Match the posts (A–D) to pictures (1–4).

- Ask learners if they have ever dressed up. Say *If you dress up, you wear a costume.* Learners answer. Ask who they would dress as if they were going to a party.
- Share ideas.
- Tell learners to read the question at the top of the blog from Eiffel_64.
- Ask learners why he is writing to his friends.
- Learners discuss in pairs.
- Share ideas. *(he is having a birthday party and wants his friends to wear superhero costumes)*
- Ask learners who they think each of his friends will dress as.
- Learners guess. Note their ideas on the board.
- Tell them to read each answer and check their predictions.
- Learners read.
- Ask them to compare in pairs and see if they were correct.
- Check answers.

Key: A 4 B 3 C 1 D 2

2 Read Eiffel_64's post again. Say *yes* or *no*.

- Tell learners to read the sentences. Tell them they will find out if each sentence is true or false.
- Read the first example together and find the sentence that gives the answer in the messages. (*You're all coming to my birthday party next weekend.*)
- Learners read again.
- Put learners into pairs to compare ideas.
- Check answers.

Key: 2 yes 3 no 4 yes

3  Write two yes/no sentences about one of the posts. In pairs, say your sentences.

- Tell learners to read the text again and write two sentences. Tell them the sentences can be true, false or one of each. Learners write sentences.
- Put learners into pairs. Learners take it in turns to read their sentences. Their partner says if the sentence is true or false.

Activity Book, page 106

See pages TB126–141.

Ending the lesson

- Tell learners they are going to create a graph of favourite superheroes.
- Put learners in pairs to think of superheroes.
- Share ideas and make a list on the board. Try to list about six to eight characters.
- Ask the learners to copy the list.
- Tell learners to do a survey of at least ten other learners (or the whole group if you have a smaller class).
- Learners should ask which superhero each person likes best and why. They put a tick next to the superhero chosen each time.
- When the learners have finished tell them to make a graph showing their results. Show them a bar chart and a pie chart and ask them to choose which one they will use.
- Put the learners in pairs to make their graphs.
- Check and monitor as they work.
- Ask learners to compare their graphs and see if they got similar results.
- Finally ask learners to write two sentences about their graphs, e.g. *Spiderman is the most popular superhero. A few people wanted to be a penguin.*

  Extra support Give learners a ready-made bar chart and ask them to try to understand the information.

Learning outcomes By the end of the lesson, learners will be able to understand and use causative *have/get* accurately.

New language the causative *have/get, script*

Recycled language *film,* vocabulary related to film and TV

Materials audio, poster paper, colouring pens

Pupil's Book, page 107

Warm-up

- Ask learners to write some problems as you say them. Dictate: *the car isn't working; my hair is too long; I need a special cake for a party.*
- In pairs, learners think about who can help in each situation.
- Say *Sometimes we need other people to help us with problems.*

Presentation

- Ask learners what kind of cake Eiffel_64 had for his party. *(a superhero cake)* Ask *Did he make the cake himself? (no). Did his mum make it? (no).*
- Ask learners to find the sentence about the cake on page 106. Write it on the board. *Mum's having a special superhero cake made for me.*
- Underline *having* and *made*. Ask *Who is making the cake? (someone at a cake shop).* Point to *having* and say *We use 'have' here.* Point to *made* and ask what kind of verb it is. *(past participle)*

Grammar look: the causative *have/get*

- Put learners into pairs. Look at the grammar title. Tell learners causative *have* or *got* means we get someone else to do something for us. They do it because we ask them.
- Tell them to read the sentence at the top left of the Grammar look box. In pairs, they answer the questions.

Key: 1 No 2 someone at a cake shop 3 Yes, probably 4 don't do it

Complete the Grammar look on page 126.

1 3.22 Read and match the script ideas (1–4) to A–D. Listen and check.

- Ask learners what we call written dialogues used to make a film. *(script)*. Tell learners to read the four beginnings of some scripts. Ask them what kind of film they think each one is. Learners discuss in pairs and suggest ideas.
- Learners read scripts A to D and match the beginnings and endings. Tell them to listen and check. Play the audio.

Key: 1 C 2 A 3 D 4 B

Track 3.22

1 Sarah moves to a dark, old house a long way from the town. One day she has the walls repainted in a beautiful green. But when she goes to eat breakfast the next morning, the colour of the paint is different.

2 A grey goat lives on a mountain and feels very lonely. But one day, he gets his hair dyed pink. Lots of people start visiting the mountain to see him and take his photo. He's the most famous animal on the hill.

3 A farmer lives in a quiet village in a little old spaceship. One day he has his lights fixed by a strange old woman. 'Your lights turn on and off now, but don't press that big red button,' she warns.

4 Two brothers were organising a birthday party. They had a cool cake made, their faces painted and lots of pizzas delivered. But when the party started, there was one problem they hadn't thought off.

2 Choose one script idea from Activity 1 and finish it.

- Put learners into groups of three. Tell them to read the four script ideas and choose one to finish. Read the example together. Ask which script it finishes. *(idea 2)*
- In groups, learners think of an ending for each story.
- Monitor and support. Learners present their ideas.

Mission Stage 1

- Ask learners to think about different film types.
- Tell them to choose one type of film.
- Look at the mind map on page 107. Ask what they need to think about. *(the type of film, the name of the film, the characters in it, the beginning and end of the story).*
- Give out poster paper and colouring pens to each group.
- Learners work in groups to make posters.

Extension Ask each group to show their mind map and summarise for the class.

Activity Book, page 107

See pages TB126–141.

Ending the lesson

- Put learners into groups of five or six. Tell them to create a film quiz. They think of five questions about films, e.g. *Who is the cowboy in Toy Story? (Woody)*
- Once learners have finished, ask each group to choose a buzzer sound, e.g. an animal noise. Choose one group to ask the class their questions. Teams make their sound if they know the answer. The fastest team to answer correctly get a point. If they are wrong, it passes to the second fastest team or is offered to the class again.
- Keep a note of the points. Repeat with other groups or keep their quizzes for later lessons.

Language practice 1

Grammar look: causative *have/get*

'Mum's having a special superhero cake made for me.'

1 Will Eiffel_64's mum make the cake herself? **Yes / No**

2 Who will make the cake? **someone at a cake shop / the boy**

3 We use *have* when we have asked someone to do something for us. We **do / don't** do it ourselves. In informal situations, we can use *get* instead of *have*.

page 126

1 3.22 **Read and match the script ideas (1–4) to A–D. Listen and check.**

1 Sarah moves to a dark, old house a long way from the town. One day she …

2 A grey goat lives on a mountain and feels very lonely. But one day, he gets …

3 A farmer lives in a quiet village in a little old spaceship. One day he has his …

4 Two brothers were organising a birthday party. They had …

A his hair dyed pink. Lots of people start visiting the mountain to see him and take his photo. He's the most famous animal on the hill …

B a cool cake made, their faces painted and lots of pizzas delivered. But when the party started, there was one problem they hadn't thought of …

C has the walls repainted in a beautiful green. But when she goes to eat breakfast the next morning, the colour of the paint is different.

D lights fixed by a strange old woman. 'Your lights turn on and off now, but don't press that big red button,' she warns.

2 Choose one script idea from Activity 1 and finish it.

At first, the goat loves seeing so many people. But the cars coming to see him are noisy, and some people leave litter on the hill.

Mission Stage 1

Make a mind map for a three minute scene.

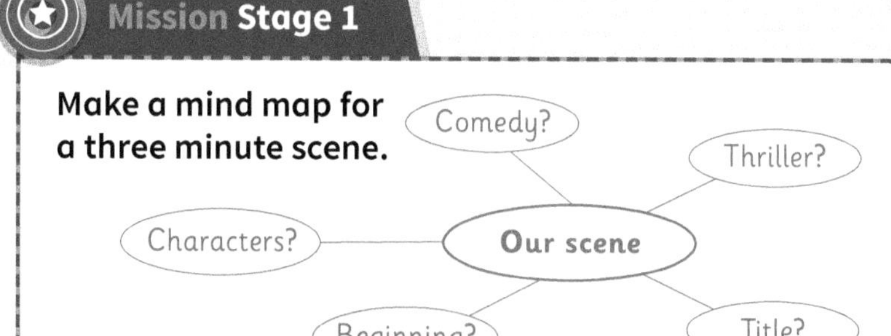

Vocabulary 2

1 3.23 **Look at the pictures.** Listen to Mark's podcast. Which idea is not in the pictures?

2 3.24 **Listen again.** Put the pictures in the order that you hear them.

A travelling to China to film

B paying famous actors

C building old rooms in a studio

D making advertisements for the film

E spending money on special effects

F buying dance shoes

3 3.25 **Complete the sentences from Mark's podcast.** Use the words in the box. Listen and check.

adverts celebrity channel heroine/hero interviewing performance programmes review series scene studio

1 I'm ________ my classmates to ask what they would do if they had $250 million to make a film.
2 I'd love to work with a famous actor. Someone who's a big ________ .
3 The ________ is the most important person in most films.
4 I'd spend the money by building lots of old rooms in a ________ .
5 I'd spend the money on ________ . It's really important that everyone knows about new films.
6 I'd love to make a TV ________ about tigers. I'd make six ________ that are each 30 minutes long.
7 That'd be great for the nature ________ .
8 So I'd have one ________ with the heroine flying above a city.
9 We're doing a dance ________ at the theatre next week.
10 Maybe Jenny can ________ it for her blog?

Learning outcomes By the end of the lesson, learners will be able to listen to understand opinions.

New language *adverts, celebrity, channel, hero/heroine, interview, review, series, scene, studio*

Recycled language vocabulary related to film and TV

Materials audio

Pupil's Book, page 108

Warm-up

- Tell learners that you are going to make a list of what happens when a film is made.
- Write some phrases on the board: *choose adverts to tell everyone about the film, choose a celebrity as the main actor, go to the studio, choose a script, look at the reviews, start filming scenes.*
- Put the learners into pairs and ask them to look at the words and check any they don't know. Either ask learners to check in the dictionary or help with the meanings. Check understanding.
- Tell learners to put the words in the order they think they happen.
- Check their ideas. *(choose a script, choose a celebrity as the main actor, go to the studio, start filming scenes, choose adverts to tell everyone about the film, look at the reviews)*

Presentation

- Tell learners they are going to listen to a podcast by Mark. He is asking students what kind of film they would like to make.
- Ask learners to look at the pictures in Activity 1.
- Share their ideas.
- Ask learners if they would choose to spend the money on any of the same things. Learners suggest ideas.

1 **Look at the pictures. Listen to Mark's podcast. Which idea is not in the pictures?**

- Tell learners to listen carefully to Mark's ideas.
- Play the audio. Put learners into pairs to compare ideas.
- Check answers.

See audioscripts on pages TB118–123.

Key: If I had that money, I'd buy cameras and costumes for the actors

2 **Listen again. Put the pictures in the order that you hear them.**

- Tell learners to listen again and think about the order they hear the ideas.
- Tell them to write the letters of the pictures as they listen.
- Play the audio. Learners listen then compare answers in pairs. Check answers.
- Track 3.24 Repeat previous track.

Key: B C D A E F

3 3.25 **Complete the sentences from Mark's podcast. Use the words in the box. Listen and check.**

- Ask learners who a hero or heroine is *(the main character of the film who is good – a hero is male and a heroine is female).* Ask them the difference between a programme and a series. *(a programme is singular, a series is a number of programmes linked together).*
- Tell learners to read the sentences from the podcast and think about which words go into the gaps. Play the podcast again. Learners listen and write the missing words.
- Check answers with the class. As you go through the answers say each word clearly so that learners can repeat.
  Fast finishers Learners say words from the box. Their partner gives them the meaning or an example.
- Track 3.25 Repeat previous track.

Key: 1 interviewing 2 celebrity 3 hero or heroine 4 studio 5 adverts 6 series, programmes 7 channel 8 scene 9 performance 10 review

Activity Book, page 108

See pages TB126–141.

Ending the lesson

- Tell half the class to stand in a circle facing outwards. Ask the others to stand in a second circle around the first, facing inwards so that learners are face to face. Ask learners to think of their favourite TV show and discuss it with their partner.
- After a minute, stop them and ask the learners in the outer circle to walk around in a clockwise direction until you clap.
- Learners move around. Clap your hands, checking they stop in front of a different partner.
- Ask them to talk about a documentary they have seen which was interesting. Learners talk to their new partner. After a minute, stop and ask the outer circle to walk around again. Repeat asking different questions each time, e.g. *Which channel do you think has the best programmes? Who is your favourite film hero or heroine? Is there a celebrity you don't like and why?*

Learning outcomes By the end of the lesson, learners will be able to understand and use the second conditional.

New language second conditional

Recycled language vocabulary related to film and TV

Materials pictures of film stills; optional – clip of a film dialogue, paper and colouring pens, Mission worksheet (Teacher's Resource Book page 86)

Warm-up

- Find some pictures of film scenes with people talking.
- Show a picture to learners. Ask *What do you think is happening? Who are the people and what happened just before the picture was taken?* Ask what the people are saying.
- Give out more pictures or show one on the board. Put learners into pairs and ask them to repeat. Tell them to imagine they are the people in the picture. Ask them to create a short dialogue of what they think the people are saying. Choose a few learners to show their picture and say their dialogue.

Pupil's Book, page 109

Presentation

- Say learners *If we made a film, I'd like you to act in it.* Ask *Are we making a film? (no) Is it possible. (yes) But are we probably making one or probably not? (probably not).*

Grammar look: the second conditional

- Learners read questions 1–5 in the box and choose the correct options in pairs.
- Ask learners to look at the example sentences again and ask *How many parts are there in the sentences? (two)* Ask *In the 'if' part, what tense is used? (past)* Ask *In the second part of the sentence, what verb form is used? (would plus infinitive)*

Key: 1 No 2 No 3 Probably not 4 Probably not 5 Not likely to happen

1 Complete the email with the words in the box. Write one word in each gap.

- Ask learners to read through the email quickly. Tell them not to worry about the gaps, but find out what Simon is asking his friend Claire. Check their ideas. *(He is asking what kind of film she would make if she had money to make a film).*
- Tell learners to write a word in each gap. Tell them to think about the grammar. Check answers.

  Extra support Give learners the missing words and ask them to match to the gaps.

Key: 1 about 2 If 3 had 4 what 5 would

EXAM TIP! Ask a strong learner to read the exam tip. Say *Sometimes when we have to fill gaps in sentences we have to think about grammar.*

Complete the Grammar look on page 127.
See pages TB125–126.

2 What would you do if you had $250 million to make a film? Write four ideas. Share your ideas. Which idea do you like best?

- Tell learners to think of a film they would like to make and what they would need, e.g. special effects, actors, scripts.
- Tell them to write four things they would spend the money on.
- Tell the class they are producers. Put learners into groups of five or six. Tell each learner to present their ideas to the producers. The producers decide which film they would like to spend money on.

  Fast finishers Learners choose celebrities they would like for their film.

3 Tell a chain story.

- Learners work in their groups again to make a story for a film. One learner writes down a sentence to describe a situation. The next learner adds another sentence to say what happens next. They continue around the group until they complete the story. Ask groups to present their stories to the class. Take a vote on the best story.

Mission Stage 2

- Ask learners to look at the pictures. Ask what it is *(a storyboard).* Give each learner a photocopy of the storyboard (Teacher's Resource Book page 86) and ask them to complete the information under each heading. They have to include all information about their scene: what type of scene it is, who the characters are, and they draw and write the first few frames of the story. They can change or add new things to the storyboard to fit their ideas.

Activity Book, page 109

See pages TB126–141.

Ending the lesson

- **SA** Ask learners to complete their self-assessment (see Introduction).

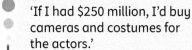

Language practice 2

9

Grammar look: the second conditional

'If I had $250 million, I'd buy cameras and costumes for the actors.'

'If there was someone well-known in my film, I think it'd be really popular.'

1 Is having $250 million to make a film possible? **Yes** / **No**

2 Is it likely? **Yes** / **No**

3 Will there be someone well known in the film? **Probably** / **Probably not**

4 Will the film be popular? **Probably** / **Probably not**

5 We use the second conditional to talk about something that is **likely** / **not likely** to happen.

page 127

1 Complete the email with the words in the box. Write one word in each gap.

had what would if ~~was~~

EXAM TIP! Look at the words that come **before and after** the gap.

Dear Claire,

I (1) was watching TV yesterday, when I decided I'd like to make a film. It'd be a documentary about our town. (2) ______ I was allowed, I'd film at the zoo. I love the animals there! If I (3) ______ a lot of money, I'd get a celebrity to be in the film. What about you? (4) ______ would you do if you had money to make a film? If you could ask any celebrity, who (5) ______ be in your film?

See you soon!

Simon

2 What would you do if you had $250 million to make a film? Write four ideas. Share your ideas. Which idea do you like best?

If I had $250 million, I'd make my film in space.

3 Tell a chain story.

If Tim had a million dollars, he'd buy a big house.

If Tim had a big house, he'd keep lots of camels there.

If Tim kept lots of camels, they'd eat all the flowers in his garden.

Mission Stage 2

In groups, make a storyboard for your scene.

If I had more money, I'd run away.

1 **Read the title and look at the pictures. What do you think the monster is?**

3.26 The Monster in our Homes

I think you're probably not aware
Of the terrible monster sitting there.
Inside your house, right under your nose,
'Cos everyone's got one, but nobody knows.

It's big and ugly and usually black,
It waits and waits, ready to attack.
When you sit down and switch it on,
You can't escape it and then you're gone.

The screen catches you and you sit and stare,
You really don't know how long you're there.
Your eyes get tired and sleepy and red,
And Mum keeps shouting, 'It's time for bed!'

Children are one of its favourite things,
It shows them heroes and monsters with wings.
Cartoons and quiz shows, movies and more,
Means that kids can't move from their place on the floor.

Learning outcomes By the end of the lesson, learners will have read a poem and understand opinions.

New language *monster, chatty, stare, think twice, skip, unfair*

Recycled language *switch on, watch TV, screen, hero, cartoon, quiz show, movie, remote, bin*

Materials audio, dice (enough for groups of 3), optional – remote control, picture of a monster

Warm-up

- Use a remote control or if you don't have one a prop e.g. a small cardboard box. Mime pressing buttons on the remote. Ask *What am I doing? (using a remote control).*
- Give a demonstration of the activity. Ask two strong learners to come to the front. Mime pressing the remote and say *Ah, a comedy programme*. Encourage the learners to make silly faces and act like they are in a comedy. Press the button again and say *Ah, the sports channel.* Encourage learners to pretend to play football.
- Put learners into groups of three. Choose one learner in each group and tell them they have control of the remote. They can use a box or pencil case as a prop. Remind them of different types of programmes (horror films, sports, nature documentaries, comedy, romantic stories, chat shows, quiz shows, news).
- Tell the other learners they are on the screen of the TV. But when their partner presses the remote the channel changes. Learners act out changing channels.

  Fast finishers Ask learners to list the different types of programmes they acted out.

Pupil's Book, page 110

Presentation

- Show learners a picture of a monster, e.g. from the film *Monsters Inc*. Ask what they are *(monsters).*
- Ask learners to look at the title of the text on page 110 and the pictures. Ask them what kind of text it is *(a poem).*
- Tell learners before they read the poem they are going to learn some new words. Ask *If someone is chatty, what do they like to do? (talk a lot).* Ask them who in the class is chatty. Stare in an exaggerated way at one of the learners they say is chatty. Ask them *What am I doing? (staring).* Say *If you stare at something you look at it for a long time.* Learners repeat *stare.*
- Ask learners what happens if you think twice *(you think about something very seriously before you do it).*
- Demonstrate skipping (or show a picture of a child skipping). Ask learners for the verb. Say *skip.* Learners repeat

1 Read the title and look at the pictures. What do you think the monster is?

- Put learners into pairs. Ask learners to look at the pictures and say what they can see. Ask them what they think the terrible monster in the poem is. Learners discuss in pairs.

3.26 The Monster in our Homes

- Tell learners to listen and read the story on pages 110–111 and find out if they are right about what the monster is.
- Play the audio. Learners read and listen.
- Ask learners to compare their ideas in pairs.
- Check answers. Tell learners *You are going to read and listen to the story again in more detail.*
- Ask them to read and find out things the monster likes to show children and things that children used to do before there was a television. Learners listen and read again.
- Put learners into pairs to share ideas. *(The TV shows them heroes, monsters, cartoons and quiz shows, movies; in the past children used to play in the streets, skip, ride bikes, read books)*

Key: The television is the monster.

Activity Book, page 110

See pages TB126–141.

Ending the lesson

- Tell learners they are going to think of some questions about the poem. Ask them to look at the poem again and try to think of some questions, e.g. *What happens to your eyes when you watch TV? What does Mum say?*
- Write the numbers 1 to 6 down the side of the board.
- Learners work in pairs and think of questions.
- Ask learners to share their ideas. Pick out six good questions and ask learners to say them again.
- Correct their ideas and write the six questions next to the numbers.
- Put learners into pairs. Ask learners to read the poem and find the answers. Now put the learners into groups of three and give each group a dice.
- Tell learners to roll the dice and read the question for that number from the board. Learners see if they can remember the answer to the question without looking.
- Learners work in groups until each question has been asked once.

  Fast finishers Learners copy the questions and write down the answers.

Learning outcomes By the end of the lesson, learners will have read a poem to understand opinions.

Recycled language *monster, chatty, stare, think twice, skip, unfair*

Materials dice (or versions of dice, e.g. 6 numbers on paper in a bag that learners pick out)

Social and Emotional Skill: identifying and expressing an opinion

- After reading, ask *Is the poem fact or an opinion? (an opinion) Do you agree that the TV is a monster? Do you want to put it in the bin?* Learners form opinions. Explain that respecting others' opinions even if we don't agree helps us discuss without arguing.
- Divide learners into two groups: one side to argue that TV is bad for you and the other that TV is good.
- Learners use examples of arguments for and against TV from the text and their own ideas. They take turns to express opinions and debate their points of view. Check they use phrases like *In our opinion, … We think … We respect what you're saying … Interesting argument, but we think … That's a good point but we don't agree …*

Warm-up

- Put learners in pairs. Remind learners of the new words they learnt by writing them onto the board: *chatty, stare*.
- Ask learners to read the poem again and find out who is chatty and who stares. *(children stare at the TV; children in the past used to be chatty)*

Pupil's Book, page 111

Presentation

- Tell learners to find more words from the text in a reading race. Put learners into groups of five and choose a captain for each team. Tell them you will give them a clue and the first person to find the answer should tell the captain who will raise their hand and give the answer.
- Say *Who is chatty?* Learners look and tell their captain to raise their hand. Choose the first learner and ask the answer. *(children in the past were chatty)* Make sure only the captains raise their hands and answer.
- Ask questions. Learners play the game.
  What is black? (the monster/TV) Who shouts 'It's time for bed'? (Mum) Who can't move? (kids watching TV) Why do kids scream and shout? (because their parents take the remote) Who rode bikes? (children in the past)
- Ask learners look at page 110 and find verbs and adjectives that have a negative meaning.
- Put learners in pairs to find them. *(terrible, attack, can't escape, ugly, stare, tired, red, shouting)*
- Ask them to look at page 111 and find verbs and adjectives that have a positive meaning. *(free, fun, played, happy, skipped, chatty)*.

  Fast finishers Learners find additional negative adjectives and verbs.

2 In pairs, talk about the questions.

- Ask learners to read the first question.
- Put them into pairs to discuss. Ask them to find examples from the poem to show why they think what they do.
- Ask learners to read the rest of the questions and discuss them. Learners work in pairs. Monitor and support. Share ideas with the class.

  Extension Put learners into threes and ask them to think about three things they really enjoy doing that isn't watching TV or doing something with a screen. Invite learners to share ideas.

Key: Learners' own answers

Activity Book, page 111

See pages TB126–141.

Ending the lesson

- Divide learners into two groups. Show a dice. Ask them to choose a number to be the bomb e.g. 2 Tell learners that each team will answer a question. If it's correct, they will roll the dice for their points e.g. if they roll 3 they get 3 points. Explain that if they roll the bomb, (number 2) they lose all their points. Ask questions. Teams take turns to answer and roll the dice. Keep the points on the board.
- Add more questions if you want, e.g. *This describes a funny programme. (Comedy) This is the written text used to make a film. (Script) A famous actor is called this. (celebrity) A film about the real world. (documentary)*
- Work out which team has the most points.

And even though it seems free and fun,
If I were you I'd get out and run.
Because there's no doubt, it can change your mind,
With the silly ideas that you might find.

Parents often say, 'Your eyes will go square.'
And some kids respond, 'I think that's unfair!'
But take the remote and they'll shout and scream,
And others I've heard can get really mean!

But there is a solution against this terrible enemy,
Just think about kids in the past generally.
They had no technology, not even a phone,
But had lots of friends and were never alone.

They played in the streets with their friends, they were happy,
They skipped, rode bikes and were very chatty.
Some rode to the library and even took out a book,
They got lost in adventures with Captain Cook.

So if you've got a house with a monster within,
I'd get rid of it now, I'd throw it straight in the bin.
I'd think twice about watching so much television,
I'd find other things to do and I'd make that my mission!

2 In pairs, talk about the questions.

1 Does the poet think the monster is good or bad? Why?
2 Why isn't it a good idea to watch too much TV?
3 How much TV do you watch?
4 What do you like to watch on TV?

Cross-curricular

1 **Look at the pictures.** How do you think they are relevant to films?

2 3.27 **Listen and read the text.** How were special effects different in the past?

Special effects in film

Have you ever watched a film and thought, 'How did the hero fly?' or 'How did they film that action on a burning ship?' Film makers make these scenes by using special effects. These are artificial images that look like they are real but are created by artists and technical experts.

Quite often the action is filmed on a green screen and then special effects are added on a computer. Sometimes the effects are so good that the experts win awards for their work.

Special effects in the past

Before the use of CGI (computer generated images) in cinema, it was difficult to make exciting special effects that looked real. Special effects artists used optical illusions and visual effects like painted sets, complicated make-up or models.

The Great and Powerful Oz has lots of amazing special effects, but there is an older version of the film called *The Wizard of Oz* which was made in 1939. There is a famous scene when a tornado (a dangerous wind storm) hits a farm in Kansas, USA. The film makers created the tornado by using a very long sock made of thin material which they filled with sand. Then they blew it round and round with a powerful electric fan! There are lots of other basic special effects in the film which at the time were very exciting.

Make your own special effects

You can make your own special effects using your mobile phone or objects at home. Try putting a pencil into a clear glass full of water and then look at the pencil through the glass – how does it look? There are lots of apps that you can use which put special effects on photos – you can be an animal or take photos and change the way they look. We can even have videos changed on our phones – why not try it?

3 **Read the text again and answer the questions.**

1 What does CGI mean?
2 When was *The Wizard of Oz* made?
3 How did they make the tornado?
4 What effects can we use on our phones?

4 **You are a film maker and you haven't got a computer.** In pairs, talk about how to make the scenes below.

- a landing on the moon
- a trip under the sea
- a snow storm

Learning outcomes By the end of the lesson, learners will be able to respond to a text, using critical thinking and emotional intelligence and understand how special effects are used in films.

New language *artificial, awards, optical illusion, sets, tornado, fan, landing, visual*

Recycled language *films, computer, special effects, material, app*

Materials picture of an award, e.g. an Oscar, optional- mobile phones or devices

Warm-up

- Show learners a picture of an award, e.g. an Oscar. Ask them who often wins awards (actors and film makers, sports people, people who have achieved something in a job or to help people). Say *If you had an award who would you give it to?* Give them some examples, e.g. *I'd give it to my friend for helping me whenever I have a problem.*
- Put learners into groups of four and ask them to tell their group who they would give an award to. Learners discuss in groups. Share ideas with the class.

  Fast finishers Learners talk about what they do well and say what they could get an award for. They discuss with a partner.

Pupil's Book, page 112

Presentation

- Tell learners they are going to read about special effects. Ask them why special effects are used in films *(to make something look real).*
- Say *If there is something that looks real but isn't real it is called an illusion. Learners repeat.* Say *Special effects are often used to show a natural disaster like a tornado.*Say *tornado*. Learners repeat.
- Ask learners where films are made *(a studio).* Tell learners that sometimes buildings are made inside a studio and these are called *sets*. Learners repeat.

1 Look at the pictures. How do you think they are relevant to films?

- Ask learners to look at the three pictures. Tell them the names of the objects: *a green screen, a fan, make up.* Learners repeat the words. Tell them the objects are used for films. Ask them to think about how the objects are used in films.
- Learners discuss in pairs. Share their ideas.

2 3.27 Listen and read the text. How were special effects different in the past?

- Tell learners read the text to find out how special effects were done in the past. In pairs, learners share ideas. Check answers.
- Ask them to look at the three pictures again and check if their ideas about how the things are used were correct.
- Learners compare ideas in pairs. *(The green screen is used to add illusions using a computer; the fan was used to create a tornado in the Wizard of Oz; make-up is used to create illusions).*
- Ask learners which techniques were used in the past and which are used now. *(the fan was used in the past; make-up was used in the past and now).*

Key: Special effects artists used optical illusions and visual effects like painted sets, complicated make-up or models.

3 Read the text again and answer the questions.

- Put learners into pairs to answer the questions. Check answers.

Key: 1 CGI = Computer Generated Images, 2 It was made in 1939, 3 using a very long sock made of thin material which they filled with sand.4 you can be an animal or take photos and change the way they look.

4 You are a film maker and you haven't got a computer. Talk about how to make the scenes below.

- Ask learners to look at the three scenes.
- Put them into pairs and ask them to think how they could create the scenes. Tell them to make a plan for each scene.
- Learners discuss. Share ideas. Ask the class which ideas they think would work best.

Key: Learners' own answers

Activity Book, page 112

See pages TB126–141.

Ending the lesson

- Play *20 questions*. Ask learners to think of a popular film or TV show that other learners will know. Put learners into groups of four.
- Learners take it in turns to be the 'hot seat'. The other learners ask questions to find the name of the film or show the person in the hot seat is thinking of. The learner they are asking can only answer *yes* or *no*, e.g. *Is it a TV show? No. So if it's a film, is it a comedy? (yes)…* Learners have to try and find the name of the film or show in 20 questions. If they reach 20 questions, they lose.

Learning outcomes By the end of the lesson, learners will be able to read to find detailed information and write part of a story.

Recycled language *monster, film, cinema*

Materials paper and pens

Warm-up

- Put learners into pairs to think of a famous film, book or story.
- Tell them to think of how they could show the main idea in three pictures only. Learners discuss their ideas.
- Ask learners to describe their three pictures. The class try to guess which story or film they are describing, e.g. *In the first picture, a boy meets an alien and they look happy to meet each other. In the second picture, the alien looks sad and is pointing to the stars because he wants to go home. In the last picture, the boy is waving and the alien is flying away. (It's ET!)*

Pupil's Book, page 113

1 Look and read. Do you need all of these things to tell a story? Which do you think is the most important?

- Ask learners to think about their favourite stories from a film or book. Put them into pairs to share the stories.
- Tell learners to look at the four words in the box. Remind them that in Key for Schools Reading and Writing Part 7, they have to write a story based on three pictures. They don't have much space, so they have to decide how to include all the parts.

Key Learners may disagree. All the elements can make an effective story.

2 Look at picture A and answer the questions.

- Put learners into pairs to answer the questions.
- Learners discuss in pairs. Share their ideas.
- Ask learners what the questions are asking about. *(the names and relationships of the characters, where they are, when it is and what happened in the picture).*

3 Read the beginning of the story. What things in picture A does this student write about?

- Tell learners to read the sentences to check what the learner has included. Learners read in pairs to share answers.
- Monitor and support. Check answers

Key: The sentences give the names and relationship of the two characters, it says where they are and what they did.

4 Look at picture B and read the middle of the story. Which type of film does the student write about?

- Tell learners to read the sentence about the middle picture and find out what type of film it is. Check answers.

Key: a monster film

5 Look at picture C. What happened? Tell your partner. Use the words below or your own words.

- Tell learners to look at the third picture and think about what is happening. Tell them they need to tell the end of the story.
- Ask them to use the words in the box.
- Learners work in pairs to describe the end of the story.
- Ask a few pairs to share their ideas with the class.

EXAM TIP! Ask a strong learner to read out the exam tip. Remind learners about the word count. Tell them if they include all the information and describe each picture clearly, they should have enough words.

6 Write about the end of the story.

- Tell learners to use their ideas and write the end of the story.

7 Swap stories. Give your friend's story a mark. 1 is poor and 5 is excellent. Write three things they can do to improve.

- Ask learners to swap sentences with their partner.
- Ask learners what is important in good story.
- Tell learners to read their partner's story and decide on what mark it should get from 1 to 5. Learners read and assess. Tell them to explain to their partner why they chose the mark and what they should do to improve it, e.g. *You didn't use a full stop at the end.*

Activity Book, page 113

See pages TB126–141.

Ending the lesson

- Put learners into groups of three. Ask them to try and remember the story in the pictures without looking. Tell each learner to do one picture each. Learners retell the story in their threes. Ask some groups to retell the story.

1 **Look and read.** Do you need all of these things to tell a story? Which do you think is the most important?

characters action a place a time names

2 **Look at picture A and answer the questions.**

1 Who are the characters? What are their names?

2 Where are they?

3 What are they doing?

3 **Read the beginning of the story.** What things in picture A does this student write about?

Last night, Oliver and his brother went to the cinema.
Oliver bought some snacks while Peter bought the tickets.

4 **Look at picture B and read the middle of the story.** Which type of film does the student write about?

... the tickets. They sat down and the monster film started.

5 **Look at picture C. What happened?** Tell your partner. Use the words in the box or your own words.

a brave hero special effects was scared
funny laughed pointed

6 **Write about the end of the story.**

Peter was scared!

7 **Swap stories.** Give your friend's story a mark. 1 is poor and 5 is excellent. Write three things they can do to improve.

EXAM TIP! Try to write between 35 and 45 words. You will **lose marks** if you write less than 35 words.

1 **Read the question and Katerina's reply. What has Tanya forgotten to include in her email?** ______

You must answer this question. Write your answer in about 100 words.
Read this message from your English-speaking friend Tanya and the notes you have made.

TO:
FROM: Tanya

Hello!

What programmes or films have you watched on TV this week? — **Describe the best one.**

I saw the first episode of the new celebrity chat show on Friday. It was on the kids' channel and it got some great reviews. Would you like to come with me to the TV studio on Saturday? — **Yes – ask what time.**

Dad says he can give you a lift or you and your mum can meet us there. Which do you prefer? — **Tell Tanya**

What shall we do after the show? It finishes at 8 pm. — **Suggest ...**

Write your email to Tanya, using all the notes.

Hi Tanya,

I watched a cool documentary about modern heroes and heroines. It was incredible! But it finished at midnight so I was really tired the next day at school.

I'd love to come with you to the studio. I'm free all day on Saturday. What time do they start filming the show?

I'm happy to get a lift with you and your dad. My mum also says we can get the underground so we can meet you at the studio. Why don't we go out for something to eat after the show? We both like that new Mexican restaurant.

Write soon, Katerina

2 **Which sentences in the reply from Katerina answer the notes on the email?**

______

______

______

3 **Add at least one other way to start and finish an email.**

Start	Finish	Sign your name
Hi Tanya,	Write soon,	Katerina

EXAM TIP! You should always put **your name** at the end of an email.

Learning outcomes By the end of the lesson learners. will be able to understand strategies for writing effectively.

New language *email, informal*

Recycled language *celebrity, chat show, channel, studio, reviews, show*

Materials paper and pens

Warm-up

- Ask learners if they often send emails. Learners respond.
- Put learners into pairs and ask them to tell their partner about the last email they sent. Ask *Who was it to? Why did you send it?* If they haven't sent an email, ask them to talk about a text message or instant message.

Pupil's Book, page 114

1 Read the question and Katerina's reply. What has Tanya forgotten to include in her email?

- Tell learners to read Katerina's email and think about which part is not clear.
- Put them in pairs to discuss.
- Check their ideas.
- Ask them to work alone and copy Katerina's email but change it so that it will be better.
- Learners write.
- Tell them to compare their answer with a partner.
- Check and suggest possible answers.

Key: She didn't answer about getting a lift clearly. It sounds as if both options are possible.

2 Which sentences in the reply from Katerina answer the notes on the email?

- Ask learners to read the notes again to find out what they need to answer. Tell them to write their sentences.
- Put learners in pairs to share answers.

3 Add at least one other way to start and finish an email.

- Tell learners to think of ways to open and end the email.
- Put learners into pairs to discuss.
- Check their ideas.

Key: Sample answers To open: Dear Tanya, Hi!, Hiya!, Hello Tanya. To close: Let me know, Love from, See you tomorrow, Bye for now!

EXAM TIP! Ask learners to read the exam tip. Remind them that they must answer all four points in the question clearly. Tell them that even though Katerina's email was very good she would lose points for missing things.

Activity Book, page 114

See pages TB126–141.

Ending the lesson

- Put learners into group of three.
- Ask them to if they have ever been to a film or TV studio. Learners respond.
- *Ask If you could go to any film set or TV programme, which one would you go to and why?* Ask learners to discuss in groups.
- Share their ideas.

Learning outcomes By the end of the lesson, learners will have used language from the unit to talk about film and TV and revised the unit language and skills.

Recycled language unit language

Materials pictures, Mission storyboards

Warm-up

- If possible, find a short film with lots of action.
- Show learners a still from the film and ask them to say what type of film they think it is. E.g. *action/comedy*.
- Show them a short clip to check if they are right. Pause the film and check answers.
- Divide the group into two and ask half the learners to turn their chairs around so they have their backs to the screen. Their partner sits facing them and the screen.
- Show the next short section of the film. The learner who can see it describes the action to their partner. Stop the film and ask learners who couldn't see it what they think happened.
- Now ask learners to a places and repeat, showing the next part of the film. Check what those who couldn't see understood.
- Now rewind and show all the students the whole of the section so they can check how well they did.

  Fast finishers Learners guess what happens in the next part of the film.

Pupil's Book, page 115

1 Complete the text. Use the words in the box.

- Ask learners to read the text quickly to find out what a celebrity has done. *(she moved into a castle and is changing it).*
- Put learners into pairs. Ask learners to look at the options in the box. Tell them to decide which words go into the gaps in pairs. Remind them to think about whether they need a grammar phrase or a vocabulary item. Check answers.

Key: 1 had/got 2 painted 3 had/got 4 built 5 had/go 6 cut

2 Complete the sentences.

- Ask learners to look at the sentences and think about the ones with the gaps. Ask what kind of sentences they are. *(second conditional).*
- Look at number one together as an example. Remind learners of the structure. Ask *How many parts is each sentence? (Two). Which tense is the in 'if' part? (past) And what's in the second part? (would).*
- Tell learners to complete the rest of the sentences 2 to 5.
- Put them in pairs to compare ideas. Check answers.

Key: 2 had seen, had 3 seen the interview, known that the celebrity has 20 dogs 4 the hero hadn't lost his phone, he would have called the president 5 If I hadn't seen the advert, I wouldn't have bought a new computer.

3 Choose ten words from this unit. Record the words using the steps below.

- Say *You've learnt a lot of new language and we've used different ways to learn the words and remember them. Let's do one more.*
- Ask *How many words will you choose? (10) Where can you look it up? (in a dictionary, online or in this book). How can you practise? (write the definition of the word and write similar words). How will you show you have learnt it? (put it in a sentence and say it to a friend).*
- Say *Now let's try it.* Tell learners to choose 10 words from the unit and follow the flowchart.
- Learners work alone. Monitor and check.
- Once they have finished, pair learners. Ask them to show their words to their partner.

Mission in action!

- Put learners back into the same groups as Mission Stage 2.
- Give back the storyboards they made at Stage 2 and tell them to look at it and plan a role play.
- Each group acts out their scene together. Monitor and support.
- Tell the groups they will present their scenes to the producers. Ask the class what kind of things the producers will look for. Share ideas, e.g. *an interesting story, a good dialogue, interesting action.* As learners agree on ideas, write them onto the board. Ask learners to copy the list and tell them to make some notes as they watch.
- Invite each group to present their scene. The rest of the class watches and makes notes.
- Finally, take a vote asking the class to decide which scene is the best.

  Alternative Instead of presenting to the whole class, if learners have access to cameras, they can film their scenes and show their mini films to the class.

Activity Book, page 115

See pages TB126–141.

Ending the lesson

- **SA** Complete the self-assessment (see Introduction).

1 Complete the text. Use the words in the box.

had/got x3 built cut painted

My favourite celebrity moved into a castle a few weeks ago – the castle was very old so she **(1)** ______ a lot of things changed. She had all of the walls in her house **(2)** ______ gold and she **(3)** ______ thick red carpets put on all the floors. In the garden, she had a golf course and swimming pool **(4)** ______ – and she **(5)** ______ some of the plants **(6)** ______ to look like elephants!

2 Complete the sentences.

1 I read the review so I didn't watch the film.

If I _hadn't read_ the review, I would have _watched_ the film.

2 I didn't see my favourite singer at the shops so I didn't have a photo taken with him.

If I ______ my favourite singer at the shops, I would have ______ a photo taken with him.

3 I saw the interview, so I know that the celebrity has 20 dogs.

If I hadn't ______, I wouldn't have ______.

4 The hero lost his phone, so he didn't call the president.

If ______

5 I saw the advert, so I bought a new computer.

______

3 Choose ten words from this unit. Record the words using the steps below.

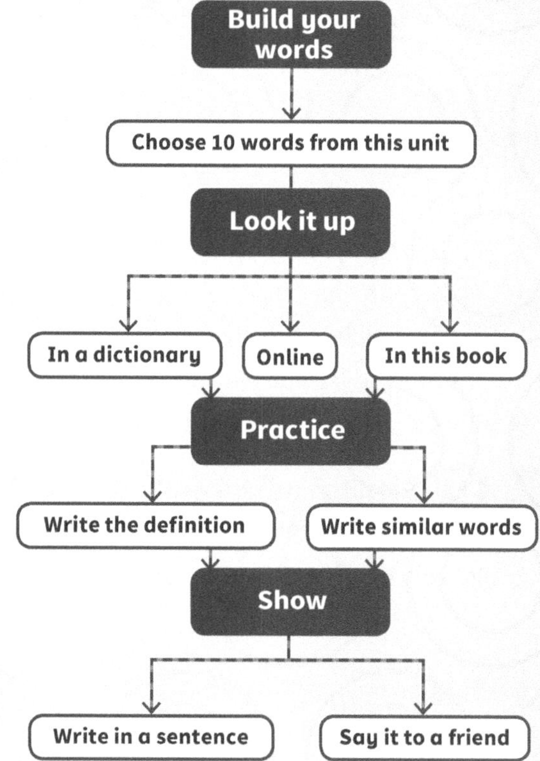

Mission in action!

- Present your scene.
- Watch and make notes.
- Vote for the best scenes!

This comedy is going to be so funny!

Review ••• Units 7–9

1 **Watch the video and do the quiz.**

2 **Choose the correct words to complete the sentences.**

Tips for visiting our town

1 You **should / mustn't** ask about the opening hours at the tourist information centre.
2 You **mustn't / have to** have a picnic on the roundabout.
3 You **shouldn't / ought to** drop litter on the pavement.
4 You **mustn't / have to** bring a horse when you take the underground.
5 You **ought to / mustn't** buy your cinema tickets at the booking office.

3 **Complete the sentences. Use *such … that / so … that*.**

1 It was ________ a funny comedy ________ I woke my cat up because I laughed so loudly.
2 The cartoon was ________ long ________ I fell asleep before it finished.
3 The action film was ________ exciting ________ I told my friends to see it too.
4 The questions on the quiz show were ________ easy ________ I only got one wrong.
5 On Thursday, I watched a film. It was ________ a terrifying horror film ________ I couldn't sleep.
6 It was ________ an interesting documentary ________ I watched it twice.

4 **Find the mistakes. Write the correct sentences.**

1 When we were children we use to go on holiday together.
____
2 I used to buying postcards from every place I went to on holiday.
____
3 In the past people were poor and they used to living in small houses.
____
4 The cinema is in town where we use to go every weekend.
____
5 I used to cycling in the countryside every day.
____

5 **A health expert is coming to your school. Say the questions as indirect questions.**

Please could you tell me … ? Do you know … ?
Would you mind explaining … ?

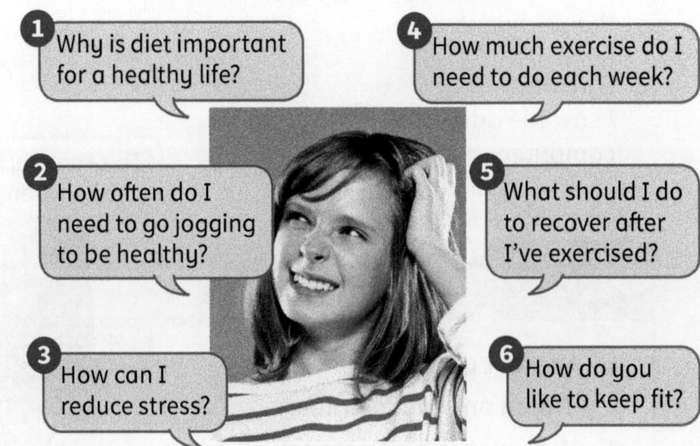
1 Why is diet important for a healthy life?
2 How often do I need to go jogging to be healthy?
3 How can I reduce stress?
4 How much exercise do I need to do each week?
5 What should I do to recover after I've exercised?
6 How do you like to keep fit?

Learning outcomes By the end of the lesson, learners will have consolidated language from Units 7-9.

Recycled language modal verbs to talk about obligation and necessity, *so* and *such*, direct and indirect questions, *used to* to talk about past habits, vocabulary to describe TV and film

Materials video

Warm-up

- Put learners into pairs.
- Tell learners to look at units 7-9 in threes and write down three questions about anything in the unit. Put the pairs into groups of four. The pairs ask and answer each other's questions.

  Fast finishers Learners ask additional questions from the units.

Pupil's Book page 116

1 Watch the video and do the quiz.

- Play the video. Learners watch and do the three unit quizzes.
- Check answers.

Key: **Unit** 7 1 B 2 C 3 A 4 A 5 B 6 C 7 A 8 B 9 C 10 A 11 B 12 B
Unit 8 1 A 2 B 3 C 4 A 5 B 6 C 7 A 8 B 9 C 10 A 11 B 12 B
Unit 9 1 B 2 C 3 A 4 A 5 B 6 C 7 C 8 B 9 A 10 C 11 B 12 A

2 Choose the correct words to complete the sentences.

- Ask learners to think about lessons and find one thing they must do, one thing they should do and one thing they mustn't do at school, e.g. *I must complete my work; I should read outside class; I mustn't forget my homework.*
- Learners work in pairs. Share ideas, checking understanding of the modal verbs.
- Tell learners to work in pairs and choose the best options in sentences 1–6. Check answers.

Key: 1 should 2 mustn't 3 shouldn't 4 mustn't 5 mustn't 6 ought to

3 Complete the sentences. Use *such … that* / *so … that.*

- Pair learners and ask to say the complete sentences filling in the gaps. Complete the first one together. Learners fill the gaps 2-6. Check answers.

Key: 1 that – C, 2 that – A, 3 so – D, 4 that – E, 5 such – F, 6 such – B

4 Find the mistakes. Write the correct sentences.

- Write two sentences on the board. *When I was a child, I used play lots of games. I use to ride my bike in the park.* Tell learners to look at the sentences and decide if they are correct or not. (~~I used play~~- I used **to** play; I ~~use to ride~~- I use**d** to ride..)
- Pair learners and tell them to look at the sentences 1-5 and correct the mistakes. Monitor and support. Check answers.

Key: 1 ~~**use**~~ **used** 2 ~~**buying**~~ **buy**, ~~**to**~~ 3 ~~**living**~~ **live** 4 ~~**use**~~ **used** 5 ~~**cycling**~~ **cycle**

5 A health expert is coming to your school. Say the questions as indirect questions.

- Ask learners *How can I have a healthy life?* Learners reply. Tell them to look at the phrases in the box and ask them to make your question more polite, e.g. *Do you know how I can have a healthy life?*
- Do the first example together. Learners complete numbers 2-6 in pairs. Check answers.

Key: (sentence can start with any of the three phrases from the word pool): 1 … why diet is important for a healthy life? 2 … how often I need to go jogging to be healthy? 3 … how I can reduce stress? 4 … how much exercise I need to do each week? 5 What I should do to recover after I've exercised? 6 … how you like to keep fit?

Activity book, page 116

See pages TB126–141.

Ending the lesson

- Write on the board *'Find someone who … 1 likes watching action films 2 used to watch cartoons 3 thinks they should do more exercise 4 has to travel by bus or underground sometimes.* Tell learners to copy the sentences. Give them five minutes to mingle and find a name to add to each sentence. Demonstrate asking the questions, e.g. *Do you like watching action films?*
- Learners mingle and discuss. At the end of the activity share which sentences are true for different learners.

Learning outcomes By the end of the lesson, learners will have consolidated language from Units 7-9.

Recycled language vocabulary to describe feelings and emotions, vocabulary to describe cities, vocabulary to describe TV and film, causative *have/got*, second conditional

Materials pictures (smiley and frowning emoticons, a TV and a town)

Warm-up

- In pairs, learners discuss their two favourite places in their town and two places they don't like and want to change.
- Share ideas.

Pupil's Book page 117

6 In pairs, talk about what the town has had done.

- Tell learners to look at the two pictures of the town. Ask *Are they the same or different? (Different).*
- Say *The government had some things changed.*
- Put learners into pairs and tell them to find the things they had done. Check ideas.

Key: Sample answers
1 They've had the palace repainted. 2 They've had the department store rebuilt. 3 They've had the gallery windows repaired. 4 They've had the sculpture/ statue cleaned. 5 They've had the tower fixed.

7 Complete the texts.

- Ask learners to look quickly at the sentences in boxes A–C without worrying about the gaps. Say each one is an imagined situation – ask them to find out what each text is about. Share their ideas *(having a lot of money, a talking rabbit, being a fruit).*
- Put learners into pairs and tell them to read again and say the missing words. Monitor and support. Check answers.
  Extra support Write the missing words on the board jumbled up for learners to add to the gaps.

Key: A 1 If, 2 would B 1 I'd / I would, 2 if
C 1 I would / I'd, 2 wouldn't

8 Complete the sentences (A–D).

- Put learners into pairs to discuss. Remind them to think of ideas to include. Ask what else they need to remember. *(organisation, grammar, vocabulary, spelling, punctuation)* Note these on the board. Ask which grammar they need to include. *(second conditional)*
- Learners write. Monitor and support.
- Put learners into groups of four and ask them to look at each other's work. Ask them to say one thing they like and one error that can be corrected.
  Extension Learners rewrite their text correcting, errors.

9 Choose and complete two of the challenges.

- Put up a picture of smiley and frowning emoticons, a TV and a town.
- Tell learners they are going to complete two challenges. Ask them to read the three challenges quickly and match the challenges 1–3 with the pictures. *(1 emoticons 2 a town 3 TV)*
- Put learners into pairs and tell them to choose their two favourite challenges.
- Ask them to complete the challenges and see who can finish successfully first.
- Learners work in pairs. Check their ideas.
  Fast finishers Learners complete the third challenge.

Key: Sample answers
Challenge 1: Bored, Relaxed, Amazed, Interested, Negative, Miserable, Annoyed, Positive, Satisifed
Challenge 3: three exciting kinds of TV programme – action, horror, thriller; two funny kinds of TV programme – comedy, cartoon: three kinds of TV programmes where you learn new things – documentary, news, quiz show; three things that help you find out about new TV programmes or celebrities – review, interview, advert

Activity Book, page 117

See pages TB126–141.

Ending the lesson

- Write a word from the unit on the board with gaps instead of vowels, e.g. *m _ n _ m _ n t*. Ask learners if they can guess what the word is by adding back the vowels. If they can't guess, give them a clue e.g. *It's a place you visit when you are sightseeing. (monument).*
- Give out 3 cards or sticky notes per learner. Tell them to think of three words they have learnt and write them down putting gaps instead of vowels.
- Tell learners to stick their notes onto the walls around the classroom.
- Ask learners to walk around in pairs looking at the sticky notes and trying to fill in the gaps and find the missing letters.
- Once learners have looked at all the words, tell them to choose any three (not their own) write in the missing letters and stick them up onto the board.
- If any notes are left, the learner who wrote it can give clues to help the class guess.
- Once all the words are on the board, point to each one and ask learners to give an example sentence using the word.

6 In pairs, talk about what the town has had done.

They've had the sculpture cleaned.

7 Complete the texts.

A

(1) ________ I found $250 million, I'd be amazed. First I'd go shopping, then I'd get some presents for my family. I think my dad (2) ________ like a helicopter!

B

If my rabbit could talk, I'd like to know what its favourite foods are. I think he likes carrots, but perhaps he prefers cake! (1) ________ also like to know (2) ________ he likes living with me, or if he'd prefer to live in the wild.

C

If I was a fruit, (1) ________ be a coconut because I'm very relaxed. I'd love to live somewhere warm – a beach would be great, too. I (2) ________ like it if people tried to eat me though!

8 Complete the sentences (A–D).

A If I was three metres tall ________

B If I found $250 million behind my sofa ________

C If my rabbit could talk ________

D If I could live anywhere in the world ________

9 Choose and complete two of the challenges.

CHALLENGE 1

Think of a feeling or emotion that starts with each of the following letters:

B-R-A-I-N M-A-P-S

CHALLENGE 2

Look at Unit 8 pages 93 and 96. What are five things that the place you live has got? What are five things that the place you live hasn't got?

CHALLENGE 3

Look at Unit 9. Find:

- three exciting kinds of TV programme.
- two funny kinds of TV programme.
- three kinds of TV programme where you learn new things.

Pupil's Book audioscripts

Unit 1

Pupil's Book, page 8

Listen to Safi and Rav packing. Do they need winter or summer clothes?

Girl: Our trip's tomorrow! And Mum says we need to pack before dinner!

Boy: She's right. Look at the timetable. Our bus to the airport's really early.

Girl: When does it leave?

Boy: At quarter past six!

Girl: Let's pack then! It's sunny in South Africa. So we'll need sunglasses and swimming costumes.

Boy: Really? It's July – so isn't it winter in South Africa?

Girl: What?! Africa's always hot.

Boy: I think it'll be cold … I'm taking a shirt with long sleeves. And my leather jacket. There are parrots in South Africa, aren't there?

Girl: Yes – and look! We might see some. We go to the forest on Wednesday.

Boy: I'll take my parrot pattern scarf then!

Girl: A scarf?! Haha! I'm taking my dress with the blue collar. It's great for hot weather.

Boy: The party dress with gold buttons?

Girl: Yes. Look – there's a party at the hotel on Tuesday afternoon. No, sorry! It isn't on Tuesday. The party's on Wednesday.

Boy: Brilliant! Look on Friday we go camping!

Girl: Camping!? I'll pack my shorts.

Boy: And I'll pack warm trousers …

Girl: Hmm … Shall we take a bag?

Boy: Yes. Look, we go whale watching on Saturday at 2:30 [half past two]. We'll need a bag for our cameras. Shall we take this one?

Girl: No, that's not the right size. Let's take the small one.

Boy: Great!

Girl: We're finished, aren't we? That was easy!

Boy: Well … I'm finished –you need to start again.

Girl: Huh!? Why?

Boy: I've checked on my computer. It is winter in South Africa in July …

Girl: What!!!!? Ohhh …

Pupil's Book, page 14

Listen and match. Put the pictures in the correct order.

Narrator: 1

Mr Winford: Come in, Sofia. How are you?

Sofia: Fine thanks, Mr Winford.

Mr Winford: So, I've marked your test and I have some good news for you …

Narrator: 2

Boy: Excuse me?

Man: Yes? Can I help you?

Boy: Yes, I'd like to change this tracksuit I bought last week …

Narrator: 3

Mum: Karen, can't you do the washing-up tonight?

Karen: Oh, Mum! I've got to read ten pages about jewellery for my history homework!

Mum: And what about your brother? …

Narrator: 4

Man: That's the King's Theatre on the left.

Woman: How long did it take to build?

Man: Well, there was a terrible fire in 1727 but after that …

Narrator: 5

Boy: Do you know the answer to question 4?

Girl: No, I'm answering question 3.

Boy: Well number 4 is really difficult! Pupil's Book, Unit 2

Unit 2

Pupil's Book, page 17

Listen, point and say the numbers.

This is my laptop. I use it to do my homework, talk to my friends around the world and listen to music.
My laptop's screen is small. It's OK, but sometimes when I watch videos on the computer with my friends, we can't all see it.
On the screen now, you can see a computer program that I'm writing … If you run the program, the computer says, 'Hello world'!
There are lots of kinds of hardware on my desk. There's the laptop and the screen, and the keyboard and printer too.
This is my keyboard. I use this a lot when I'm doing my homework.
This is my printer. I use my printer a lot for my homework too, when I need to print something to give to my teacher.
It's bright orange! I love my mouse.
Here's my dad's mobile phone. It's next to my computer. He always loses it – that's why he's connected it to that cute frog toy!
There's a disc and its box too. The disc is very new. I got it yesterday. There's a new piece of music software on the disc. The software means my computer can make the sounds of a piano or guitar or anything. Listen to this …

Pupil's Book, page 18

Listen to Tom talking to a friend about a technology show. What's the address of the show's website?

Boy: Hey Sarah – Are you going to the tech show on Saturday?

Sarah: I hope so. If my mum says it's OK, then I'll go.

Boy: Cool! What'll you look at, if you go?

Sarah: Well … my keyboard isn't working so I want to look at the new ones. I think I'll buy one, if it's not too expensive. And the School Science club is going to the fair, so if I go, I'll see all my friends!

Boy: Really? Are Dale and Brian going then?

Sarah: Yes, they are. And they're very excited. Dale said he wants to look at the printers. He says that there'll be printers there that can make toys! And Brian wants to look at the mice.

Boy: Are there animals at the fair then?

Sarah: Haha! No – the computer mice!

Boy: Oh! I see.

Sarah: Courtney'll go too, if she finishes her homework in time. She wants to see the mobile phones. Her brother emailed them to ask about the phones there, and there are going to be some really cool ones.

Boy: He emailed them? What's their address?

Sarah: It's 'information@technology.com'. They've got a website too. It's www.technology.com.

Boy: Brilliant. Maybe I'll have a look when I get home. What about Scott?
Sarah: Well, he wants to see the dogs.
Boy: Dogs?! You said there aren't any animals at the fair?
Sarah: Well, they're robot dogs!
Boy: Wow! That sounds great. I hope you can go!
Sarah: I know I'll have fun if I do!

Unit 3

Pupil's Book, page 32

Listen. Match four commentaries to the photos (A–D).

1: There are three minutes left. Bolt for Team City has the ball. But here's Waldek for Team United. He takes the ball from Bolt and runs at the goal. Team City can't stop him. Can Wakdek shoot? Yes he can! He hits it hard and high, and it's a goal!! A brilliant goal from Waldek! Team United are winning by two goals to one. The coach is jumping up and down. His team have worked hard and they're winning. He must be delighted. Shall we watch the goal again?

2: The Silver Beach surfing competition will start in about 35 minutes. I can see Daisy Brass, the world champion, jogging. She's training because she knows that she needs to be fit and strong. Riding a surfboard across the waves is hard work. Now she's picking up her special surfboard, one of the most expensive in the world – it cost $1 million. It's no surprise that Daisy has asked a police officer to look after it while she trains! She wouldn't be happy if someone stole it.

3: This could be the most important point today! If Tim wins one point, he'll win the Lemonade Cup. Tim starts, Hugh hits it back well ... but the ball might go into the net! No. The ball goes over the net and Tim hits it hard with the middle of his racket. Hugh runs to the net, and wow! – he hits the ball – but no! –The ball falls two meters outside the court. Tim wins the point and the Lemonade Cup! He may be this garden's greatest ever tennis player! He lifts his racket in the air. He's delighted!

4: The world's ten fastest cyclists are here on their bicycles, waiting for the race to begin ... They start quickly. Jessica Cage is in front of the other cyclists on the track. Birch and Noble are behind her. But wait! Birch and Noble have fallen! Birch may have made a mistake and hit Noble. And the other cyclists could ride into Noble here. Oh no! They've fallen too! There are nine cyclists on the track now, but they're OK. It's good that they're wearing helmets to protect their heads! Cage is still cycling. She hasn't seen the accident! She finishes the track and wins the race ...

Pupil's Book, page 37

Look at the example answer and listen. What will the children learn?

Good morning. I'm your instructor Dan and I hope you'll enjoy today's lesson for beginners. I can see some new faces, so welcome to Summer Surf Camp!
First I want to give you some advice for this week. It will help you become a better surfer!
Everything starts with the food you eat. Half of your food needs to be water, fruit and vegetables and the other 50% is a little meat and some sugars. So, no burgers, chips and ice-cream I'm afraid! If you want help choosing your meals, I'll be in the Main Hall after 6pm, Monday to Friday.
Keeping fit and making your shoulders, arms and legs stronger is also very important. So, use the gym after every lesson. We think 45 minutes a day is enough! Your gym coach is Bob Vanya, that's V-A-N-Y-A. He's there every day.
Surfing might look hard on your knees but after the first day you may find that your stomach hurts. You will improve if you follow this advice. So come on surfers, let's go!

Unit 4

Pupil's Book, page 43

Listen and choose the correct answer.

Boy: Hey Maria – Look at this.
Maria: Oh, wow! Is this a new computer game?
Boy: Yes, it is. You have to ask people what's wrong, then you decide how to make them feel better.
Maria: Really! What's wrong with this man then? The man with a shark on his hand.
Boy: He injured his hand when he was feeding his shark. The shark's his pet. I've made an appointment for the man to meet the doctor and have the shark removed. But now, I need to find some water to put the shark in!
Maria: I see. What's wrong with this patient? The man who's having his heart checked.
Boy: Well, he has a problem with his girlfriend. That's why he's so sad. Look! He's got a broken heart.
Maria: How are you going to make him feel better?
Boy: I don't know. Maybe I can give him some flowers and some chocolates...
Maria: Good idea! That woman's going to the emergency door quickly, isn't she? Do you know why there's a fire?
Boy: I think there was an accident and her pet monster made the fire.
Maria: Did the monster break the woman's ankle, too?
Boy: Yes. She had another accident when she was playing with the baby monster. It's very strong, even though it's a baby.
Maria: And what about this patient? The one with the big hands.
Boy: He was making dinner. But while making a sandwich, his knife slipped and he cut his hand.
Maria: It looks very painful. It must hurt a lot.
Boy: Yes ... you need to be careful when you're using knives, don't you?
Maria: Haha!

Pupil's Book, page 52

Listen. Who's talking?

Example
Boy: Do you remember your first day at school, Kitty?
Girl: Yeah, I didn't know anybody! I felt sick all morning!
Boy: Ah, poor you.

1
Mum: Don't forget Dad's birthday! I gave him socks last year.
Young girl: I know Mum! He never wears them! How about a DVD this year?

2
Woman: All our cows go out to the fields in the day. They come in when the sun goes down. Their milk is excellent!

3
Man: Well, yes I would like to speak to the manager! I don't think it's all right to serve food that is not cooked.

4
Boy 1: See you at the club later, then?
Boy 2: Ah, I can't play football tonight, Rob. Got a bad knee!

5
Man: Listen up, class! When we get to the top of the hill we'll stop and you can have your picnic lunch. OK?

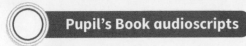

2 2.09 **Read the instructions and the options A, B and C. What do you think the question is? Listen and check.**

Narrator: You hear a student talking about a film she watched. What was the film about?
Girl: Is it difficult to watch TV with your family? Well, last night Mum wanted to watch that history film about a king in Greece who had an accident. My cousin and I wanted to watch the story about a guy who has an operation. Guess what! We watched the cartoon. Boring!

6 2.12 **Listen and choose the correct answer.**

Narrator: What did the woman buy for her grandson?
Woman: Excuse me, can you help me? I need to buy a present for my grandson, it's his birthday next week.
Assistant: What about this scooter? My little brother loves his!
Woman: I think it might be a little too expensive. Do you have any wallets?
Assistant: No, sorry. But the World Cup is soon and we do have these footballs …
Woman: He'd love one of those! I'll take one, please.

Unit 5

Pupil's Book, page 56

2 2.14 **Listen to five conversations. How many times do you hear the word 'broccoli'?**

Narrator: 1 What's Claire's favourite dinner?
Dad: Claire, it's Mum's birthday party next week. What shall we make for our family dinner?
Claire: I know. Let's have steak and broccoli! … That's my favourite food to have for dinner.
Dad: Well, it is Mum's birthday … but steak's very expensive – so I don't think we can have that.
Claire: Oh yes – I see. Well, why don't I ask our family what they'd like to have?
Dad: Good idea. You should ask Mum first! Then your sisters and your brother.
Narrator: 2 What would Mum like to have for dinner?
Claire: Hey Mum. What would you like to have for your birthday dinner next week? Dad and I are going to cook.
Mum: Well – anything healthy is great for me. You know, I prefer to eat healthy food. Maybe we could have fish and some vegetables?
Claire: Oh OK. So would you rather have salmon or steak?
Mum: I'd rather have salmon. Fish is good for my heart! And we could have cabbage with it. I love all vegetables: cabbage … potatoes … beans … broccoli.
Narrator: 3 Which vegetable doesn't Emma like?
Claire: Hi Emma!
Emma: Hi Claire.
Claire: It's Mum's birthday next week. Would you like to have salmon and cabbage for her birthday dinner?
Emma: UHHHH, YUK! NOOOOOO!
Claire: What? Salmon?
Emma: No, salmon's OK … but the other thing…
Claire: Cabbage?
Emma: Ugggggh, I don't want that! It's disgusting! I hate it.
Claire: OK. So you don't want salmon and cabbage then?
Emma: No, I prefer not to have cabbage. I'd rather have another vegetable. Maybe mushrooms or carrots?
Narrator: 4 Which carrots would Karen prefer?
Claire: What's your favourite food, Karen?
Karen: Well … I like hot and spicy food … anything with a strong taste – so something with chilli, garlic and onions …
Claire: Do you like broccoli? …
Karen: It's OK. But I prefer carrots to broccoli. I love carrots if they're cooked with chilli and onion!
Narrator: 5 Which food can't Tom eat?
Tom: Morning, Claire! It's only a week until Mum's birthday, isn't it?
Claire: Yes! It's very exciting! … Umm … Dad and I are going to make her birthday dinner. What would you like to eat for it? Would you prefer to have mushrooms, carrots or broccoli? …
Tom: I'd prefer to have carrots, but I love all vegetables!
Claire: And do you like salmon?
Tom: Umm … I don't know actually.
Claire: You don't know?
Tom: Well, you know I can't eat fish, don't you? I feel ill if I have it … So I've never tried salmon …
Claire: Oh no! We can't have salmon for dinner then! But what can we have …

Pupil's Book, page 58

3 2.16 **What are the answers to the riddles? Listen. Then write your own.**

1
Girl: I can slice apples to make you a pie. Or I can cut onions and make you cry. What am I?
Boy: A knife!
2
Girl: Every day's a fry-day if you are me. What am I?
Boy: A frying pan!
3
Girl: While you become full, I become empty. What am I?
Boy: A dish!
4
Girl: When the oven roasts a chicken, or when it roasts another meat, I sometimes sit above it. Cooking healthy things to eat. What am I?
Boy: A saucepan!
5
Girl: Thirsty, tired people love to see me. I help them by boiling water for their tea. What am I?
Boy: A kettle!

Pupil's Book, page 63.

3 2.21 **Listen to the conversation. Write two places you hear for each day.**

Girl: Hi Tim. How was your holiday?
Tim: It was great! We went on a cooking tour last week.
Girl: Oh yeah, because your dad's a chef. Where did you stay?
Tim: Well, on Tuesday the hotel was full, but there was an apartment opposite. We had fresh fish for dinner! It was great!
Girl: Oh! And what did you see on Wednesday? A castle?
Tim: No! We went to the Museum of Food and Drink. I bought this picture of a woman selling garlic. Do you like it?
Girl: Very nice. Did you visit anything on Thursday?
Tim: Dad usually cooks at the TV studio. But this time we went to the Town Hall to cook roast chicken!
Girl: Did you come home on Friday?
Tim: No, we got lost and couldn't find the train station! So, we went to that famous park and ate strawberry and chocolate ice cream.
Girl: And what happened on Saturday?

Tim: Well, I often go to a café on Saturday, but this week Dad took me to a farm to try some steak and mushroom pie. I won't be hungry for a week now!

Unit 6

Pupil's Book, page 67

Listen and point to the things in Ela's house. Say the numbers.

There are lots of reasons why I like my house. First, there are lots of beautiful things here. Above the stairs is a cool bulb. It's huge and it looks like it was made by a spider! It makes the house nice and bright. Even the small things in the house were designed carefully. In the living room, there's a plug that looks like the sun!
In my bathroom, there are some cool things too. For example, the sink looks like a shell! When I wash my hands, I always think of the sea. Most of the house is very new, but in the bathroom above the shell sink there are some very old tops. They were my grandmother's – and they're more than 100 years old! I think that the most beautiful things in my house – or on my house?! – are the big candles in the garden on the roof. When I light them at night they look amazing.
Another reason that I love my house is that it's very easy living there. For example, there are some big curtains in front of my house's big windows – and when you want to open or close the curtains, you can press a button!
The most useful thing in my house is in the kitchen. It's the dishwasher. The dishwasher makes it easy for my family to wash the dishes!
Also, my dustbin's connected to the kitchen. So when you throw something away in the kitchen, it falls into the dustbin outside! On Wednesdays, someone come to collect the rubbish. It's Wednesday today so there's a black bag of rubbish outside the house!
My house is always very comfortable too. In the winter, the house isn't cold because of the heating.
And in the summer, the house is cool too. That's because there's air conditioning in the bedroom and living room.
Finally, I like my house because it's environmentally friendly. Most of our electricity comes from the sun!

Pupil's Book, page 70

Listen to the podcast. Who always uses recycled paper?

Girl: Today's podcast is a debate: my brother versus my grandma. The question: When was life better for the environment? Now, or when my grandma was young? So first, let's talk about recycling. BROTHER VERSUS GRANDMA!

Boy: These days, everyone recycles a lot, don't they? I always sort out my plastic and glass and so on. Then I take them to the area where the dustbins are, outside my flat. I recycle by making things out of old bottles too. But Grandma, you couldn't recycle, could you?

Grandma: No, when I was young, there weren't any recycling bins. But we made less rubbish too. We bought sweets in paper bags – today, every sweet is wrapped in plastic, and the sweets are put in plastic bags too. Then, when you pay for the sweets, they give you another bag to take them home in, don't they?! I think people today are better at throwing their litter away though. I never did this, but after picnics, people sometimes left their litter in the park. That made me so angry…

Girl: BROTHER VERSUS GRANDMA! OK. Next, let's talk about travelling to school. Alex, since you started school you've travelled by car, haven't you?

Boy: Yes, my dad drives me to school every day. The drive takes a long time because there are awful traffic jams. People should use more public transport like trains and buses. Then the roads would be less busy. People would save money too – Mum always says that petrol's very expensive when she fills up the car.

Grandma: When I was young, I walked to school on a beautiful path through the park. I didn't drive because my family didn't have a car. It was safe to walk because there were very few cars on the roads. And the air was cleaner then, wasn't it? There weren't many cars so there wasn't much pollution.

Girl: BROTHER VERSUS GRANDMA! OK – let's talk about saving electricity. Grandma, go!

Grandma: When I was young, I didn't worry about the environment. But we used less electricity than young people now – we didn't have computers or big TVs or DVD players or mobile phones. I think that people today use much more electricity, don't they?

Boy: Yes, but I always turn lights off when I leave rooms to save electricity. When I'm cooking with my mum, we always cover the saucepans. That helps to save gas, doesn't it? I try to help the rainforest too – so that fewer trees are cut down, I always use recycled paper.

Girl: BROTHER VERSUS GRANDMA

Girl: So when was life better for the environment? Now, or when my grandma was young? Vote now to decide!

Review Units 4–6

Pupil's Book, page 78.

Listen. Write the sentences.

Narrator: 1
Speaker: The cyclist was hit while she was going to school.
Narrator: 2
Speaker: Her leg was injured and her bike was damaged.
Narrator: 3
Speaker: The girl was taken to hospital.
Narrator: 4
Speaker: She was kept at the hospital until she felt better.

Unit 7

Pupil's Book, page 84

Listen. Where did the boy fall asleep?

Girl: Hey Brian – What's in that bag?

Boy: My sports clothes! I've just been to the sports centre with my Mum.

Girl: Really?

Boy: Yes, we started going three weeks ago. My mum said she was feeling worried because we're moving house and my grandma's ill … so she wanted a way to reduce stress. We go to the sports centre together to relax and keep fit.

Girl: But isn't it boring?

Boy: No! This sport centre's so fun that I'd like to go every day. You can do exercise there, like running or swimming. But … well …. it's different to other sports centres too … When you do exercise it's like being in a video game, or a film.

Girl: Why?

Boy: Umm … well … when we go jogging we wear special glasses. It feels like we're running away from a monster! Or we're jogging over a rainbow …

Girl: No way!

Boy: Yeah! It's so fun that my mum and I always laugh a lot.

Girl: Amazing!
Boy: And while my mum goes to the gym to lift weights, there's a big swimming pool where I go to swim with sharks.
Girl: That sounds dangerous!
Boy: No it's not! The swimming pool is built above the sharks' pool, so you're not in the same water. But it's so exciting that I can swim for ages without feeling tired.
Girl: That sounds fun!
Boy: It is! And after we exercise, there are lovely places to sit and recover.
Girl: What are they like?
Boy: Well, there's a little pool that we go to when we've got tired, aching legs. It looks like a space ship! Also, there's a garden on the roof. It's such a relaxing place that I once fell asleep there! It's great – you can just sit, breathe deeply and listen to the river. …
Girl: What?! There's a river on the roof, too?
Boy: Haha! Just a small one.
Girl: Awesome!
Boy: There's a café on the roof too – but I haven't been.
Girl: Do you think it's nice?
Boy: I don't know … they've only got healthy food. They say a good diet is important, so they haven't got cake or ice cream.
Girl: Wow! Maybe my mum and I should go to the sports centre too? My mum always says she wants to look after her health better …

Pupil's Book, page 90

6  Listen to the conversation. Answer the questions from Activity 5.

Female: Hi Yuri, what's the matter? You don't look very well. Have you got a cold?
Male: Hi Sophie, I'm very tired actually. I'm not sleeping enough at the moment.
Female: Oh! Why not? Are you worried about your science test?
Male: Yes, it's tomorrow. I had a Maths test yesterday and History today. If I don't sleep well, I won't get a good mark. I read an article that said on average 47 per cent of primary school children around the world need more sleep!
Female: That's a lot. But Yuri, are you eating the right kind of food to help you concentrate too?
Male: Oh yes, don't worry, eating healthy food and getting the right kind of exercise is not a problem for me. In fact, playing football is a great way to stop me feeling worried.
Female: Well, maybe you shouldn't use your mobile phone or tablet late at night.
Male: Really? Why's that?
Female: Because it sends too much light to your eyes and that sends a message to your brain to stay awake!
Male: Oh, I see. I'll stop messaging my friends late at night then.
Female: Great! I think good sleep helps your memory too so I'm sure you'll be fine in the end for that test.
Male: Thanks, Sophie. You've given me some really good advice. I feel better already!

Unit 8

Pupil's Book, page 94

2 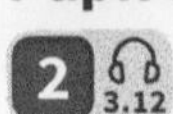 Listen to a radio show called Charlie's Challenge and check your answers to Activity 1.

Boy: Hello and welcome to Charlie's Challenge! My name's Charlie!
Girl: And my name's Charlie, too!
Boy: Today, we're at the Museum of Modern Art in New York – and our challenge is to find out as much as we can about this amazing gallery in five minutes.
Girl: So, let's begin. Are you ready Charlie?
Boy: Yes, Charlie!
Girl: I'm starting the clock – we've got five minutes – Go!
Boy: Excuse me, could you answer some questions about the gallery, please?
Man: I'm sorry but I don't work here – you should ask that woman. She's themanager.
Boy: OK – thanks … Excuse me – would you mind answering our questions about the museum, please?
Woman: Yes, of course.
Girl: Thank you!
Woman: What can I tell you?
Girl: First, do you know how many paintings there are in the museum?
Woman: That's a good question. The number changes every day. Paintings travel all the time, to different galleries – but today there are probably about 2,300 paintings here. There are lots of beautiful sculptures, drawings and films in the museum too.
Boy: Interesting! Now, could you tell us how old the museum is?
Woman: The Museum of Modern Art is about 90 years old, but the building we're in today opened in 2004.
Girl: Could you tell me how much tickets are for children, please?
Woman: Well, the tickets for adults are $25. But the tickets for children under 16 years old don't cost anything – they're free.
Girl: Wow! That's great.
Boy: Now, could you tell us what your favourite painting here is?
Woman: Of course! There are so many amazing and famous pictures here … but my favourite is a picture called 'The Starry Night'. It's by the Dutch painter Vincent Van Gogh.
Girl: 'Starry'– is that S-T-A-double-R-Y?
Woman: Yes.
Girl: And if people want to find out more, what should they do?
Woman: Well, they can visit our website, at www dot MoMA dog org, that's www dot M–o–M–A dot O–R–G.
Girl: Do you know if they can they phone you too?
Woman: Yes, we're on 212 708 9400.
Boy: Oh no! Our time is up. Thank you so much for your help!
Woman: You're welcome.
Girl: Well … We've learned lots of new things in today's Charlie's Challenge. See you next week!

Pupil's Book, page 100

3  Listen and write the correct answers.

Guide: Hello and welcome to Timanfaya National Park. The park is about 51 square kilometres in size and as you can see we are in the mountains. The mountains are called the Montañas del Fuego or Fire Mountains and this is because there are more than 100 volcanoes here. The ground is very hot, but don't worry we are all very safe!
So, we're in the car park and this is where the bus tour starts … we …
Man: Excuse me, could you tell me if we can walk through the park?

Guide: I'm sorry no. We need to look after the mountains but the driver will stop at different places so that you can take photos. If you want to take a camel ride, you need to go to the booking office and they can help you. … So, on the bus there will also be information for you to listen to and …

Man: Sorry, could you tell me if the information will be in English?

Guide: Yes, in fact you can choose your language. … So, when we get back to the car park here you can have lunch. The restaurant here has traditional food and it's cooked over a large hole in the ground. The food is very good and cooked by local people. Right, let's all get on the bus …

Unit 9

Pupil's Book, page 108

1 3.23 **Look at the pictures. Listen to Mark's podcast. Which idea is not in the pictures?**

Mark: Did you know that making some films costs more than $250 million dollars? That's right! $250 million! So today I'm asking my classmates what they'd do if they had $250 million to make a film. Here's what they said. Hi! I'm making a show for the school podcast. Could I ask you a question?

Girl 1: Yeah. Cool!

Mark: What would you do if you had $250 million dollars to make a film?

Girl 1: $250 million?! I'd love to work with a famous actor. Someone who's a big celebrity … like umm, Selena Gomez or, I don't know … George Clooney.

Mark: You'd have to pay them a lot of money!

Girl 1: Yes, the hero or heroine is the most important person in most films. If there was someone famous in my film, it'd be really popular.

Mark: What would you do if you had $250 million dollars to make a film?

Boy 1: I'd love to make a drama film about history.

Mark: OK.

Boy 1: So I'd spend the money by building lots of beautiful old rooms in a studio. You know, with huge paintings and big gold chairs!

Boy 2: Well … If I had that money, I'd buy cameras and costumes for the actors. And I'd spend the money on adverts. It's really important that everyone knows about new films. My favourite singer could be in the advert – that'd be expensive … and so, so cool!

Girl 3: Well, I wouldn't make a film – I'd make a TV series about tigers. There'd be six programmes that are each 30 minutes long.

Mark: That'd be great for the nature channel. What would you spend the money on?

Girl 3: On visiting China with some cameras and travelling around. I'd love to put lots of cameras around a forest to film the tigers. That'd be amazing.

Boy 3: I'd spend the money on special effects. I'd love to make a film about people who can fly. So I'd have one scene with the heroine flying above a city, and another where she flies into a volcano …

Boy 4: I'd love to make a film with my dance group.

Mark: That sounds cool!

Boy 4: Yeah, we're doing a dance performance next week actually.

Mark: That's great! Maybe Jenny can review it for her blog? And what would you spend the money on?

Boy 4: Well it'd be great to have some new dance shoes. If I only bought the shoes, could I keep the change?

Mark: Haha! Why not?

Pronunciation Answer Key

Unit 1 Plural pronunciation of 's'

3 1.04 **Listen and repeat. Then listen again and write the words.**

- Learners draw a table with seven lines. Tell them to listen and to write the words under the sound /z/ or /s/. Play the audio.
- Ask them to read the words in pairs to practise the sounds.

Track 1.04

days	trainers	tights	suits	keys	snacks
jobs	jeans	shoes	newspapers	cups	

Key: /z/ days, trainers, keys, jobs, jeans, shoes, newspapers /s/ tights, suits, snacks, cups

Unit 2 Syllabus stress in two-syllable words

4 1.17 **Listen and repeat. Then listen again and underline the stress in each word.**

Key: 1 laptop 2 keyboard 3 software 4 handbag 5 raincoat 6 hardware 7 printer 8 program 9 tracksuit 10 costume

Unit 3 Contracted forms

1 1.26 **Listen and repeat. Then listen again. Which verb form do you hear?**

Track 1.26

1 You shouldn't do that.
2 I can't climb that tree!
3 I wouldn't do that if I were you.

Key: 1 shouldn't 2 can't 3 wouldn't

Unit 4 Sentence stress

1 2.05 **Listen and repeat. Then listen again and underline the stressed words.**

Key: 1 How long have you been ill? 2 I've been ill for a while. 3 How long have you had a fever? 4 I've had it since last week.

Unit 5 Verb endings in the past

1 2.18 **Listen and repeat. Then listen again and write the words in the correct column.**

- Learners draw a table, with three lines. They listen and write the words under the sound /id/, /t/ or /d/.
- Learners write sentences to practise the different endings.

Track 2.18

1 My uncle cooked a delicious meal last night.
2 It rained and rained all weekend.
3 I planted some vegetables last week.
4 My mum roasted the potatoes for dinner. They were yummy!
5 I climbed up a mountain with my friend.
6 We watched a great film yesterday!

Key: **/id/** melted, planted, roasted **/t/** cooked, watched **/d/** boiled, rained, climbed

Unit 6 Schwa

1 2.25 **Listen and repeat. Then tick the words or phrases with unstressed syllables.**

Track 2.25

- See audioscript on Pupil's Book, page 119.

2 2.26 **Listen again and underline the unstressed syllables.**

Key: 1 dishwasher – schwa 2 the dishwasher – schwa 3 The dishwasher is in the kitchen. – schwa 4 curtains – no schwa 5 the curtains – schwa 6 We've had the curtains for a long time. – schwa

Unit 7 /b/ /v/ /w/

3 3.03 **Listen and repeat. Then write the words in the correct column.**

- Remind learners that 'b', 'v' and 'w' sound different in English. Ask them to draw a table with three lines. Tell them to listen and write the words under the sounds /v/, /b/ or /w/. Play the audio.
- In pairs, learners write sentences for practice.

Track 3.03

1 positive	3 negative	5 embarrassed
2 worried	4 bored	6 clever

Key: **/v/** positive, negative, clever **/b/** bored, embarrassed **/w/** worried

Unit 8 Intonation in questions

1 3.15 **Listen and repeat. Which questions are pronounced politely?**

Track 3.15

1 Do you know where the train station is, please?
2 Where's the train station?
3 When does the restaurant open?
4 When does the restaurant open?
5 How many friends are coming to your party?
6 How many friends are coming to your party?

Key: 1 polite 2 impolite 3 impolite 4 polite 5 impolite 6 polite

Unit 9 Word stress

3 3.21 **Listen and repeat. Then underline the stressed syllables.**

Key: 1 cartoon 2 action 3 broccoli 4 amazed 5 sightseeing 6 gallery 7 soap opera 8 embarrassed 9 onion 10 accident

Grammar look Answer Key

Pupil's Book, page 120

Unit 1 Comparative adjectives, adverbs and *as … as*

1 Complete the sentences.

Key: 1 the wettest 2 the most beautiful 3 the tallest 4 heavier than 5 worse than 6 closer … than

Unit 1 The present simple with future meaning

1 Complete the sentences. Use the correct form of the words in the box.

Key: 1 We'll 2 leaves 3 starts 4 is

Pupil's Book, page 121

Unit 2 The zero and first conditional

1 Match the sentence halves.

Key: 1 d 2 c 3 a 4 b 5 e

Unit 3 The passive (present simple)

1 Complete the sentences. Use the words in brackets and the present simple passive.

Key: 1 is grown 2 are sold 3 is played 4 is made 5 are lost 6 am paid

Pupil's Book, page 122

Unit 3 Modal verbs

1 Complete the sentences with *can('t), could(n't), may, might, would* or *shall*. Sometimes more than one answer is possible.

Key: 1 can't 2 could 3 might/may/could 4 shall/can/may 5 might/may/could 6 can 7 Would 8 couldn't

Unit 4 Present perfect with *how long, for* and *since*

1 Choose the correct words to complete the sentences.

Key: 1 two weeks 2 14 years 3 last weekend 4 January 5 23 years 6 the age of nine

2 Ask and answer questions. Use the ideas below.

Key: Learners' own answers

Pupil's Book, page 123

Unit 4 Present continuous for future plans

1 Read the sentences and say '*future*' or '*now*'.

Key: 1 future 2 future 3 now 4 now 5 future 6 now

Unit 5 *rather* and *prefer*

1 Use one phrase from each box to make sentences.

Key: I'd rather stay at home tonight. She'd prefer salmon to steak. Would you prefer to drive or catch the train? I prefer swimming to writing. Would you rather watch a film or go for a pizza? He prefers walking to school to cycling.

Unit 5 The passive (past simple)

1 Complete these sentences. Use the word in brackets and the present simple or the past simple.

Key: 1 was played / was watched 2 was given 3 was built 4 is collected / is recycled / is taken

Pupil's Book, page 124

Unit 6 *a lot of, lots of, a few, a little, many, much*

1 Correct the sentences.

Key: 1 We haven't got <u>much</u> time. 2 I drink <u>a little</u> water.
3 There are <u>a lot of</u> things we need to discuss.
4 There isn't <u>much</u> traffic. 5 I've only got <u>a little</u> money.
6 How <u>many</u> pairs of shoes

Unit 6 Tag questions

1 Write the tag questions.

Key: 1 do they? 2 can't you? 3 doesn't he? 4 have you? 5 isn't she? 6 can you? 7 are they?

Pupil's Book, page 125

Unit 7 *needn't, have to, should, ought to, must, mustn't*

1 Complete the sentences with *need(n't), (don't) have to, should(n't), ought to* or *must(n't)*.

Key: 1 should / have to / need to / ought to / must 2 shouldn't 3 don't need to / don't have to 4 should / ought to 5 have to / must / ought to 6 should / ought to 7 should / need to / ought to

Unit 7 *so/such … that*

1 Match the sentence halves.

Key: 1 D 2 E 3 B 4 F 5 C

Pupil's Book, page 126

Unit 8 Indirect questions

1 Rewrite the following as indirect questions. Start with the phrase in brackets.

Key: 1 Could you tell me where you live? 2 I was wondering if you are doing anything at the weekend. 3 I can't remember what we did last weekend. 4 I'd like to know what you thought of the film.

Unit 8 *used to / didn't use to*

1 Rewrite these sentences. Use the correct form of *used to*.

Key: 1 I like hot weather now, but I didn't use to in the past. 2 My brother used to play football regularly until he broke his leg. 3 My hair used to be black. 4 Did you use to go on holiday with your parents when you were a child? 5 When I was younger, I didn't use to get up late.

Unit 9 Causative *have/get*

1 Put the words in order.

Key: 2 I might have my bedroom painted blue. 3 Has Michael had his bike fixed yet? 4 I get my teeth polished every six months. 5 You should have your computer checked for viruses.

Unit 9 The second conditional

1 Write second conditional sentences.

Key: 2 If she spoke English, she could get a job in Canada. 3 If I had enough/more free time, I would learn to play a musical instrument. 4 If I knew Tom's email address, I would send him a message. 5 If my uncle weren't so old, he could be an airline pilot. 6 If my eyesight was better, I could read more quickly. 7 If I had enough money, I would buy a Mercedes. 8 If I weren't afraid of heights, I'd climb mountains.

Activity Book Answer Key

Unit 1

Page 5

1

Key: 2 tie 3 jewellery 4 suit 5 swimming costume 6 tracksuit

2

Key: 2 tights 3 blouse 4 jumper 5 jewellery 6 handbag 7 trainers

3 4.02

Key: 1 no 2 yes 3 no

Page 6

1

Key: 2 happy 3 awesome 4 cheap 5 talented 6 dirty

2 

Key: 1 Valeria 2 Grace 3 Santiago 4 Valeria 5 Grace 6 Santiago

Page 7

1

Key: 1 more quickly 2 is smaller than 3 as ugly as 4 less expensive 5 is bigger than 6 closer

2

Key: 2 (the) most interesting 3 nicer 4 better 5 hotter 6 worse

3

Key: **Sample answers** Jacob is colder than Catalina. Julieta is braver than Jorge. Yesim is as tall as Elif. Climbing a tree is more dangerous than walking. Jin is speaking more angrily than Li.

Page 8

1

Key: 1 button 2 collar 3 chain 4 leather 5 pattern 6 label

2

Key: 1 silk 2 sleeves 3 size 4 cotton 5 tried on

3

Key: Learners' own answers

Page 9

1

Key: 1 begins 2 leaves 3 don't start 4 isn't

2

Key: 1 opens 2 ends 3 starts/begins/is

3

Key: 1 Ezgi 2 Pablo 3 Ezgi

4

Key: Learners' own answers

Page 10

1

Key: 4 1 3 6 5 2

2

Key: 1 no 2 yes 3 yes 4 yes 5 yes 6 no

3

Key: 2 c, grey suit 3 a, gold trainers 4 d, blue and orange jumper

Page 11

4

Key: 1 to 2 than 3 with 4 took 5 as 6 sat 7 too

5

Key: Learners' own answers

Page 12

1

Key: 1 They used wool and leather. 2 They are cheaper than natural textiles (and some have special qualities, e.g. swimwear dries faster). 3 Fleece is made from recycled plastic bottles. 4 It is better than wool because it is waterproof. 5 Smart textiles can light up, change colour and grow.

2

Key: Learners' own answers

3

Key: Learners' own answers

Page 13

1

Key: 1 A 2 A 3 A 4 C 5 B 6 C

Page 14

1 4.03

Key: 1 C 2 B 3 A 4 C 5 A 6 C

Page 15

1

Key: 1 smaller than 2 more slowly than 3 is better than 4 as scared

2

Key: 1 The film starts at 2 pm. 2 The bus leaves at 17:14. 3 Kieron finishes work at 4 pm today. 4 My class ends at 12:00. 5 The football match begins after lunch.

3

Key: 2 size 3 suit 4 jumper 5 label 6 swimming costume

4

Key: Learners' own answers

Unit 2

Page 17

1

Key:

V	S	P	Y	X	G	Z	K	G	C	U	O
M	O	C	O	S	B	C	E	U	P	Y	H
O	O	Y	R	B	Y	P	Y	J	R	I	G
U	J	B	D	E	R	S	B	T	I	S	M
S	K	O	I	I	E	P	O	T	N	A	K
E	G	X	N	L	G	N	A	W	T	Q	F
M	V	T	W	E	E	M	R	O	E	V	Z
T	R	U	T	E	S	P	D	R	R	Z	B
R	I	E	F	C	I	H	H	Y	D	X	S
H	H	B	S	N	L	M	Y	O	E	I	G
L	A	P	T	O	P	D	S	C	N	W	O
M	A	U	Y	C	X	H	O	G	V	E	R

1 keyboard 2 laptop 3 mobile phone 4 mouse
5 printer 6 screen

2

Key: 1 b 2 d 3 a 4 c

3

Key: 1 laptop 2 mouse 3 screen 4 keyboard
5 disc

4

Key: Learners' own answers

Page 18

1 4.04

Key: 1 reply, message 2 football, ball
3 bottle, brother 4 work, expensive

2 4.05

Key: 1 C 2 A 3 A 4 C

Page 19

1

Key: 2 won't 3 will you 4 will 5 isn't 6 miss

2

Key: 2 doesn't practise 3 are 4 works
5 won't go 6 help

3

Key: 1 She won't go in the water if there's a shark.
2 If you drink too much milkshake, your stomach will hurt.
3 If he goes to the cinema on Saturday night, his friends won't be there. 4 If you don't have a ticket, you can't travel.

4

Key: Learners' own answers

Page 20

1

Key: 2 downloaded 3 turn on 4 text 5 click
6 chatting 7 turn off 8 upload 9 install 10 enter

2

Key: Learners' own answers

Page 21

1

Key: 1 will meet – 1st 2 click – Zero 3 phones – Zero
4 will eat – 1st

2

Key: 1 If you drop a ball, it bounces. 2 If it snows tomorrow, I'll go snowboarding. 3 If you tidy your room, I'll give you some money. 4 If people don't cut their hair, it grows.

4

Key: Learners' own answers

5

Key: 2 love 3 like 4 I'm not sure 5 prefer
6 enjoy taking 7 don't like

Page 22

1

Key: 4 1 5 2 3

2

Key: 1 yes – the date of the paper is 28th May and the competition was announced at the beginning of May
2 yes – his parents teach him 3 no – everyone said if he enters he'll win 4 no – she joined the Academy last month
5 no – Azra is very quiet 6 yes – Burak was very unhappy when Azra won

3

Key: Learners' own answers

Page 23

4

Key: Learners' own answers

5 4.06 ★

Key: 1 A 2 C 3 C 4 A

Page 24

1

Key: 1 c 2 d 3 a 4 b

2

Key: 1 application 2 program 3 download 4 laptop

3

Key: Learners' own answers

4

Key: Learners' own answers

Page 25

1

Key: Learners' own answers

2

Key: Learners' own answers

Page 26

1

Key: 1 B 2 C 3 C 4 A 5 B 6 A 7 B

Page 27

1

Key: Learners' own answers

2

Key: 2 f 3 b 4 c 5 a 6 e

3

Key: Learners' own answers

4

Key: 1 keyboard, hardware 2 click, mouse, enter 3 text, email 4 download, disc, laptop

5

Key: Learners' own answers

Unit 3

Page 29

1

Key: 1 cycling 2 diving 3 gymnastics 4 surfing 5 boxing 6 golf

2

Key: 1 cricket 2 rugby 3 athletics 4 water skiing 5 ice hockey

3

Key: Learners' own answers

Page 30

1

Key: jellyfish

2

Key: tank, wetsuit, mask

3 ★

Key: 1 C 2 B 3 C 4 B

Page 31

1

Key: 2 is used 3 is played 4 Is ... practised 5 are taught 6 are shown

2

Key: 1 More than 3 million bikes are sold every year in the U.K. 2 Chinese food is served with rice.
3 Is Japanese spoken by many people in your school?
4 Ice hockey isn't played in a swimming pool.
5 Tablets and phones aren't used in tests.

3

Key: Learners' own answers

Page 32

1

Key: 2 cyclist 3 track 4 surfboard 5 goals
6 train

2

Key: Learners' own answers

3 4.07

Key: 1 coach 2 court 3 hit 4 net 5 racket

Page 33

1

Key: 2 may not 3 could 4 Shall 5 Can 6 will

2

Key: 1 will/can 2 might 3 Shall/Can 4 might

3

Key: 1 2 football and basketball 2 1 athletics

4

Key: 1 because 2 also 3 like 4 for example

5

Key: Learners' own answers

Page 34

1

Key: Correct order: Cynisca and her brother (Top left), Cynisca with her horses, the charioteer in chariot race, Cynisca's brother tells her she can't go into the stadium (bottom right) Agilsilaus runs out of the stadium to tell Cynisca she's won, the statue of Cynisca links

2

Key: 2 Archidamas, King of Sparta 3 Agisilaus
4 chariot racing 5 396 BCE 6 four-horse chariot race

3

Key: Learners' own answers

Page 35

4

Key: Learners' own answers

5 ★

Key: 1 A 2 C 3 C 4 A

Page 36

1

Key: Learners' own answers

2

Key: Learners' own answers

Page 37

1 4.08

Key: 1 Valley 2 July 3 stadium 4 tennis 5 37750

Page 38

1

Key: 1 of 2 the 3 Did 4 the 5 some 6 not

Page 39

1

Key: 2 isn't / is not used 3 are played 4 are worn
5 is done 6 is taught

2

Key: 1 might 2 Shall 3 can 4 could 5 will

3

Key: Learners' own answers

4

Key: 1 surfboard / surfing 2 athletics coach 3 helmet / boxing 4 goal / ice hockey 5 racket

5

Key: Learners' own answers

Review Units 1–3

Page 40

1

Key: 1 c 2 a 3 e 4 b 5 d

2

Key: 1 older 2 opens 3 'll (will) 4 upload/share 5 are

3

Key: 2 If you will click – If you click 3 A point scored – A point is scored 4 Felipe is teach – is taught by 5 May he play tennis well? – Can he play tennis well? 6 It can rain tonight – it may/might/could rain tonight

4

Key: 1 athletics, tracksuit 2 download, mobile phone 3 collar, tie 4 screen, laptop 5 racket, court

Page 41

2

Key: She has asked her to go cycling, said what clothes she needs and given details of where they'll meet. She hasn't said how Abigail can conntact her.

3

Key: 1 Hey Abigail! Hello Abigail! 2 How's things? How's tricks? 3 Do you fancy going …? How about going …? 4 From, Eliza Bye for now, Eliza

2

Key: Learner's own answers

Unit 4

Page 43

1

Key: Top row: emergency door, patient, heart, painful Bottom row: break, ankle, cut, injured

2

Key: Learners' own answers

3

Key: Learners' own answers

Page 44

1

Key: Sample answers 1 You could slip on the banana skin! 2 Be careful! You might cut yourself. 3 Look out! You may hurt the mouse.

2 4.09

Key: 2 4 3 1

3 4.10

Key: 1 C 2 C 3 C 4 A

Page 45

1

Key: 2 haven't seen 3 have broken 4 Has [Noa] visited 5 hasn't played 6 How [long] have [you] been

2

Key: 1 I haven't seen you since we were five. 2 How long have we been in the car? 3 He hasn't eaten since breakfast. 4 They have lived in Sydney for three years.

3

Key: 2 have 3 has 4 Have 5 haven't 6 since

4

Key: Learners' own answers

Page 46

1

Key: 2 bandage / lie down / rest 3 flu / prescription / pill / feel / better

2

Key: 1 flu 2 lie down 3 rest 4 medicine 5 operation 6 bandage 7 prescription 8 pills 9 feels better

3

Key: Learners' own answers

Page 47

1

Key: 2 isn't going 3 Are [they] escaping 4 Is [she] going / isn't swimming 5 is buying 6 Are [we] going / 're flying

2

Key: 1 Ezgi – she had a high temperature
2 Pablo – he fell off his bike and broke his leg

3

Key: 1 8 2 no age – when she was little 3 Ezgi
4 Pablo – he can't think of anything to start and says 'no', then he thinks of a story

4

Key: Learners' own answers

5

Key: 1 Ezgi, how old are you? 2 Where do you live?
3 Did you go to hospital?

Page 48

1

Key: 1 Chloe is excited because the programme is showing a robbery at a bank she knows. 2 The two men are the criminals who robbed the bank. 3 Joshua hurt himself when he fell. 4 Joshua didn't follow his cousin and sister over the bridge because he cut his knee and it was bleeding and painful. 5 Joshua doesn't jump into the river because it is full of crocodiles.

2

Key: Across 1 rope 5 cousin 6 pounds
Down 2 painful 3 flu 4 Monday

Page 49

3

Key: Learners' own answers

4

Key: Learners' own answers

Page 50

1 4.11

Key: 1 7th November 2 Warsaw 3 Paris 4 Physics 5 radium 6 Physics 7 Chemistry 8 1934

2

Key: Learners' own answers

Page 51

1

Key: 1 A 2 C 3 C 4 B 5 B 6 A

Page 52

1 4.12

Key: 1 A 2 B 3 C 4 A 5 C

Page 53

1

Key: 1 haven't watched / since 2 hasn't walked / for 3 've been / since 4 How long has / had 5 've been / for 6 has gone

2

Key: 2 are / wearing 3 are / getting 4 is taking 5 are coming 6 not buying 7 I'm shopping

3

Key: Learners' own answers

4

Key: 1 d 2 e 3 a 4 c 5 b

5

Key: Learners' own answers

Unit 5

Page 55

1

Key: 2 broccoli 3 chilli 4 onion 5 salmon 6 garlic

2

Key: 1 steak 2 oil 3 garlic 4 herbs 5 chilli

3

Key: Learner's own answers

Page 56

1

Key: 1 A 2 C 3 C 4 B 5 A 6 C 7 C 8 B

2

Key: Learner's own answers

Page 57

1

Key: 2 prefer 3 rather 4 prefer 5 prefer 6 rather

2

Key: 2 Kieron and Caleb would **rather not** play with Tyler today.
3 We**'d** rather sit outside than inside.
4 Maria would prefer **to have** a dog than a baby sister.
5 Juan would prefer not **to** go to school today. Juan would **rather** not go to shcool today.
6 Would James **prefer** to play basketball or football?

3

Key: Learners' own answers

4 4.13

Key: 1 Would you rather have cake or fruit? 2 Would you prefer to see a crocodile or a bear? 3 Would you rather go with Ed Sheeran or Emma Watson?

Page 58

1

Key: 2 cut 3 fry 4 dish 5 kettle 6 frying pan 7 carrots 8 boiled 9 sliced

2

Key: Learners' own answers

3 4.14

Key: 1 A 2 A 3 B 4 C 5 B

Page 59

1

Key: 1 was 2 Were 3 weren't 4 were 5 wasn't 6 Was

2

Key: 2 were placed 3 was boiled 4 were removed 5 were cut off 6 were eaten

3

Key: 1 Ezgi 2 Pablo

4

Key: 1 EX 2 E 3 P 4 E 5 EX 6 E 7 EX

5

Key: Learners' own answers

6

Key: really

Page 60

1

Key: 1 They think the show is brilliant. 2 The show is called 'Cooking with Carlos'. 3 He cooks different recipes on the show. 4 Juana hasn't watched it because she doesn't like it and thinks Carlos talks about it too much; she is probably jealous. 5 She puts worms in his cooking pot to embarrass him on the show.

2

Key: Learners' own answers

3

Key: Learners' own answers

Page 61

4

Key: Learners' own answers

5 ★

Key: Juana because she gives lots of details.

6

Key: Learners' own answers

Page 62

1

Key: 1 cooked rice, biscuit, potato, pasta, bread 2 apple, carrot 3 Learners' own answers

2 4.15

Key: 1 pear 2 green 3 milk 4 lemon

3

Key: Learners' own answers

Page 63

1 4.16

Key: 1 F 2 D 3 H 4 C 5 A

Page 64

1

Key: Learners' own answers

Page 65

1

Key: 1 Would you rather eat inside or outside?
2 Daniela prefers strawberry jelly to ice cream.
3 Facundo would rather go to the cinema.
4 We prefer to spend times with our friends.
5 I'd rather not eat cabbage soup.

2

Key: 1 were fried 2 was made 3 weren't added 4 wasn't told 5 was given 6 was cooked

3

Key: 1 steak / onion 2 boiled / roast 3 sliced / dish 4 fry / salmon / garlic 5 kettle

4

Key: 1 Sample answer Cut cheese (and if you like tomatoes) into slices. Cut the bread into slices. Put butter on the bread. Add the cheese (and tomatoes) into the bread.) 2 Learners' own answers

Unit 6

Page 67

1

Key: 2 electricity 3 plugs 4 heating 5 air conditioning 6 dishwasher 7 sink 8 a tap 9 rubbish 10 dustbin 11 bulbs 12 candles

2 4.17

3

Key: Learners' own answers

Page 68

1

Key: 1 to 2 in 3 with 4 for 5 and 6 from 7 have/need 8 is 9 town 10 you

2 4.18

Key: David

3 4.19

Key: 1 C 2 A 3 G 4 H 5 B

Page 69

1

Key: 2 many 3 a lot of 4 much 5 a little 6 lots of

2

Key: 1 countable – many 2 countable – lot
3 uncountable – much 4 uncountable – lot of
5 uncountable – much 6 countable – a few

3 4.20

Page 70

1

Key: petrol, traffic jam, pollution, area, litter, recycle, path, public transport, gas, rainforest

2

Key: 1 rainforest – A 2 traffic jam – C
3 public transport – C 4 recycling – B 5 litter – B

3 4.21

Page 71

1

Key: 2 can you? 3 wasn't it? 4 didn't you?
5 aren't they? 6 has he?

2

Key: 2 didn't you? 3 wasn't it? 4 weren't you?
5 did you? 6 haven't you? 7 didn't he? 8 aren't I?

3

Key: 1 you prefer to travel / or by public transport?
2 pollution a problem / you live?

4

Key: Ezgi – B

5

Key: Learners' own answers

6

Key: 1 convenient 2 transport 3 pollution
4 traffic jam

Page 72

1

Key: Learners' own answers

Page 73

2 4.22

Key: 1 11 2 8:30 3 plants 4 lunch (food)

3

Key: Learners' own answers

Page 74

1

Key: 1 Rainforest 2 African grasslands 3 Desert
4 Polar

2 4.23

Key: bees birds frogs hedgehogs

3 4.24

Key: 1 yes 2 yes 3 no 4 yes 5 no 6 no

4

Key: Learners' own answers

Page 75

1

Key: Learners' own answers

2

Key: Learners' own answers

3

Key: Learners' own answers

Page 76

1

Key: Learners' own answers

Page 77

1

Key: 1 a lot 2 much 3 a lot 4 many 5 a few 6 a little

2

Key: 1 d 2 a 3 e 4 b 5 c

3

Key: Learners' own answers

4

Key: 1 area 2 public transport 3 litter 4 candles 5 heating

5

Key: Learners' own answers

Review Units 4–6

Page 78

1

Key: 1 'm 2 wasn't 3 have 4 can't 5 rather 6 few 7 to

2

Key: 2 Bautista ~~**didn't eat**~~ meat – hasn't eaten 3 I ~~**cook**~~ – I'm cooking 4 then put **them** in – then put in 5 Guadalupe ~~**was put**~~ – put 6 There's ~~**alot**~~ of litter – a lot 7 I put too ~~**much**~~ herbs – many 8 You have ~~**much**~~ candles – a lot of

3

Key: 1 slicing / broccoli / bandage 2 traffic jam / pollution / public transport 3 chilli / saucepan / dustbin

Page 79

1

Key: Learners' own answers

2

Key: **Sample answers** What? a litter pick up
When? while Sam was chatting with James
Where? in the local park Why? James walked into a dustbin / they found a strange object

3

Key: Learners' own answers

Unit 7

Page 81

1

Key: 1 relaxed 2 annoyed 3 embarrassed 4 bored 5 miserable 6 positive

2

Key: 1 amazing 2 interested 3 worried 4 negative

3

Key: Learners' own answers

Page 82

1 4.25

Key: a spider

2 4.26

Key: amazed, bored, satisfied, worried

3 4.27 ★

Key: 1 A 2 A 3 B 4 C 5 C

4 4.28

Key: Learners' own answers

5

Key: Learners' own answers

Page 83

1

Key: 1 needn't 2 have to 3 should 4 ought to 5 must 6 mustn't

2

Key: 1 should, B 2 have to, D 3 mustn't, A 4 needn't, C

3

Key: 2 must 3 likes 4 mustn't 5 ought to

Page 84

1

Key: 1 jogging 2 ache 3 recover 4 stress 5 exercise 6 keep fit 7 gym 8 health 9 diet 10 breathe deeply

3

Key: Learners' own answers

Page 85

1

Key: 1 such, that 2 so, that 3 such, that 4 so, that

2

Key: 1 so 2 so 3 such 4 so 5 that 6 such 7 that

3

Key: 1 What about you? 2 Do you like going to the gym? 3 How much water do you like to drink? 4 Do you like to sleep a lot? 5 Do you like to sleep a lot? 6 What do you think about spending a lot of time outside? 7 What about you?

4

Key: 1 do to keep fit 2 such a quick sport 3 do to reduce stress 4 talk to my parents

5

Key: Learners' own answers

Page 86

1

Key: 2 He was worried the wolf might kill the calves. 3 Cody decided to leave Buck to protect the calves. 4 He didn't like it. He was bored and lonely. 5 He wanted to see and talk to someone. 6 The men came to help him. 7 She suspected that he was lying. 8 Nobody believed Buck when he cried 'Wolf', so they didn't come and the wolves killed the calves.

2

Key: Learners' own answers

Page 87

3

Key: 1 no 2 yes 3 yes 4 yes 5 no 6 yes

4

Key: Learners' own answers

Page 88

1

Key: Sample answers 1 sad/ sad, angry, 2 disappointed/ sad 3 Learners' own answers

2

Key: Learners' own answers

3 4.29

Key: The girl in conversation 1 and the first boy in conversation 4.

4 4.30

Key: A E F

Page 89

1

Key: 1 B 2 C 3 B 4 A 5 C

Page 90

1 4.31

Key: 1 A 2 C 3 B 4 A 5 A

Page 91

1

Key: 2 must 3 needn't 4 should / ought to
5 have to / must 6 mustn't

2

Key: 1 Josh is so cold that he's wearing three jumpers!
2 I ran so fast yesterday that my legs ache today.
3 It's such a friendly dog that everyone stops to say hello.
4 We're so happy that we're going to cry.
5 Alicia is such a fast swimmer that she wins every race.
6 We're such good students that we always get ten out of ten.

3

Key: 2 annoyed, Breathe deeply 3 miserable, aches
4 embarrassed, jogging 5 worried, healthy diet

4

Key: Sample answers To look after my health, I always eat healthy food and do lots of exercise. I go to the doctor when I'm ill. When I'm stressed, I think about happy things.

Unit 8

Page 93

1

Key: 1 music festival 2 monument 3 sculpture
4 palace 5 collection 6 tower

2

Key: 1 sightseeing 2 department store 3 gallery
4 cruise

3

Key: Learners' own answers

4

Key: Learners' own answers

Page 94

1

Key: 1 puppy flower sculpture 2 spider sculpture
3 boat in bottle 4 department store 5 photo of city

2 ★

Key: 1 A 2 C 3 B 4 B

Page 95

1

Key: 2 what I can see 3 where Sarah is 4 how much it costs

2

Key: (in any order) Do you know where I can take great photos? Do you know when the museum is open? Could you tell me where I can buy concert tickets? Do you know where the sculpture is?

3

Key: You can take great photos from the hill in Artxanda. The museum is not open on Monday, but you can go the other days and at the weekend. You can buy concert tickets in the centre of the city at the department store. The sculpture is next to the river.

4 4.32

Key: a no b no c yes

Page 96

1

Key: 2 tourist information centre 3 opening hours
4 car park 5 cash machine 6 signpost 7 pavement
8 underground 9 roundabout

2 4.33

Key: 1 hotel 2 bridge 3 museum 4 river 5 park

Page 97

1

Key: 1 I used to hate broccoli. 2 Which sports did you use to play? 3 Shakira used to live in Colombia. 4 When I was three, I didn't use to do homework.

2

Key: 1 The world's tallest tower used to be in New York. 2 This train station used to be an art gallery. 3 Did this monument use to be gold? 4 People didn't use to use cash machines.

3

Key: 1, 2 and 4

4

Key: like, peaceful, castle, monuments, typical

5

Key: Learners' own answers

6

Key: 1 what's, surname 2 how, spell 3 study, English, school 4 where, come

Page 98

1

Key: 1 box of chocolates 2 tennis racket 3 toothbrush 4 apple juice 5 black tie 6 clothes

2

Key: Learners' own answers

3

Key: 2 He's a secret detective. 3 He thinks Arabella Von Thursday stole it 4 Learners' own answers. 5 They say they know where the Black Diamond is.

Page 99

4

Key: 1 A 2 B 3 B 4 C

5

Key: Learners' own answers

Page 100

2

Key: 1 Locations 2 What to do 3 Sumatran wildlife 4 Local culture 5 When to go

3

Key: 1 coastal plains, forested valleys, rivers, mountains 2 Tourism is helping to protect the park and in this way it is also helping to protect these beautiful big cats. 3 Learners' own answers

Page 101

1

Key: 1 B 2 C 3 A 4 C 5 A 6 C

Page 102

1

Key: 1 FOR 2 TO 3 THERE 4 BUT 5 IF 6 ON

Page 103

1

Key: Learners' own answers

2

Key: Learners' own answers

3

Key: 1 b 2 d 3 a 4 c

4

Key: Learners' own answers

5

Key: 1 pavement 2 rock concert, booking office 3 roundabout, underground, car park 4 signpost, gallery 5 department store, opening hours

6

Key: Learners' own answers

Unit 9

Page 105

1

Key: 1 cartoon 2 comedy 3 drama 4 the news 5 quiz show

2

Key: Learners' own answers

Page 106

1

Key: Learners' own answers

2 4.34

Key: 1 A 2 B 3 C 4 C

Page 107

1

Key: 2 had 3 having 4 have 5 had 6 have

2

Key: 1 Get/Have, washed 2 Have/Get, wrapped 3 gets/has, brushed 4 get/have, painted

3

Key: Learners' own answers

4

Key: Learners' own answers

Page 108

1

Key: review, scene, hero, celebrity, channel, interview, series, programme, studio, advert, performance

2

Key: 1 advert 2 celebrity 3 programme 4 channel 5 review 6 interview 7 studio 8 performances

3

Key: 1 series 2 celebrity 3 adverts 4 channel 5 hero Mystery word: scene

Page 109

1

Key: 1 met, 'd be 2 became, would move 3 were, would you go 4 wouldn't speak, lived 5 would watch, wasn't 6 Would you make, could

2

Key: Learners' own answers

3

Key: in the centre, at the back, on the left, on the right, at the front

4

Key: Learners' own answers

5

Key: Learners' own answers

Page 110

1

Key: Sample answers The writer says it's a monster. The writer says the TV is sitting there. It's big and ugly. It's ready to attack. You can't escape it. The screen catches you.

2

Key: Tick ALL the boxes.

3

Key: black/attack, stare/there, red/bed, wings/things, floor/more, square/unfair, phone/alone, happy/chatty, television/mission.

4

Key: 2

Page 111

5

Key: Learners' own answers

6

Key: Learners' own answers

7 4.35

Key: 1 A 2 B 3 B 4 A 5 A 6 B

Page 112

1

Key: Learners' own answers

2

Key: Learners' own answers

3

Key: Learners' own answers

Page 113

1

Key: **Sample answer** Kim saw an advert on TV for a lovely handbag. Mum said, 'It's time to go to the supermarket.' While they were shopping, Kim bought one of the handbags. In the evening, Kim wore it and went out with her friends. She had a great time.

Page 114

1

Key: **Sample answer**
Hi Sahar,
Wow, what an interesting project! Of course I'd love to help you. Let's do it on Thursday after school. I can come to your house at about 4 pm.
I think the cartoon show *The Simpsons* would be a good choice because even if Bart is naughty, the other characters are really funny. His dad is so lazy, but Lisa is my favourite! She's more intelligent than she seems. Why don't we go and see that new comedy film? It's on at the cinema near my house. The tickets are cheaper on Thursday evenings too.

Call me later.

Jim

Page 115

1

Key: 2 had/got, fixed 3 to have / to get, made 4 had/got, dyed 5 having/getting, taken 6 had/got, stolen

2

Key: 1 C 2 A 3 F 4 B 5 E 6 D

3

Key: Learners' own answers

4

Key: Learners' own answers

5

Key: 1 interview, heroine 2 The news, channel 3 review, action film 4 performance, horror movie 5 studio, quiz show

Review Units 7–9

Page 116

1

Key: 1 should 2 ought to 3 so 4 such a 5 used 6 the last sightseeing tour is 7 how many people work 8 had

2

Key: 2 must to go: You must go to the gym more often if you want to be as strong as Hulk!
3 don't must do: You don't have to do your homework tonight because it's the weekend.
4 use to be: There used to be a tourist information centre on King Street, but there isn't now.
5 used to was: I used to be embarrassed when I sang, but now I don't mind.
6 would see: If you saw a monster reading the news, you'd be amazed.

3

Key: A 5 worried B 6 breathe C 2 sculpture D 1 roundabout E 4 cartoon F 3 celebrity

Page 117

1

2

Key: Questions: What would you rather do? Where would you like to eat? Anyway, could you tell me what time your train arrives? Learners' own answers

3

Key: Learners' own answers

4

Key: Learners' own answers